Letters from the Front

World War I 1916 – 1918

WWI LETTERS TO HOME

FROM BROTHERS CHARLES AND HICKMAN VERNON

Together with other memories and stories

of the Vernon Family of Joondanna

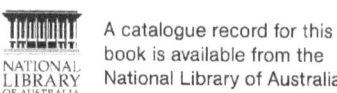 A catalogue record for this book is available from the National Library of Australia

Copyright © 2025 Lyn Brown
All rights reserved.
ISBN-13: 978-1-923174-74-0

Linellen Press
265 Boomerang Road
Oldbury, Western Australia
helen.iles.linpress@gmail.com

Contents

Letters from the Front 1

Letters to Jeannie McDonald Banks From Soldiers at The Front 89

The Vernon Families of Joondanna 135

Photo Album 195

Vernon Family Tree 247

Molesworth (wife) v. Molesworth 259

Foreword

This collection of photos, letters, part letters, postcards and crockery was given to me by my mother Marjory Gardiner, nee Vernon, daughter of Hickman and Jean. The letters to Jean were lent to me by my cousin Jan (nee Williams). Additional material was collected from the deceased estate of Charles Vernon's son Gordon.

The letters were sent during the course of the First World War, mostly from France and Belgium, by brothers Charles & Hickman Vernon to their widowed mother Laura and sisters Florence and Dorothy who at the time lived in Harper Street in Midland. Some of the letters were written in pencil and the photographs of these are very faint, however I am happy with the transcriptions. Any grammar or spelling mistakes in original correspondence have been left verbatim.

The Bairnsfather crockery is a souvenir of the war and was given to my Mother by her Grandmother Laura. I assume it was brought home from England by Charles, who stayed on in the UK after the War to train as a telegrapher.

The entire collection of letters and postcards has been donated to the State Library of Western Australia and can be viewed online (Charles & Hickman Vernon papers www.slwa.gov.au/), or in person on request. The Bairnsfather crockery has been donated to the Museum of Western Australia.

Both collections have been donated on behalf of the Vernon Family of Joondanna.

In correspondence from Charlie and their mother, the spelling of Hickey's name is Hickie, whereas in Hickey's own correspondence, he spells his name with an 'ey' ending. In any of my comments in this work I have used his preferred spelling, the other spelling will appear when the correspondence has been written by others.

Thanks to all family members who contributed their stories to the "Growing Up Vernon" section and to my husband Dave Brown for his patience, his work on our family tree and his research many years ago into the Molesworth connection.

Lyn Brown (nee Gardiner)

Granddaughter of Hickey

Cover Photo

Hickman Molesworth Vernon

Charles Molesworth Vernon
&
Hickman Molesworth Vernon

The brothers enlisted a day apart – Charles (Charlie) on 1 February and Hickman (Hickey) on 2 February 1916 at Blackboy Hill Training Camp in Greenmount, Western Australia, where they spent almost four months training.

Charlie (1/2/1893 – 4/8/1975) Enlistment number 25410, left Melbourne, Australia as a Gunner in 3 Divisional Ammunition Column 3, 1 – 8 Reinforcement aboard the HMAT *Baramba* A37 on 27 June 1916, arriving in Plymouth, England and was sent to France on 24 November 1916, the same day as Hickey.

He was wounded in action in September 1917 but returned to active service on the same day. He was hospitalised only once, in June 1918, with influenza.

He returned to England from France and repatriated to Australia on 3 May 1919 on the Troopship SS *Leicestershire*.

Hickey (12/4/1895 – 31/1/1977) Enlistment number 24611, was in the army cadets 38th Battery Australian Field Artillery for three years and was still serving when he enlisted. He left Melbourne, Australia as a Driver in 3 Divisional Ammunition Column 1 – 8 Reinforcement aboard the same ship as his brother, HMAT *Barambah* A37 on 27 June 1916, arriving in Plymouth, England, where he spent around five months before being sent to France on 24 November 1916.

From his records, it appears Hickey spent all of his time in France apart from leave in England and one stay in Bath War Hospital, England.

Both Brothers were awarded two medals, The British War Medal & The Victory Medal

His time in active service was dogged with illness, and he was hospitalised at least seven times with varying conditions such as influenza, boils, scabies, bronchitis and finally pyrexia when he was invalided to the UK and repatriated on 25 January, 1919, on the troopship SS *Ceramic*.

MANIFESTO
TO AUSTRALIAN SOLDIERS
From Mr. W. M. HUGHES, Prime Minister of the Commonwealth.

SOLDIERS OF AUSTRALIA!

AFTER more than two years of heroic effort, the tide of battle, which so long ran strongly with the enemy, who had been prepared for and deliberately provoked war, turns slowly but surely in our favour. The results of the Great Offensive, during which you have added fresh lustre to the glorious name of Anzac, have shown that if the Allies but press resolutely on, decisive victory must crown their heroic labours.

BUT though the valour and dash of the Allied forces have pushed her legions back along a wide front, the day of decisive victory is not yet in sight. No one of you who knows the tremendous resources of the enemy, his courage, his determination, will say that Germany is yet defeated.

YET she must be defeated.

THE world yearns for peace, but any peace would be but a hollow mockery, unless the great disturber of the world's peace were first beaten to her knees. Until Germany is driven headlong from France and Belgium, and decisively beaten on her own soil, she will never consent to the peace that the Allies want and are determined to have.

IN order to ensure decisive victory the Allies have decided to put every available man into the field, so that their Armies may be kept at full strength, and every man in the trenches be kept fit by frequent reliefs.

The Path to Victory.

WHEN you know all this, you know also that the path of victory lies stretched in front of you. You know it is on the Western Front that the crushing blow must be delivered. You know that more men are needed, and **the British Empire must supply them.**

FRANCE for nearly two years endured the brunt of the most ferocious batterings of the enemy. The bones of her gallant sons strew the soil of their dear France like shells on the sea shore. She has covered herself with imperishable glory. She was never so great as in this supreme hour of her trial. Despite their great losses, her glorious soldiers still fight on with unshaken resolution, and will fight while one Frenchman, capable of bearing arms, remains alive.

NOW is the hour when **our** race must prove itself worthy of its traditions and its heritage.

This is our War, Soldiers!

THIS is Australia's war just as much as France's or Belgium's. Our liberties and our national existence are equally, nay, more, at stake. Australia must do her share. Britain has told us what she expects us to do; it is not more than we can or ought to do, it is, indeed, much less proportionately than she herself has done.

W... hundred thousand troops. Britain has five million under arms. If we had done as much we should have enlisted five hundred thousand instead of little more than half that number.

VOLUNTARY recruiting has, unfortunately, proved quite inadequate to supply the necessary number of men during the past three months.

THOUGH VOLUNTARYISM FAILS, AUSTRALIA MUST NOT FAIL. DUTY, HONOUR, AND SELF-INTEREST ALIKE POINT THE PATH WE MUST TREAD.

The Spirit of Patriotism: The Duty of Free Men.

UPON the citizens of Australia, the freest democracy the world has ever known, there rests a grave and solemn responsibility. They are called upon to show themselves worthy of their great privileges. The sacred duty of every free man is to fight in the defence of his country. Men ought not to wait to be compelled to do their duty, they ought rather to run to the ranks on the first sound of the tocsin.

IT was this spirit, soldiers, that inspired you to enlist. It was this spirit that spurred you to your great deeds on Gallipoli and in France. It is this spirit that now upholds you, and urges you on.

Voluntaryism has Failed.

I HAD hoped that this spirit so permeated Australian manhood that we should only need to ask for men to be overwhelmed with recruits; but during these past five months the number of men offering themselves has been steadily falling off, and is now a mere fraction of those required for drafts.

The Government Proposals.

IN these circumstances the Government has decided that the deficiency between the number of men required and the monthly quota must be made up by compulsion. On the twenty-eighth of this month, the citizens of Australia will be asked to vote "Yes" to the following question:—

"Are you in favour of the Government having in this grave emergency, the same compulsory powers over citizens in regard to requiring their military service for the term of the war outside the Commonwealth, as it now has in regard to military service within the Commonwealth?"

If the citizens and soldiers of Australia approve, the Government will thereafter provide that either by voluntary enlistment or by compulsion the regular monthly reinforcement shall be trained and sent abroad to maintain the Australian Army.

Exemptions.

THE Government consider that the number of fit single men without dependents is sufficient, when supplemented by voluntary recruiting, to carry us through the war. The Government believe that it will not be necessary to call up married men. The following classes of single men will be exempt:—

(1) ALL UNDER 21 YEARS OF AGE;
(2) ONLY SONS;
(3) SINGLE MEN WHO ARE THE SOLE SUPPORT OF DEPENDENTS;
(4) WHEN ONE OR MORE MEMBERS OF A FAMILY HAVE ENLISTED, THE REMAINING MEMBERS UP TO AT LEAST ONE HALF OF THE WHOLE FAMILY, WILL BE EXEMPT.

There will also be exemptions for the number of men requisite to carry on certain vital industries.

OTHER men who claim exemption for special reasons will have their cases heard by non-military tribunals, with appeal to a State Judge, and final appeal to a Justice of the High Court of the Commonwealth.

No State to make up any deficiency in the others.

NO State of the Commonwealth which has furnished its own quota of reinforcements by voluntary recruiting or by compulsion will be required to make up the deficiency of any other State.

For the term of the War only.

THE power asked for to compel military service abroad will be granted to the Government for the term of the war only.

Australia's duty to Britain and her Allies.

SOLDIERS, if the people of Australia vote "No," they encourage the enemy, they abandon you, they desert France that has shed its blood in the common cause, they desert Belgium, they leave unavenged those foul outrages inflicted upon women, children and helpless noncombatants of the Allied nations; they repudiate the debt they owe to Britain, under the wing of whose mighty navy they have lain secure and safe from all the horrors of this war. Indeed they cover Australia with the mantle of eternal shame; the glorious name of Anzac becomes a tarnished and dishonoured thing.

Australia Looks to You.

SOLDIERS of Australia, your fellow citizens, confronted with the greatest crisis in their history, look to you for a lead. Your votes are being taken first. I appeal to you who have gone out to fight our battles, who have covered the name of Australia with glory, to lift up your voices and send one mighty shout across the leagues of ocean, bidding your fellow citizens do their duty to Australia, to the Empire, to its Allies and to the cause of liberty and vote "Yes."

W M Hughes

Prime Minister.

8 February 1916, Enlistment Record for CHARLES

Enlisted at Blackboy Hill, Greenmount, WA

Full Service record attached to this is available online at: discoveringanzac-s.naa.gov.au/   (Search for Charles Molesworth Vernon)

2 February 1916, Enlistment Record for HICKMAN

Enlisted at Blackboy Hill, Greenmount, WA

Full Service record attached to this document is available online at: discoveringanzacs.naa.gov.au/ (Search for Hickman Vernon)

Charles Vernon 1916
Taken at Midland Junction Studio

1916 Hymn Book issued to troops

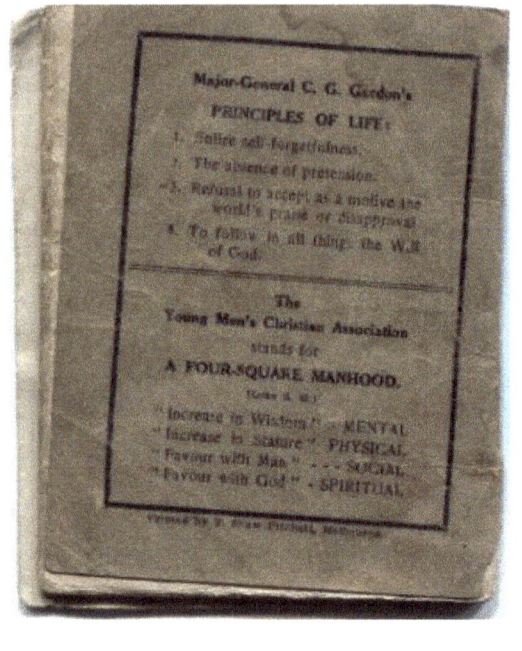

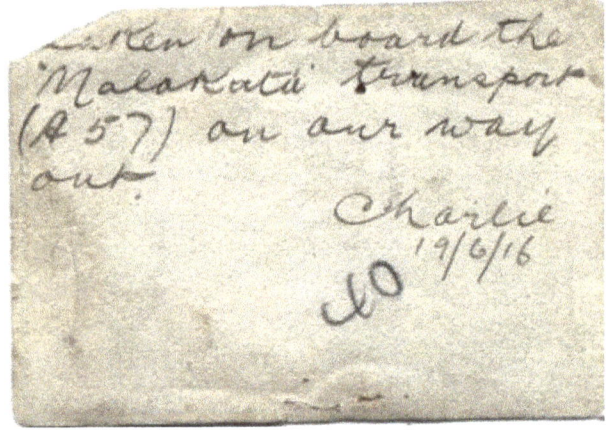

Hickey (L) & Charlie
Taken on board the "Malakuta"
(A57) on our way out.
Charlie 19/6/16

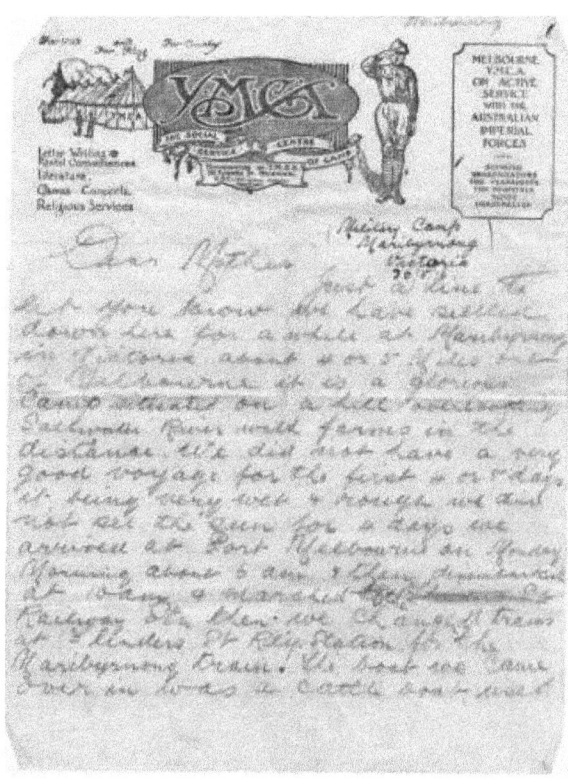

30 May, 1916
Letter
From Charles to their mother, Laura

Dear Mother

Just a line to let you know we have settled down here for a while at Maribyrnong in Victoria about 4 or 5 miles out of Melbourne it is a glorious camp situated on a hill overlooking Saltwater River with farms in the distance. We did not have a very good voyage for the first 4 or 5 days it being very wet and rough we did not see the sun for 4 days we arrived at Port Melbourne on Monday morning about 6am and then disembarked at 10am and marched to the railway station then we changed trains at Flinders St railway station for the Maribyrnong train. The boat we came over in was a cattle boat used …

… for transporting horses so you can guess we did not have too comfortable of a trip although we enjoyed it alright she did not have any horses on board this trip. The name of the boat was the "Malakutu" (A. 57.) We are attached to the 1st Reinforcements (D.A.C.) Divisional Ammunition Column and expect to be leaving here for England about the end of the month, so ought to have a good trip out of it. I was only sea sick once and that was on the roughest day when you could keep nothing on the table but it calmed down on the last couple of days, the sea being nice and calm. We went into Melbourne last night and had a good look round although there was a big mist all round. It is such a nice place compared with Perth.

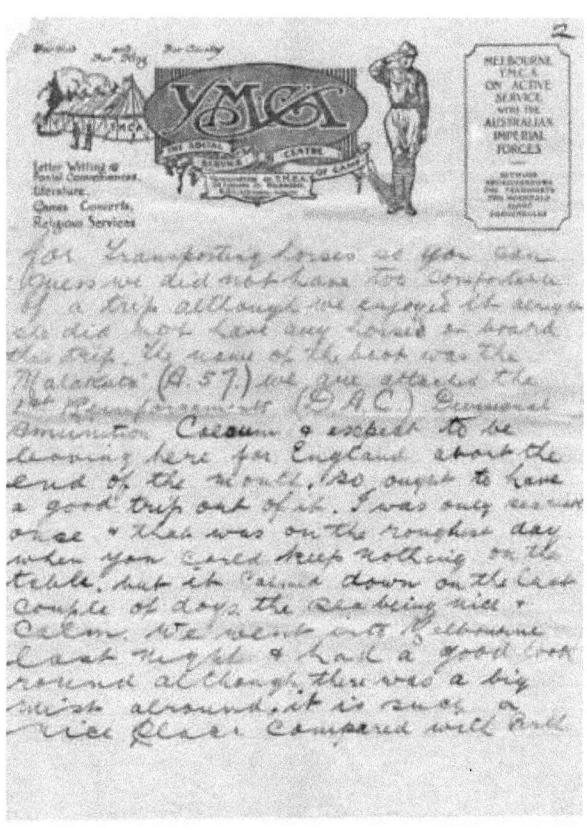

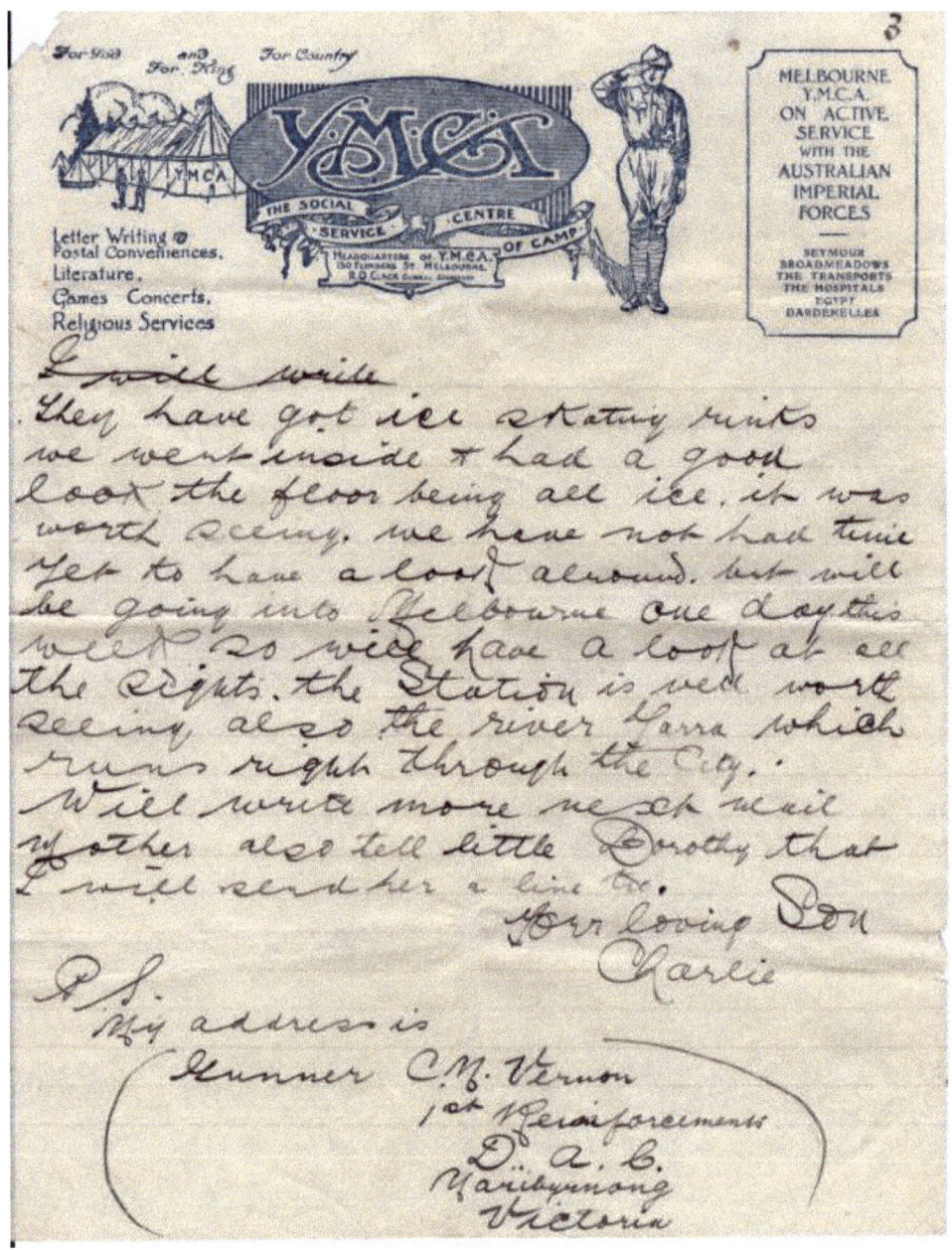

They have got ice skating rinks we went inside and had a good look, the floor being all ice, it was worth seeing. We have not had time yet to have a look around but will be going into Melbourne one day this week so will have a look at all the sights. The station is well worth seeing also the river Yarra which runs right through the City. Will write more next mail Mother, also tell little Dorothy that I will send her a line too.

Your loving Son Charlie

PS my address is: Gunner C.M. Vernon, 1st Reinforcements, D.A.C., Maribyrnong, Victoria

16 June 1916
Postcard – Concertina-type postcard:
From Hickey to Laura

Photos of Ferntree Gully and Warburton, Victoria

26 June 1916
Postcard
From Charlie to Laura

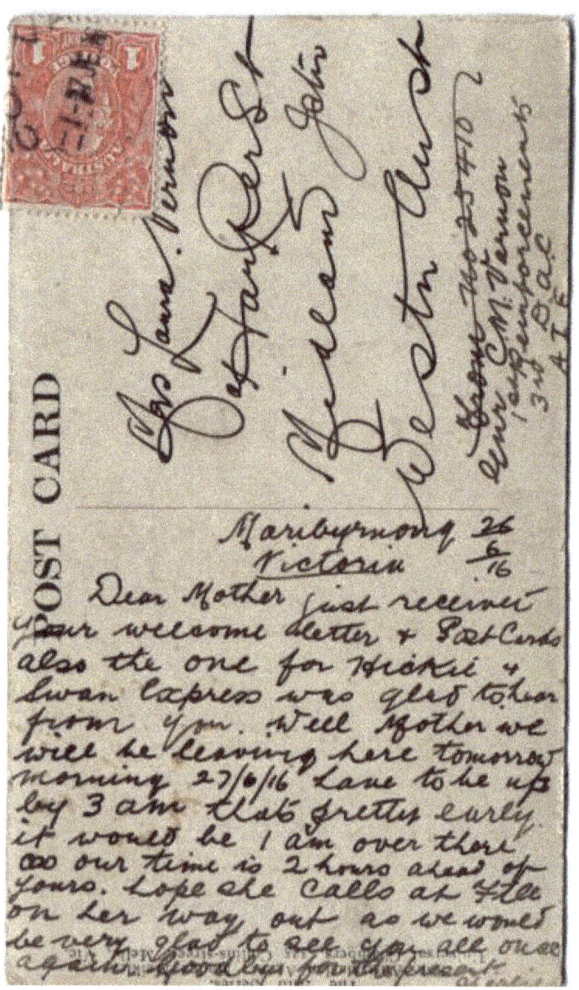

Maribyrnong 26/6/16

Dear Mother

Just received your welcome letter & postcards also the one for Hickie and Swan Express was glad to hear from you. Well Mother, we will be leaving here tomorrow morning 27/6/16 have to be up by 3am that's pretty early it would be 1am over there ooo our time is 2 hours ahead of yours. hope she calls at F'tle on her way out as we would be very glad to see you all once again. Good-bye for the present, Charlie

17 July 1916 at Sea
Card
From Hickey to their sister Dorothy (Dorrie)

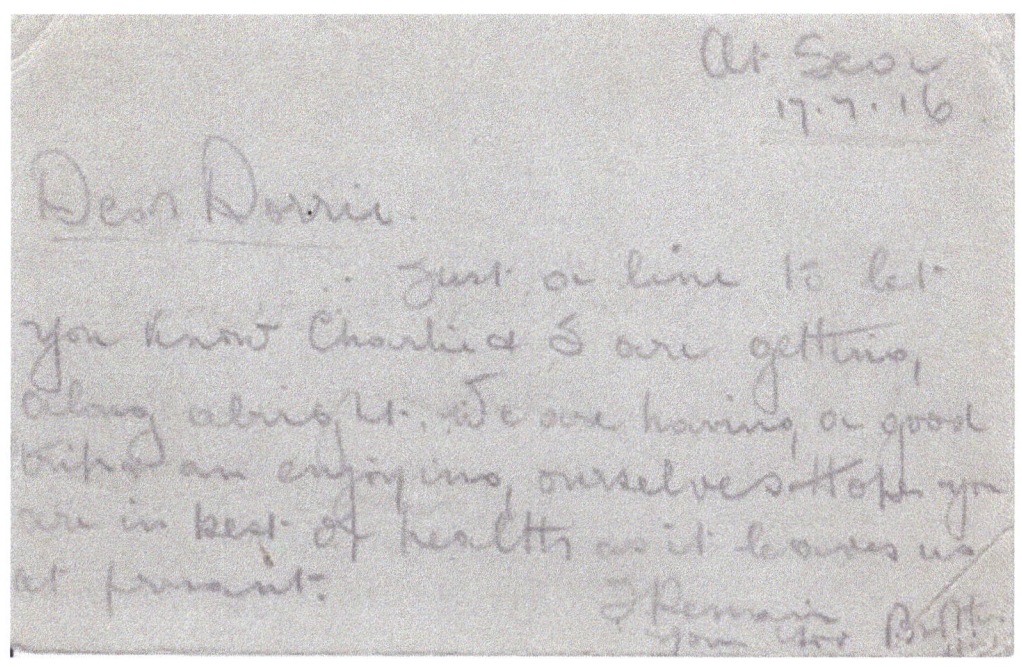

Dear Dorrie

Just a line to let you know Charlie & I are getting along alright. We are having a good trip and enjoying ourselves.

Hope you are in best of health as it leaves us at present.

I remain your loving Brother Hick

Cape Town South Africa
28/7/16

To dear little Dorrie wth best love from her loving brother Charlie

27 July 1916
Postcard
From Charlie to Dorothy

We landed here this morning after being a month on the water. We went for a route march today and had a splendid time by the people on the March being given oranges and teacakes etc. Climate here is similar to West Aust. Best love Charlie

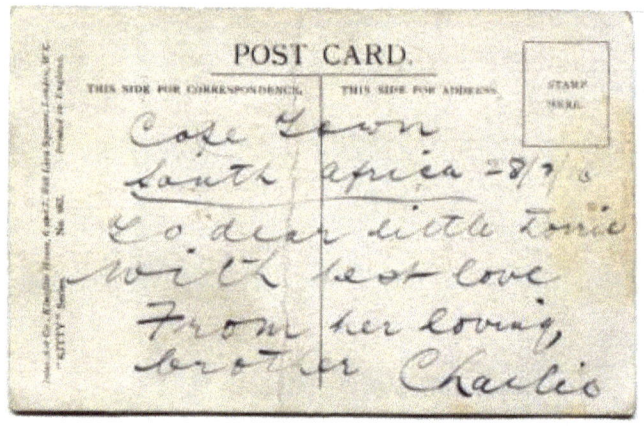

Cape Town
South Africa
To dear little Dorrie
with best love from her loving brother
Charlie

27 July 1916
Photo
From Charlie to Laura

Taken at Sea Point Cape Town S Africa

Charlie, Eric, Hickie, Tom. The view is of Sea Point Table mountain is to the left of this it is not shown in this photo.

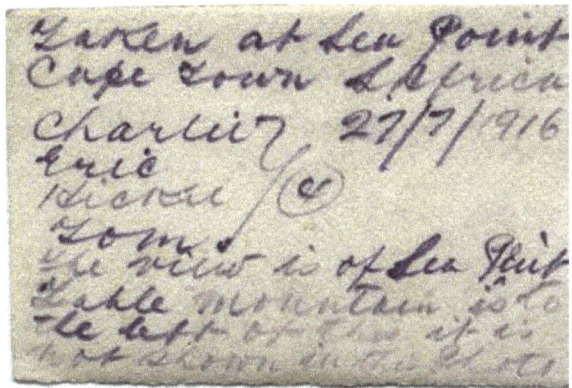

27 July 1916
Postcard
From Charlie to Laura

Cape Town
Arrived here all well with love
Charlie, Hickie & Eric

7 August 1916
Letter
From Charlie to Laura

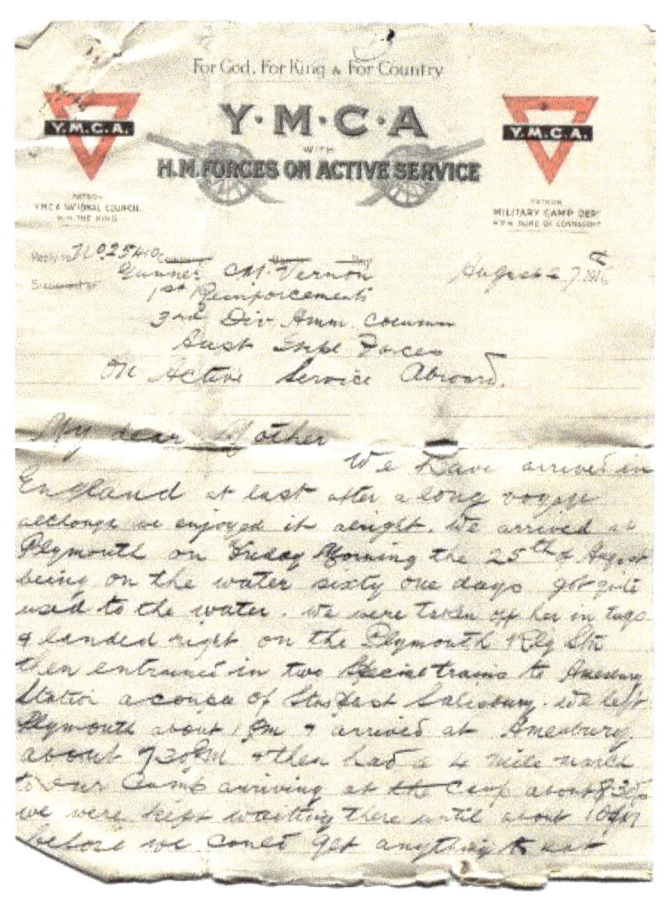

No 25410 Gunner C.M. Vernon 1st Reinforcements

3rd Division Amm. Column Aust Impl Forces

On Active Service Abroad

My Dear Mother

We have arrived in England at last after a long voyage al-though we enjoyed it alright. We arrived at Plymouth on Friday morning the 25th of August being on the water sixty one days, got quite used to the water. We were taken off her in tugs and landed right on the Plymouth Rly Stn then en-trained in two special trains to Amesbury, about 7.30pm and then had a 4 mile march to our camp, arriving at the camp about 8.30pm we were kept waiting there until about 10pm before we could get anything to eat…

…although we were up from 3.15 am the same day we were given a snack at Exeter the place where the big Rwy smash was not so long ago, the people made us very welcome they half filled our water bottles with hot tea and gave us all a bun each. It was a lovely train journey the scenery was simply beautiful all farming places and little villages all along the track with the exception of a large town here and there. We also seen a lot of rabbits along the track and hares. An aeroplane flew over us as we were coming along the first one I had seen but when we arrived at the camp we seen plenty they are flying about over us all day. The aviation school is not far from here. We are camped near the Stonehenge and the chestnut tree where the village…

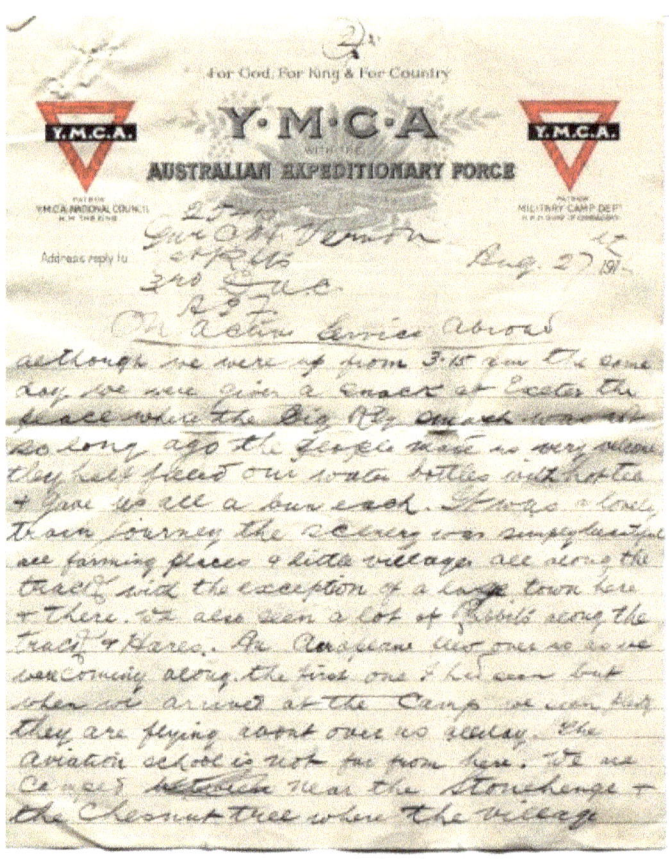

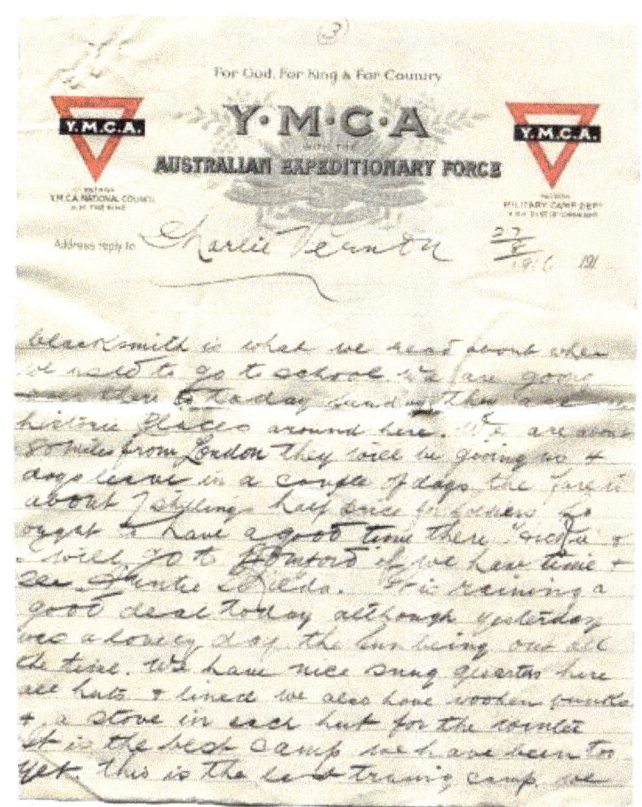

…blacksmith is what we hear about when we used to go to school. We are going over there today Sunday they are all historic places around here. We are about 80 miles from London they will be giving us 4 days leave in a couple of days the fare is about 7 shillings half price for Soldiers so ought to have a good time there. Hickie and I will go to Romford if we have time and see Auntie Hilda. It is raining a good deal today although yesterday was a lovely day the sun being out all the time. We have nice snug quarters here all huts & lined we also have wooden bunks and a stove in each hut for the winter. It is the best camp we have been to yet. this is the last training camp we…

…have before going over to France. I received your letter the next day we arrived dated June 24th written over two months ago one from dear little Dorothy they were read-dressed from Maribyrnong. Hickie got one also the arrangements with the letters are not too good. The name of the camp is Larkhill Camp Salisbury Plains Wiltshire. It runs right through for miles there are about 2 1/2 million men here. The camps are all scattered about the Australians are all together here and the English are in another part of the camp. We past through three counties Devonshire, Somersetshire, Dorsetshire & Wiltshire on the way from Plymouth. Yesterday Sunday we went over to the village blacksmith…

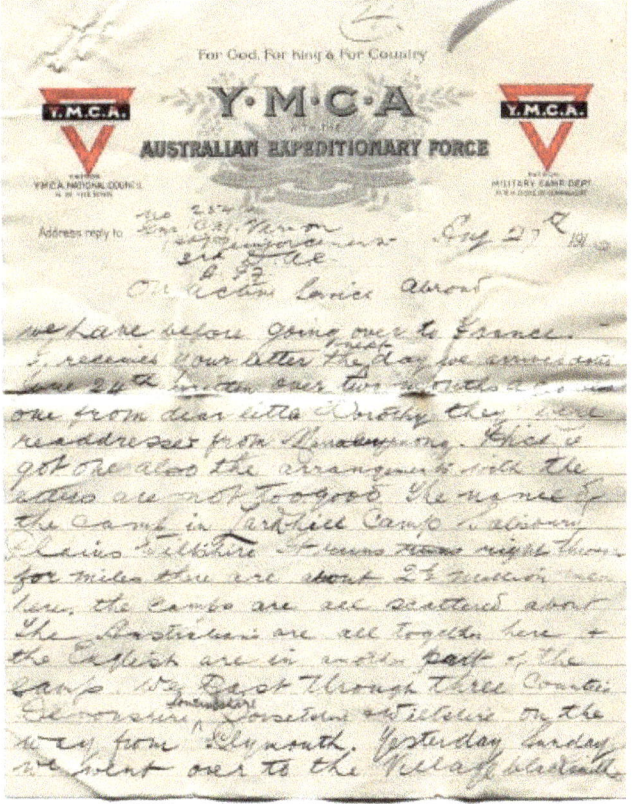

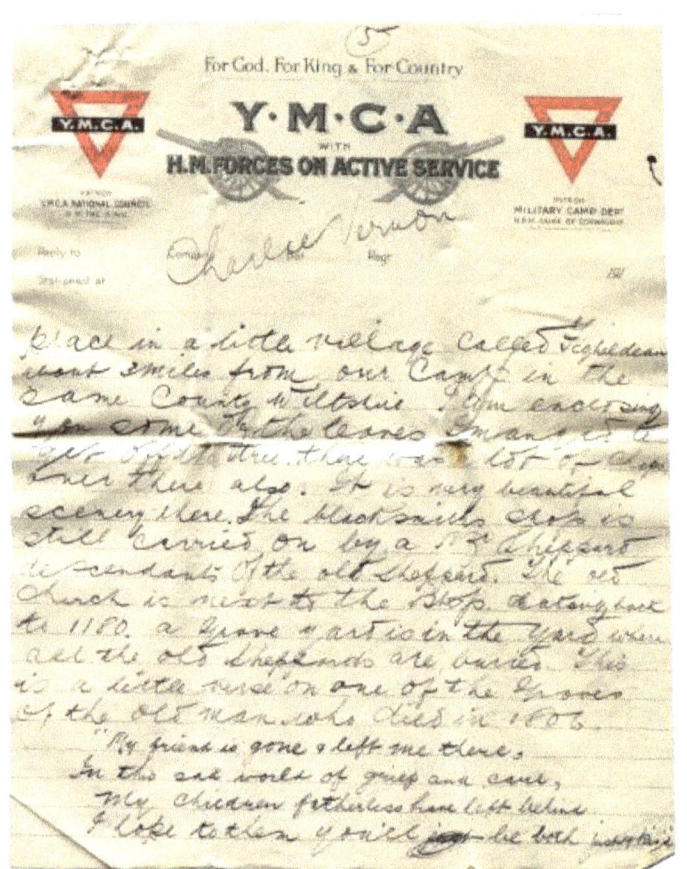

place in a little village called Figheldean almost 3 miles from our camp in the same county Wiltshire. I am enclosing you some of the leaves I managed to get off the tree, there was a lot of chaps over there also. It is very beautiful scenery there.

The blacksmith's shop is still carried on by a Mr Sheppard, descendants of the old Sheppard. The old church is next to the shop dating back to 1180.

A graveyard is in the yard where all the old Sheppards are buried. This is a little verse on one of the graves of the old man who died in 1806.

"My friend is gone & left me there, In this sad world of grief and care, my children fatherless have left behind, I hope to them you'll be both just and kind"….

His father, mother, two brothers, four sisters and his daughters are all buried around the same part of the cemetery. We spent the Sunday in the little village and had afternoon tea in a little shop underneath the chestnut tree. We also stopped there for tea and went to the old church in the evening which was very nice. The people are very nice here. All the places look very ancient the roofs are all roofed with hay but they look very snug and comfortable one of them has got 1666 on it that's pretty old this place will always do me. I like it very much but I don't think we will be here very long as I believe by the time you get this letter Mother we will be at the front. We are getting four days leave on Thursday we are…

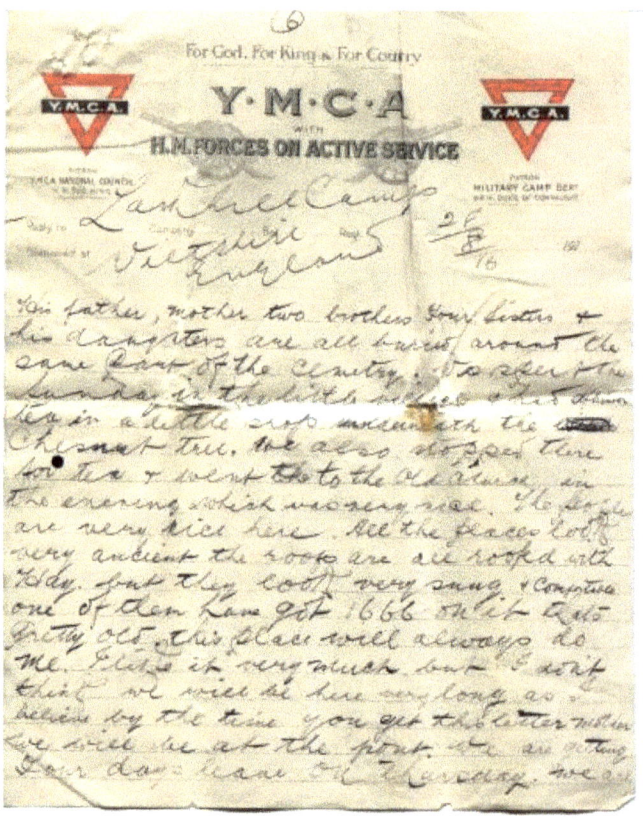

...all taken into London and then dismissed so Hickie and I will go and see Auntie Hilda for a day if we are able. Our money does not go far here as things are twice as dear as in Australia when we left. Some things are three or four times as dear. In the letter little Dorrie sent me, she said the roof of the old hut was leaking and you were going to get Willie to fix it. If you think it is too wet there mother dear for you and little Dorrie you can let the place for a few shillings and rent a nice comfortable place anywhere you like you need not run short as you can take the money out of that of mine. Well mother I think I will now conclude this letter trusting you and little Dorrie are in the best of health as it leaves us at present. Will write next mail. Trusting it will not be long before we are both back again to the old home. I remain your loving son Charlie.

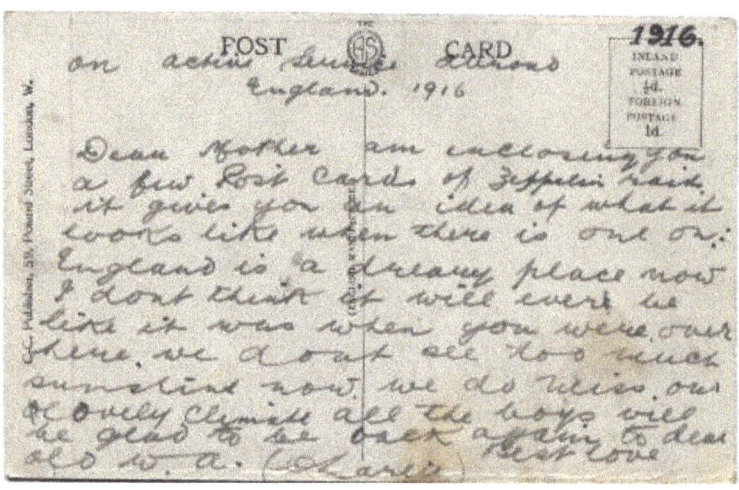

1916
Postcards
From Charlie to Laura

on active Service around England 1916

Dear Mother, am enclosing you a few postcards of Zeppelin raids, it gives you an idea of what it looks like when there is one on. England is a dreary place now I don't think it will ever be like it was when you were over here, we don't see too much sunshine now we do miss our lovely climate all the boys will be glad to be back again to dear old WA. Best love (Charlie)

"HOT STUFF"
German Raider brought down in flames, somewhere in Essex. September 24th, 1916.
Sanctioned by Censor, Press Bureau, September 30th, 1916.

"FRIGHTFULNESS."
"The military depots and fortifications were lavishly bombarded, and good results were clearly discerned." — Extract from German official report.
Sanctioned by Censor, Press Bureau, October 18th, 1916.

4 September 1916
Postcard
from Charlie to Dorothy

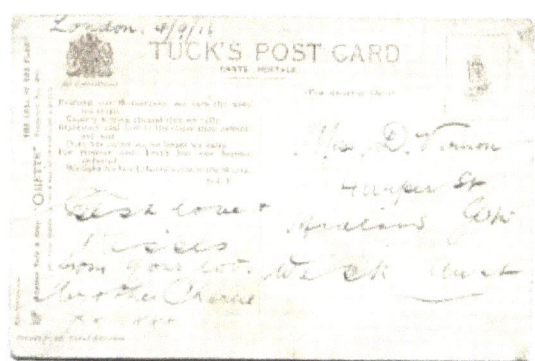

London 4/9/16
Best love & kisses from your loving brother
Charlie xxxxxx

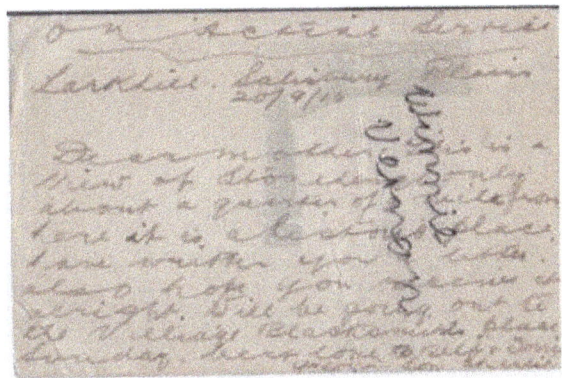

20 September 1916
Postcard
From Charlie to Laura

ON ACTIVE SERVICE Larkhill, Salisbury Plains (later graffiti compliments of Hickey's daughter Winnie!)

Dear Mother, this is a view of Stonehenge only about a quarter of a mile from here it is a historic place. Have written you a letter also hope you receive it alright. Will be going out to the Village Blacksmiths place

30 September 1916
Postcard
From Charlie to Laura

Larkhill Camp 30/9/16 Salisbury Plains
England
Dear Mother this is only a section of the camp here. Am sending you a few other P.Cards of views around here
Charlie

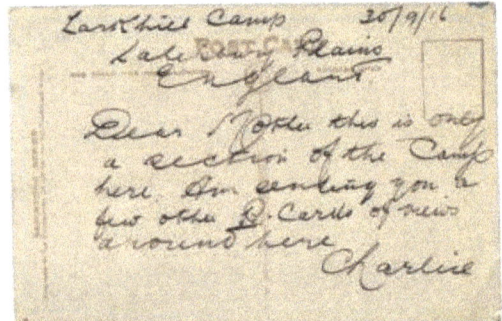

7 November 1916

Postcards
From Charlie to Dorothy

November 1916 (translated from French)
Postcard
From Charlie to Laura

Miss Edith Cavell - Lamentably murdered by a German Officer

Condemned to death by a military court in Belgium for helping English and Belgian soldiers escape, Miss Edith Cavell of Norwich, a volunteer nurse, is brought to the Execution Post on October 12 at daybreak. She falls unconscious. The German officer gives his soldiers the opportunity to fire; they hesitate to shoot at the panting woman. The monster pulls his revolver and leans over the victim and coldly shoots.

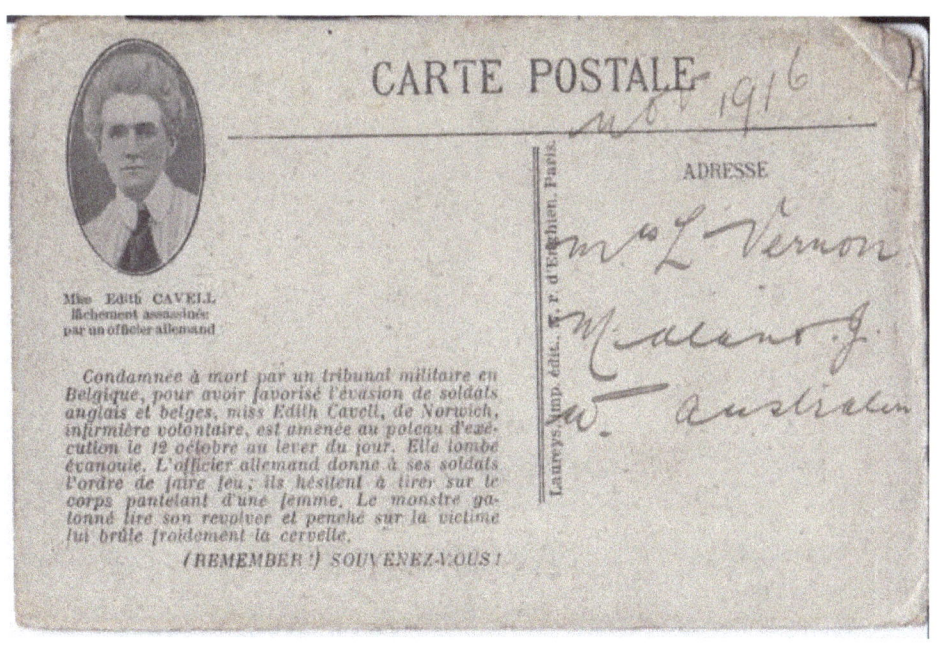

25 December 1916
Postcard
From Charlie to Dorothy

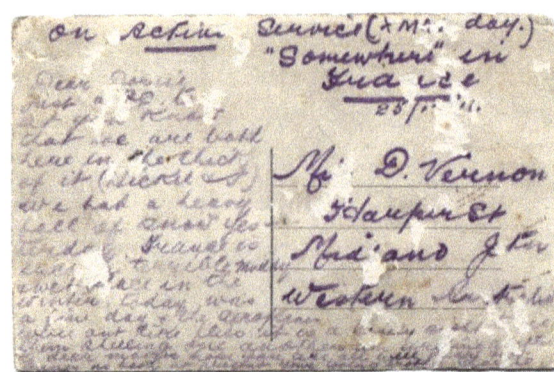

On Active Service (Xmas Day) "Somewhere in France 25/12/1916

Dear Dorrie

just a … to let you know that we are both here in the thick of it (Hickie & I) We had a heavy fall of snow yesterday. France is such a terribly muddy and wet place in the winter. today was a fine day and the aeroplanes where out like flies it is a lovely sight to see them shelling one another. am writing a letter to dear mother hope you are all well as we both are at present. Your loving brother Charlie

December 1916
Christmas Card
From Hickey - Probably to his Mother, Laura

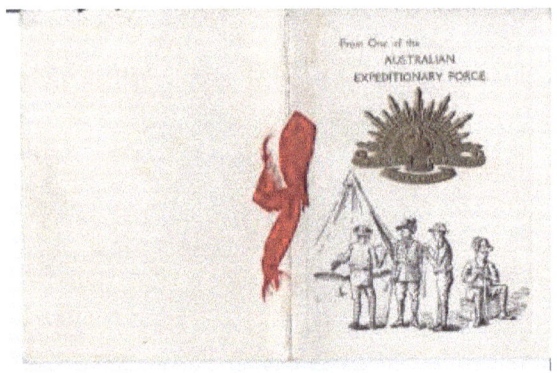

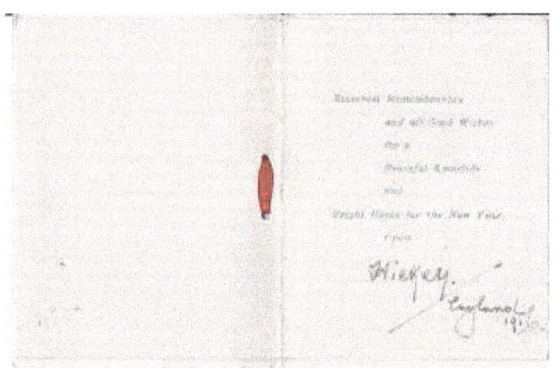

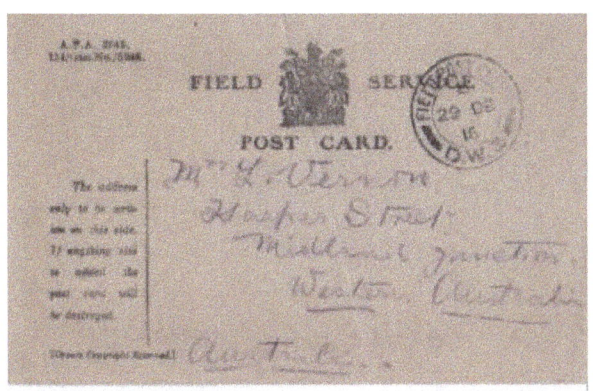

24 December 1916
Field Service Postcard
From Hickey to Laura

Standard form, date and signature only.
Addressed to Mrs Laura Vernon, Midland Junction, W.Australia

"I am quite well, I have received your letter"

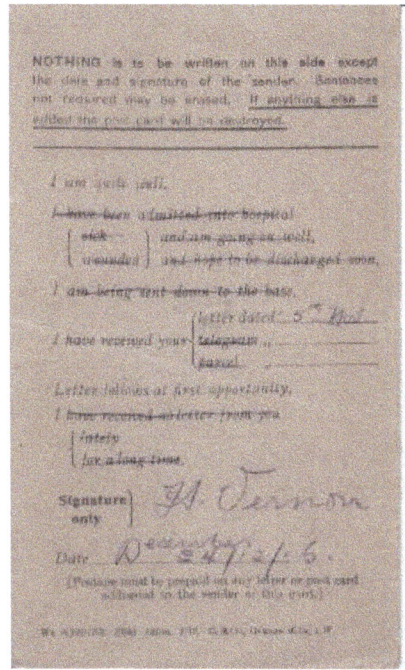

25 December 1916
Christmas Card
From Charlie to Laura

Your loving son Charlie

Salisbury Plain England

29 December 1916
Postcard
from Charlie to Dorothy

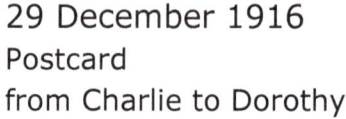

18 January 1917
Postcard
From Charlie to Dorothy

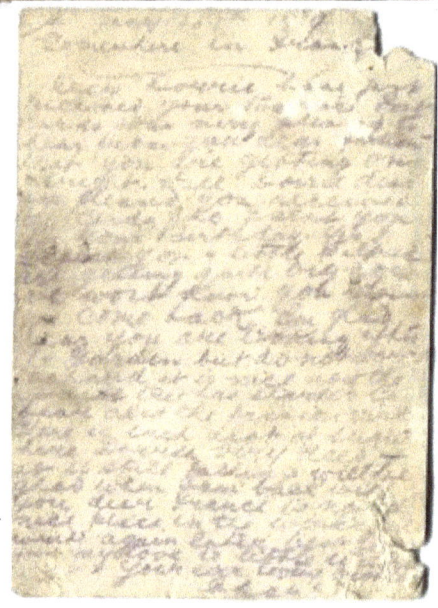

January 18th 1917

Somewhere in France

Dear Dorrie, have just received your terrific postcards was very pleased to hear from you dear mention that you are getting on alright. Well Dorrie dear am pleased you received the cards that I sent you for your birthday. Yes I expect you and little Wilfred are getting a bit big now, I won't know you when I come back. Am glad that you are looking after the garden but do not work too hard it is nice to know the apricot tree has started to bear also the passion vine. There is such a lot of snow here Dorrie very deep. I will be glad when I am back with you dear France is not a nice place in the winter. I will write again later. Give my love to little Wilf, your ever loving brother Charlie

Undated Photo

Taken in France. Hickey is marked with an "X"

1917 Belgium
Group Photo - Taken near Nieuve Eglise

Hickman Molesworth Vernon

6 January 1917
Part Letter
From Charlie to their sister Florence (Florrie)

"SOMEWHERE IN FRANCE"

Dear Florrie

Just a line to let you know that I am still alive here and making the best of it. Well Florrie dear it is a good while since I last received your kind and welcome Post Card. Hope you and dear Mother and dear little Dorothy are keeping well and making the best of things till Hickie and I are back again to the dear old Home. Am very sorry one of us did not stop home with dear Mother and dear little Dorothy considering they are both all alone but I trust that the day is not far off when we are altogether again. Hope this spring will end this war most of the French people seem to think it will. The weather here is still very wet and dreary. We did not have too bad a Xmas although we were working all day we work 7 days a week so you can see we do not get any time off at all. We had Bully Beef for our Xmas dinner the meat they cooked was not done in time

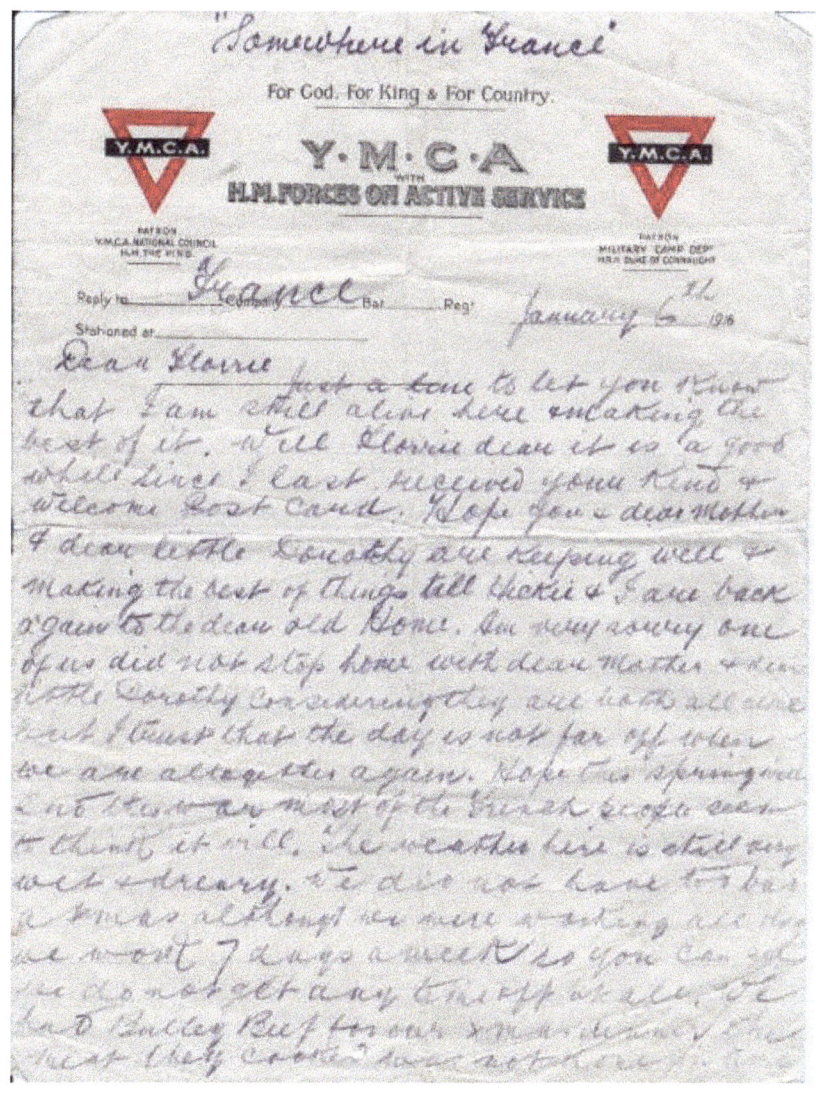

12 February 1917
Belgium

Embroidered Postcard
From Charlie to Dorothy

To Dear Dorrie with best love & kisses from your loving brother Charlie

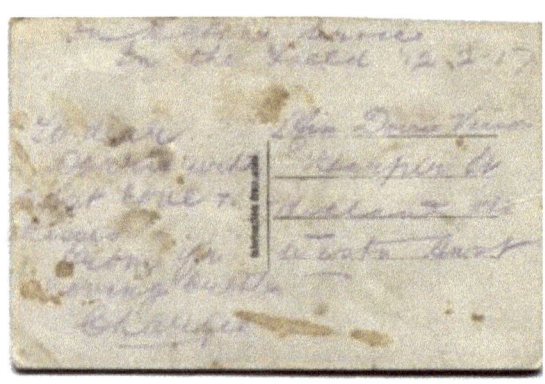

15 February 1917
Embroidered Silk Postcard
From Hickey to Dorothy

"SOMEWHERE IN FRANCE"

Dear Dorrie. Hoping this card finds you all in best of health as it leaves us all at present. Well Dorrie things are just about the same since I last wrote although the weather is now getting much warmer and so you can guess we are not sorry. Do not forget to write and let me know how you are all getting along. With fondest love. From Hick

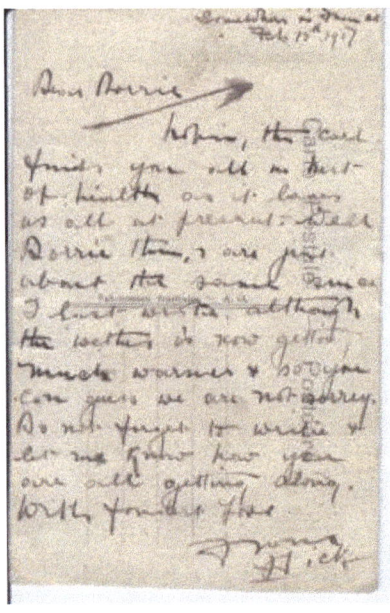

8 March 1917
Field Service Postcard
To Laura From Hickey

Standard form, date and signature only.

I am quite well, I have received your letter dated December 4th

17 March 1917
Leave Pass

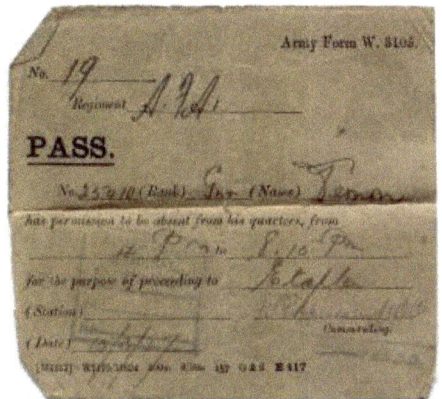

 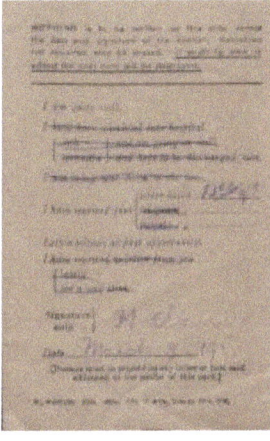

17 March 1917
France
Embroidered Postcard
From Charlie to Laura

To my dear Mother with best love from your loving son Charlie no.25410

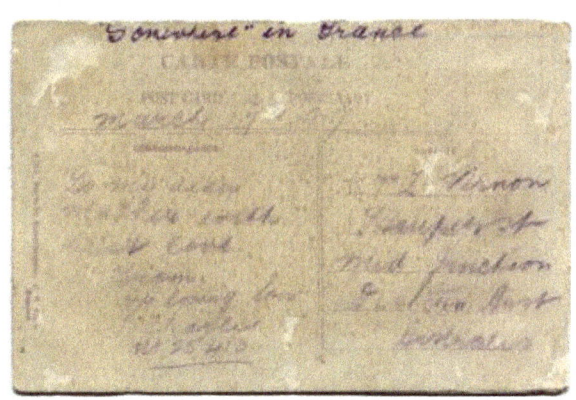

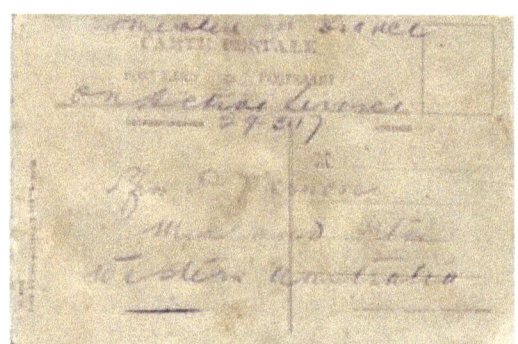
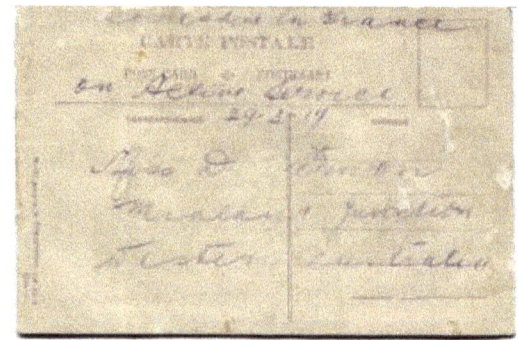

29 March 1917 France
Embroidered Postcards
From Charlie to Dorothy

April 1917 (translated from French)
Postcard
From Charlie to Laura

"Somewhere in France"

The Sentry – The Sentry braves death, a duty that a soldier fills effortlessly

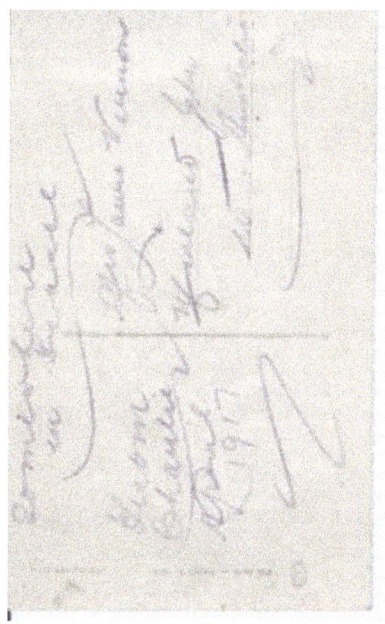

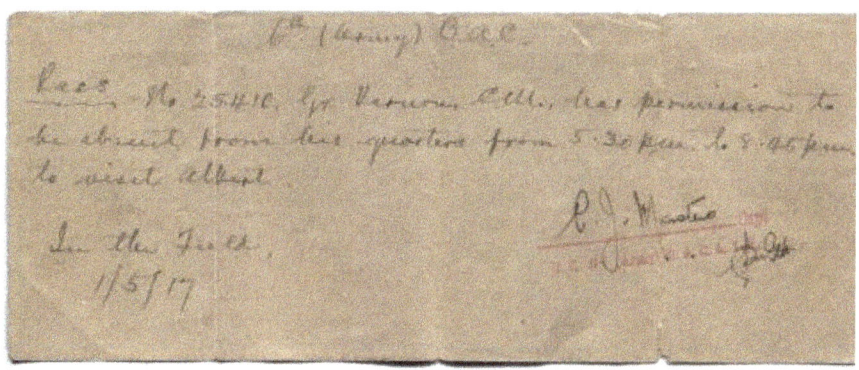

1 May 1917

Leave Pass

Pass No 25410 Gr Vernon CM., has permission to be absent from his quarters
from 5.20pm to 8.45pm to visit Albert

In the Field 1/5/17

29 May 1917 France
Postcards
From Charlie to Dorothy

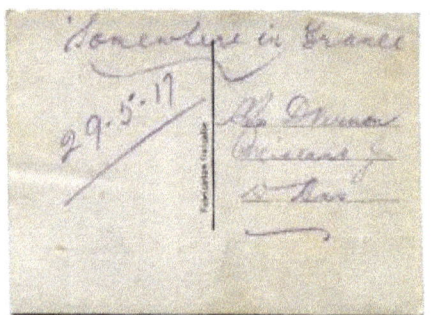 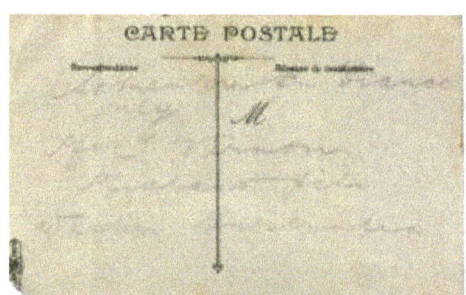

July 1917 France

Postcard
From Charlie to Laura

2 September 1917
Somewhere in France
(Translated from French)

Postcard
From Charlie to Dorothy

Translation: "A scrap of paper that is only good for throwing in the bin say the Germans, do you prefer my pockets?"

5 September 1917 Belgium
Letter from Charlie to Laura
Page 1

Ypres

September 5th 1917

My dear Mother

Just a little to let you know that Hickie & I are quite well since last writing to you Mother dear. We have moved to this section of the firing line. It was a pretty rough place at Nieuwpoort Belgium. I am giving this letter to one of the boys going on leave who is going to post it for me in England. The weather is glorious now, lovely and warm but its such a changeable climate. Tomorrow perhaps might …

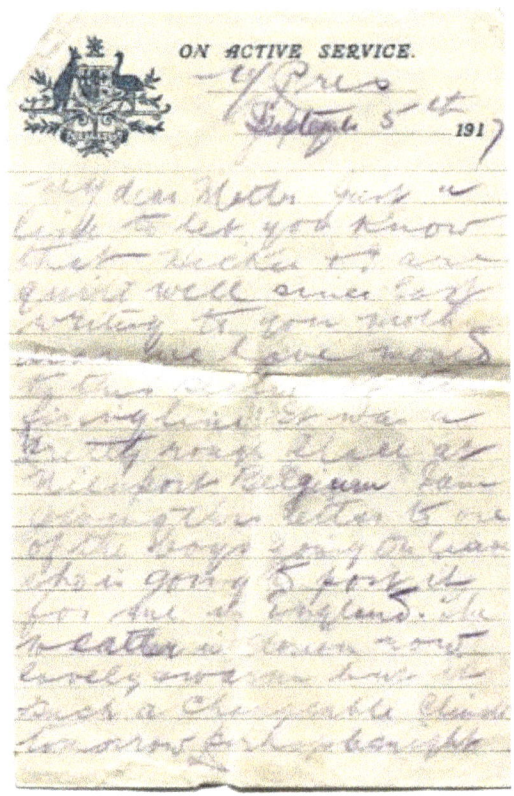

page 2

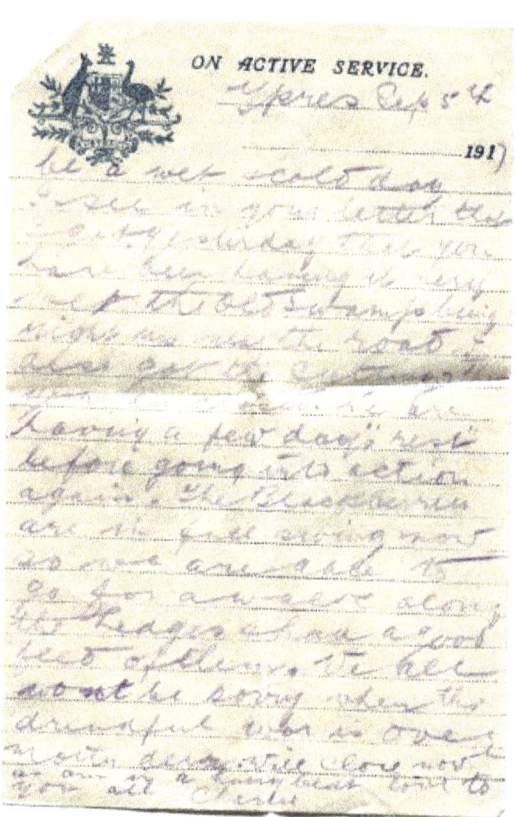

…be a cold wet day.

I see in your letter that I got yesterday that you have been having it very wet, the old swamp being right up near the road. I also got the cutting that you enclosed. We are having a few days "rest" before going into action again. The blackberries are in full swing now so we are able to go for a walk along the hedges and have a good feed of them. We all won't be sorry when this dreadful war is over Mother dear. Will close now as am in a hurry, best love to you all Charlie

28 September 1917
Postcard
From Hickey to Dorothy

Dear Dorrie, We arrived in London today from France and am having a good time. Hope you are all keeping well at home. This is a great place Dorrie and Australians get treated very well whilst they stay in England.

With fondest Love Hickey

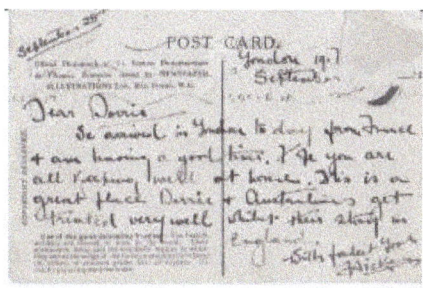

Carlisle 1 October 1917
Postcard
From Charlie to Dorothy

Dear Dorrie, We are having a nice time on our holiday am going back to France today week best love dear, your ever loving brother Charlie

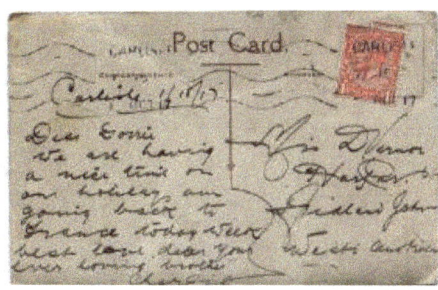

Carlisle 1 October 1917
Postcard
From Charlie to Florence

Dear Florrie, just a line to let you know we are on leave and am having a good time in Glasgow. With best love dear your ever loving brother Charlie

 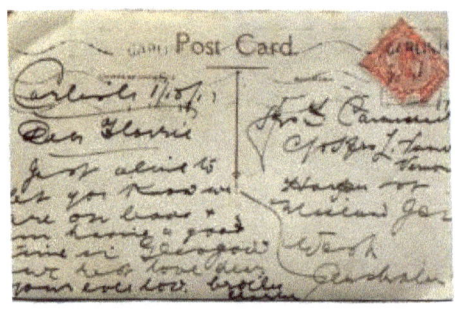

Carlisle 1 October 1917
Postcard
From Charlie to Laura

Dear Mother

We went out & seen this on Sunday. Best love Charlie

London 9 October 1917
Postcard
From Hickey to Dorothy

Dear Dorrie

Wishing you a Merry Christmas and a Happy New Year, 1917-1918, Hickey

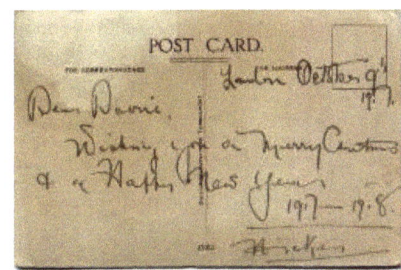

17 October 1917
Melbourne
Notice From AIF to Laura

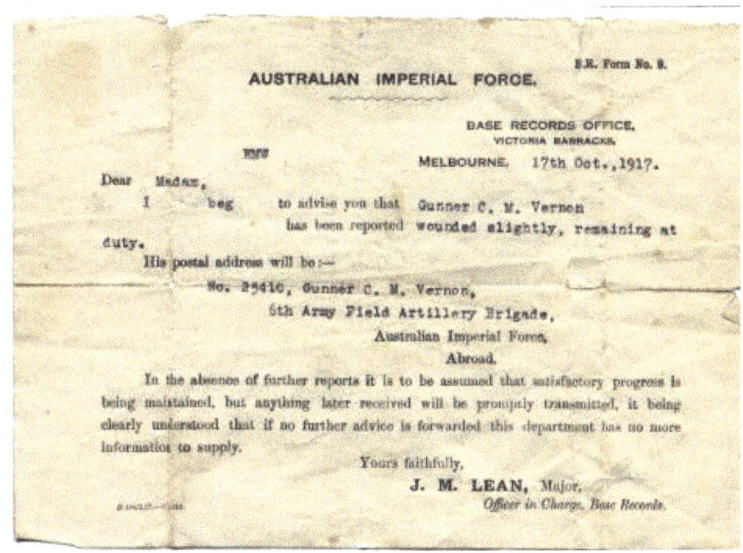

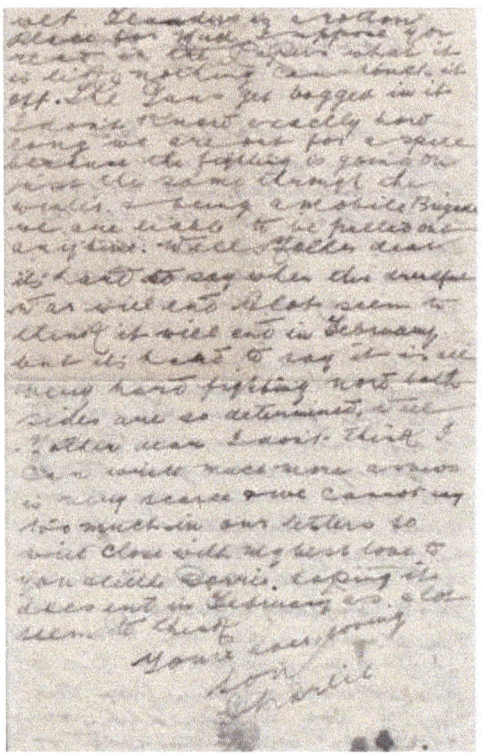

27 November 1917
Letter
From Charlie to Laura

SAME OLD ADDRESS SOMEWHERE IN BELGIUM

My dear Mother

Just a line or two to let you know that we are quite well and hope that you are all the same.

Well Mother dear I received a letter from Florrie yesterday am pleased she is getting along alright also little Wilfie as it was a long while since I last got a letter from her. Florrie says she goes out kangaroo hunting now and again. Don't we wish we were back in dear old Australia.

It must be nice for Florrie now that she has got a piano it is good company especially in the bush where she is. Am pleased that you are able to get a pass now and again from the Mng. Coy. The weather over here is still very cold and ...

.... wet. Flanders is a rotten place for mud. I suppose you read in the papers what it is like, nothing can touch it off. The guns get bogged in it. I don't know exactly how long we are out for a spell because the fighting is going on just the same through the winter and being a mobile brigade we are liable to be pulled out anytime.

Well Mother dear its hard to say when this dreadful war will end. A lot seem to think it will end in February but it's hard to say it is all very hard fighting now both sides are so determined.

Well Mother dear I don't think I can write much more as news is very scarce and we cannot say too much in our letters so will close with my best love to you and little Dorrie.

Hoping it does end in February as a lot seem to think.

Your ever loving Son Charlie

5 February 1918
Field Service Postcard to Laura

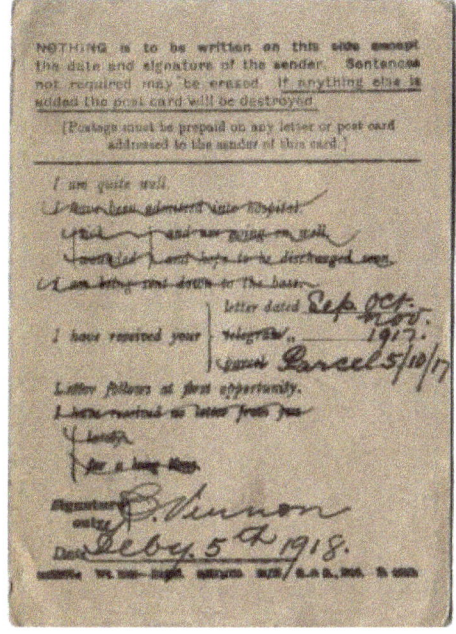

14 February 1918
Embroidered Postcard to Laura

"Somewhere" in Flanders

Best love from your loving son Charlie

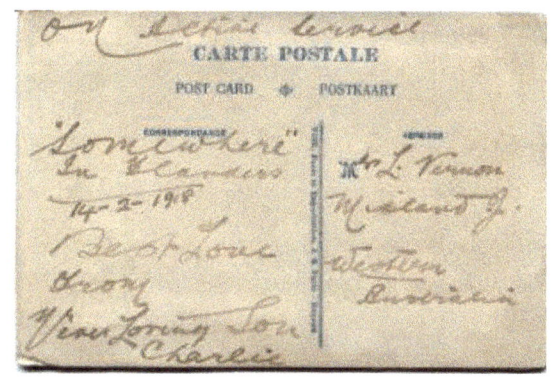

April 1918
Part Letter to Laura

ON THE BATTLEFIELD NORTHERN FRANCE WESTERN FRONT

Pages 5 & 6 of a letter

"...the same. I believe Arthur Gardner had his foot crushed on his way up here so he is in an hospital somewhere. Eric Diffen is in England in hospital. The weather is getting a bit better now. Well Mother dear I will now close this letter hoping it soon sees an end to this War. Best love, Your ever loving son Charlie. Give my love to Dorrie."

Overleaf: "on The Battlefield Northern France Western Front April 1918"

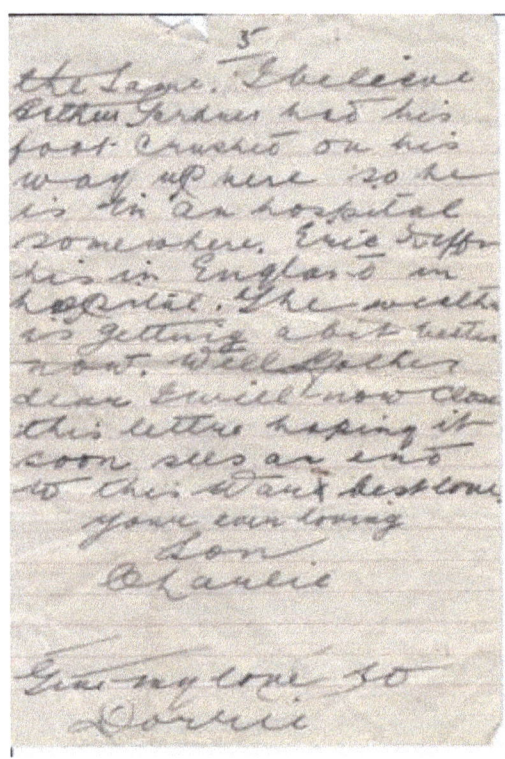
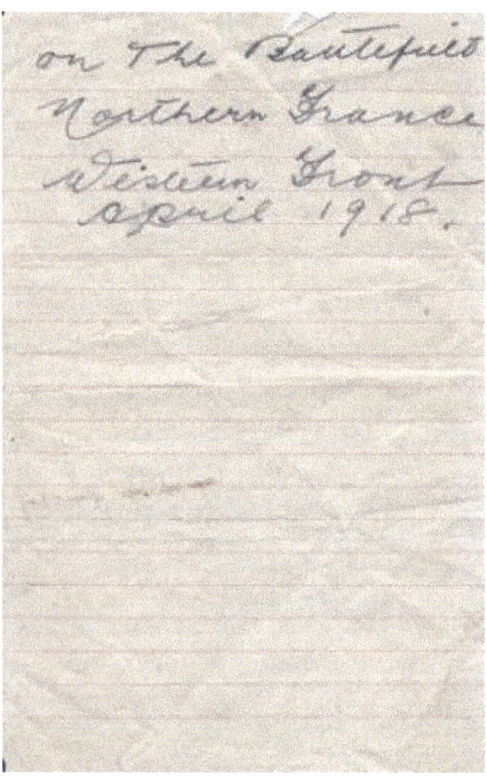

18 June 1918
France
Postcard
From Charlie to Laura

June 06 1918
Letter to Laura

WESTERN FRONT AMIENS SECTOR SOMEWHERE IN FRANCE JUNE 16 1918

My dear Mother, am now able to give you a bit of an idea of the work we have been doing since I came back from "Blighty" leave last October. After a couple of days we managed to find our unit which is a difficult thing at times when coming back from leave as they move about such a lot they were at a place called Merville having pulled out of that terrible place called Ypres of which one will never forget…

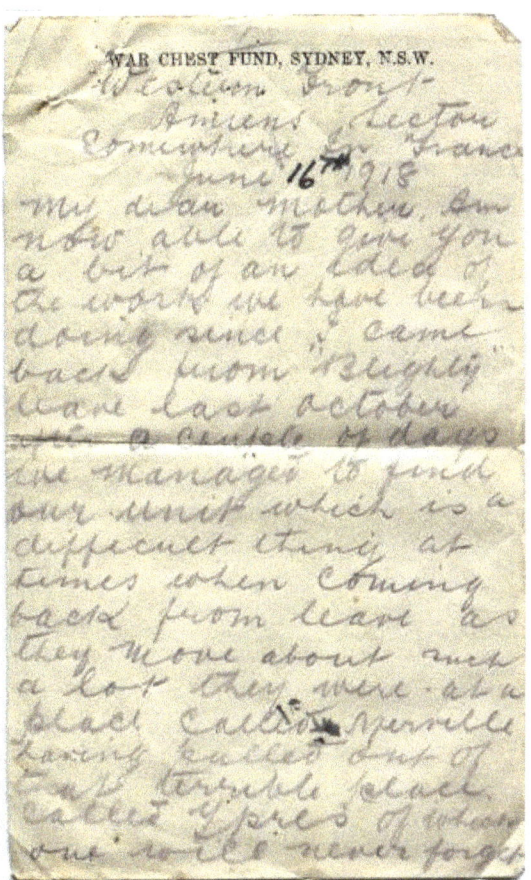

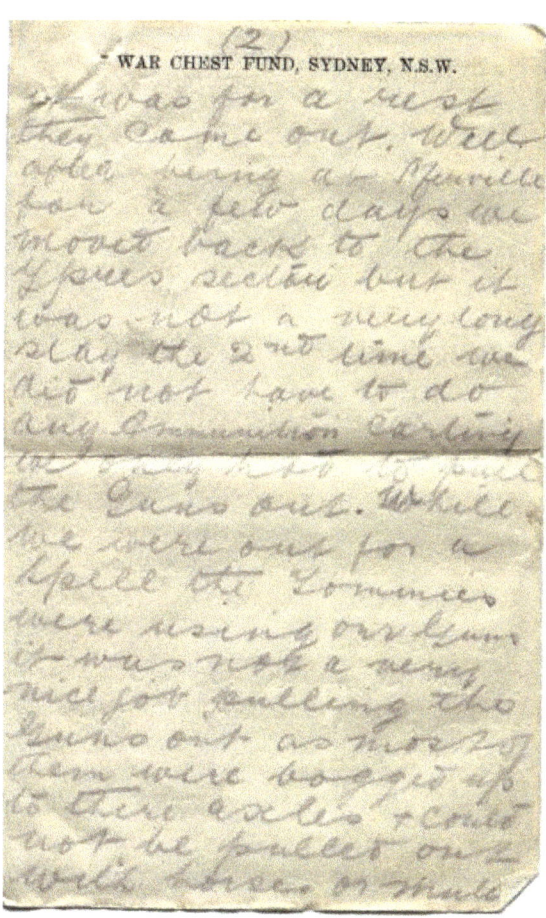

… it was for a rest they came out. Well after being at Merville for a few days we moved back to the Ypres sector but it was not a very long stay the 2nd time we did not have to do any ammunition carting, we only had to pull the guns out. While we were out for a spell the Tommies were using our guns, it was not a very nice job pulling the guns out as most of them were bogged up to there axles & could not be pulled out with horses or mules

June 06 1918
Letter to Laura (cont.)

WESTERN FRONT AMIENS SECTOR SOMEWHERE IN FRANCE JUNE 16 1918

but had to be man handed with drag ropes of course there was heavy shelling going on around us most of the time.

We did not have any casualties on these guns while pulling them out it was when we were hauling out an old "Tommy" Battery of which all the crew were either killed or wounded, we (a party of 20) went up about 2 a.m. in the morning of course we all had a good Rum issue before we started otherwise I do not think we would have managed to stand the strain, well we were more unfortunate on these guns, in fact before …

…we started pulling them out a "Tommy" officer whose Battery was near by told us not to attempt to pull those guns out as they were observed too much by the enemy anyhow we had to obey our officers orders so after we replaced some of them with new wheels (I can tell you the guns were knocked about a good deal with shell fire) we layed planks across the shell holes which are that close to one another it is almost impossible to find a track through them. Well Mother it was just beginning to break of day & we had only got one of the guns half way across towards a bit of a road when …

June 06 1918
Letter to Laura (cont.)

WESTERN FRONT AMIENS SECTOR SOMEWHERE IN FRANCE JUNE 16 1918

…we observed old Fritz's observation Balloon going up. Well he wasn't up for very long when a battery of his opened fire my word his Gunners were accurate he was landing shells all around us. Well we got orders from our officers to make for a dugout. We jumped from shell hole to shell hole. Well out of our 20 one was killed and 4 were wounded we were lucky getting out so light considering how close the shells landed to us our Sergeant who was with us received the "Croix de Guerre" French decoration, Well the next morning at the same time a larger party…

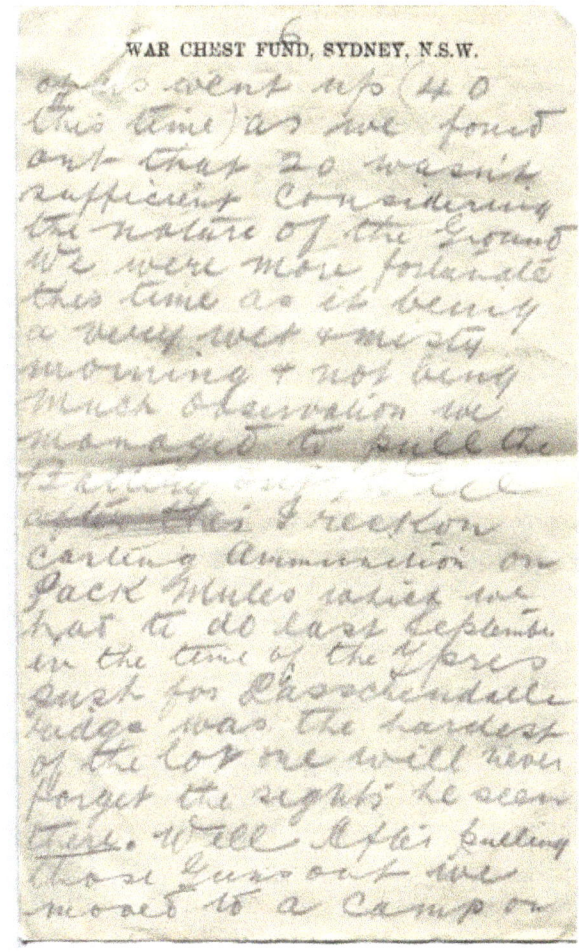

… of us went up (40 this time) as we found out that 20 wasn't sufficient considering the nature of the ground. We were more fortunate this time as it being a very wet and misty morning and not being much observation we managed to pull the battery out, well I reckon carting ammunition on pack mules which we had to do last September in the time of the Ypres push for Passchendalle ridge was the hardest of the lot one will never forget the sights he seen there. Well after pulling those guns out we moved to a camp on …..

June 06 1918
Letter to Laura (cont.)

WESTERN FRONT AMIENS SECTOR SOMEWHERE IN FRANCE JUNE 16 1918

…the slopes of Mont Kemmel which as you know is well in the hands of the enemy (also Merville) well we stayed there for a while until we got more reinforcements as we were very short at the time one driver looking after 6 to 8 animals instead of 2 after getting up to strength we moved to Neuve Eglise which is in the Messines sector we spent our Xmas in this place it being our 2nd Xmas in France in fact Neuve Eglise is in Belgium. I hope we do not have to spend a third one…

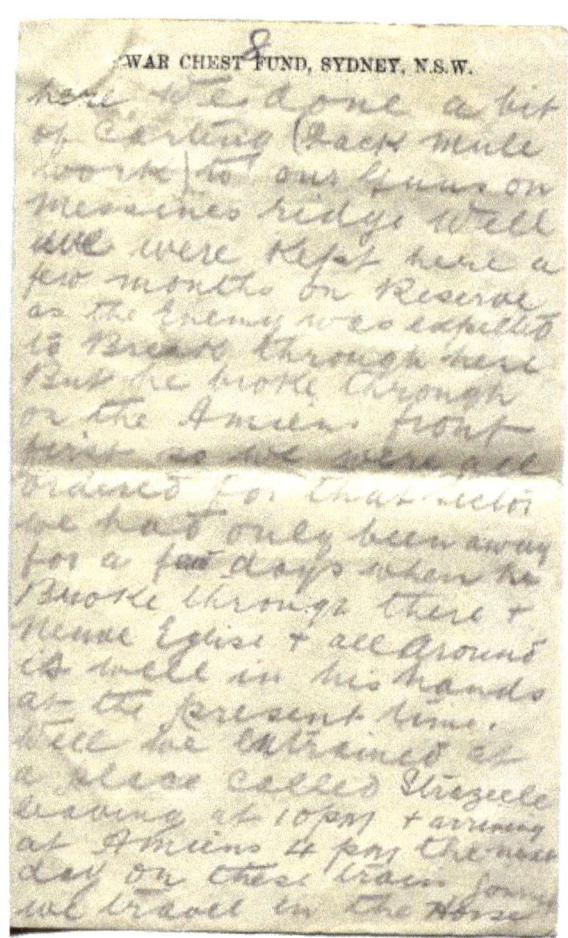

…here. We done a bit of carting (pack mule work) to our guns on Messines ridge Well we were kept here a few months on Reserve as the Enemy was expected to break through here but he broke through on the Amiens front first so we were all ordered for that sector. We had only been away for a few days when he broke through there & Neuve Eglise & all around us is well in his hands at the present time. Well we entrained at a place called Strazeele leaving at 10pm and arriving at Amiens 4pm the next day. On these trains we travel in the Horse …

June 06 1918
Letter to Laura (cont.)

WESTERN FRONT AMIENS SECTOR SOMEWHERE IN FRANCE JUNE 16 1918

…trucks with our mules in fact all troops travel in these trucks. Well after disentraining we harnessed up and moved off about 6pm passing through the lovely town of Amiens with its beautiful Cathedral overlooking the city it was a pity to see the people moving away with that ever they could get hold of. Old Fritz was shelling it when we were passing through towards the line some of the places were knocked about then since we last seen it I believe it has been shelled a good deal more.

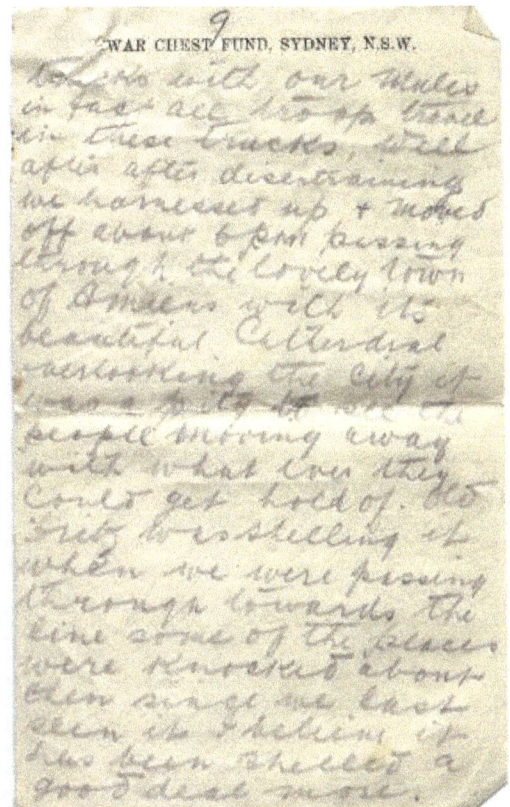

Postcards to Mother - addressed but no message. from "Somewhere in France"

49

18 June 1918
Postcard
From Charlie to Laura

"But we also tried hard to kill ourselves before we could get up the line, by tearing like mad up and down a lot of sand hills in full fighting order."

15 July 1918
Letter from Charlie to Laura

"Somewhere" in France Western Front

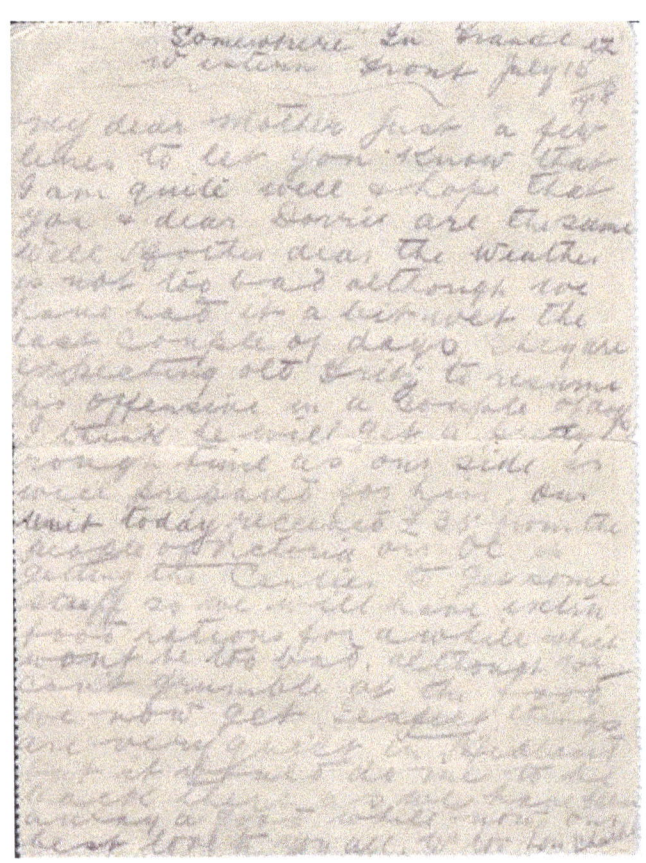

My dear Mother just a few lines to let you know I am quite well and hope that you and dear Dorrie are the same. Well Mother dear the weather is not too bad although we have had it a bit wet the last couple of days. They are expecting old Fritz to resume his offensive in a couple of days. I think he will get a pretty tough time as our side is well prepared for him. Our unit today received £35 from the people of Victoria. Our OC is getting the canteen to get some stuff so we will have some extra food rations for a while which won't be too bad, although we can't grumble at the food we now get. I expect things are very quiet in Midland but it would do me to be back there - as we have been away a good while now, our best love to you all. W love Charlie

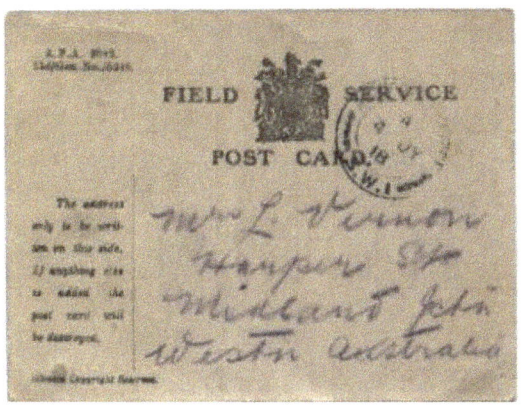

3 July 1918
Service Card
From Charlie to Laura

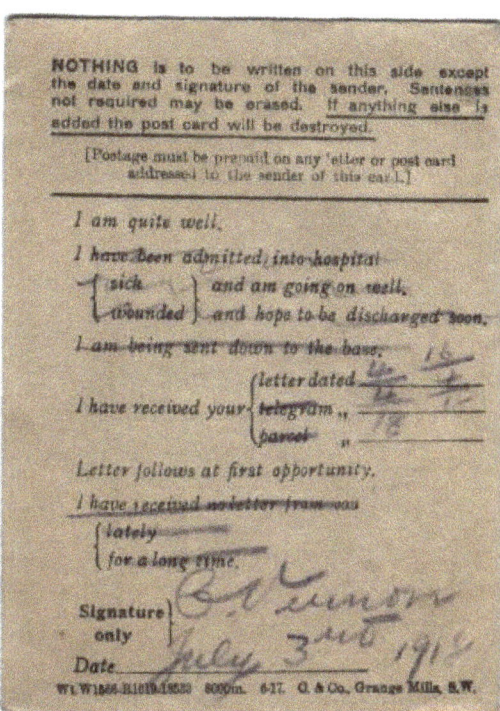

19 August 1918
Embroidered Post Card
From Hickey to Dorothy

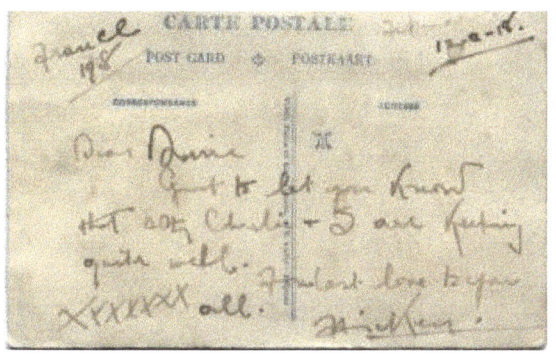

Dear Dorrie, Just to let you know that both Charlie and I are keeping quite well. Fondest love to you all xxxxxxxxx

Hickey

1 October 1918
Entrance Card & Souvenir
Postcard from Windsor Castle

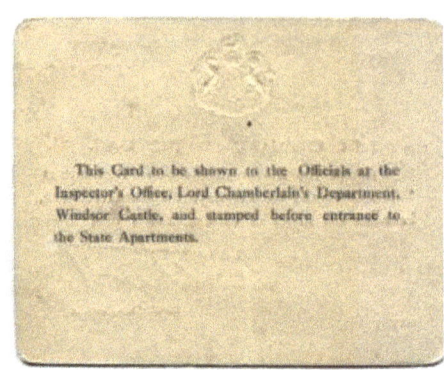

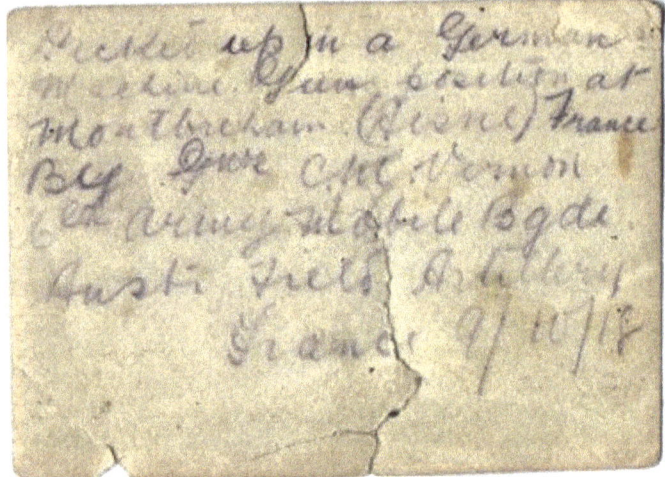

Picked up in a German machine gun position at Montbrehain (Aisne) France by Cnr C.M. Vernon 6th Army Mobile Bgde Aust Field Artillery France 9/10/18

09 October 1918
Photo unknown couple

14 October 1918
Letter to Australian Corps
From General Sir H.S.Rawlinson

25410
Dvr C.M. Vernon
6th Army Field Artillery Brigade
Amiens France

Fourth Army No. G.S.2/23.

Australian Corps.

Since the AUSTRALIAN CORPS joined the Fourth Army on the 8th April, 1918, they have passed through a period of hard and uniformly successful fighting of which all ranks have every right to be proud.

Now that it has been possible to give the AUSTRALIAN CORPS a well-earned period of rest, I wish to express to them my gratitude for all that they have done. I have watched with the greatest interest and admiration the various stages through which they have passed, from the hard times of FLERS and POZIERES to their culminating victories at MONT ST. QUENTIN and the great Hindenburg system at BONY, BELLICOURT Tunnel and MONTBREHAIN.

During the Summer of 1918 the safety of AMIENS has been principally due to their determination, tenacity and valour.

The story of what they have accomplished as a fighting Army Corps, of the diligence, gallantry and skill which they have exhibited, and of the scientific methods which they have so thoroughly learned and so successfully applied has gained for all Australians a place of honour amongst nations and amongst the English speaking races in particular.

It has been my privilege to lead the AUSTRALIAN CORPS in the Fourth Army during the decisive battles since August 8th, which bid fair to bring the war to a successful conclusion at no distant date.

No one realises more than I do the very prominent part that they have played, for I have watched from day to day every detail of their fighting, and learned to value beyond measure the prowess and determination of all ranks.

In once more congratulating the Corps on a series of successes unsurpassed in this great war, I feel that no mere words of mine can adequately express the renown that they have won for themselves and the position they have established for the Australian nation not only in France but throughout the world.

I wish every Officer, N.C.O. and Man all possible good fortune in the future, and a speedy and safe return to their beloved Australia.

H. S. RAWLINSON,
General,
Commanding Fourth Army.

H.Q., Fourth Army,
14th October, 1918.

2 November 1918
Postcards
To Dorothy from Charlie

On Active Service Somewhere in France

Best Love

Charlie

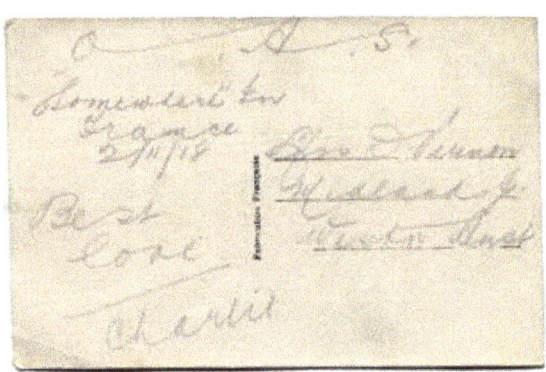

3 November 1918
Postcards
To Florence from Charlie

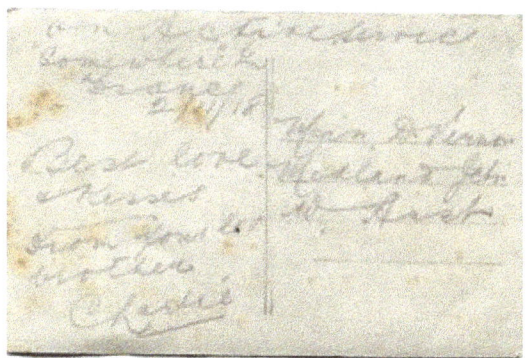

Best love and kisses from her brother Charlie

On Active Service Somewhere in France Best Love

Charlie

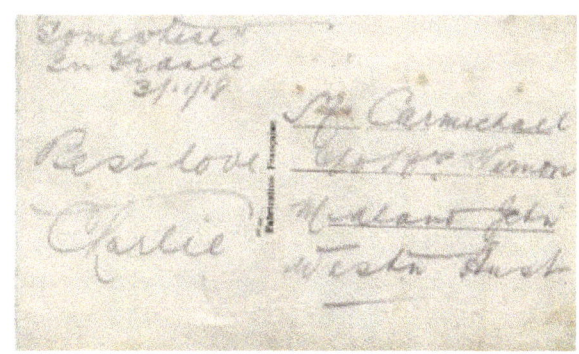

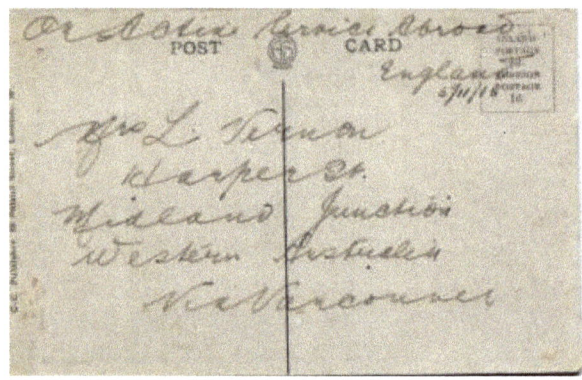

3 November 1918
Postcard
To Florence from Charlie

On Active Service Somewhere in France 3/11/18
Best Love
Charlie

6 November 1918
Postcard
To Laura from Charlie Via Vancouver

On Active Service abroad England
6/11/18
Best Love
Charlie

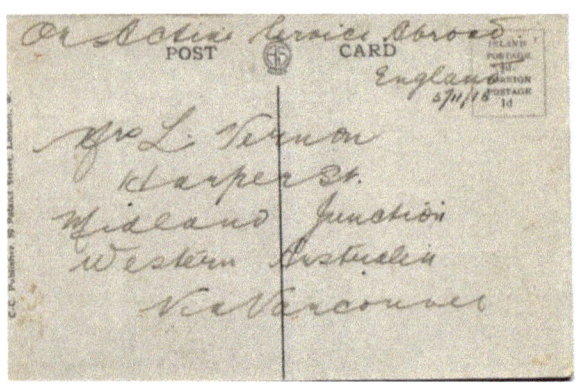

8 November 1918
Letter
To Laura from Charlie

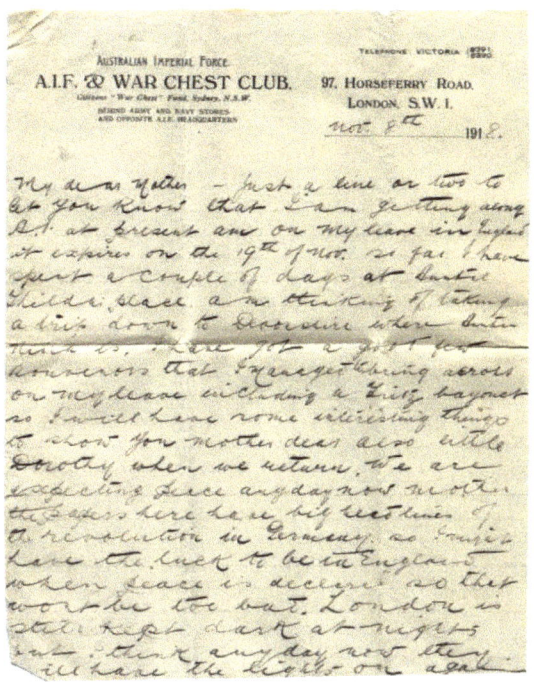

My dear Mother - just a line or two to let you know that I am getting along A1 at present am on my leave in England it expires on 19 Nov. So far I have spent a couple of days at Auntie Hilda's place am thinking of taking a trip down to Devonshire where Auntie Nina is. I have got a good few souvenirs that I managed to bring across on my leave including a Fritz bayonet so I will have some interesting things to show you mother dear also little Dorothy when we return. We are expecting peace any day now mother the papers here have big headlines of the revolution in Germany so I might have the luck to be in England when peace is declared so that won't be too bad. London is still kept dark at nights but I think any day now the will have the lights on again

Well Mother dear we will have a lot to tell you of the war when we get home once again. We had a fairly rough time of it in France the 8th of August until recently as we had to follow up the enemy across very rough roads & tracks as he mined the roads & bridges. Hickie is in camp at Sutton Veny I have sent him a letter to try and get a few days off I expect I will see him any day now. I have not seen him since the end of August. A. Hancock had the morning off so we had a look at the Museum & Westminster Abbey which I reckon are worth seeing. Am sending you & Dorrie in a registered envelope a couple of little brooches that I bought in France. Well Mother dear by the time you receive this I think the war will be over.

So will now close with my fondest love to you all.

Yr loving son Charlie

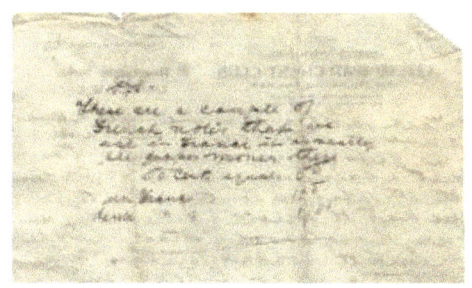

PS

These are a couple of French notes that we use in France it is really all paper money there

50 cents equals 5s5d
un franc equals 10s5d
deux franc equals £1.10s8d

11 November 1918
Letter to all Ranks of Fourth Army from General Sir H.S.Rawlinson

Fourth Army, No. G.S. 125.

TO ALL RANKS OF THE FOURTH ARMY.

The Fourth Army has been ordered to form part of the Army of Occupation on the RHINE in accordance with the terms of the Armistice. The march to the RHINE will shortly commence, and, although carried out with the usual military precautions, will be undertaken generally as a peace march.

The British Army through over four years of almost continuous and bitter fighting has proved that it has lost none of that fighting spirit and dogged determination which has characterized British Armies in the past, and has won a place in history of which every soldier of the British Empire has just reason to be proud. It has maintained the highest standard of discipline both in advance and retreat. It has proved that British discipline, based on mutual confidence between officers and men, can stand the hard test of war far better than Prussian discipline based on fear of punishment.

This is not all. The British Army has, during the last four years on foreign soil, by its behaviour in billets, by its courtesy to women, by its ever ready help to the old and weak, and by its kindness to children, earned a reputation in France that no army serving in a foreign land torn by the horrors of war, has ever gained before.

Till you reach the frontier of Germany you will be marching through a country that has suffered grievously from the depredations and exactions of a brutal enemy. Do all that lies in your power by courtesy and consideration to mitigate the hardships of these poor people who will welcome you as deliverers and as friends. I would further ask you when you cross the German frontier to show the world that British soldiers, unlike those of Germany, do not wage war against women and children and against the old and weak.

The Allied Governments have guaranteed that private property will be respected by the Army of Occupation, and I rely on you to see that this engagement is carried out in the spirit as well as in the letter.

In conclusion I ask you one and all, men from all parts of the British Empire, to ensure that the fair name of the British Army, enhanced by your exertions in long years of trial and hardship, shall be fully maintained during the less exacting months that lie before you.

I ask you to show the world that, as in war, so in peace, British discipline is the highest form of discipline, based on loyalty to our King, respect for authority, care for the well-being of subordinates, courtesy and consideration for non-combatants, and a true soldierly bearing in carrying out whatever duty we may be called upon to perform.

Rawlinson.
Genl.

H.Q., FOURTH ARMY,
11th November, 1918.
Commanding Fourth Army.

PRINTED IN FRANCE BY A.P. AND S.S.   PRESS A—11/18—8609X—20,000.

14 November 1918
Letter to all Servicemen
From Field Marshall Lord William Birdwood

To the Officers, Non-Commissioned Officers, and Men of the Australian Imperial Force.

It is now just four years that we have been serving together, often through days of hardship and peril, and often through times of well-deserved success.

During this time I hope and think we have come to know each other well, and I trust have realised how rightly we have confidence in each other.

No words of mine can possibly express all I feel for the magnificent work which has been done by the Australian soldier during these long four years. It is well known and recognised, not only throughout the British Empire, but throughout the world—and now we have peace in sight, and peace after a victory in which the Australian soldier has taken so large a share.

Even then, with peace there are still difficult times before us. Faith in our recent foe cannot quickly be established, and it may be that for some little time yet we shall be able to relax no precautions, until we are assured of the complete and honest fulfilment of our terms.

Then will come the difficult time of demobilisation, and it is regarding this that I wish to make a personal appeal to every single member of the A.I.F. in the full confidence that it will be met as every other appeal to face and tackle the strongest positions has ever been met by the Australian soldier. Never has the name of Australia stood higher than it does now throughout the world, thanks to the bravery of her soldiers, and it is up to every one of us to see that this is maintained, and that no reproach can be cast on the Australian Flag owing to any behaviour of ours.

The time of demobilisation will undoubtedly be difficult and irksome—I fully realise what great personal self-restraint will certainly be required—but if each individual of us makes up his mind to do his best during these times, realising the good name we bear, I feel confident that all will go off well.

I want you to remember that everything possible will be done to look after and help the troops during this period, while every energy will be strained to get men back to their homes as soon as this possibly can be done. You will have to realise, however, that there is a great shortage of shipping, and that there must be a considerable inevitable delay.

Play the game, boys, during this time, as you have always done, and add still more to the deep debt of gratitude which will always be acknowledged to you by the Empire and remembered by me as your comrade and commander.

In the Field,
14th November 1918.

W.R. Birdwood

19 November 1918
Ration Books

Dear Mother

This is the ration book that was issued to me when I went on leave to England

Charlie

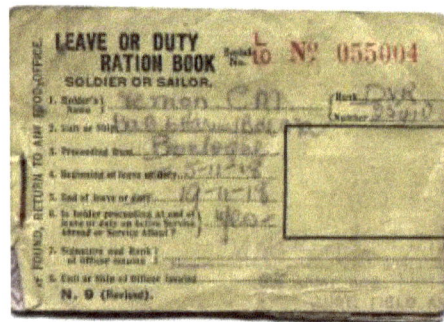
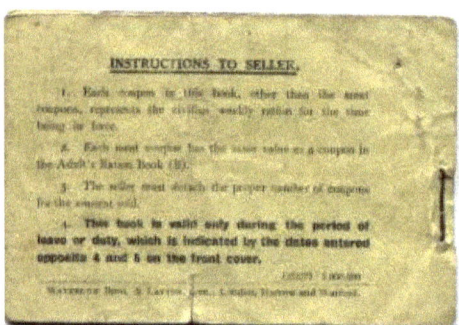

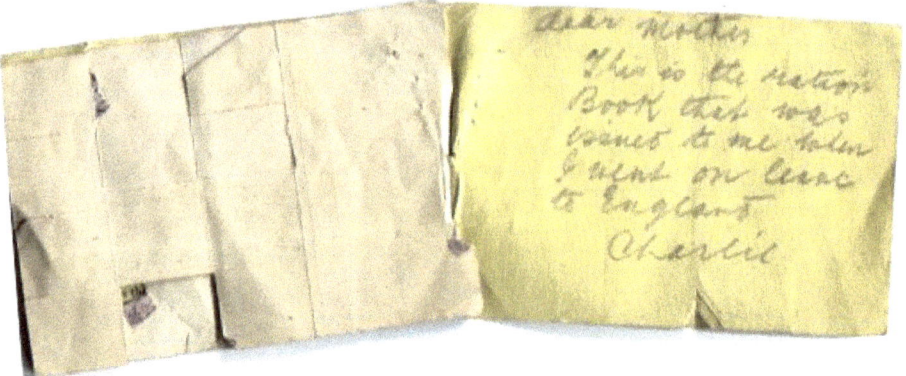

12 November 1918
Postcards
To Laura from Charlie

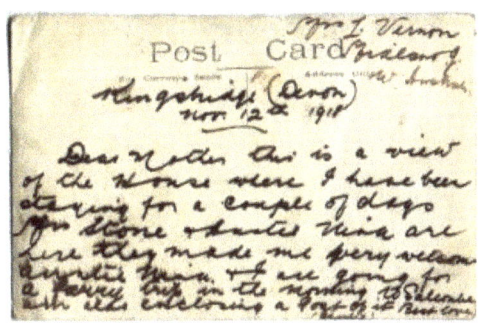

Kingsbridge (Devon)

Nov. 12th 1918

Dear Mother this is a view of the house where I have been staying for a couple of days. Mrs Stone and Auntie Nina are here they made me very welcome. auntie Dini & I are going for a ferry trip in the morning to Salcombe. with this enclosing a post of it Best love Charlie

Kingsbridge, (Devon 12/11/18)

This is another view of a little place not far from here

fondest love to you all Mother dear we will soon be home to you once again

Yr loving son Charlie

November 1918
Postcard from Charlie

This town we have also been through there was some talk before I left France about the sister camp being there after the war.

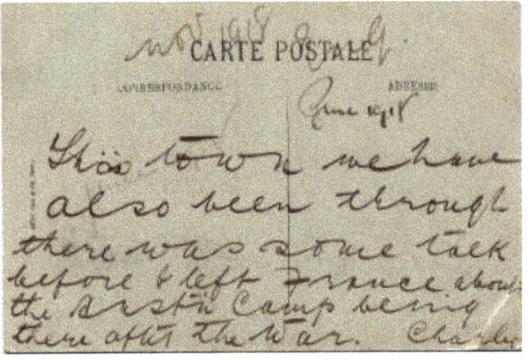
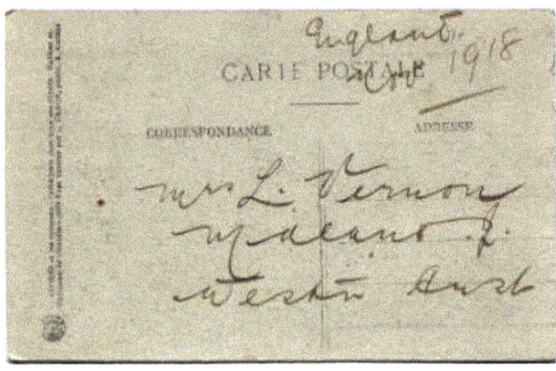

November 1918
Postcard
From Charlie to Laura

15 November 1918
Empty Envelope
From Charlie to Laura

On the back *"Touring Brakes leaving ALF & War Chest Club London".*

Handwritten "London 15/11/1918"

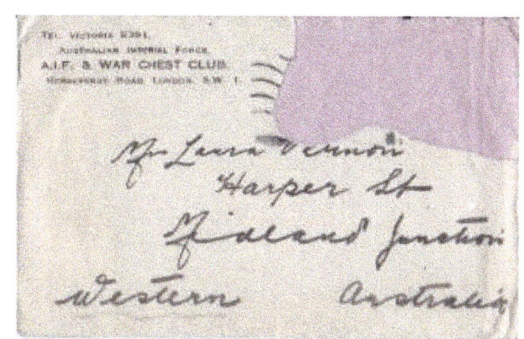

22 November 1918
Embroidered Silk Postcard
From Hickey to Dorothy

O.J.B Worminster England. Dear Dorrie, with fondest love XXXXXX Hickey

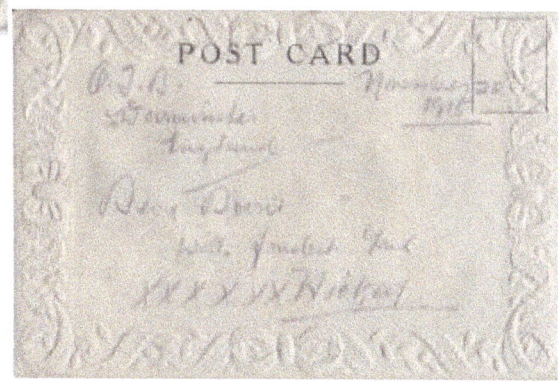

16 & 28 November 1918
Postcards
From Charlie to Dorothy

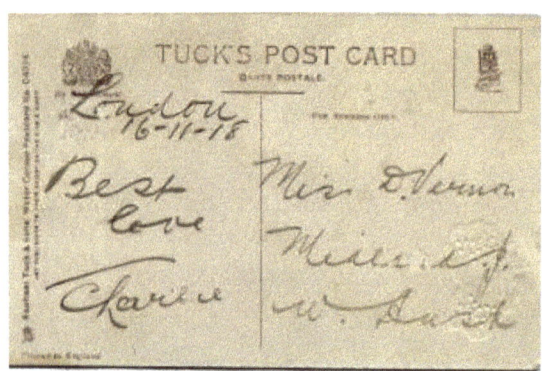

London 16/11/18
Best love
Charlie

Somewhere in France
28/11/1918
Best love to all
Your brother Charlie

23 November 1918
Letter
From Charlie to Laura

FRANCE

Dear Mother, Just a few lines to let you know that I arrived back here last night. We did not have a too bad of a trip across. It is very cold over this way now but one must expect it for this time of the year. All the ponds and creeks are beginning to freeze. We have still got our mules to look after until we hand them over one won't like parting with them after having them so long, (Ref page 74)

I do not think it will be long now …..

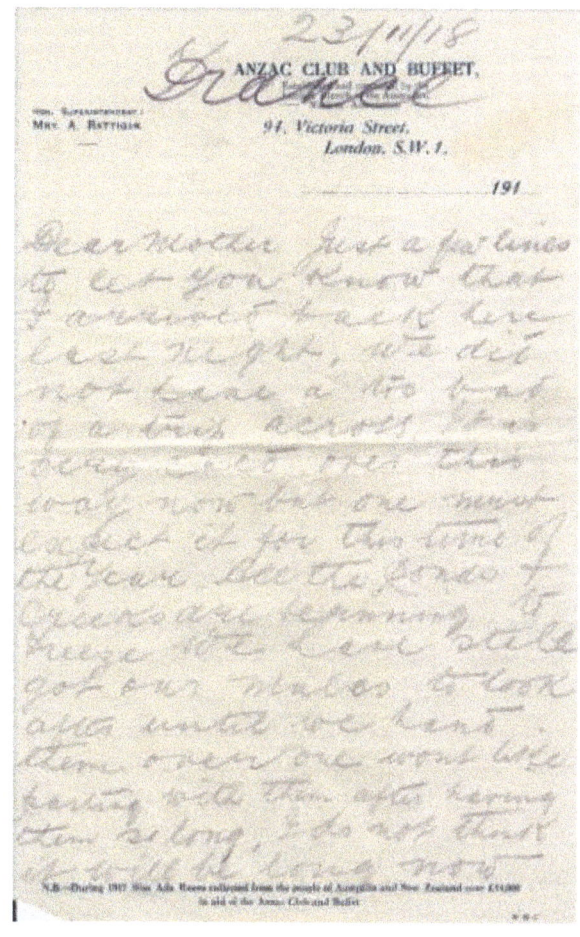

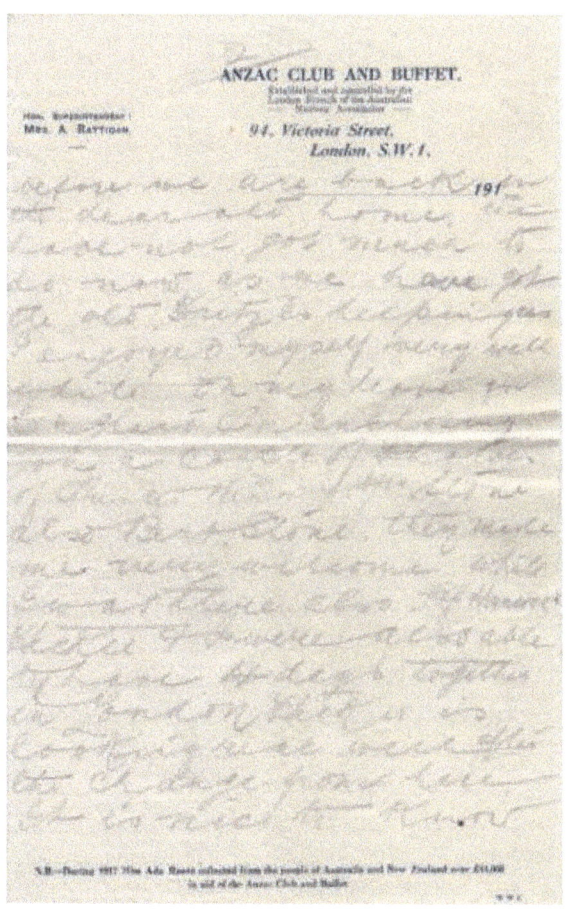

(2 …cont)….before we are back in the dear old home. We have not got much to do now as we have got the old Fritz'es helping us. I enjoyed myself very well while on my leave in England. Am enclosing you a couple of photos of Auntie Nina and Mrs Stone, also Bert Stone. They made me very welcome while I was there also Mrs Hancroft. Hickie and I were also able to have 4 days together in London. Hickie is looking real well after the change from here. It is nice to know….

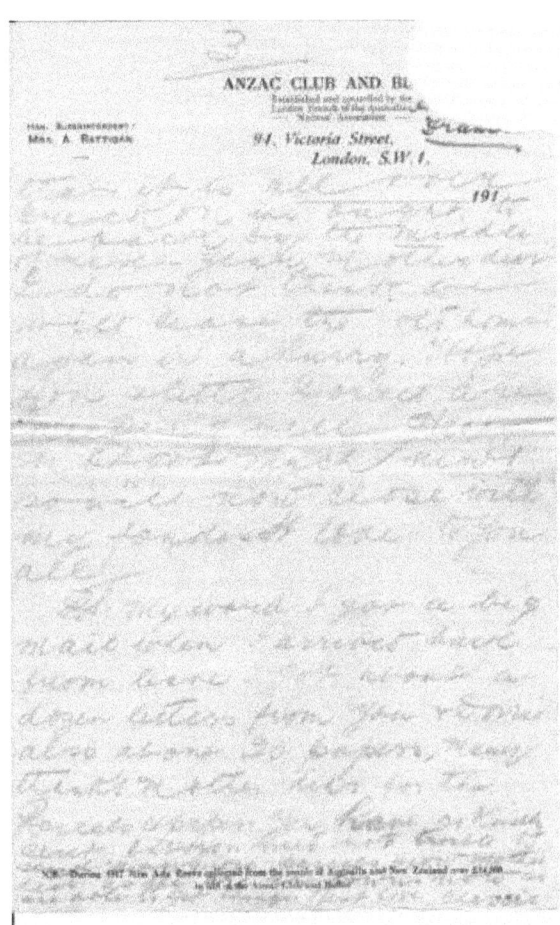

Undated Part Letter
From Charlie to Dorrie

…. you have still got the old cat. I have not got much more news at present to tell you Dorrie but don't forget to write to me as I would like to know how you are getting on. We ought to be leaving here about the end of the month for England, so will be able to see the world a bit before returning to our dear old W.A. I remain Your loving brother Charlie. PS will you ask Mother would she mind sending me the Swan Express as I would like to know how things are getting on in Midland. Charlie

(3…cont)….that it is all over. I reckon we ought to be back by the middle of next year Mother dear. I do not think we will leave the old home again in a hurry. Hope you and little Dorrie are keeping well. Have not got much news so will now close with my fondest love to you all.

PS. My word I got a big mail when I arrived back from leave I got about a dozen letters from you and Dorrie also about 20 papers. Many thanks Mother dear for the parcels and papers you have so kindly sent but you need not trouble to send any more parcels now Mother dear as we are in towns now so able to get things. Best love, Charlie

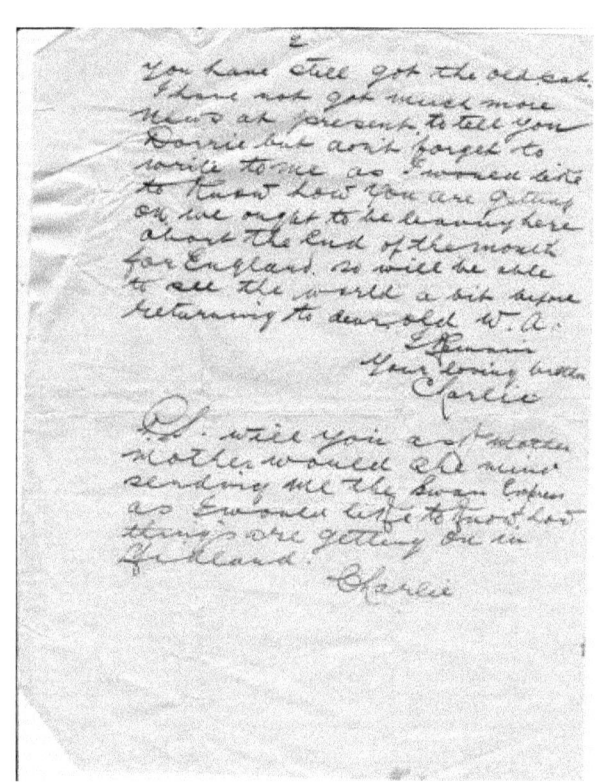

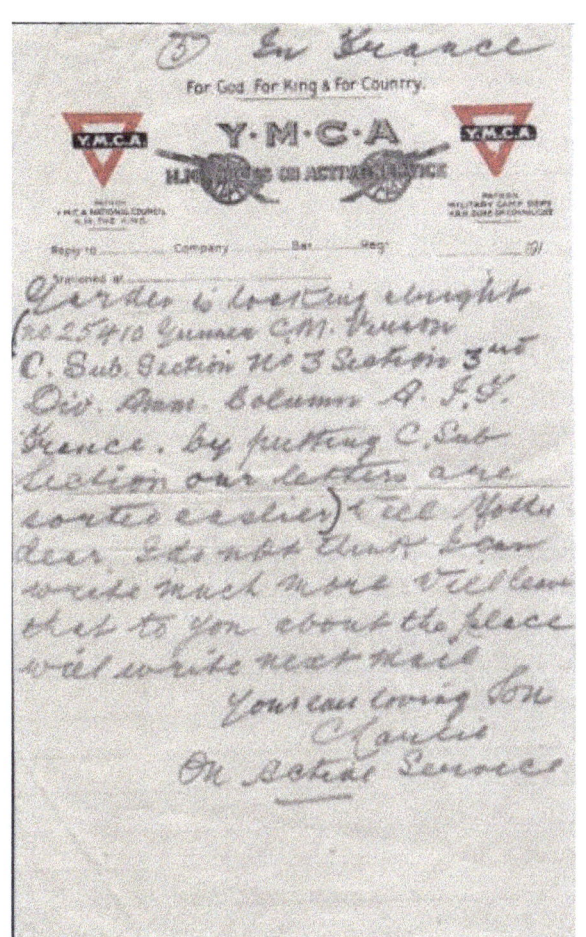

**Undated Part Letter
From Charlie to Laura
In France**

page 5 of a letter

….garden is looking alright. (no 25410 Gunner CM Vernon C.Sub.Section No 3Section 3rd Dev. Amm. Column A.I.F. France. By putting c.Cub Section our letters are sorted easier) Well Mother dear I do not think I can write much more. Will leave that to you about the place will write next mail. Your ever loving Son Charlie, On Active Service

19 December 1918
Part letter
From Charlie to Dorrie

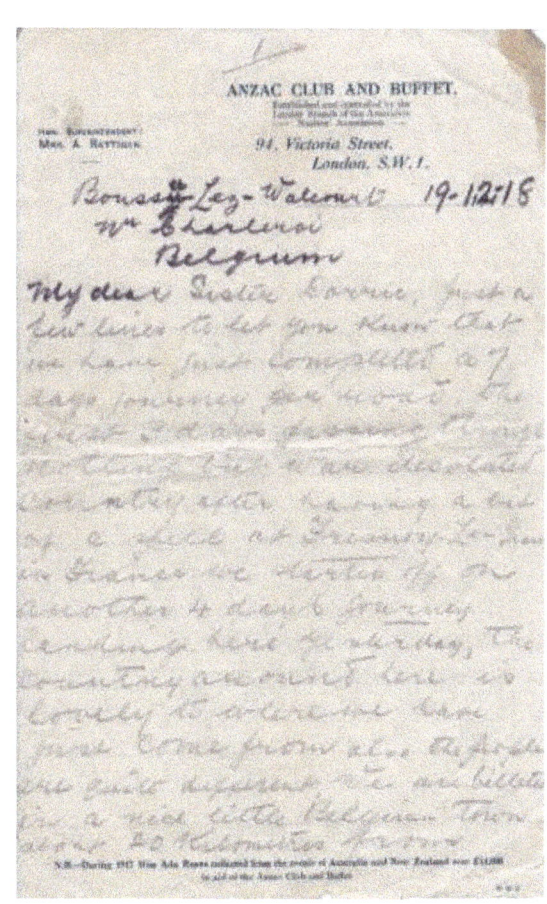

Boussé les Walcourt Nr Charleroi, Belgium

My dear Sister Dorrie, Just a few lines to let you know that we have just completed a 7 day journey per road, the first 3 days passing through nothing but war desolated country after having a bit of a spell at Fresnoy-Le-Grande in France we started off on another 4 days journey landing here yesterday. The country around here is lovely to where we have just come from also the people are quite different. We are billeted in a nice little Belgium town about 20 kilometres from …..

22 December 1918
Letter
From Charlie to Laura

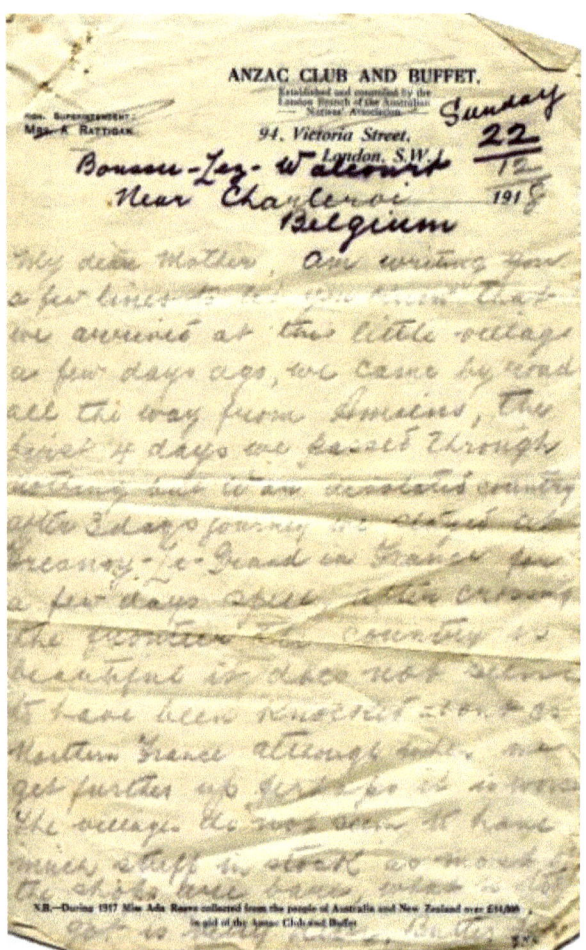

Boussu-Lez-Walcourt

Near Charleroi, Belgium

My dear Mother, am writing you a few lines to let you know that we arrived at this little village a few days ago, we came by road all the way from Amiens, the first 4 days we passed through nothing but war desolated country, after 3 days journey we stayed at Fresnoy-le-Grand in France for a few days spell, after crossing the frontier this country is beautiful it does not seem to have been knocked about as Northern France although when we get further up perhaps it is worse. The villages do not seem to have much stuff in stock as most of the shops are bare, what is to get is very dear, butter for…

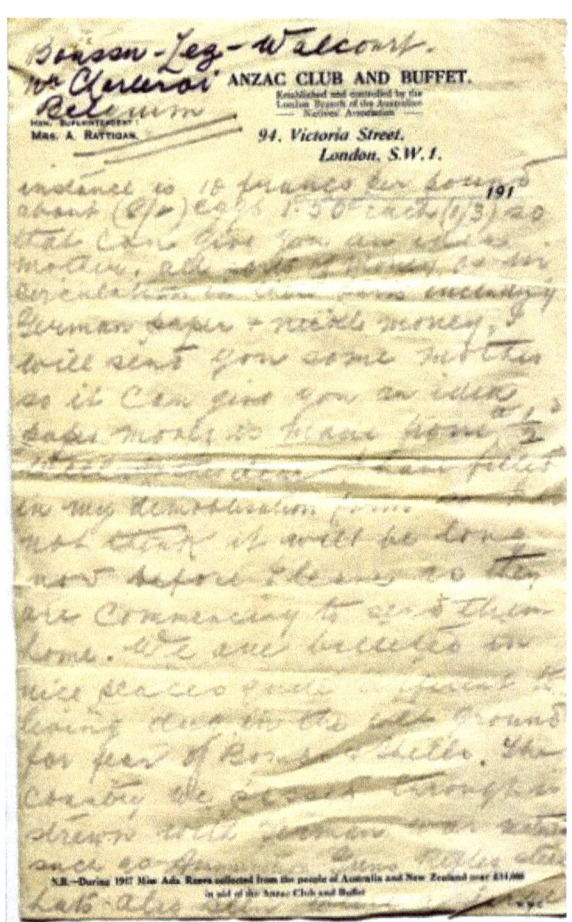

…instance is 10 francs per pound ((about 8/-) eggs 1.50 each (1/3) so that can give you an idea Mother. all sorts of money is in circulation including German paper & nickel money, I will send you some Mother so it can give you an idea. Paper money is made from a "1/2". Well Mother dear I have filled in my demobilisation form so do not think it will be long now before I leave as they are commencing to send them home. We are billeted in nice places quite different to living dug in the wet ground for fear of bombs and shells. the country we passed through is strewn with German war material such as ammunition, guns, rifles, steel hats also seen where a large….

22 December 1918
Letter
From Charlie to Laura (Cont)

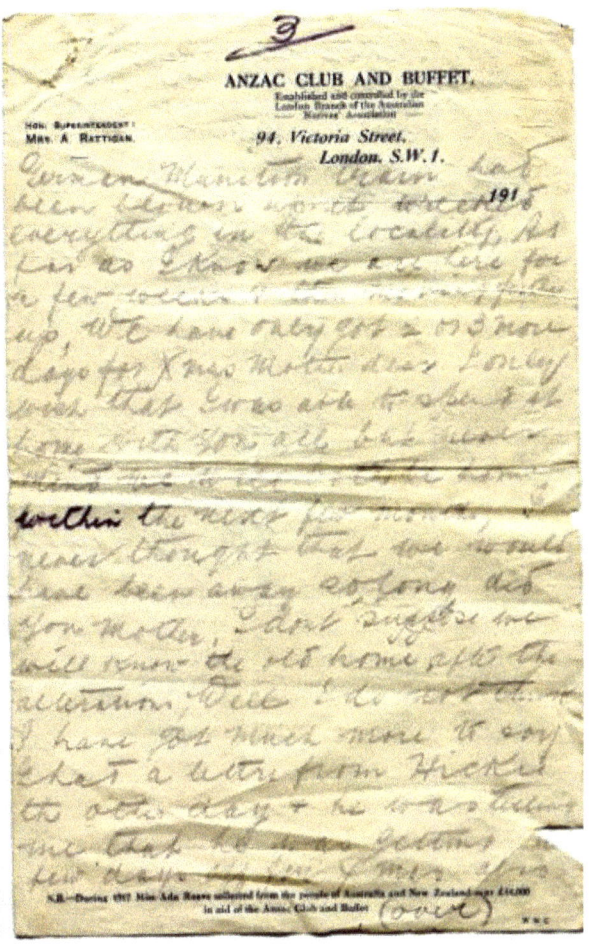

... German Munitions train had been blown up, it wrecked everything in the locality, as far as I know we are here for a few weeks and then moving farther up, We have only got 2 or 3 more days for Xmas Mother dear I only wish that I was able to spend it home with you all but never mind we will both be home within the next few months, I never thought that we would have been away so long did you mother,

I don't suppose we will know the old home after the alterations, Well I do not think I have got much more to say, I had a letter from Hickie the other day and he was telling me that he was getting a few days off for Xmas also...

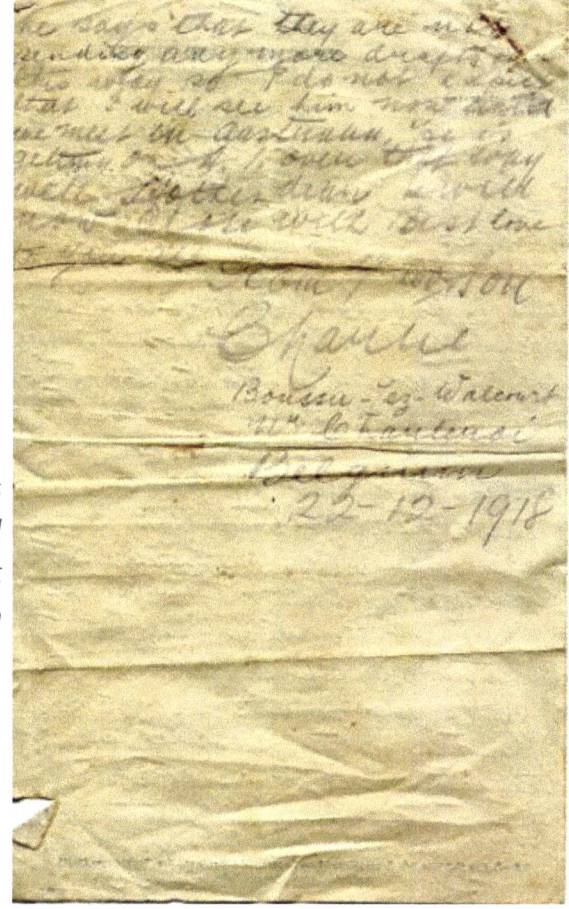

...he says that they are not sending any more drafts this way so I do not expect that I will see him now until we meet in Australia, He is getting on A.1. over that way Well Mother dear I will now close with Best love to you all

From your son

Charlie

Boussu-les-Walcourt Nr Charleroi, Belgium

22-12-1918

30 December 1918
England
Postcard
From Hickey to Laura

Dear Mother

I expect to be leaving here for Australia early in January, so you can expect me home about the end of February. I am on the Boat Roll but of course, cannot say exactly the date when we will sail. No doubt they will let you know sometime before I arrive.

This is a little village near where we are camped. As you can see it is not much of a place. We are having some very wet and cold weather at present. Charlie is keeping A1 over in France. Well my fondest love to you and little Dorrie.

Hickey

Undated Postcard

Best love from Mother

Undated Christmas Card
From Laura to Hickey

Dear Khaki Boy O' Mine

To Dearest Hickie From Mother with love and many kisses

A Happy Xmas & prosperous New Year

Front opens out from the middle to reveal pressed flowers and message inside.

(Note pressed flowers still intact!)

Undated Postcard
From Dorrie to Hickey

Dear Hickie, Hoping these few lines find you all in the best of health as it leaves mother & I at present. Hope you have a very happy birthday & let's all hope by the time the next one comes around you will be with us once again. I remain your ever loving sister Dorrie xxxxxx

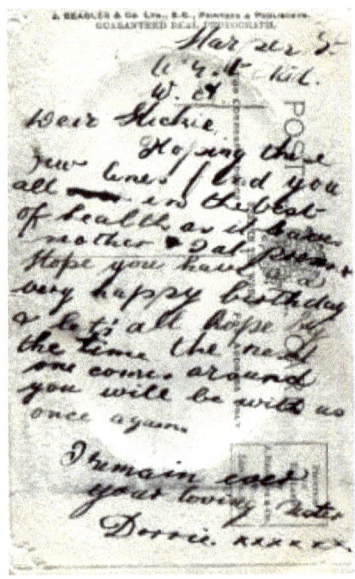

Undated Postcard
From Mother & Jessie - probably to Laura

Grotto Cottage, 13 Winfield Street, Bungay (UK), to cousin (presuming Laura in Midland Junction, WA).

Dear Cousin, with our fondest love and every good wish for a brighter and more prosperous New Year

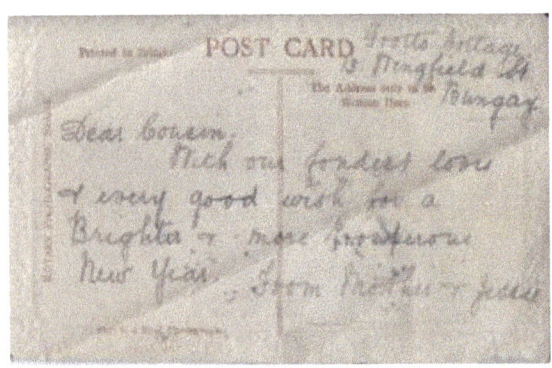

22 January 1919
Photo-Postcard
From Charlie to Dorrie

Photo of Charlie with his mules: (photo appears to have been cut to fit a frame)

"Darkie, Nigger, Myself taken at Bousse-les-Walcourt near Charleroi Belgium 11.1.19"

Dear Dorrie, This is a photo of my pair of mules that I have driven during my stay in France and Belgium, many a load of ammunition they have lumped up to the guns, also they done a lot of pack work at Ypres. A lot of us had our photos taken with the mules as we are losing them in a day or two.

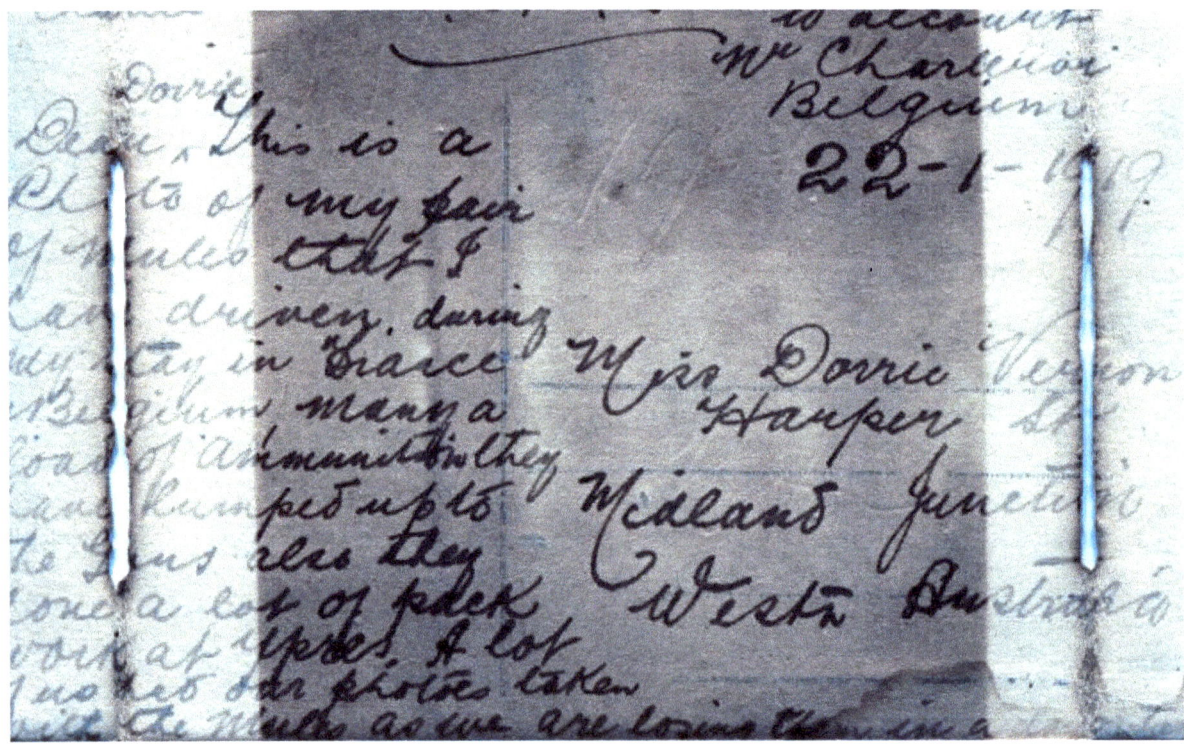

REF: BBC WWI "When the end of war was declared in 1918, millions of soldiers looked forward to finally returning home. But their horses and mules faced a far less certain future.

The healthiest and youngest animals were brought back to the UK - 25,000 remained in the British army while more than 60,000 were sold to farmers. Horses and mules in the next class down were auctioned off to farmers on the continent for an average of £37.

The oldest and most worn-out horses were sent to the knacker's yard for meat and fetched £19 – a necessary move when severe food shortages hit Europe at the end of the war."

27 March 1919
Letter
From Charlie to Laura - 5 pages

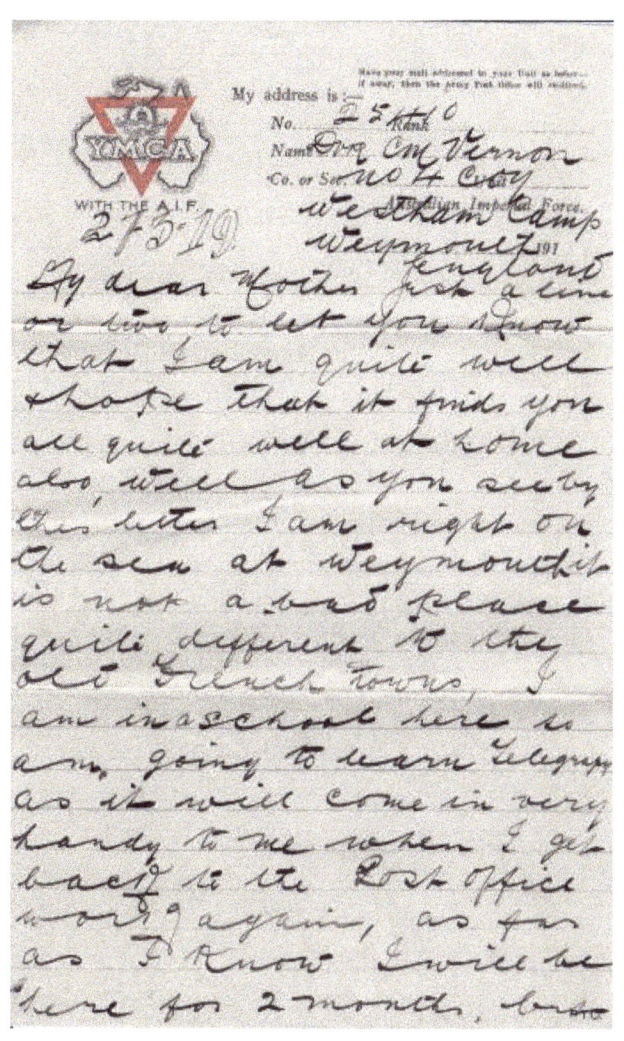

From 25410 DVR CM Vernon, No 4 Coy, Westham Camp, Weymouth England

My dear Mother, Just a line or two to let you know that I am quite well and hope that it finds you all quite well at home also.

Well as you see by this letter I am right on the sea at Weymouth it is not a bad place quite different to the old French towns, I am in a school here so am going to learn Telegraphy as it will come in very handy to me when I get back to the Post Office work again, as far as I know I will be here for 2 months but….

page 2

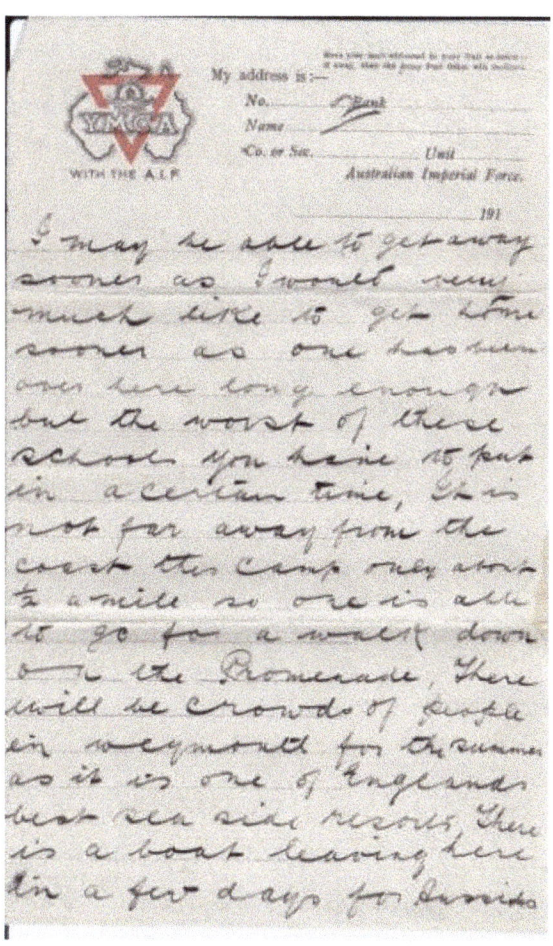

….I may be able to get away sooner as I would very much like to get home sooner as one has been over here long enough but the worst of these schools you have to put in a certain time. It is not far away from the coast this camp, only about half a mile so one is able to go for a walk down on the Promenade. There will be crowds of people in Weymouth for the summer as it is one of England's best sea side resorts. There is a boat leaving here in a few days for Aussie….

27 March 1919
Letter
From Charlie to Laura – 5 pages (cont)

page 3

…. but it is not taking any West Australians on board.

I had a letter from Auntie Nina yesterday and she was telling me that she would very much like to go out to Australia and that she is writing to you mother to see if you could manage to put her up. She also mentioned that she is writing to Uncle Marchie to see if he could give her something towards her passage out. Well mother it is nothing to do with me but if you would like her out there as company you could write and tell her as she ….

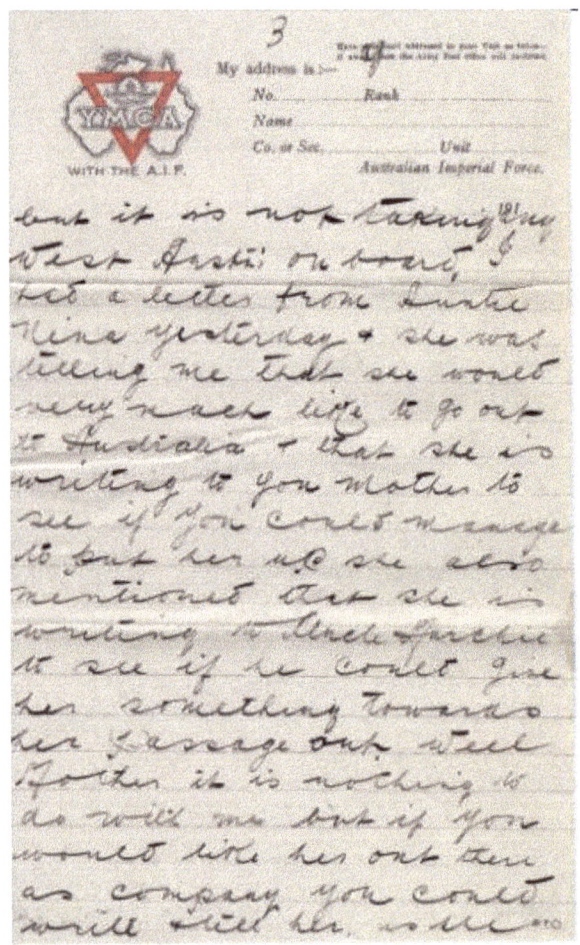

page 4

….tells me in her letter that she thinks the climate would suit her. There is plenty of picture shows etc. about here so am able to put in the evenings somehow. This month as you know we get the cold winds and I can assure you it has been a bit on the cold side the last few days, but today the sun has been out a good deal which makes it more pleasant. I expect Hickie felt the heat very much after this climate. It will be winter on your side when I arrive so that won't be too bad.

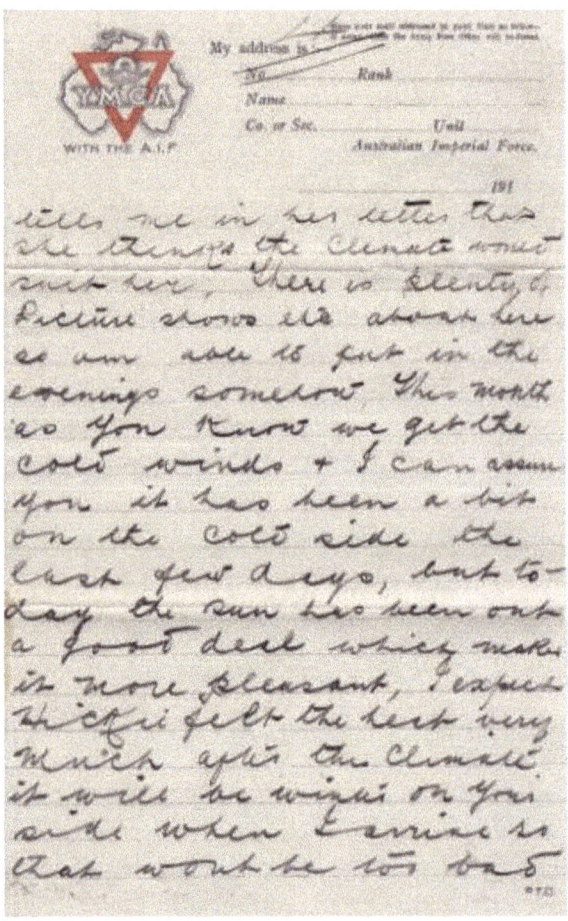

27 March 1919
Letter
From Charlie to Laura - 5 pages (cont)

page 5

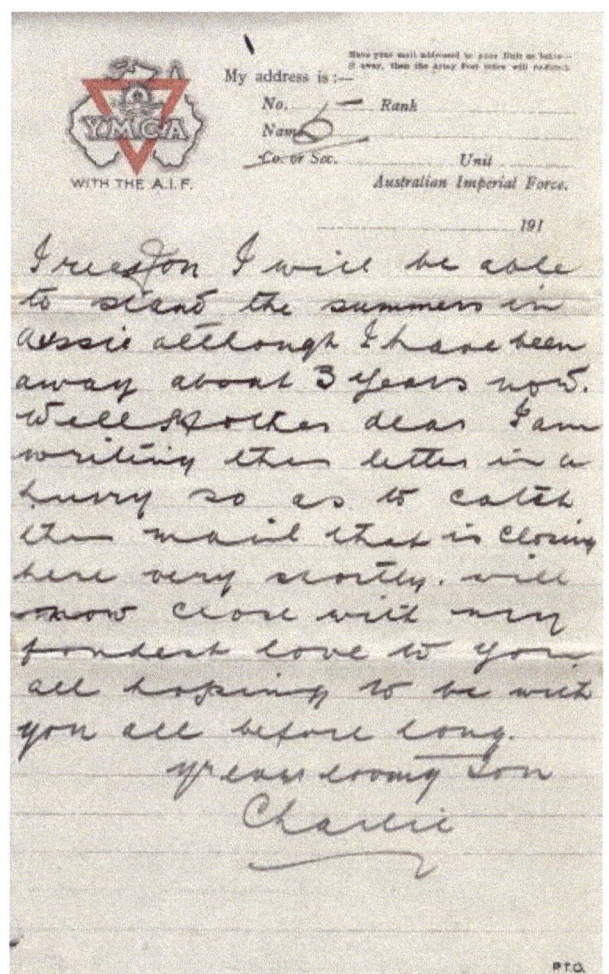

….I reckon I will be able to stand the summers in Aussie although I have been away about 3 years now. Well Mother dear I am writing this letter in a hurry so as to catch the mail that is closing here very shortly. Will now close with my fondest love to you all hoping to be with you all before long.

Your loving son Charlie

Undated Part Letter
(after January 1919 as Hickey is back in Australia)
From Charlie to Laura

Monte Video Camp Weymouth England

…..about the middle of Nov. from Romford. Am enclosing a ration book that are issued to us when we go on leave but we very seldom use them. There is going to be a procession of our troops on Anzac Day through London. I expect things will be lively in Perth on that day. Well Mother dear I haven't got much news yet to say so will bring this short letter to a close. Hoping it finds yourself, Dorothy and Hickie in the best of health, as it leaves me the same. your loving son Charlie

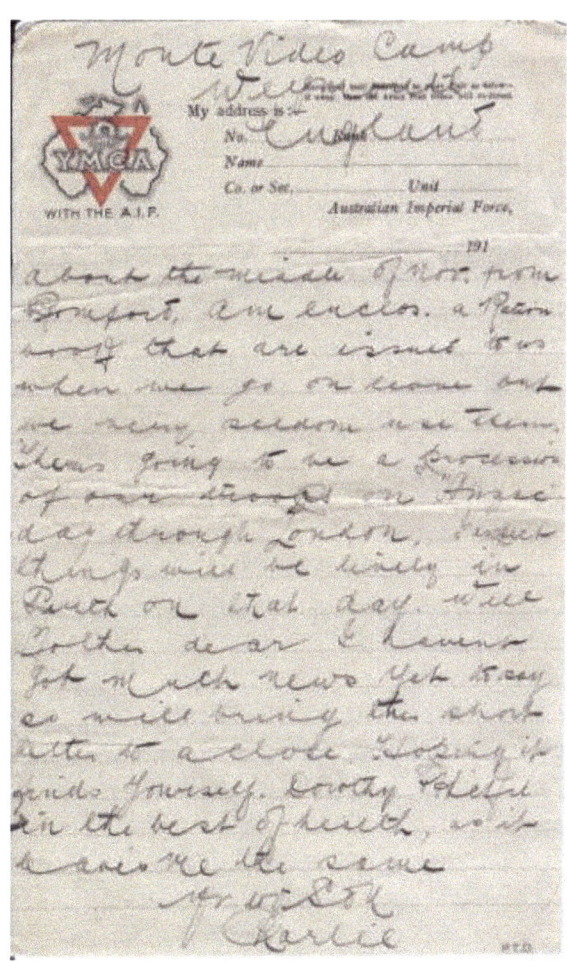

17 April 1919
Part Letter
From Charlie to Laura

No 25410 Dvr. CM Vernon 6th (army) Field Artillery Brigade No 4 Coy Westham, Weymouth

My dear Mother. Am writing you a few lines to let you know that I am quite well and hope it finds you and all at home the same. Well Mother dear I have just had 5 days leave and went up to Bungay and seen Cousin Jessie she made me very welcome I had the weekend there so on Sunday she took me for a walk out to Earsham a place I think you know well. She showed me that house on the left hand side of the road as you go from Bungay …

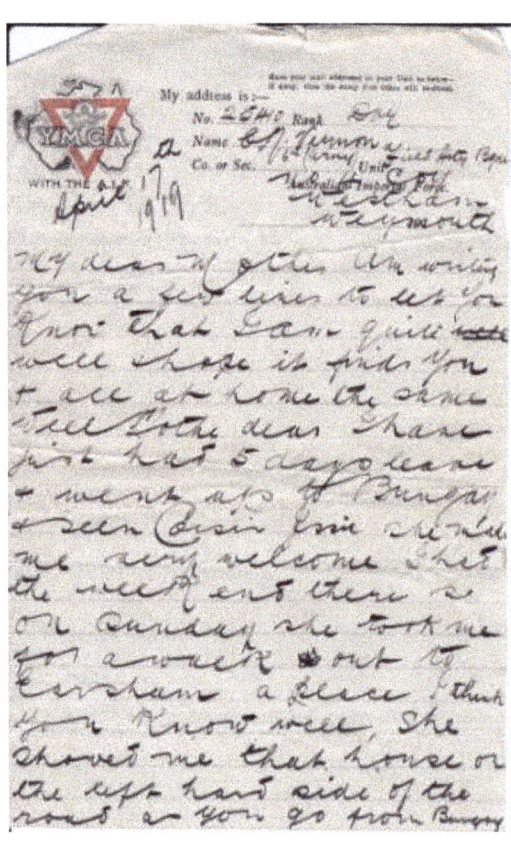

TWO BLANK POSTCARDS

Double pages There is nothing on the front - the umbrella in each folds up as you open the card.

SOUVENIRS FROM WWI
Bairnsfatherware Crockery

Extract from "In Search of the Better 'Ole" The life, The Works and the Collectables of Bruce Bairnsfather", by Tonie & Valmai Holt:

"Bruce Bairnsfather was an English cartoonist who created the best known cartoon character of the First World War - 'Old Bill' and he drew what many consider the most enduring cartoon of all time - the "Better 'Ole".

To those who experienced the privations of the years 1914 - 1918, the value of Bairnsfather's contribution to the morale of the nation, through laughter, is without question. To many, he was 'the man who won the war.'"

Charlie and Hickey's mother, Laura Vernon, had a set of Bairnsfatherware crockery. It was more than likely to have been purchased as a gift for her in London by Charlie, who stayed on for several months after the war.

The set was handed down to Marjory, Hickey's daughter, and some pieces, in particular the salad bowl and jug, were used in our daily lives.

All remaining pieces (1 dinner plate, 4 side plates, 1 large circular bowl, 5 side plates, 1 jug, 4 cups, 4 saucers, 2 oval bread baskets, 1 large octagonal bowl and 3 broken plates) have been donated to the Museum of Western Australia on behalf of the Vernon Family of Joondanna.

Large Salad Bowl
Caption: Coiffure in the trenches "Keep yer 'ead' still, or I'll ave yer blinking ear off"

Back of Salad Bowl

Medium Sized Jug
Caption: The Historical Touch "Well Alfred 'ow are the cakes?"

Dinner Plate.

Caption: "Give it a good 'ard 'un Bert. You can generally 'ear 'em fizzing a bit first if they are agoin' to explode"

Plate detail

Back of plate

Side Plate
Caption: "Keeping his hand in"

Side Plate
Caption: "I likes me drop o' rum"

Side Plate

Side Plate

Cups

Captions

Left: "What time do they feed the sea lions?"

Right: "Dear   At present we are staying on a farm"

Captions

Left: "When the 'ell is it goin' to be strawberry?"   Right: "Where did that one go to?"

Cups - reverse

Saucers

85

Large Octagonal Bowl

Bread Baskets

Detail - Bread Baskets

1915 - 1917

Letters to Jeannie McDonald Banks From Soldiers at The Front

Jeannie in the apple tree.
(This photo is mentioned in a letter to Jean from W. Cousins' sister)

Sept 1915-Feb 1916

From H GIBSON

Sept 1916 - 1919

From W COUSINS

1 September 1915
Letter to Jean – From H Gibson

B Company
4th Battalion
1st Infry Brigade 1st A.I.F
1/9/15
Dear Miss Jean

I have had the good fortune to receive the hold-all which you so kindly made, and for which please accept my thanks.

I am sorry that I cannot tell you that I am suffering from wounds, my complaint being the very ordinary one of being "run down". However, wounds or no wounds, I can assure you that I appreciate your kindness and that your little note certainly did not fail the attempt to 'cheer me up'. I may tell you that I am in a very fine hospital it having been formerly a palace. The rooms are quite 25ft high. In the open space are beautifully ornamented columns. The petitions are made of eastern lattice-work which is very complicated and highly ornamental. the floor is all of tiles. The skylights are of stained glass. Altogether I can assure you that we have first class accommodation here.

A concert is being organised tonight and I must go down later on and see what's doing. I cannot speak too highly of our nurses and the way they attend on us.

Well Miss Jean I hope that this will find you in the best of health so with all best wishes I will bring my letter to a close.

Yours etc H Gibson

Helouan (or Helwan), Cairo, Egypt. 1915. Exterior of the Al Hayat Hotel, used at the time as an Australian convalescent depot.

Opened to guests a month over four years previously, in January 1915 the 500-room Heliopolis Palace became Cairo's main military hospital. Renamed the 1st Army General Hospital (1st AGH), it was operated by the Australian Army Medical Corps. It was reorganised to provide accommodation for 1,000 sick, every door on every corridor opening to rooms of neat white beds and the grand dining-hall converted into a great convalescent ward with room for one hundred. Even so, within a very short time the hospital had to expand into additional premises, including buildings at the aerodrome, Luna Park and Heliopolis Sporting Club. Why was so much room required? Because Egypt was receiving the wounded from the ongoing campaign in the Dardanelles, including the landings at Gallipoli. Hospital ships transported the injured and dying the five or six days it took to get to Alexandria, from where patients were forwarded to local hospitals or onto Cairo.

1 September 1915
Letter to Jean
From H Gibson (Cont.)

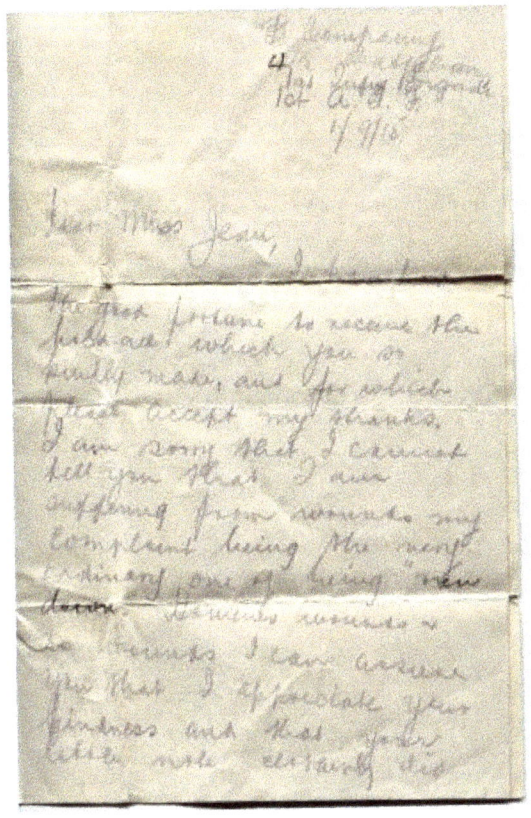

5 February 1916
Letter to Jean – From H Gibson

Dear Miss Jean,

I am in receipt of your letter and I hope you will overlook my neglect in not answering same sooner. However if I were to tell you of all the multitudinous duties which we have to perform I think you would not mind.

When I first opened your very interesting letter I was rather puzzled by the criss cross symbols at the bottom. It was the first time I had ever seen this at the end of a letter addressed to me. It was reminder ……

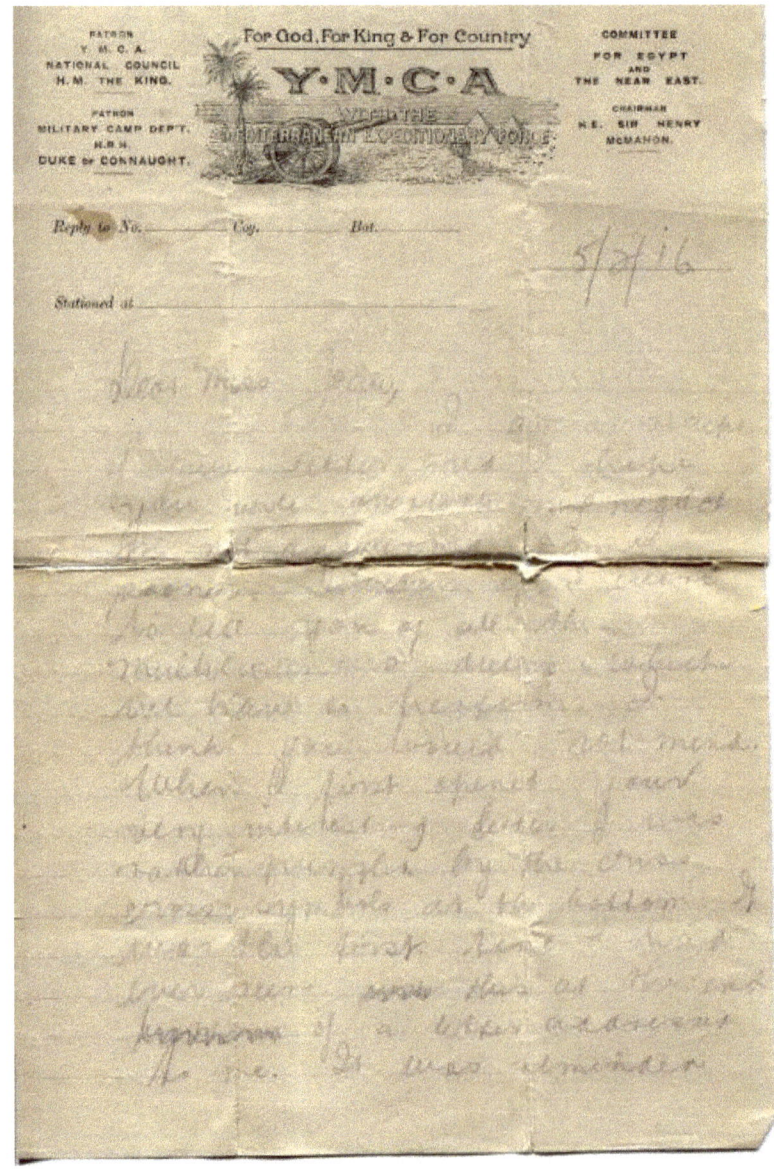

5 February 1916
Letter to Jean – From H Gibson (Cont.)

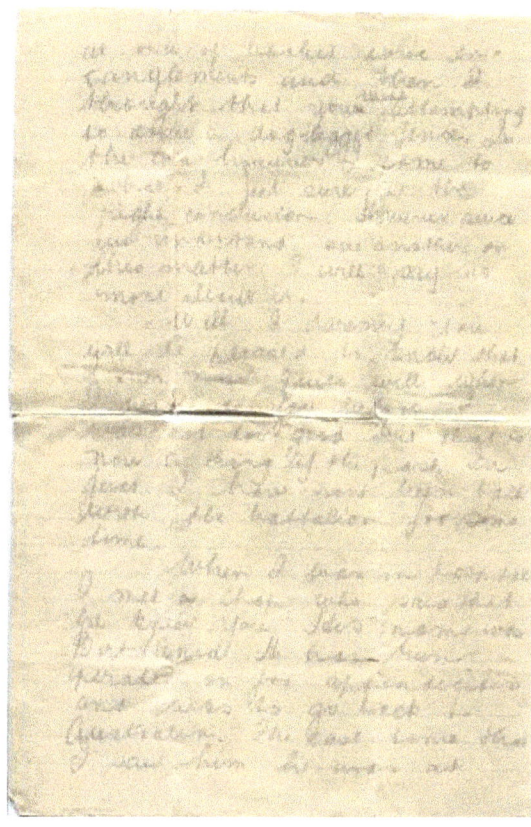 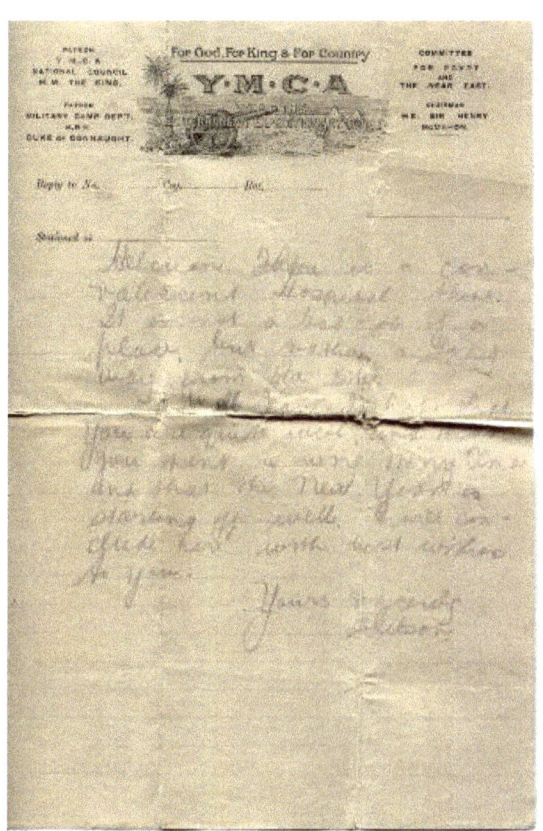

…..at once of barbed wire entanglements and then I thought that you were attempting to draw a dog-legged fence. In the end however, I came to what I feel sure is the right conclusion. However since we understand one another on this matter I will say no more about it.

Well I daresay you will be pleased to know that I am now quite well. When I wrote to you before I was not too good but that is now a thing of the past. In fact I have now been back with the battalion for some time.

When I was in hospital I met a chap who said that he knew you. His name was Bert Lanis. He has been operated on for appendicitis and was to go back to Australia. The last time I saw him was at Helouan. There is a convalescent hospital there. t is not a bad sort of a place but rather a long way from the city.

Well Jean I hope that you are quite well and that you spent a very Merry Xmas and that the New Year is starting off well. I will conclude here with best wishes to you.

Yours sincerely

H Gibson

24 September 1916
Letter to Jean
From Pte Wm Cousins

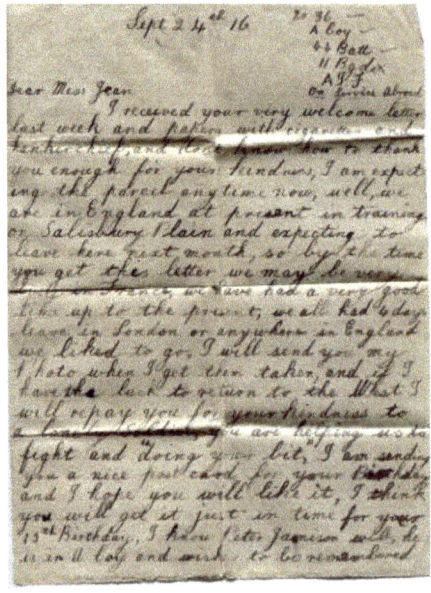
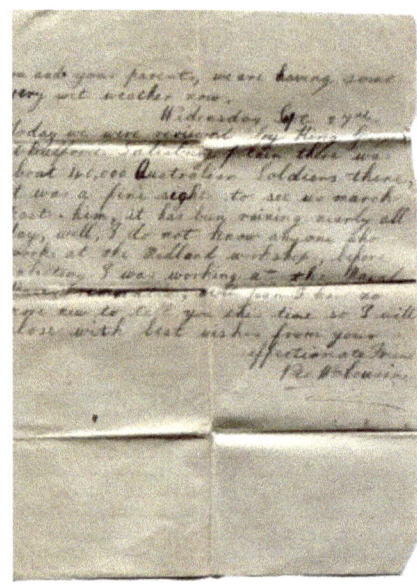

Sept 24th 16

No 36 ACoy

44 Bgde

AIF

On Service Abroad

Dear Miss Jean

I received your very welcome letter last week and papers with cigarettes and handkerchief, and don't know how to thank you enough for your kindness, I am expecting the parcel any time now, well, we are in England at present in training on Salisbury Plain and expecting to leave here next month, so by the time you get this letter we may very busy in France, we have had a very good time up to the present, we all had 4 days leave in London or anywhere in England we liked to go, I will send you my photo when I get them taken, and if I have the luck to return to the West I will repay you for your kindness to a lonely soldier, you are helping us to fight and "doing your bit". I am sending you a nice postcard for your birthday and I hope you will like it, I think you will get it just in time for your 13th Birthday, I know Peter Jamison well, he is in A Coy and wishes to be remembered to you and your parents, we are having some very wet weather now.

Wednesday Sept 17.

Today we were reviewed by King George in Bulford, Salisbury Plain there was about 40,000 Australian soldiers there, it was a fine sight to see us march past him, it has been raining nearly all day, well I do not know anyone who works at the Midland workshop, before enlisting I was working at the Naval Bases, Fremantle, well Jean I have no more news to tell you this time so I will close with best wishes from your affectionate Friend

Pte Wm Cousins

3 December 1916
Letter to Jean
From Pte Wm Cousins

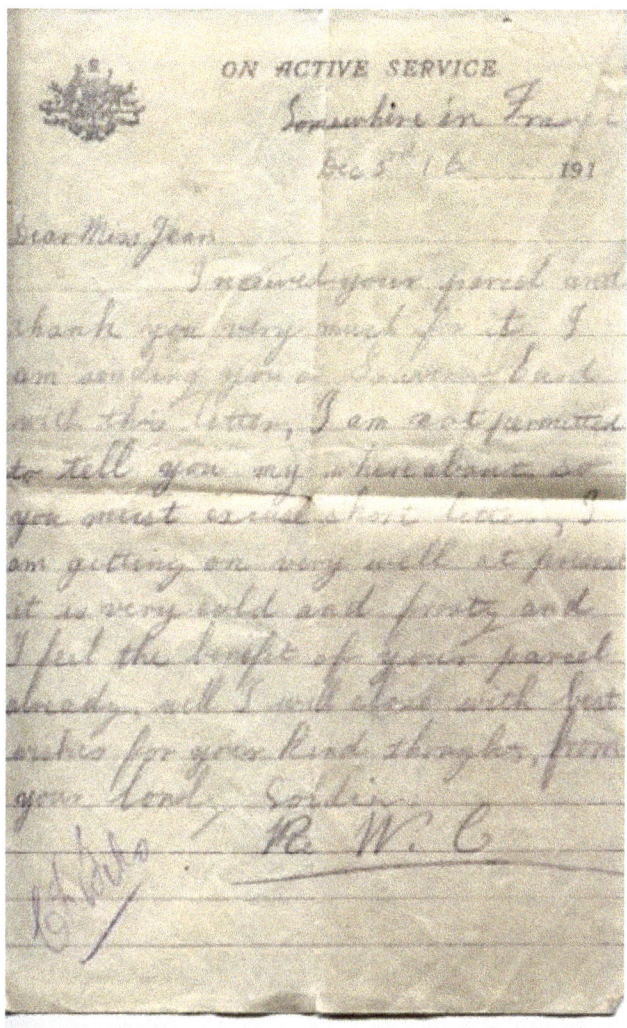

Somewhere in France Dec 3rd, 16

Dear Miss Jean

I received your parcel and thank you very much for it. I am sending you a Souvenir back with this letter. I am not permitted to tell you my whereabouts so you must excuse short letter. I am getting on very well at present it is very cold and frosty and I feel the benefit of your parcel already, well I will close with best wishes for your kind thoughts, from your lonely Soldier,

Pte W. C.

6 January 1917
Letter to Jean
From Pte Wm Cousins

France

Jan 6th 1917

Dear Miss Jean

I received your very welcome letter last week whilst in the Trenches, also Xmas card which is very nice. I received your Western Mail this week dated Nov 3rd 16. We'll move out of the trenches now for a few days rest, the Boys were very cool when under heavy fire, I am very glad you got the Birthday card alright, I sent a Xmas card from here and several letters. I hope you have received them all, our colours if I am allowed to tell you are Blue and White cut oval shape, I am getting on very well at present and hope you are also, I do not know Pte P. Carter.

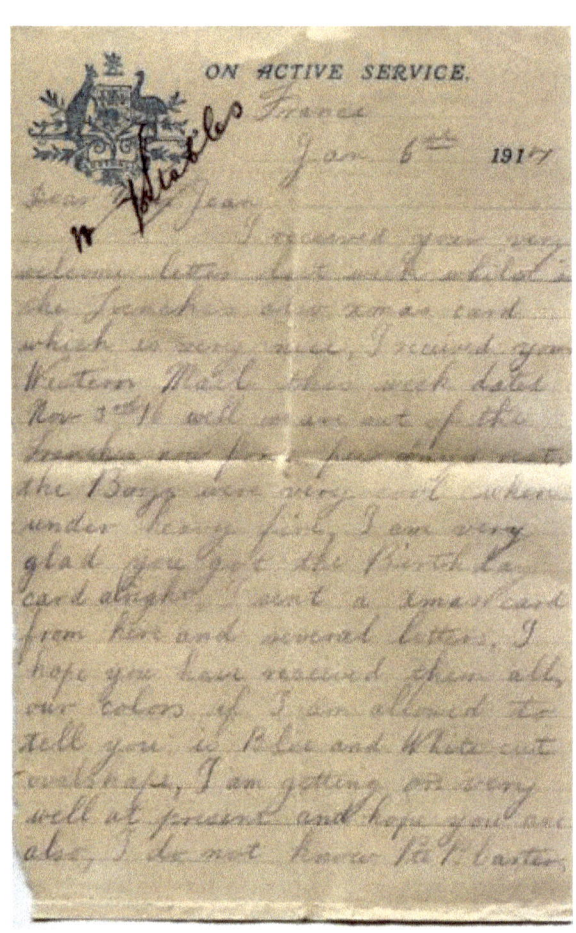

Well Jean I am not allow to tell you where we are but it must have been beautiful city one time, well I think I have told you all for the present so I will close with love from your affectionate Friend

Pte W. Cousins

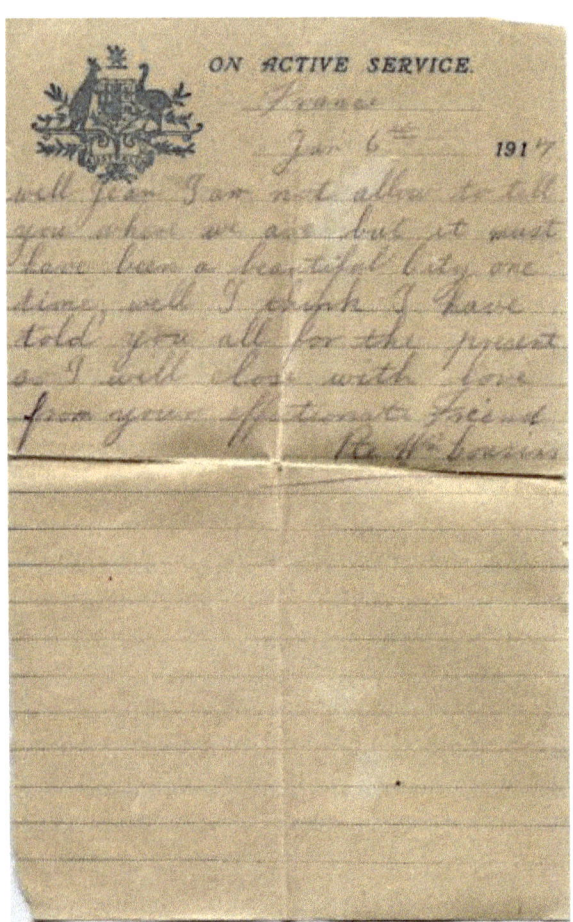

27 March 1917
Letters to Jean and her Mother
From Pte Wm Cousins

2 Letters in one, to Jean's mother, Jean Banks senior and one to Jean.

France

March 27 1917

Dear Mrs Banks and Jean

Just a few lines to let you know I received your parcels (2) whilst in the trenches and I can assure you they came in very handy, we have had a very severe winter. I saw Peter Jamison and gave him your message, he said he was very glad to hear everything was OK and wished to be remembered to you. About Percy Carter, I do not know him, I do not think he is in this Battalion but I am making enquiries….

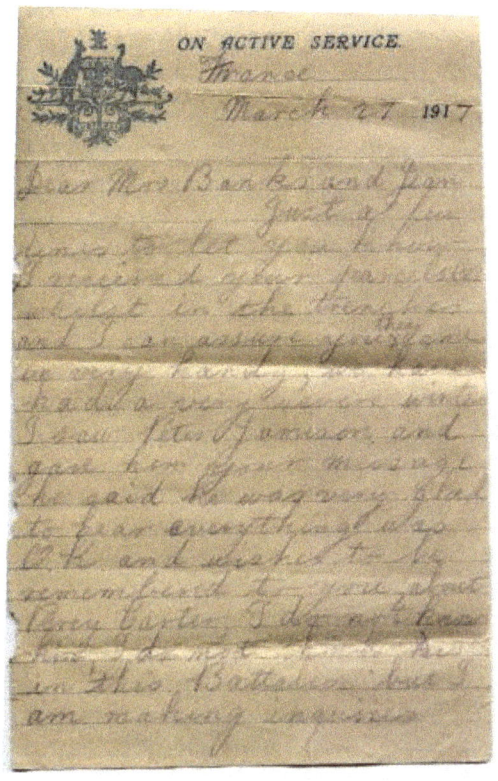

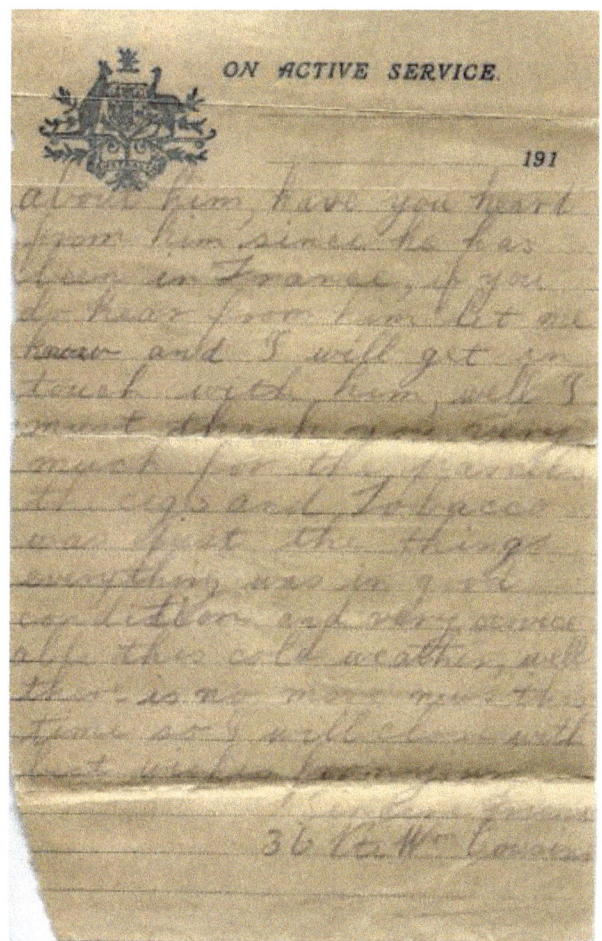

……about him, have you heard from him since he has been in France, if you do hear from him let me know and I will get in touch with him, well I must thank you very much for the cigs and tobacco was just the thing, everything was in good condition and very serviceable this cold weather, well there is no more news this time so I will close with best wishes from your sincere friend

36 Pte Wm Cousins

27 March 1917
Letters to Jean and her Mother
From Pte Wm Cousins (Cont.)

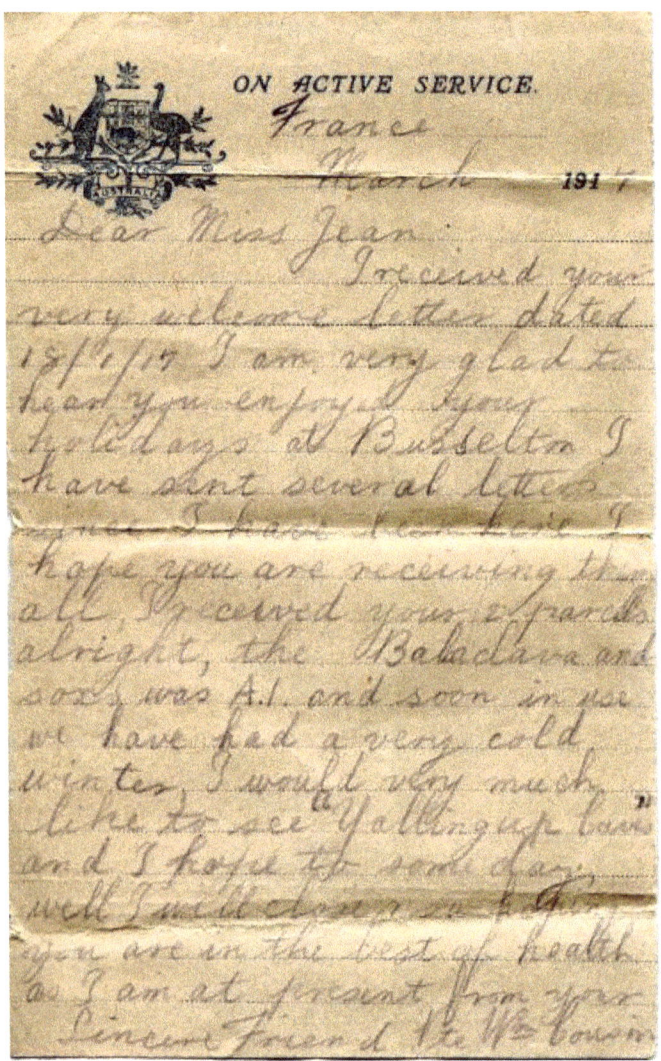

Dear Miss Jean

I received your very welcome letter dated 18/1/17. I am very glad to hear you enjoyed your holidays at Busselton. I have sent several letters since I have been here I hope you are receiving them all, I received your 2 parcels alright, the Balaclava and sox was A.1. and soon in use we have had a very cold winter, I would very much like to see "Yallingup Caves" and I hope to some day. Well I will close now, hoping you are in the best of health as I am at present.

from your sincere friend

Pte Wm Cousins

8 May 1917
Letter to Jean
From Pte Wm Cousins

France

May 8th 1917

Dear Miss Jean

I received your welcome letter dated 9/3/17 also the parcel for which I thank you very much, I was very sorry when I heard Peter was wounded and hope he will soon be alright again, we are having some very nice weather now and it is about time too, it has been a very hard winter, have you heard from Percy Carter, since no-one seems to know him here, I hope he will turn up again, you seem to be getting on very well at school, the country is beginning to look very nice now the summer is coming again, I have just had a letter from my sister in England, she has been very upset as it was reported in the Australian papers that I had been seriously wounded, so if you have seen it yourself you will know it is a mistake as I am quite well up to the time of writing, you can guess how pleased she was when she heard from me, she is my only sister and next of kin, well I have no more news this time so I will close with best wishes from your soldier friend Wm Cousins

(please remember me to your mother)

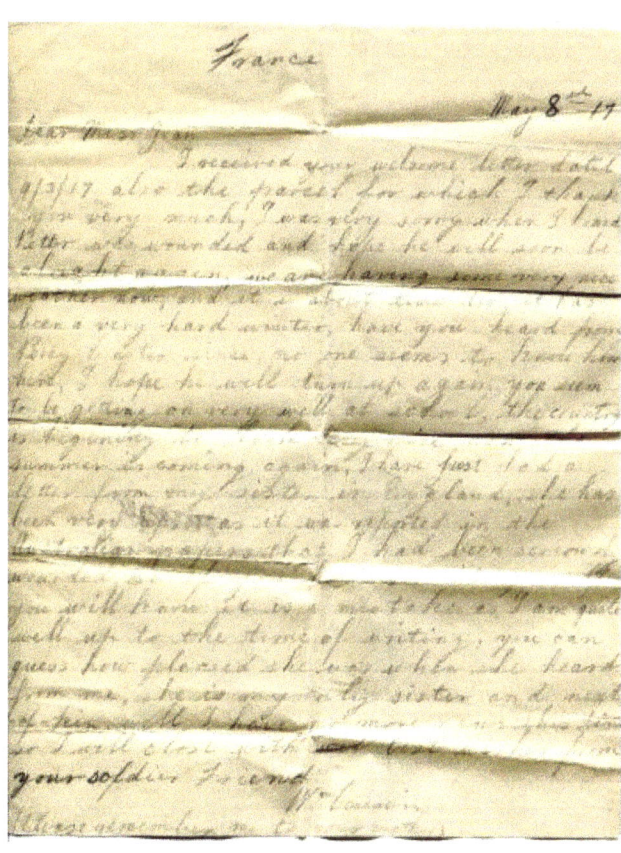 

12 September 1917
Letter to Jean
From Pte Wm Cousins

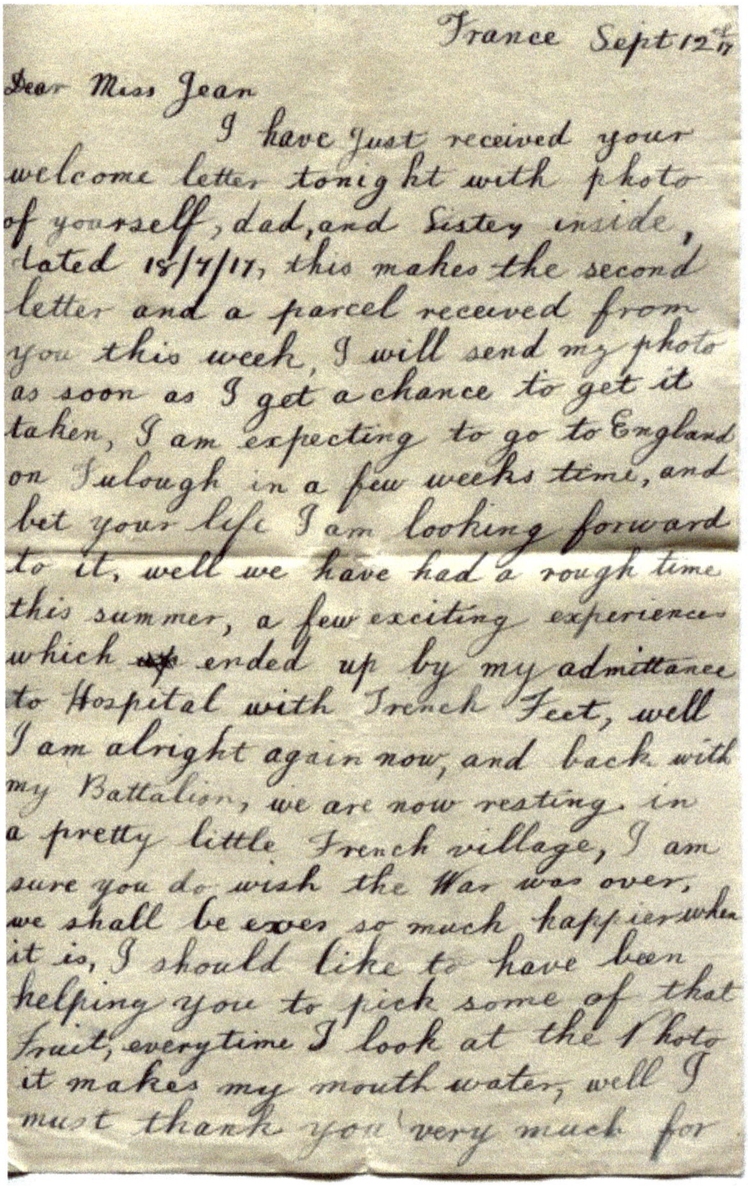

France Sept 12th 17

Dear Miss Jean

I have just received your welcome letter tonight with photo of yourself, dad and sister inside, dated 18.7.17, this makes the second letter and a parcel received from you this week, I will send my photo as soon as I get a chance to get it taken, I am expecting to go to England on furlough in a few weeks time, and bet your life I am looking forward to it, well we have had a rough time this summer, a few exciting experiences which ended up by my admittance to Hospital with Trench Feet, well I am alright again now, and back with my Battalion, we are now resting in a pretty little French village, I am sure you do wish the War was over.

we shall be very so much happier when it is, I should like to have been helping you to pick some of that fruit, every time I look at the photo it makes my mouth water, well I must thank you very much for …

France Sept 12th 17

Dear Miss Jean

I have just received your welcome letter tonight with photo of yourself, dad, and Sistey inside, dated 18/7/17, this makes the second letter and a parcel received from you this week, I will send my photo as soon as I get a chance to get it taken, I am expecting to go to England on Fulough in a few weeks time, and bet your life I am looking forward to it, well we have had a rough time this summer, a few exciting experiences which ended up by my admittance to Hospital with Trench Feet, well I am alright again now, and back with my Battalion, we are now resting in a pretty little French village, I am sure you do wish the War was over, we shall be ever so much happier when it is, I should like to have been helping you to pick some of that fruit, everytime I look at the Photo it makes my mouth water, well I must thank you very much for

12 September 1917
Letter to Jean
From Pte Wm Cousins (Cont.)

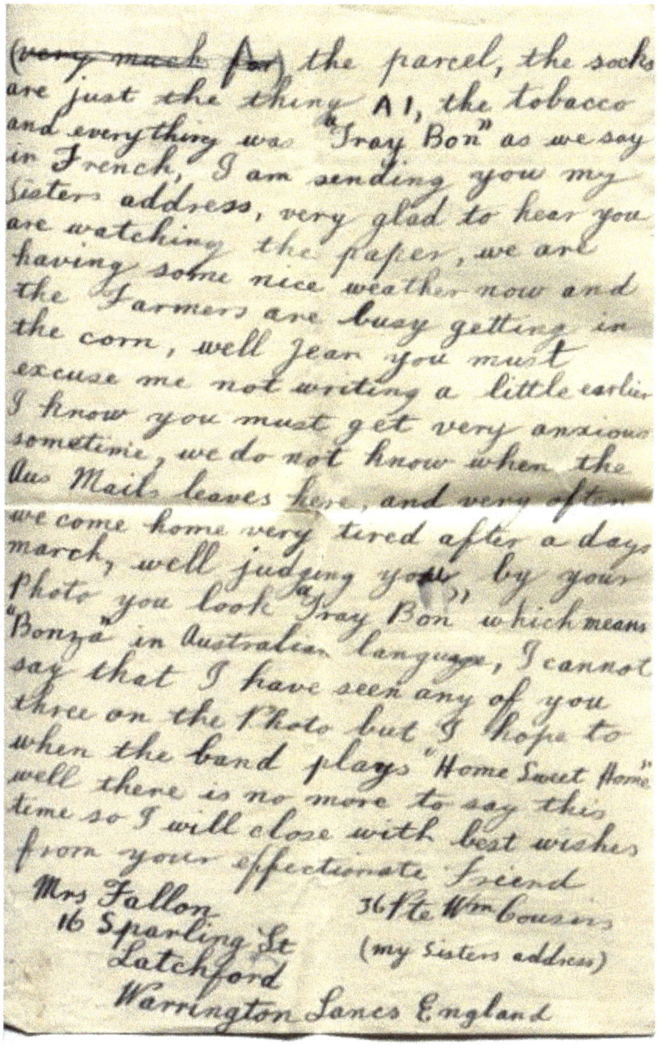

…the parcel, the socks are just the thing A1, the tobacco and everything was "Tray Bon" as we say in French, I am sending you my sisters address, very glad to hear you are watching the paper, we are having some nice weather now and the Farmers are busy getting in the corn, well Jean you must excuse me not writing a little earlier I know you must get very anxious sometime, we do not know when the Aus Mail leaves here, and very often we come home very tired after a days march, well judging you by your photo you look "Tray Bon" which means "Bonza" in Australian language, I cannot say that I have seen any of you three on the Photo but I hope to when the band plays "Home Sweet Home". Well there is no more to say this time so I will close with best wishes from your affectionate friend

36Pte Wm Cousins

(my sisters address) Mrs Fallon

16 Sparling St Latchford
Warrington
Lancs
England

7 November 1917
Letter to Jean
From Pte Wm Cousins

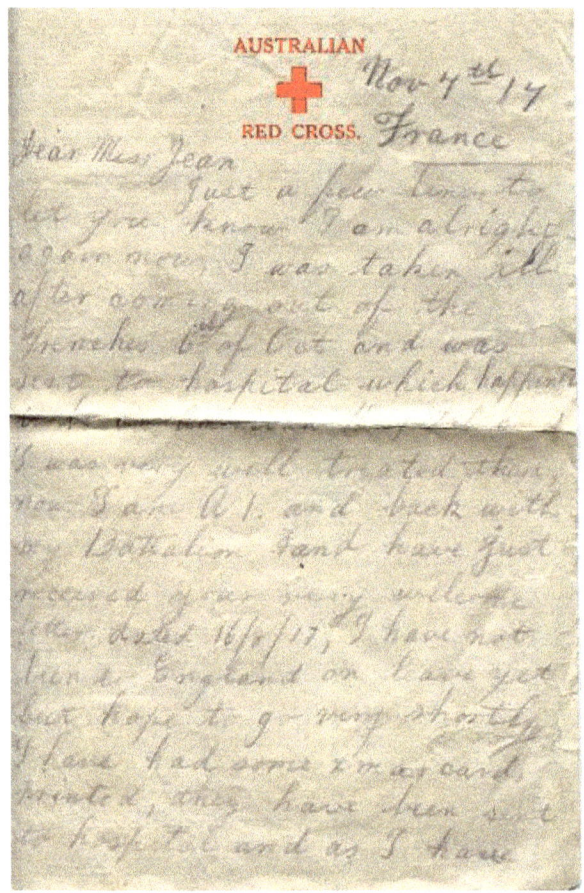 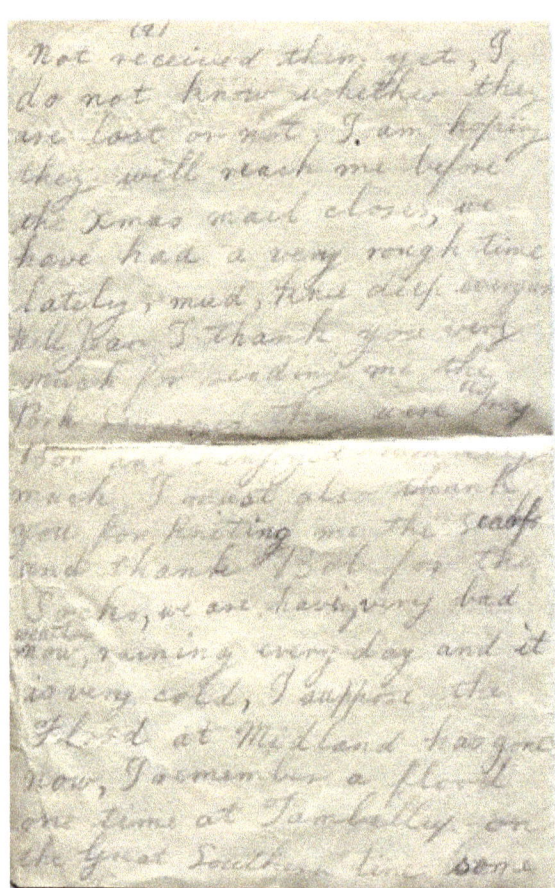

Dear Miss Jean

Just a few lines to let you know I am alright again now, I was taken ill after going out of the trenches 6 of Oct and was sent to hospital which happened to be an American hospital and I was very well treated there, now I am A1. and back with my Battalion and have just received your very welcome letter dated 16/8/17, I have not been to England on leave yet but hope to go very shortly, I have had some xmas cards printed, they have been sent to hospital and as I have not received them yet I do not know whether they are lost or not. I am hoping they will reach me before the Xmas mail closes, we have had a very rough time lately mud, knee deep everywhere. Well Jean I thank you very much for sending me the pork sausages they were "Trey Bon" and I enjoyed them very much, I must also thank you for knitting me the scarf and thank Bob for the socks, we are having very bad weather now, raining every day and it is very cold, I suppose the flood at Midland has gone now, I remember a flood one time at Tambellup on the Great Southern line some…..

7 November 1917
Letter to Jean
From Pte Wm Cousins (Cont.)

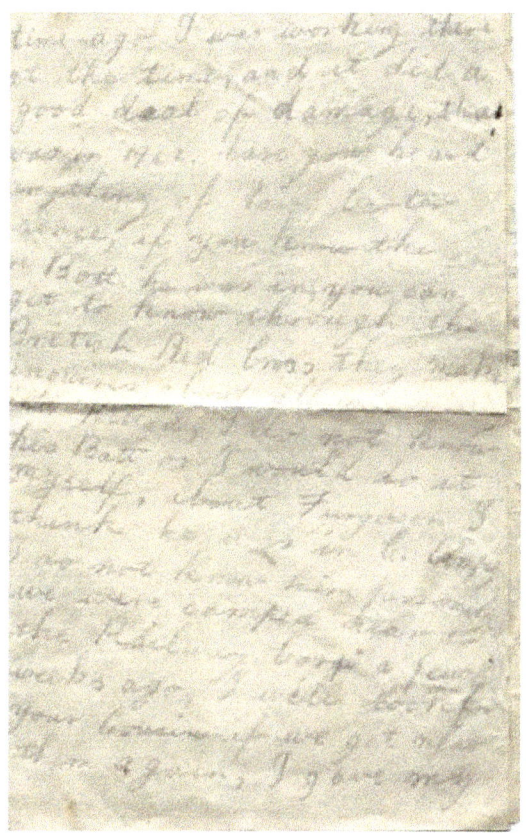 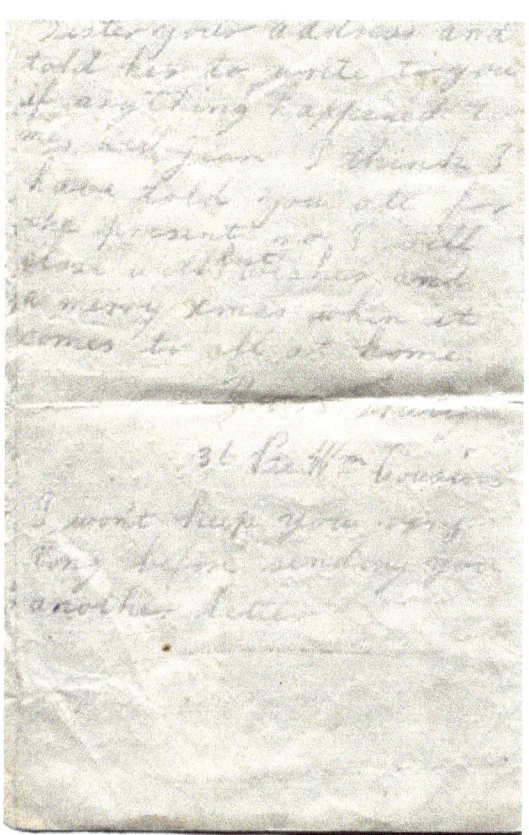

…..time ago. I was working there at the time and it did a good deal of damage, that was in 1912. Have you heard anything of Percy Carter since, if you know the Batt. he was in, you can get to know through the British Red Cross they make inquiries about all missing and killed, I do not know his Batt or I would do it myself, about Ferguson I think he was in C Company I do not know him personally we were camped near to the Railway Corp a few weeks ago, I will look for your cousin if we get near them again, I gave my sister your address and told her to write to you if anything happened to me, well Jean I think I have told you all for the present so I will close with best wishes and a merry xmas when it comes to all at home

Yours Truly

36 Pte Wm Cousins

I won't keep you very long before sending you another letter.

2 December 1917
Letter To Jean
From Pte Wm Cousins

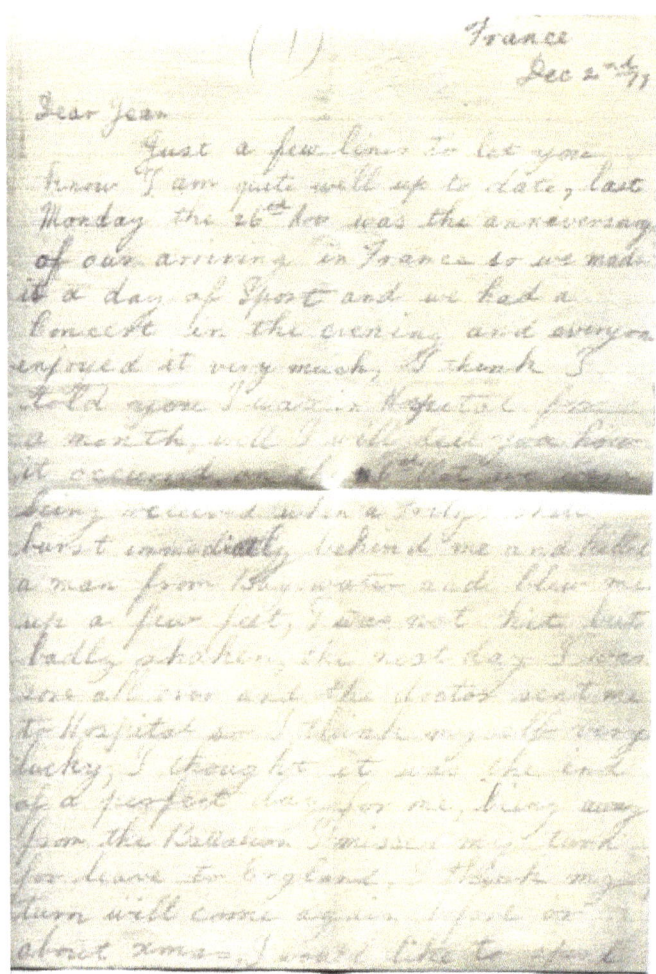

Dear Jean

Just a few lines to let you know I am quite well up to date, last Monday the 26th Nov was the anniversary of our arriving in France so we made it a day of sport and we had a concert in the evening and everyone enjoyed it very much, I think I told you I was in hospital for a month, well I will tell you how it occurred, on the 6th Oct we were being relieved when a forty shell burst behind me and killed a man from Bayswater and blew me up a few feet, I was not hit but badly shaken, the next day I was sore all over and the doctor sent me to Hospital so I think myself very lucky, I thought it was the end of a perfect day for me, being away from the Battalion I missed my turn for leave to England, I think my turn will come again before or about Xmas, I would like to spend …

2 December 1917
Letter To Jean
From Pte Wm Cousins (Cont.)

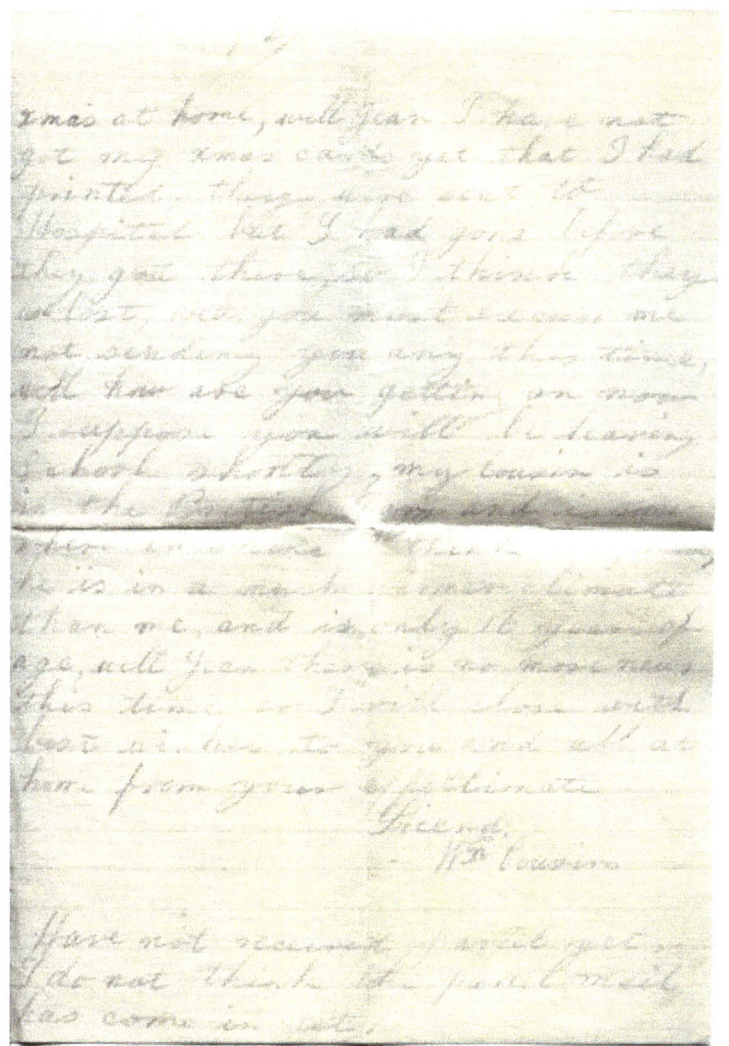

…Xmas at home, well Jean I have not got my Xmas cards yet that I had printed, they were sent to Hospital but I had gone before they got there, so I think they are lost, well you must excuse me not sending you any this time, well how are you getting on now. I suppose you will be leaving school shortly, my cousin is in the British Navy and is somewhere in China. I think at present, he is in a much warmer climate than me, and is only 16 years of age, well Jean there is no more news this time so I will close with best wishes to you and all at home from your affectionate Friend Wm Cousins

Have not received parcel yet, I do not think the parcel mail has come in yet.

31 December 1917
Letter to Jean
From Pte Wm Cousins

Dear Miss Jean

Since writing you my last letter I have been wounded in the left shoulder and I am progressing favourably. I suppose you have seen it in the paper by this time and I am now in the Australian hospital at Dartford just outside London, before coming to this hospital I was in the King George Hospital London. I got there just in time for Xmas and I can tell you I had a jolly good time there, it is very cold here at present but we have not had any snow yet, well I suppose you are having some nice weather now in the West, and enjoying yourself in the Swan, swimming or boating. I suppose you know Charles Cornish of Midland he was killed near Messines, by the time you get this letter I will be pretty well right again and perhaps in France as my wound is not serious, when I am alright I shall be staying with my sister for a fortnight on furlough then back to the Boys again, I wonder whether you get all my letters. I sent you one from France about the 2nd Dec, excuse me not sending you any views of France as we are not allowed to send them, I did not receive your parcel, if it came after I left they Boys will divide it between …

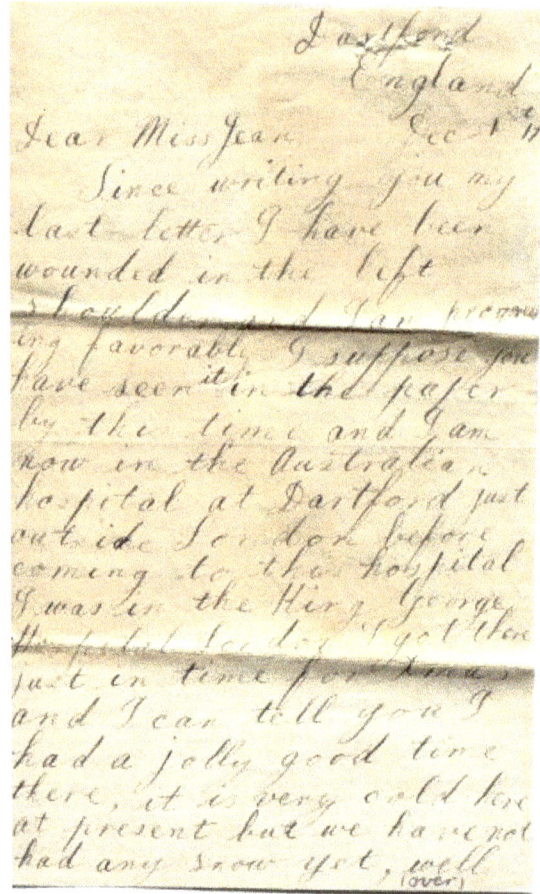

31 December 1917
Letter To Jean
From Pte Wm Cousins (Cont.)

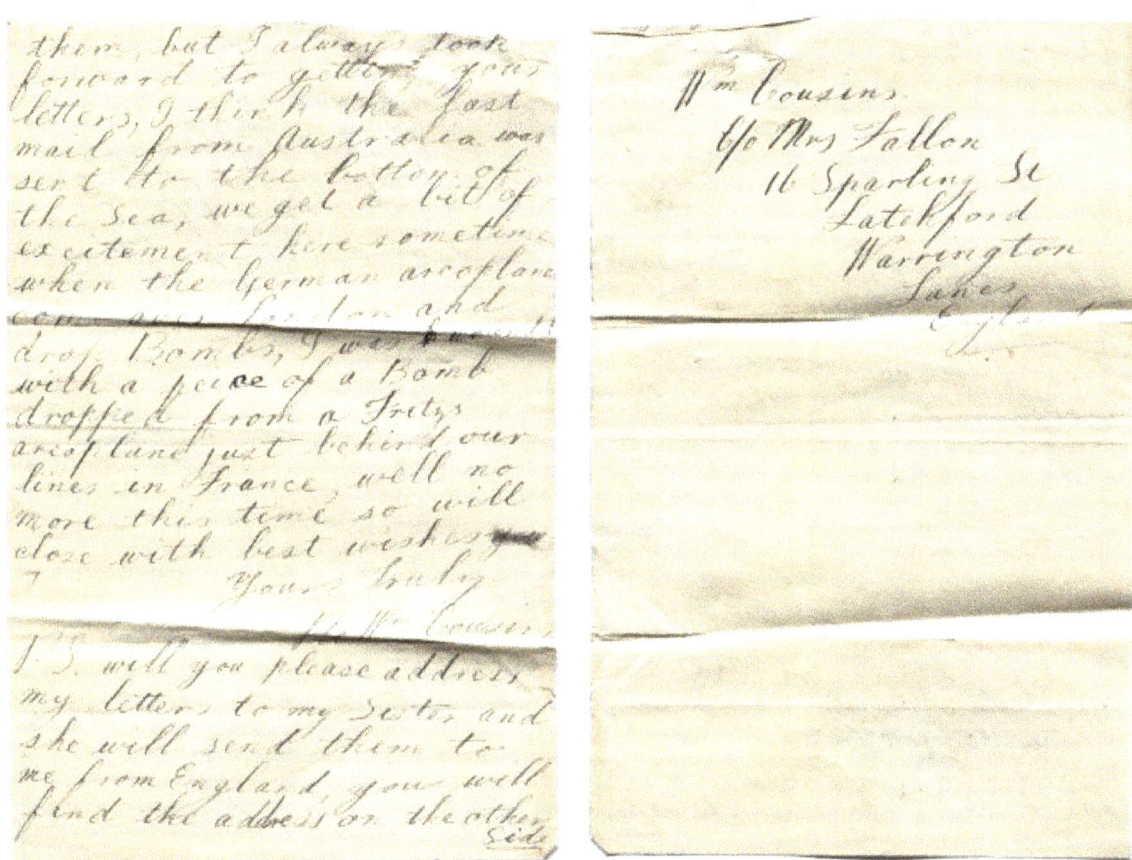

….them but I always look forward to getting your letters, I think the last mail from Australia was sent to the bottom of the sea, we get a bit of excitement here sometimes when the German aeroplanes come over London and drop Bombs, I was wounded with a piece of a bomb dropped from a Fritz's aeroplane just behind our lines in France, well no more this time so will close with best wishes

Yours Truly

Pte Wm Cousins

P.S. will you please address my letters to my sister and she will send them to me from England, you will find the address on the other side

"Wm Cousins

℅ Mrs Fallon
16 Sparling St
Latchford
Warrington, Lancs
England

29 March 1918
Letter to Jean
From Mrs P Fallon, Sister Of Pte Wm Cousins

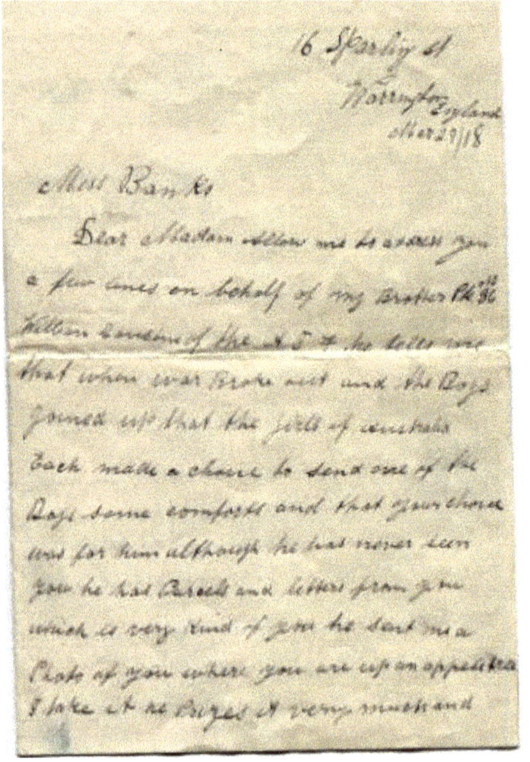

16 Sparling St
Warrington
England
Mar 29/18

Miss Banks

Dear Madam Allow me to address you a few lines on behalf of my brother Pte Wm William Cousins of the A.I.F. he tells me that when war broke out and the boys joined up that the girls of Australia each made a chance to send one of the boys some comforts and that your choice was for him although he has never seen you he has parcels and letters from you which is very kind of you he sent me a photo of you where you are up on appletree I take it no prizes it very much and he told me to take great care of it and other cards of yours as he is living in hope of taking them back to Australia when the war is over. he has had fourteen days leave he spent seven of them with me and the other in Devonshire with a cousin and he enjoyed himself very much he is now learning signaling on Salisbury Plains where he expects to for a while and then perhaps he will be going out to the front again to join the boys again of which he talks so much I hope he will have a safe return so that he will be able to shake the hand of the little girl who looked after him. Allow me to close with fondest love from his sister

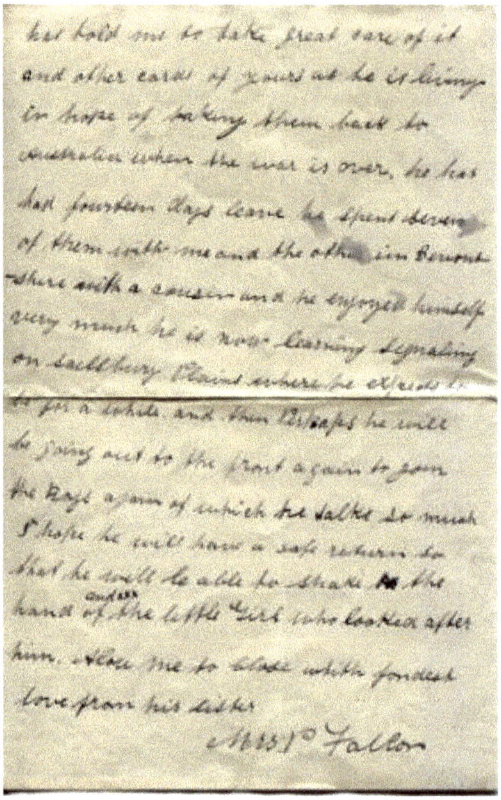

Mrs P. Fallon

P.S.
he wants you to send your letters to me so that I can forward them to him as he is being moved about a lot lately

29 March 1918
Letter to Jean
From Mrs P Fallon, Sister Of Pte Wm Cousins (Cont.)

16 Sparling St
Warrington
England
Mar 29/18

Miss Banks

Dear Madam allow me to address you a few lines on behalf of my Brother Pte No 36 William Cousins of the A.I.F., he tells me that when war broke out and the Boys joined up that the girls of Australia each made a choice to send one of the boys some comforts and that your choice was for him although he has never seen you he has parcels and letters from you which is very kind of you he sent me a photo of you where you are up an apple tree. I take it he prizes it very much and has told me to take great care of it and other cards of yours as he is living in hope of taking them back to Australia when the war is over. He has had fourteen days leave he spent seven of them with me and the other in Bermontshire with a cousin and he enjoyed himself very much he is now learning signalling on Salisbury Plains where he expects to be for a while and then perhaps he will be going out to the front again to join the boys again of which he talks so much. I hope he will have a safe return so that he will be able to shake the hand and xxx the little girl who looked after him. Allow me to close with fondest love from his sister,

Mrs P Fallon

PS he wants you to send your letters to me so that I can forward to him as he is being moved about a lot lately.

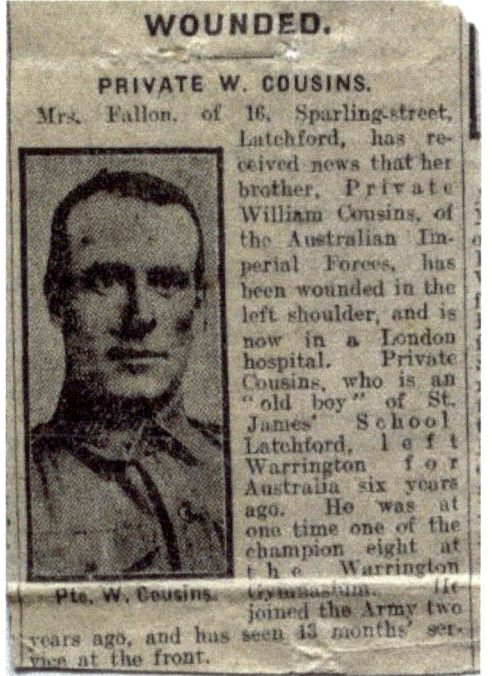

27 April 1918
Letter to Jean
From Pte Wm Cousins

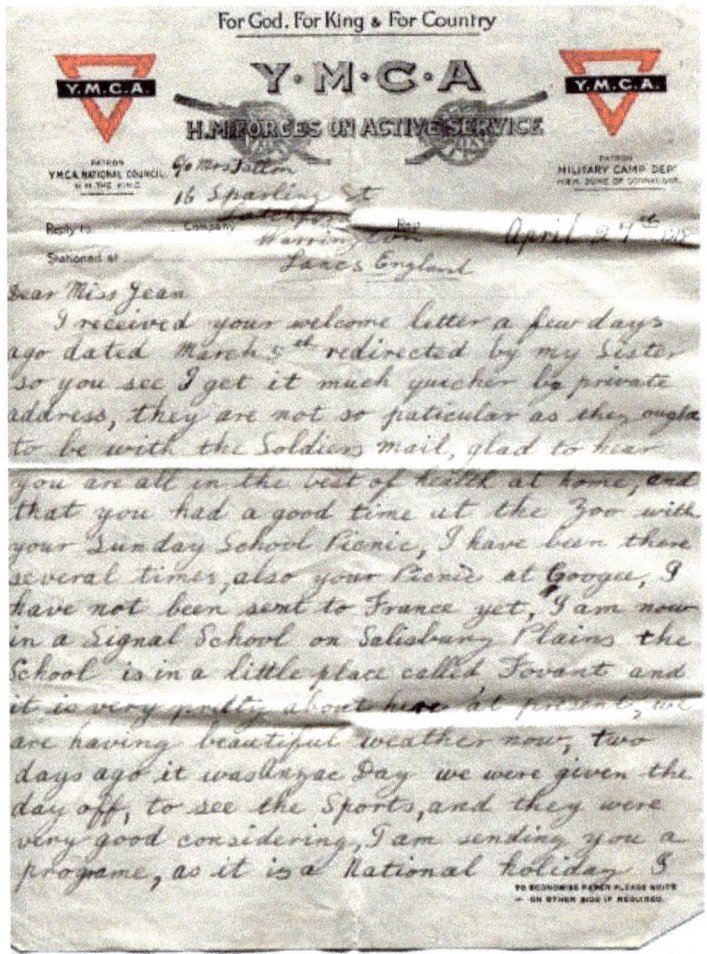

Dear Miss Jean

I received your welcome letter a few days ago dated March 5th redirected by my sister so you see I get it much quicker by private address, they are not so particular as they ought to be with the Soldiers mail, glad to hear you are all in the best of health at home, and that you had a good time at the zoo with your Sunday School Picnic, I have been there several times, also your picnic at Coogee, I have not been sent to France yet, I am now in a Signal School on Salisbury Plains the school is in a little place called Fovant and it is very pretty about here at present, we are having beautiful weather now, two days ago it was Anzac Day we were given the day off, to see the sports, and they were very good considering, I am sending you a program as it is a National holiday I…..

27 April 1918
Letter to Jean
From Pte Wm Cousins (Cont.)

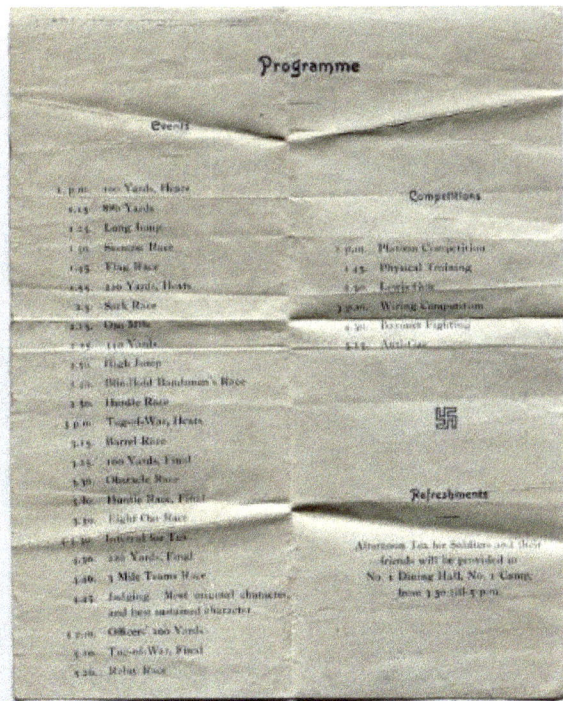

(Hope you received my sister's letter with photo)

….suppose you had a holiday too, I also received your letter dated 14 January, glad you had a good time at Busselton and good weather. I bet it was a bit hot New Years day, yes I did have a "Tray Bon" time on furlough, glad to hear Peter Jamison is home again remember me to him when you see him, sorry Percy Carter was reported missing and killed. I made many inquiries about him but no-one seemed to know him, there is some very heavy fighting going on at present in France and the 44th Batt has been in the thick of it, and has done some very good work, I see by the casualty list that some of my Platoon have been killed and wounded, it is "No Bon" in France at the present time, you make my mouth water when you talk about lime juice and soda and I suppose you had some "Ice cream" in it too.

I can get plenty water and snow here, but I think the water is quite cold enough without the snow, sorry to hear Bob pinched all your wool, never mind I hope we are not here another winter well Jean I think I have told you all for the present so I will close with love and best wishes from your Soldier Friend Pte Wm Cousins

same address

1 July 1918

Letter to Jean

From Pte Wm Cousins

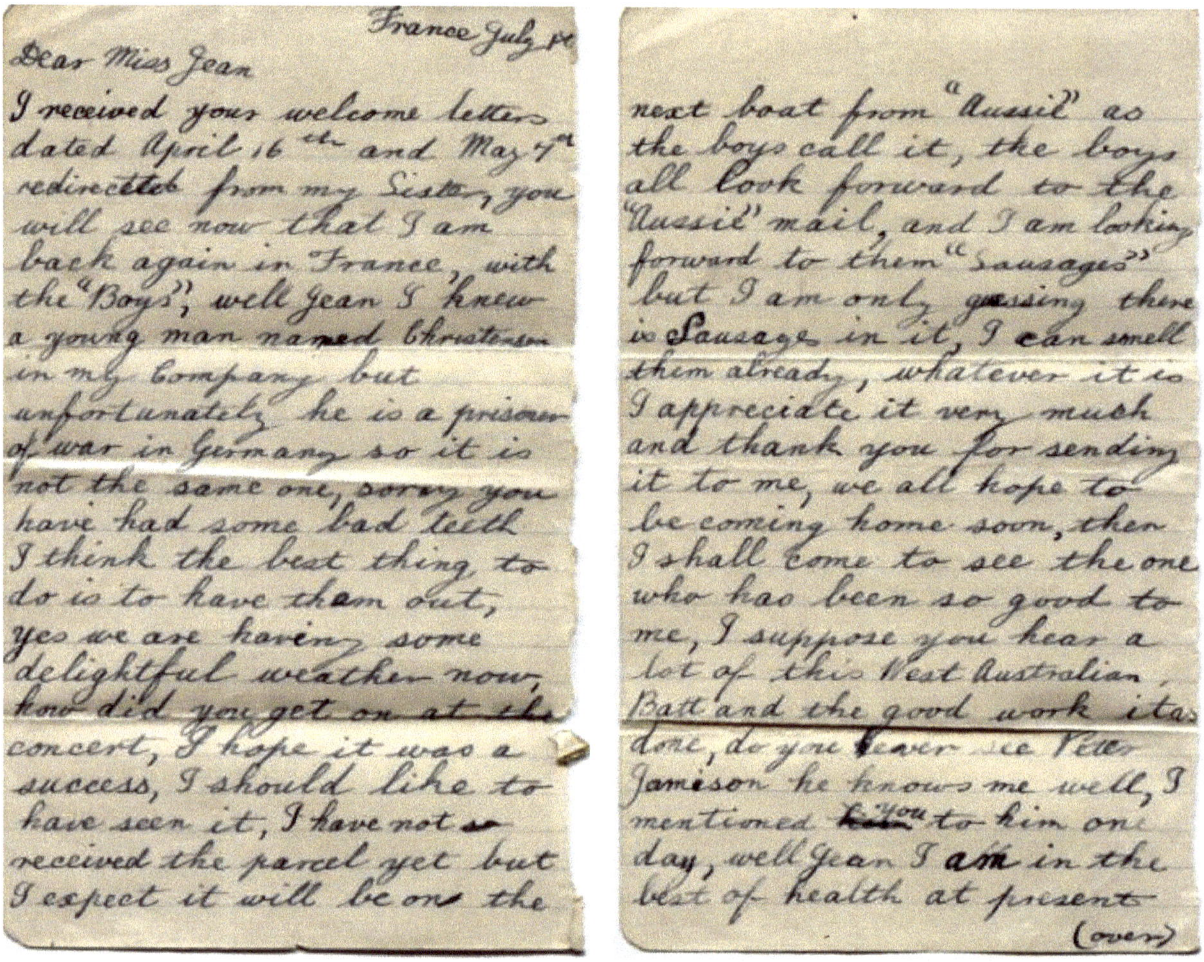

France July 1st

Dear Miss Jean

I received your welcome letters dated April 16th and May 7th redirected from my Sister, you will see now that I am back again in France, with the "Boys", well Jean I knew a young man named Christenson in my Company but unfortunately he is a prisoner of war in Germany so it is not the same one, sorry you have had some bad teeth I think the best thing to do is to have them out, yes we are having some delightful weather now, how did you get on at the concert, I hope it was a success, I should like to have seen it, I have not received the parcel yet but I expect it will be on the next boat from "Aussil" as the boys call it, the boys all look forward to the "Aussil" mail, and I am looking forward to them "Sausages" but I am only guessing there is Sausages in it, I can smell them already, whatever it is I appreciate it very much and thank you for sending it to me, we all hope to be coming home soon, then I shall come to see the one who has been so good to me, I suppose you hear a lot of this West Australian Batt and the good work its done, do you ever see Peter Jamison he knows me well, I mentioned you to him one day, well Jean I am in the best of health at present

(over)

France

July 1st

Dear Miss Jean

I received your welcome letters dated April 16th and May 7th redirected from my Sister, you will see now that I am back again in France, with the "Boys", well Jean I knew a young man named Christenson in my company but unfortunately he is a prisoner of war in Germany so it is not the same one, sorry you have had some bad teeth I think the best thing to do is have them out, yes we are having some delightful weather now, how did you get on at the concert, I hope it was a success, I should like to have seen it, I have not received the parcel yet but I expect it will be on the next boat from "Aussie" as the boys call it, the boys all look forward to the "Aussie" mail and I am looking forward to them "sausages" but I am only guessing there is sausages in it, I can smell them already, whatever it is I appreciate it very much and thank you for sending it to me, we all hope to be coming home soon, then I shall come to see the one who has been so good to me, I suppose you hear a lot of this West Australian Batt and the good work its done, do you ever see Peter Jamison he knows me well, I mentioned you to him one day, well Jean I am in the best of health at present….

1 July 1918
Letter to Jean
From Pte Wm Cousins (Cont.)

….my wound is well healed up and does not cause me any trouble, well I must close now as we cannot say much now we are in France so good-bye for the present from your affectionate friend

Pte W Cousins

36 Pte William Cousins

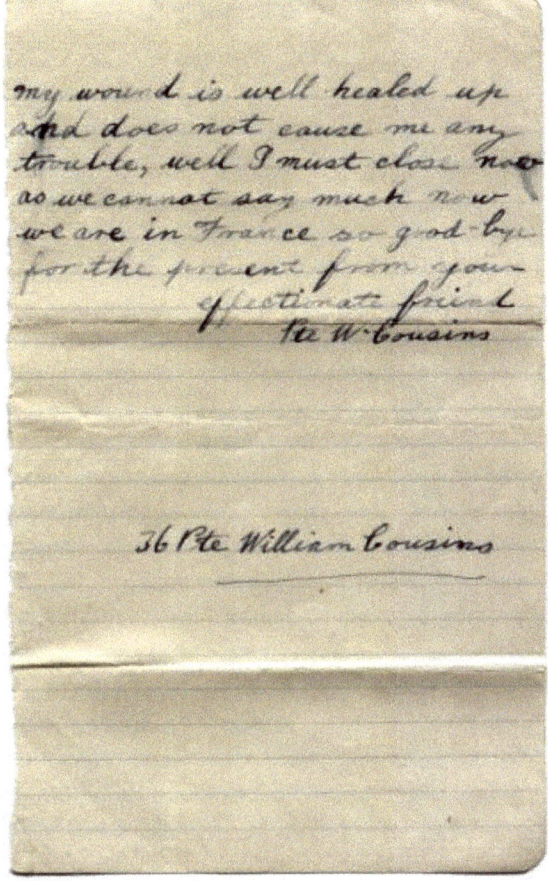

21 July 1918
Letter to Jean
From Pte Wm Cousins

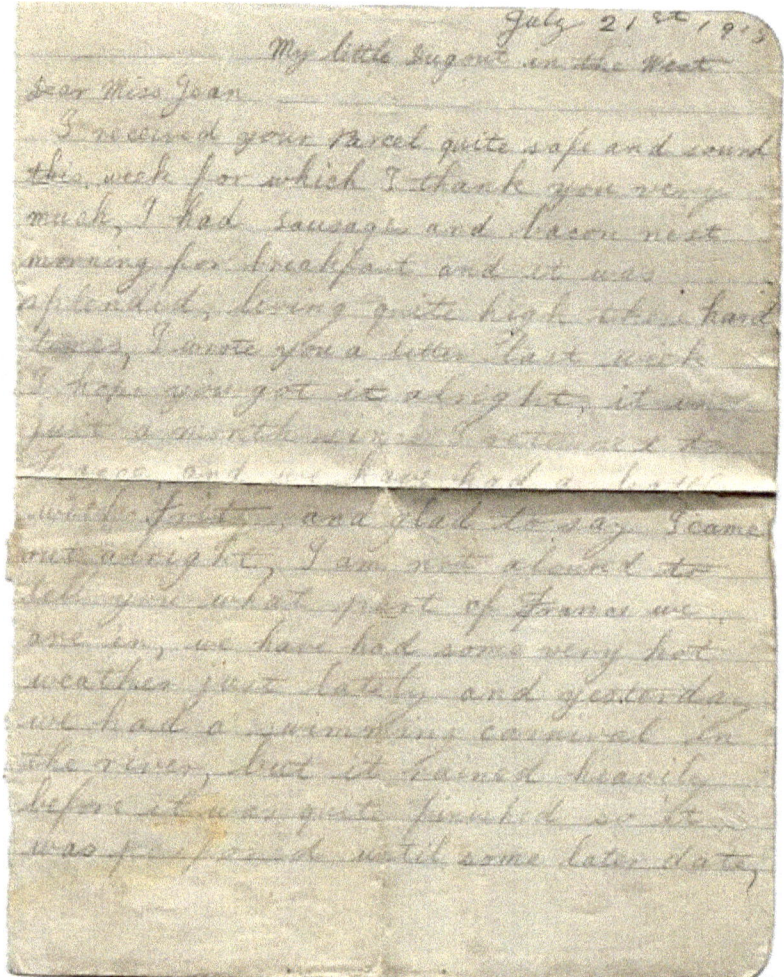

My little dugout in the West

Dear Miss Jean

I received your parcel -quite safe and sound this week for which I thank you very much, I had sausages and bacon next morning for breakfast and it was splendid, living quite high these hard times, I wrote you a letter last week I hope you got it alright, it is just a month since I returned to France, and we have had a battle with Fritz, and glad to say I came out alright, I am not allowed to tell you what part of France we are in, we have had some very hot weather just lately and yesterday we had a swimming carnival in the river, but it rained heavily before it was quite finished so it was postponed until some later date….

21 July 1918
Letter to Jean
From Pte Wm Cousins (Cont.)

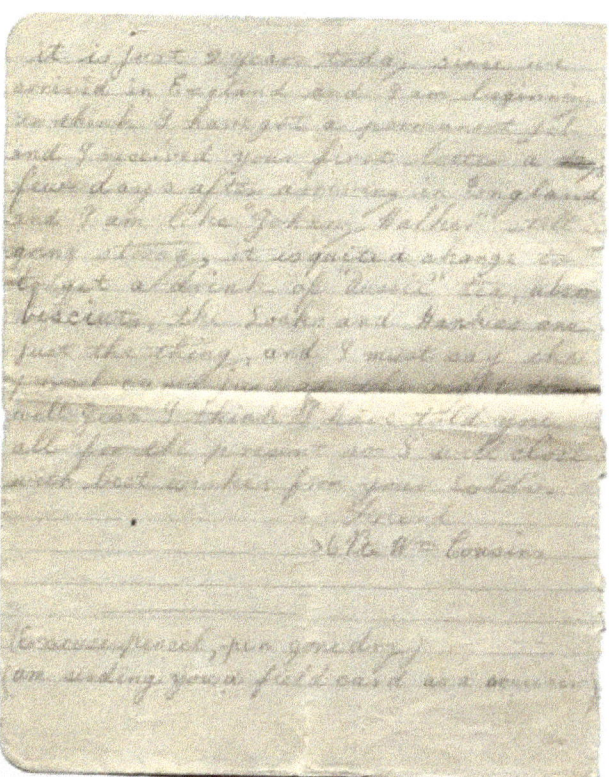

…it is just 2 years today since we arrived in England and I am beginning to think I have got a permanent job and I received your first letter a few days after arriving in England and I am like "Johnny Walker" still going strong, it is quite a change to get a drink of "aussie" tea, also biscuits, the socks and Hankies are just the thing, and I must say the parcel came just at the right time, well Jean I think I have told you all for the present so I will close with best wishes from your soldier Friend

36 Pte Wm Cousins

(excuse pencil, pen gone dry)

(am sending you a field card as a souvenir)

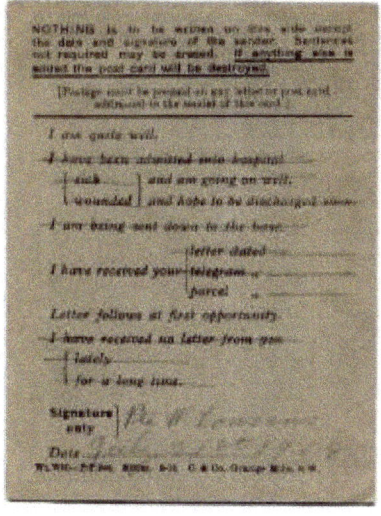

18 October 1918
Letter to Jean
From Pte Wm Cousins

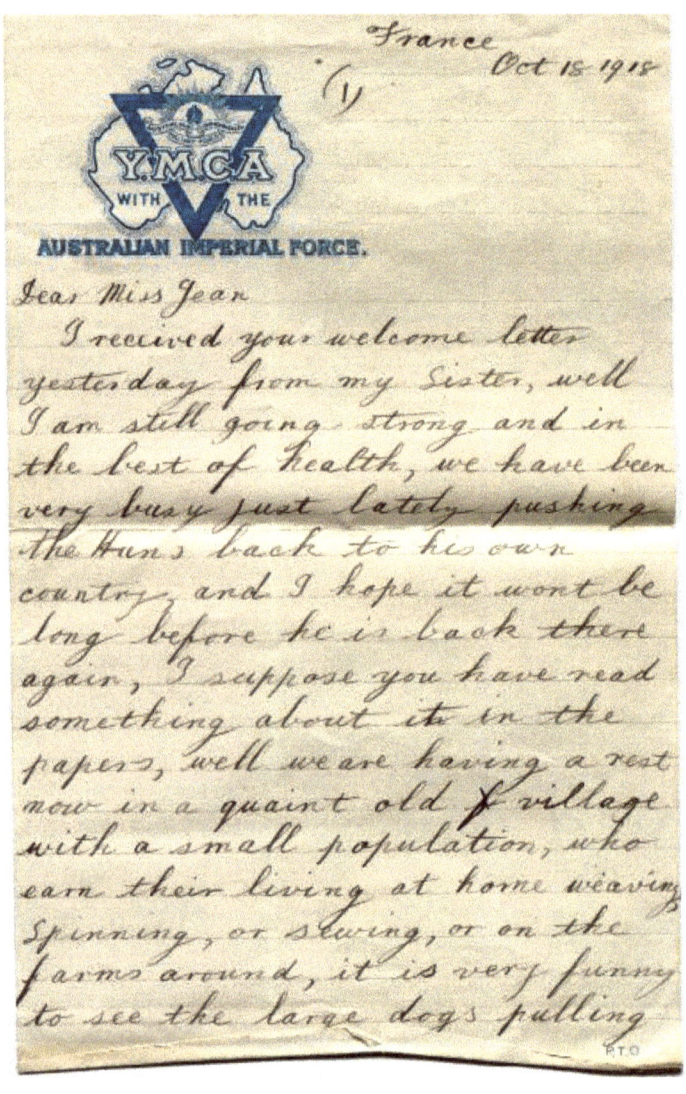

Dear Miss Jean

I received your welcome letter yesterday from my sister, well I am still going strong and in the best of health, we have been very busy just lately pushing the Huns back to his own country and I hope it won't be long before he is back there again, I suppose you have read something about it in the papers, well we are having a rest now in a quaint old village with a small population who earn their living at home weaving, spinning or sewing, or on the farms around, it is very funny to see the large dogs pulling…

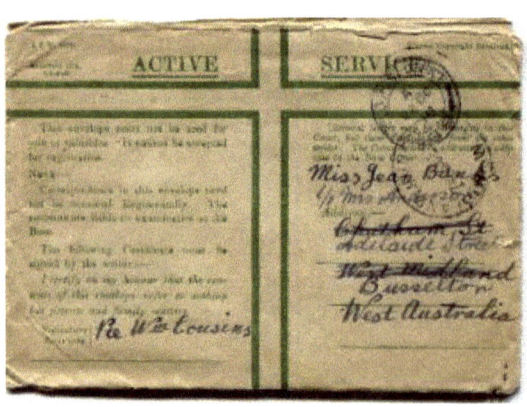

18 October 1918
Letter to Jean
From Pte Wm Cousins (Cont.)

….. a small cart for street hawking, the dog is a very useful animal in this country and works very hard, I saw one the other day engaged in the making of butter at a farmhouse, the churn was inside the house, outside was a large wheel lifted about a foot from the ground, the dog is put inside the wheel, and as the dog walks the wheel goes around, it does this many hours a day, I have been in many Churches and cathedrals since I have been in France and they are all very nice inside, well I am very glad to hear your concert was a great success,

…

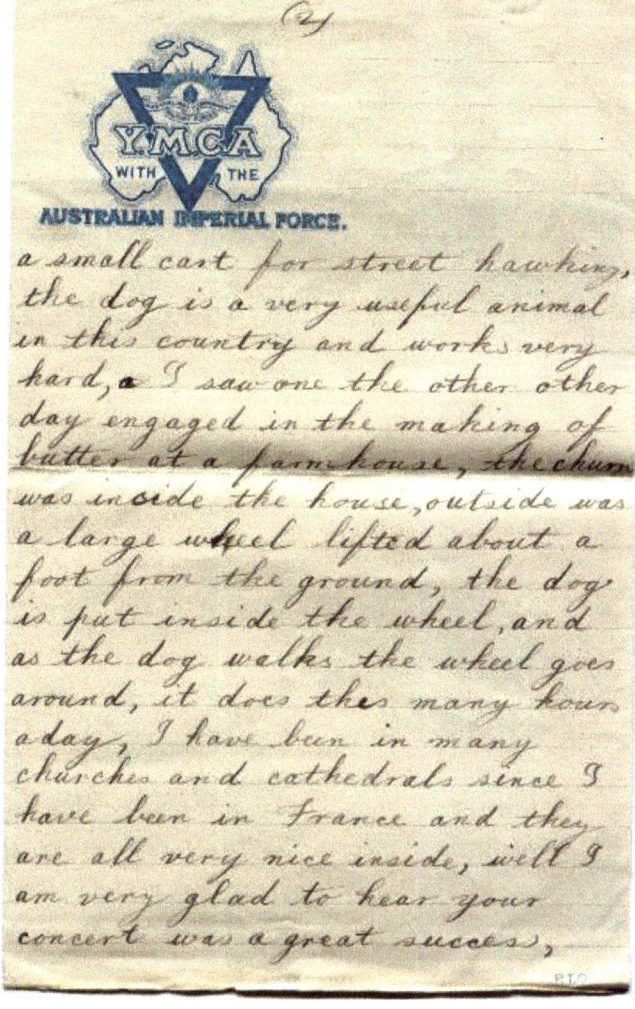

18 October 1918
Letter to Jean
From Pte Wm Cousins (Cont.)

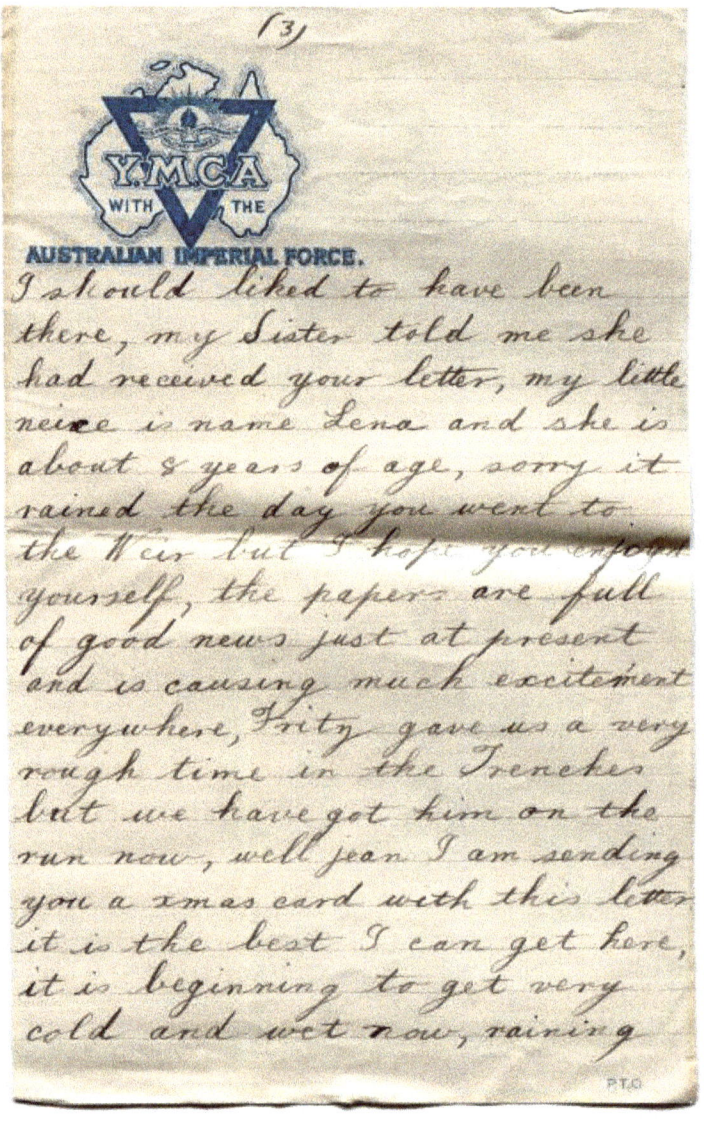

…I should liked to have been there, my Sister told me she had received your letter, my little niece is name Lena and she is about 8 years of age, sorry it rained the day you went to the Weir but I hope you enjoyed yourself, the papers are full of good news just at present and is causing much excitement everywhere, Fritz gave us a very rough time in the trenches but we have got him on the run now, well Jean I am sending you a xmas card with this letter it is the best I can get here, it is beginning to get very cold and wet now, raining …..

18 October 1918
Letter to Jean
From Pte Wm Cousins (Cont.)

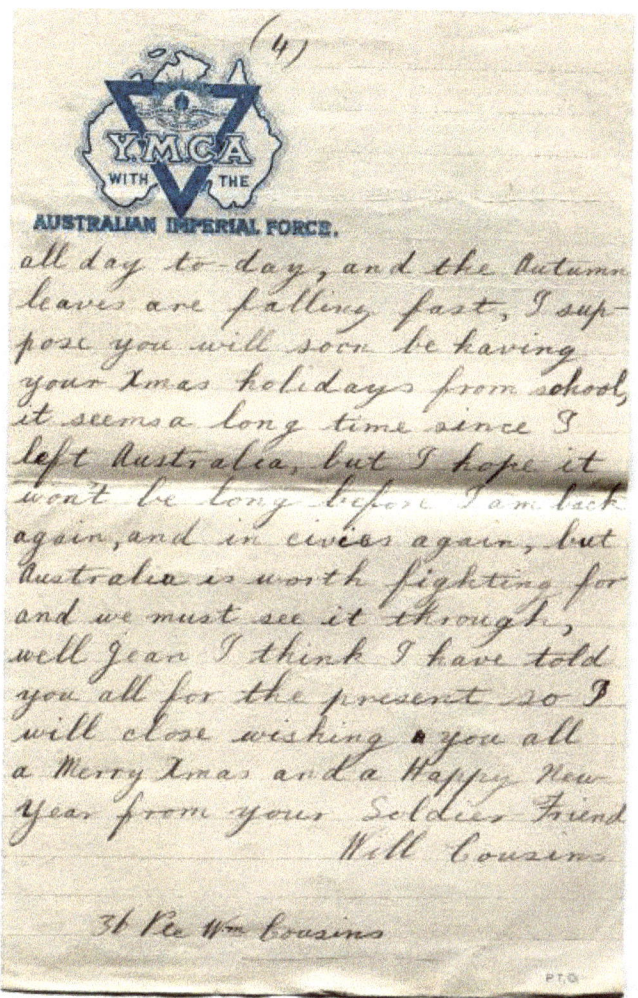

...all day today, and the Autumn leaves are falling fast, I suppose you will soon be having your Xmas holidays from school, it seems a long time since I left Australia, but I hope it won't be long before I am back again, and in cities again, but Australia is worth fighting for and we must see it through, well Jean I think I have told you all for the present so I will close wishing you all a Merry Xmas and a Happy New Year from your Soldier Friend Will Cousins

36 Pte Wm Cousins

31 October 1918
Letter to Jean – From Mrs P Fallon, Sister Of Pte Wm Cousins

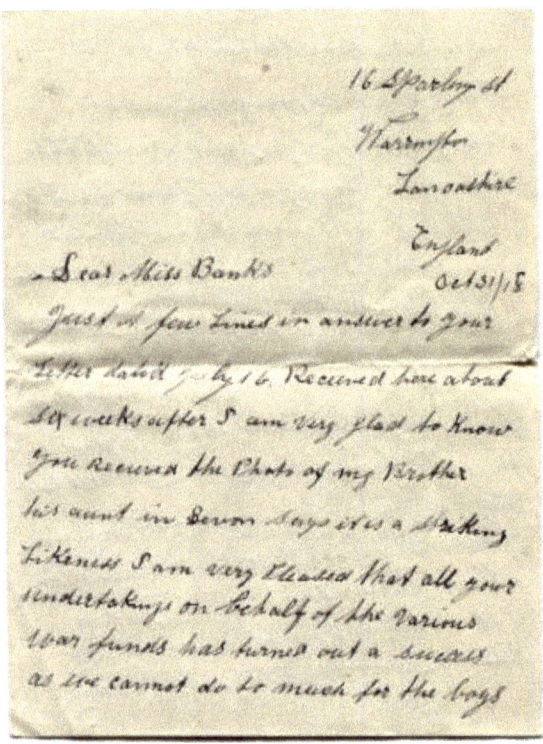

England
Oct 31/18
16 Sparling St
Warrington
Lancashire

Dear Miss Banks

Just a few lines in answer to your letter dated July 16. Received here about six weeks after I am very glad to know you received the photo of my brother his aunt in Devon says it is a striking likeness. I am very pleased that all your undertakings on behalf of the various war funds has turned out a success as we cannot do to much for the boys…

…who is risking their lives for us.

I had a letter from my brother on Saturday he says they have had a rough time but they are having a rest now he is quite well as I write I have received two letters from Australia one is stamped August 31 which I think is yours and one August 24 I think is from Mr Julian, Willie receives all his letters from Australia. Dear Madam we wish the war was over I don't think it will last very long now as everything is going in our favour what rejoicing there will be when it is over how nice it would be if it should happen at Christmas well let us hope it won't be much longer…

31 October 1918
Letter to Jean
From Mrs P Fallon, Sister Of Pte Wm Cousins (Cont.)

…as it is a terrible affair we have one of the largest hospitals in England here called lord derby their is a great many Australian boys here wounded but they don't seem to worry.

Dear Jean I think your bob is a bit greedy having two strings to her bow but don't be disappointed as there will be a boy left when the war is over.

Dear Jean our little girl's name is Lena her Uncle Willie calls her dimples as when she laughs she has two dimples in her cheeks she is sending you a Christmas card hoping when you receive it we shall have joyous news

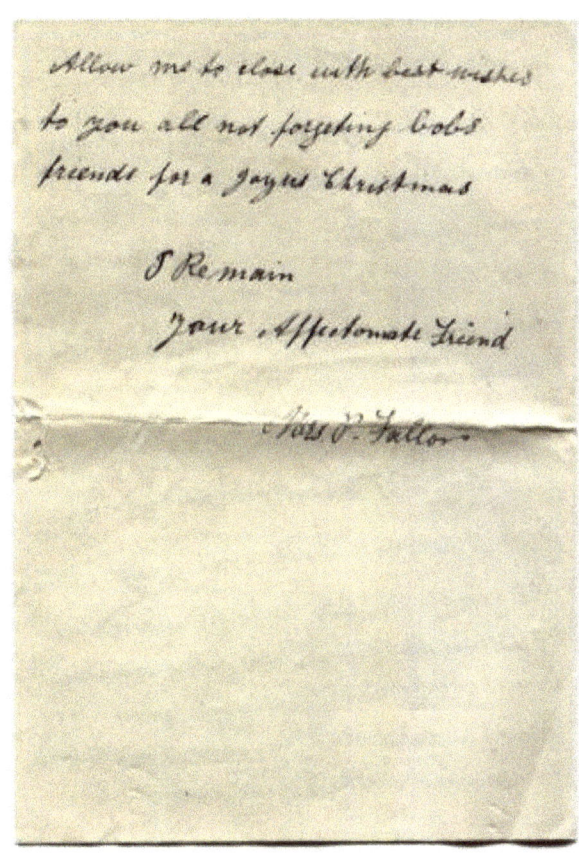

Allow me to close with best wishes to you all not forgetting bob's friends for a joyous Christmas

I remain

your Affectionate Friend

Mrs. P. Fallon

8 November 1918
FRANCE
Letter to Jean
From Pte Wm Cousins

Dear Miss Jean

I received your welcome letter dated August 26th, since writing you my last letter, prospects are much brighter and I think the end of the war is very near, won't it be a great day, I guess you will have a holiday that day, I am sending you 24 postcard views of Amiens Cathedral in a seperate packet, I hope you will get them alright they are very interesting, Jean that picture of Charlie Chaplin must have been very funny, it is a long time since I saw any movies there is no picture places…

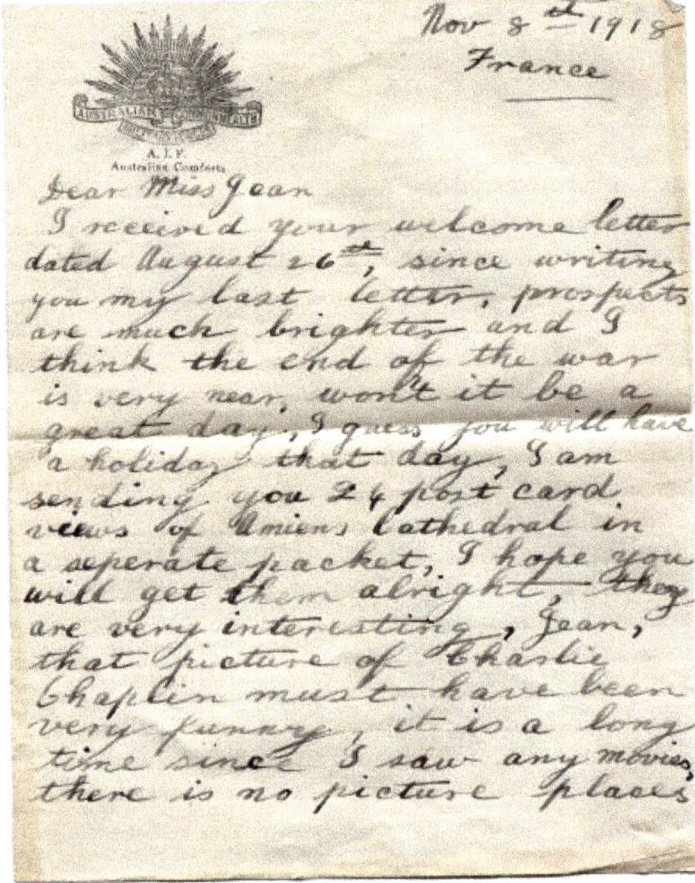

8 November 1918
FRANCE
Letter to Jean
From Pte Wm Cousins (Cont.)

….near where we are billeted, we have a concert party visiting us occasionally, glad to hear you had a good time at the school social, it is getting very cold and wet now, and Xmas will soon be here, I sent you a card with my last letter, hope you got it, my little niece says she has sent you one also, we are still billeted in the same village, well Jean I have no more to say this time so I will close with best wishes from your soldier Friend

Will Cousins

Wishing you a Merry Xmas and a Happy New Year

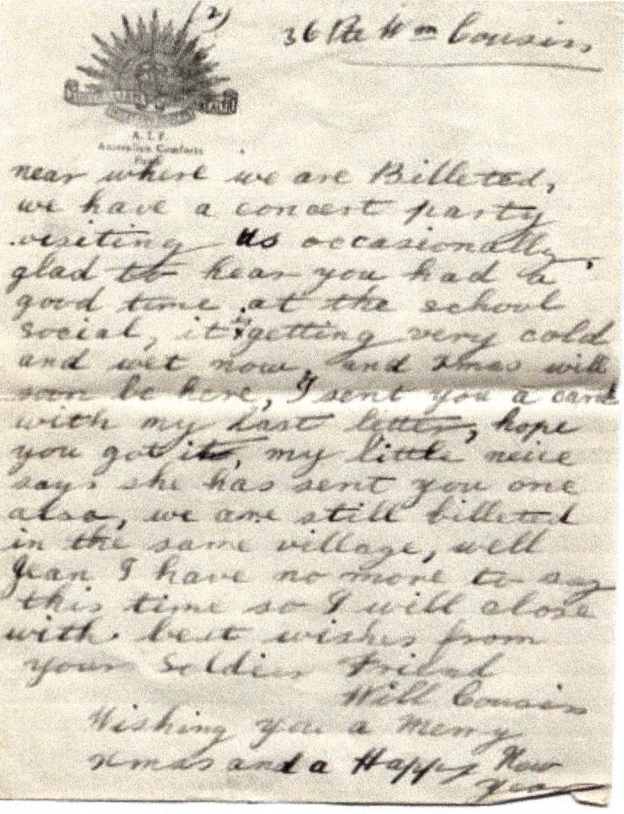

7 December 1918
France
Letter to Jean
From Pte Wm Cousins

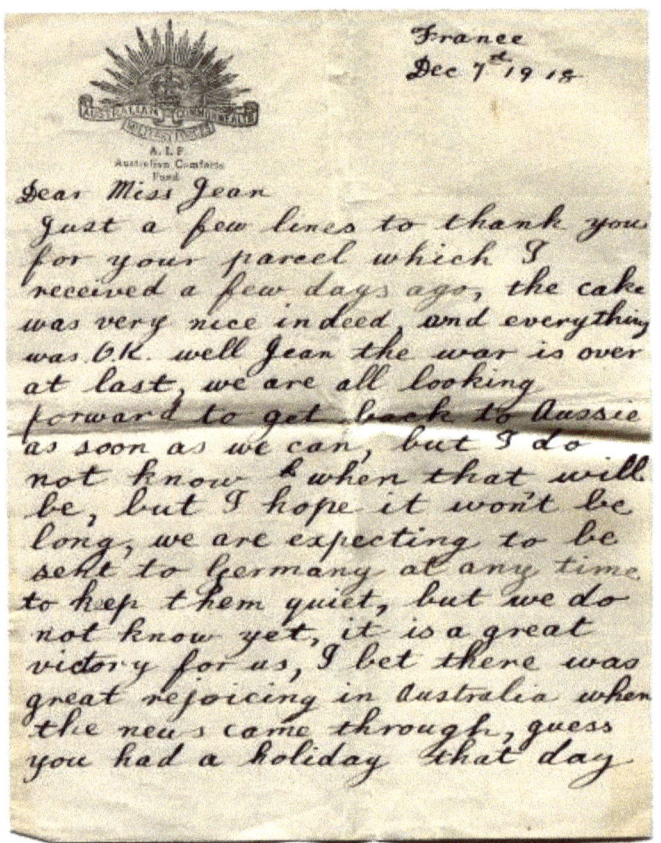

Dear Miss Jean

Just a few lines to thank you for your parcel which I received a few days ago, the cake was very nice indeed, and everything was OK. well Jean the war is over at last, we are all looking forward to get back to Aussie as soon as we can, but I do not know when that will be, but I hope it won't be long, we are expecting to be sent to Germany at any time to keep them quiet, but we do not know yet, it is a great victory for us, I bet there was great rejoicing in Australia when the news came through, guess you had a holiday that day…..

7 December 1918
France
Letter to Jean
From Pte Wm Cousins

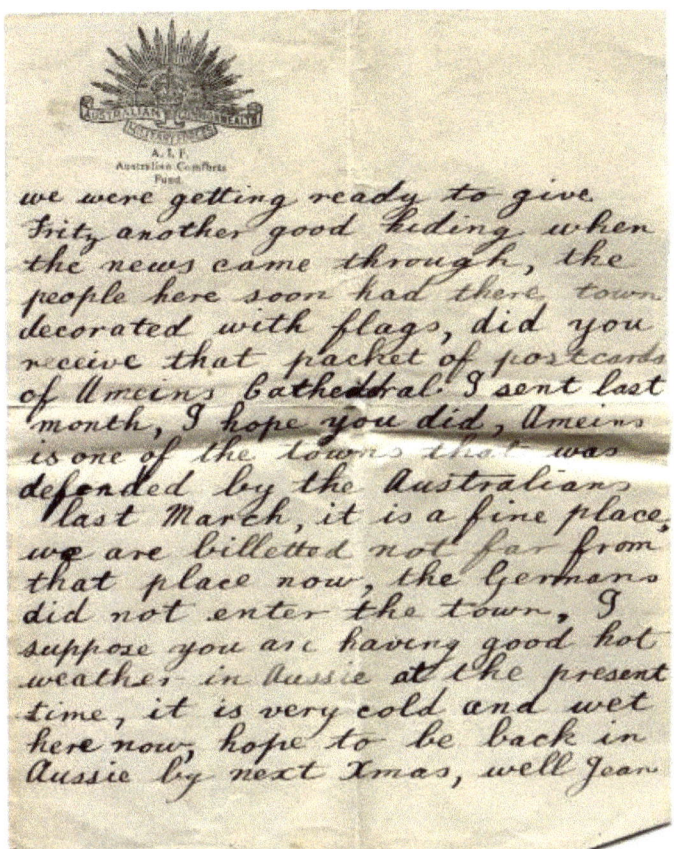

… we were getting ready to give Fritz another good hiding when the news came through, the people here soon had their town decorated with flags, did you receive that packet of postcards of Amiens Cathedral I sent last month, I hope you did, Amiens is one of the towns that was defended by the Australians last March, it is a fine place, we are billeted not far from that place now, the Germans did not enter the town, I suppose you are having good hot weather in Aussie at the present time, it is very cold and wet here now, hope to be back in Aussie by next Xmas, well Jean …

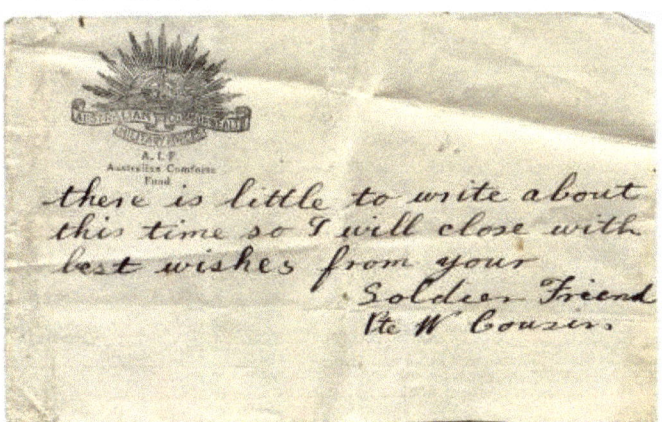

… there is little to write about this time so I will close with

best wishes from your

Soldier Friend

Pte W Cousins

11 March 1919
France
Letter to Jean
From Pte Wm Cousins

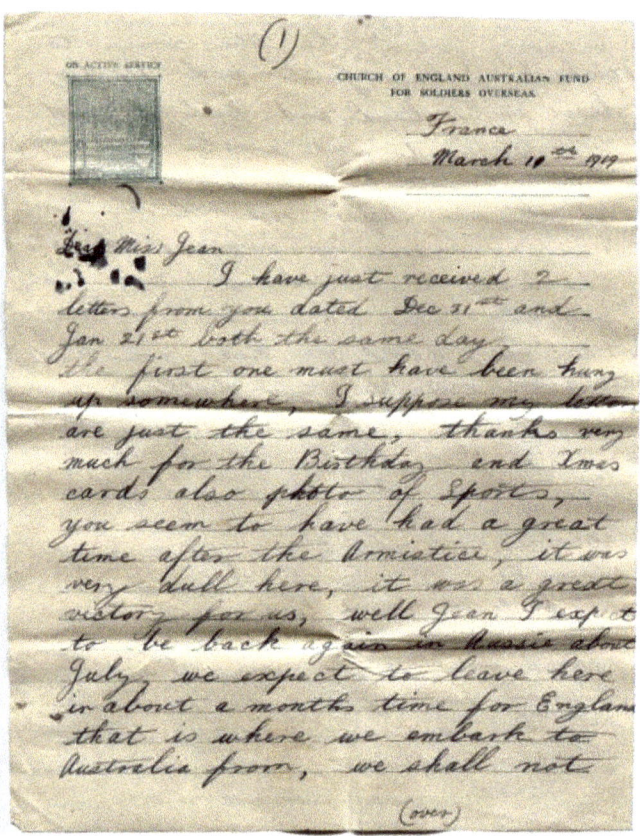

Dear Miss Jean

I have just received 2 letters from you dated Dec 31st and Jan 21st both the same day, the first one must have been hung up somewhere, I suppose my letters are just the same, thanks very much for the Birthday and Xmas cards also photos of sports you seem to have had a great time after the Armistice, it was very dull here, it was a great victory for us, well Jean I expect to be back again in Aussie about July we expect to leave here in about a months time for England, that is where we embark to Australia from, we shall not…

…be sorry when the time comes to embark, I have just had 14 days leave in England and had a good time there, do not write any more letters to me here as I may be on the way before one returns here, I will be sure to come and see you when I get back, will let you know when we are in England. I am very glad to hear you had a good time on your holidays at Busselton, have never been there myself, it is getting very miserable here now, we have nothing to do and plenty of time to do it in, just waiting to be demobilised, I think our first draft leaves here next week, I am on the 2nd draft which leaves a few weeks later, most of the first draft are married men, it is just about the beginning of Spring now and the trees are budding out, but we are still getting plenty of rain, and mud, we are camped now in Picardy, and we are not very…

11 March 1919
France
Letter to Jean
From Pte Wm Cousins (Cont...)

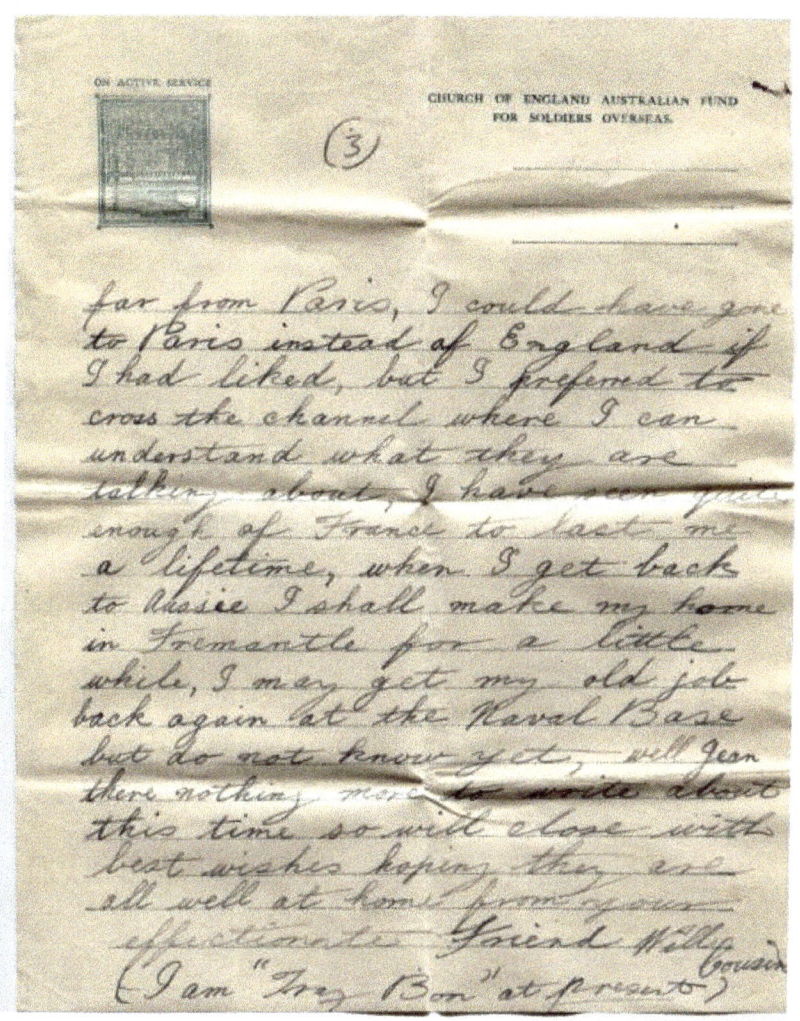

...far from Paris, I could have gone to Paris instead of England if I had liked, but I preferred to cross the channel where I can understand what they are talking about, I have seen quite enough of France to last me a lifetime, when I get back to Aussie I shall make my home in Fremantle for a little while, I may get my old job back again at the Naval Base but do not know yet, well Jean there nothing more to write about this time so will close with best wishes hoping they are all well at home from your affectionate friend Will Cousins

(I am "Tray Bon" at present)

11 May 1919

Salisbury Plains, England

Letter to Jean

From Pte Wm Cousins

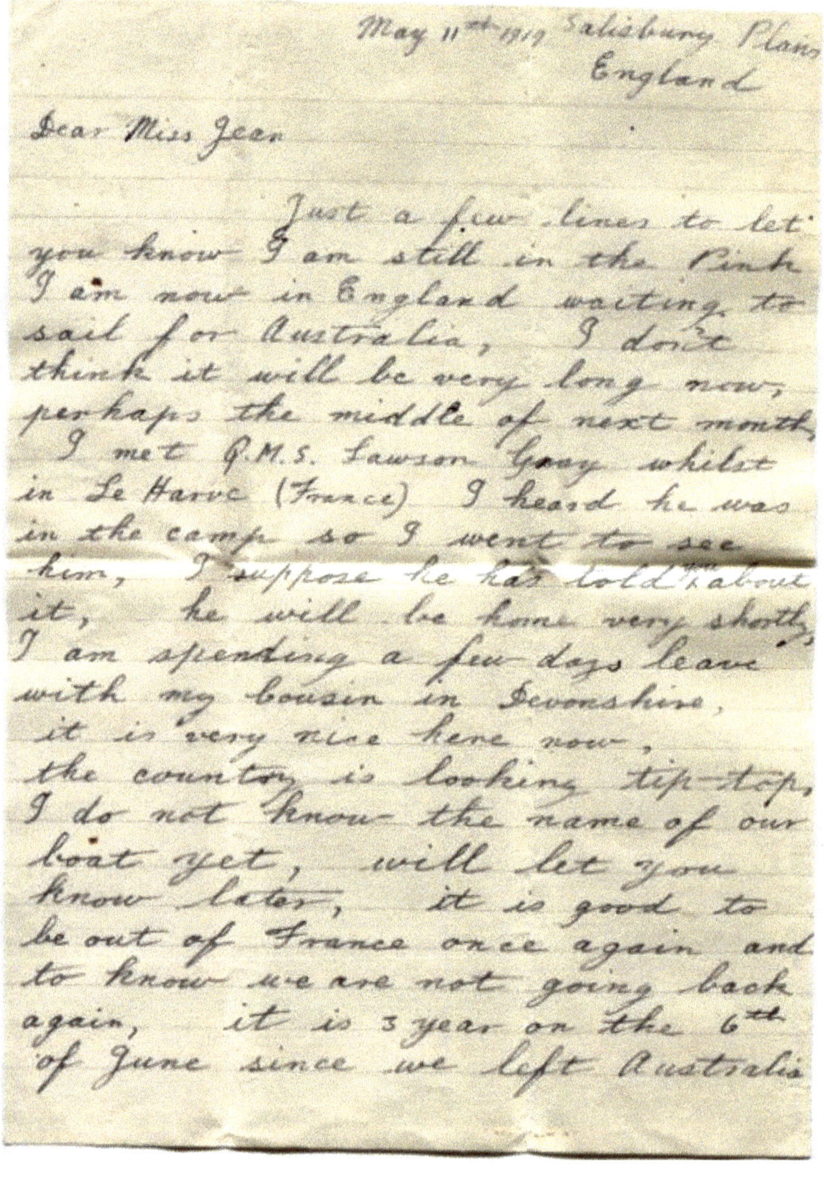

May 11th 1919 Salisbury Plains
England

Dear Miss Jean

Just a few lines to let you know I am still in the Pink I am now in England waiting to sail for Australia, I don't think it will be very long now, perhaps the middle of next month, I met Q.M.S. Lawson Gray whilst in Le Harve (France) I heard he was in the camp so I went to see him, I suppose he has told about it, he will be home very shortly, I am spending a few days leave with my Cousin in Devonshire, it is very nice here now, the country is looking tip-top, I do not know the name of our boat yet, will let you know later, it is good to be out of France once again and to know we are not going back again, it is 3 year on the 6th of June since we left Australia

Dear Miss Jean

Just a few lines to let you know I am still in the Pink. I am now in England waiting to sail for Australia, I don't think it will be very long now, perhaps the middle of next month, I met Q.M.S. Lawson Gray whilst in Le Havre (France). I heard he was in the camp so I went to see him, I suppose he has told you about it, he will be home very shortly. I am spending a few days leave with my Cousin in Devonshire, it is very nice here now, the country is looking tip-top. I do not know the name of our boat yet, will let you know later, it is good to be out of France once again and to know we are not going back again, it is 3 year on the 6th of June since we left Australia, …

Note: Lawson Gray is Jean's first cousin, son of her mother's sister Margaret.

11 May 1919
Salisbury Plains, England
Letter to Jean
From Pte Wm Cousins (Cont.)

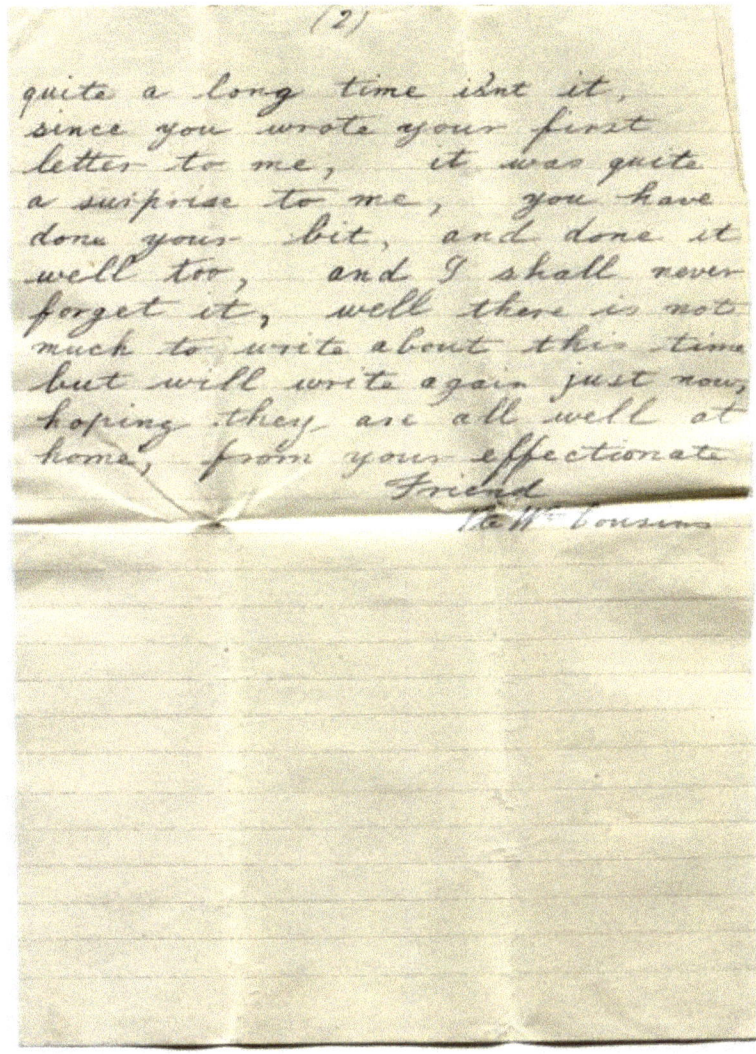

… quite along time isn't it, since you wrote your first letter to me, it was quite a surprise to me, you have done your bit, and done it well too, and I shall never forget it, well there is not much to write about this time but will write again just now, hoping they are all well at home, from your affectionate Friend

Pte Wm Cousins

28 May 1919
Codford, England
Letter to Jean
From Pte Wm Cousins

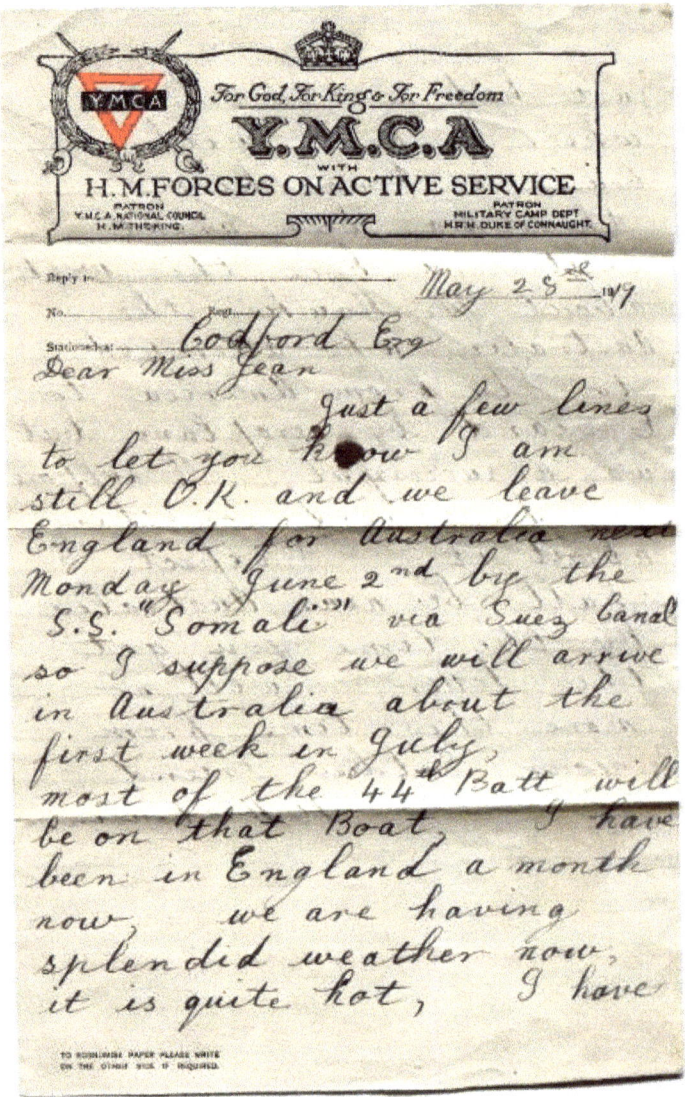

Dear Miss Jean

Just a few lines to let you know I am still O.K. and we leave England for Australia next Monday June 2nd by the S.S. "Somali" via Suez Canal so I suppose we will arrive in Australia about the first week in July, most of the 44th Batt will be on that Boat, I have been in England a month now, we are having splendid weather now, it is quite hot, I have…

28 May 1919
Codford, England
Letter to Jean
From Pte Wm Cousins (Cont.)

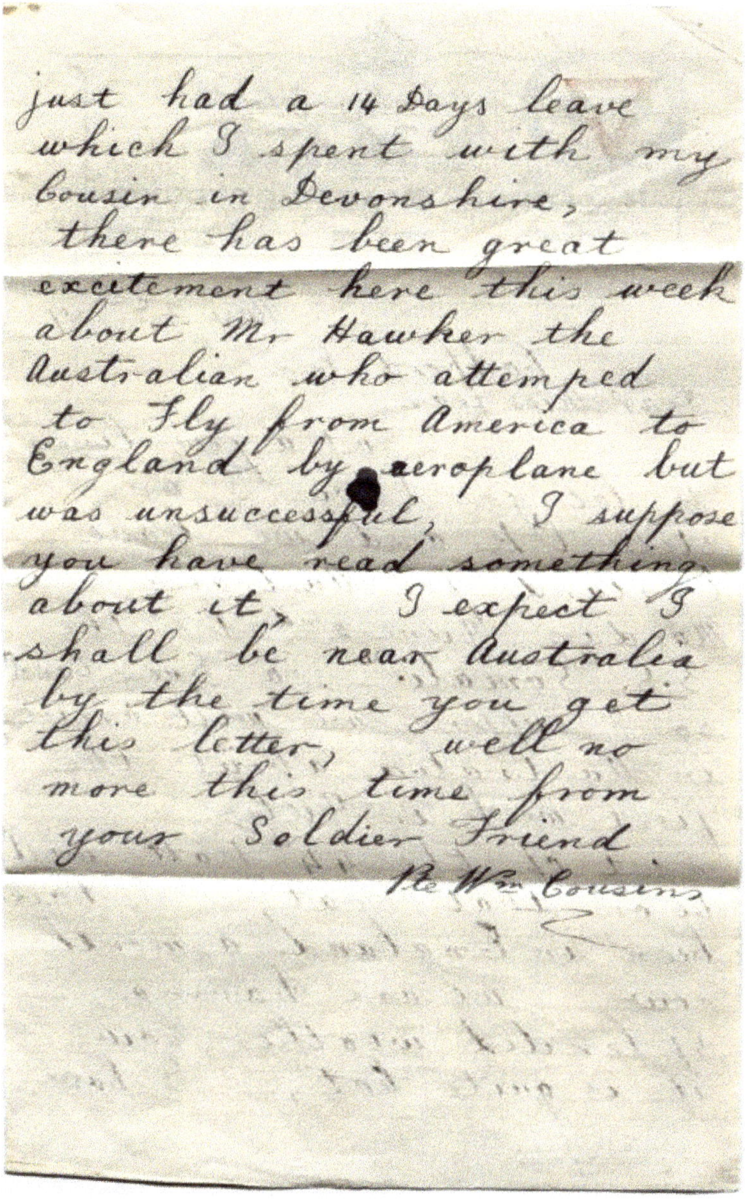
just had a 14 Days leave
which I spent with my
cousin in Devonshire,
there has been great
excitement here this week
about Mr Hawker the
Australian who attemped
to Fly from America to
England by aeroplane but
was unsuccessful, I suppose
you have read something
about it, I expect I
shall be near Australia
by the time you get
this letter, well no
more this time from
your Soldier Friend.
Pte Wm Cousins

... just had a 14 days leave which I spent with my Cousin in Devonshire, there has been great excitement here this week about Mr Hawker the Australian who attempted to fly from America to England by aeroplane but was unsuccessful, I suppose you have read something about it, I expect I shall be near Australia by the time you get this letter, well no more this time from your Soldier Friend

Pte Wm Cousins

Undated Letter
To Jean From Her Cousin Lawson Gray

(Note: Letter is sent Registered mail from Perth, assume Lawson must have sent from France to his parents in WA to forward to Jean)

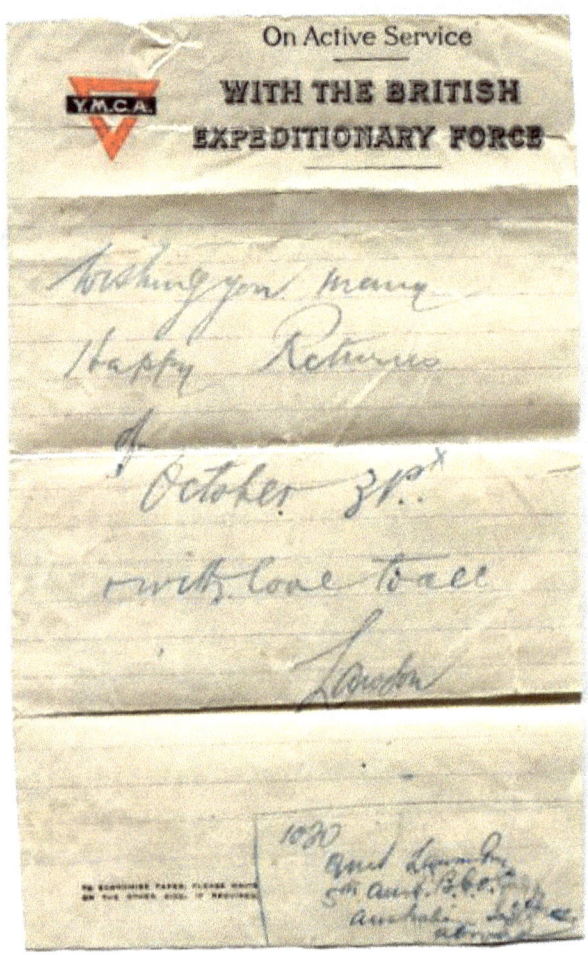

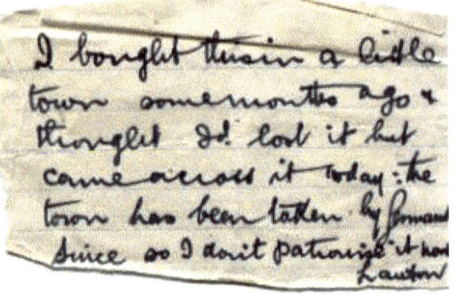

Wishing you many Happy Returns of October 31st

With love to all,
Lawson

1020 Lawson Gray, 5th Aust. B Coy Australian (unreadable) abroad

I bought this in a town some months ago & thought I'd lost it but came across it today, the town has been taken by Germans since so I don't patronise it now. Lawson

Cakes for Soldiers

WWI 1917

This article, originally published in the Sunday Times (Sydney), on Sunday 30 September 1917, encouraged its readers to 'send a good big home-made cake to your soldier at the front or in camp.' They reported that these recipes were economical and simple to make:—

There followed recipes for "SOLDIERS' PLUM CAKE", "QUEEN CAKES", "ROCK CAKES" and "SOLDIERS GINGERBREAD' with instructions on how to keep your cake fresh on its journey:

"When sending your cake to the front; you may be quite sure that it will keep perfectly fresh if you pack it in greaseproof paper in an airtight tin. Before using the tin make sure that it is dry and free from stale crumbs. Scald the tin out first, wipe it out well, and let it air thoroughly before use."

Source: https://remembering-the-past-australia.blogspot.com/2018/10/cakes-for-soldiers-wwi-1917.html

The Vernon Families of Joondanna

A Collection of Memories and Photos
of Family Members

The Vernon Families of Midland and Joondanna

Charles Molesworth Vernon and his wife Laura (nee Azzoni) lived for many years in Midland, Western Australia at Number 11 Harper Street.

They had six children:

- William Mendle, born Islington London, UK 1886;
- Robert Molesworth born Melbourne, Victoria, 1887;
- Florence Henrietta Molesworth, born Islington London, UK, 1890;
- Charles Molesworth, born Bethnal Green, London,UK, 1893;
- Hickman Molesworth, 1895, and
- Dorothy born Midland Junction, Western Australia 1904.

Their father died in 1907, the result of an accident while bathing in Spencer's Brook at Mokine, Western Australia.

The eldest son William married Ethel May Wass from Dongara, W.A. and they had eight children:

- Reginald,
- Ernest
- Douglas,
- Rona Myrtle,
- Daphne June,
- Edward William,
- Raymond Cyril,
- Henrietta, and
- Margaret.

All were born in Western Australia.

Robert never married and died young in 1912, aged 25.

Florence had an illegitimate son, Wilfred Harold in 1913. She later married Charles Edward Carmichael who she divorced 1923. In 1924, her daughter Mary Patricia Carmichael was born and at the age of 10 was killed in a road accident. According to hearsay, Florence went 'roo shooting' collecting the skins to sell.

Wilfred served in WWII and returned home "shell-shocked". He lived an itinerant life, staying periodically with his grandmother Laura and Aunt Dorothy.

Florence, Charlie and Hickey were very good swimmers and competed in the Swim Through Guildford, organised by the Guildford and District Amateur Club. Hickey won the junior championship at the age of 15. He was the first lad under the age of 16 to win this event.

Dorothy – "Dorrie" – never married and lived next door to Hickey and his wife Jean, with her mother and Florence's son Wilfred.

The following stories deal with Charles and Hickman Vernon's families.

Charles and Hickman survived the horrors of WWI and returned home physically sound. However, as we now know and acknowledge, war has a deep psychological effect on those who have served, and Charlie and Hickey were no exceptions.

After the war, Charlie remained in England for six months and trained as a telegrapher. When he returned to Australia, he joined what is now Australia Post and remained there for all his working life.

He purchased a house in Prowse Street, West Perth where he lived with his mother before moving to Joondanna, where he owned a large amount of land.

On 1 December 1928, he married Hilda St Claire from Kiama, NSW and they settled in Joondanna. They had three children:

- Mavis Gwendoline,
- Beryl Isabel, and
- Gordon Charles St Claire.

None of his children married or had children.

Charlie became a well-known eccentric in Joondanna. His block was a full acre and he built his house before the roads were gazetted. Once the roads were built (Joondanna Drive and Baden Street), his house was back to front so the rear of his house faced Joondanna Drive and the front of his house was in the middle of his block! He had a quarter acre directly in front of his house which faced on to Baden Street and half an acre adjacent which faced on to both Joondanna Drive and Baden Street. Charlie planted pine trees on his block, none of which stand today but during the writer's childhood, most Christmases, while he was still able, he climbed the tallest tree and hung coloured lights which you could see for miles.

Charlie owned several properties including houses in West Perth, Midland, Greenmount and Scarborough. Some of Hickey's children lived in the Scarborough house as newlyweds – sometimes with one family in the front and the other in the back of the house, writer's parents included. I can remember the house and the large backyard.

The brothers' mother Laura moved from Prowse Street in West Perth to a small house opposite Charlie's land in Baden Street, Joondanna, next door to Hickey's house, where she lived out her later years with her daughter Dorrie and Florence's son Wilfred.

Charles & Hilda Vernon
Mavis Gwendoline, Beryl Isobel
& Gordon Charles St Clair Vernon

Charles met Hilda St Clair when she was visiting a family friend who was a neighbour of the Vernon families in Baden Street.

Hilda Gertrude St Claire was born 13 April 1894 in Rose Valley, NSW.

**Charles & Hilda
Wedding Day 1st December 1928.**

A day at the beach, Charlie, Hilda, Jean and Hickey (obscured)

Hilda

December 1926
Letter to Hilda from her mother

(spelling and grammar as written)

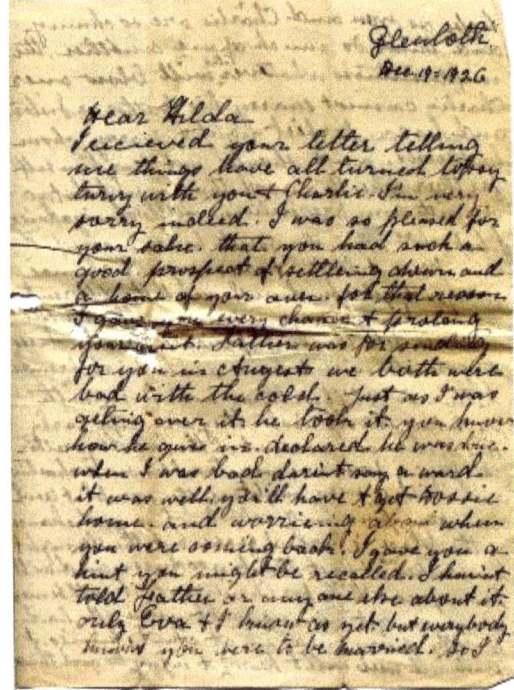

"Glenloth"

Dec.19-1926

Dear Hilda

I received your letter telling me things have all turned topsy turvy with you & Charlie. I'm very sorry indeed. I was so pleased for your sake that you had such a good prospect of settling down and a home of your own for that reason I gave you every chance to prolong your visit. Father was for sending for you in August we both were bad with the colds, just as I was getting over it he took it you know how he gives in. declared he was done. when I was bad daren't say a word it was well you'll have to get Dossie home and worrying about when you were coming back. I gave you a hint you might be recalled. I haven't told father or anyone else about it, only Eva & I know as yet but everybody knows you were to be married. so I…..

… hope as you and Charlie are so chummy and think so much of one another, the unpleasantness whatever it is will blow over. Charlie cannot marry his Mother or Sister and has a perfect right to marry whom he pleases and should not deny himself for their sake. Its a good thing you didn't go on with any preparations and took my advice. I hope Mrs Wilson & yourself had a successful and plesent trip. it was a great chance for you to get round and see all the different places. I'm glad you get on so well with the Stuarts tell them I appreciate their kindness to you. its nice to have such kind friends. Suthie is still with us and busy with packing the apricots. they are ripe early the flying foxes are very troublesome shouting and baiting every night an they wouldn't leave any. busy poisoning rabbits too a good chance as the place is bare of grass. but the drought has brocken up at last. Thank goodness. and will have green hills for Christmas. it will be over when you get this no doubt you've all had a jolly merry xmas up at aunt Annies. I trust all were well & hearty & enjoy the good things ….

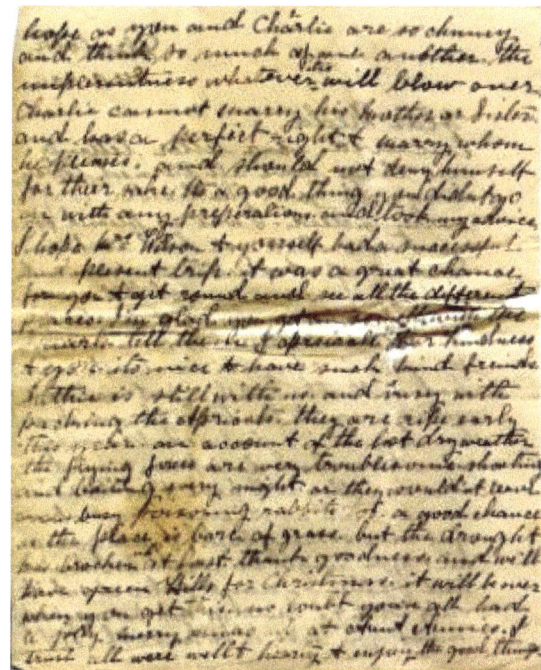

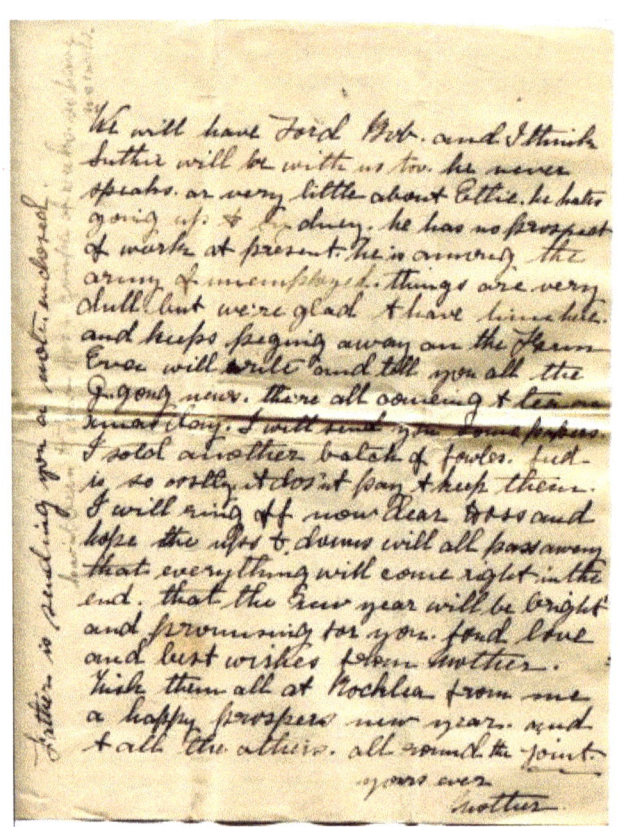

…We will have Fred Gub. and I think Suthie will be with us too. he never speaks. or very little about Ettie. he hates going up to Sydney. He has no prospect of work at present. he is among the army of unemployed. things are very dull. but we're glad to have him here. and keeps peging away on the farm Eve will write and tell you all the G.gong news. there all coming to tea on Xmas day. I will send you some papers. I sold another batch of fowles, feed is so costly it does'nt pay to keep them. I will ring off now dear Doss and hope the ups & downs will all pass away that everything will be bright and promising for you. fond love and best wishes from mother. Wish them all at Rocklea from me and a happy prospers new year. and to all the others. all round the joint. yours ever Mother

Father is sending you a note. enclosed.

haven't been to town for a couple of weeks so have no cards

Letter from Hilda to her sister Eva

undated, circa 1950–1960

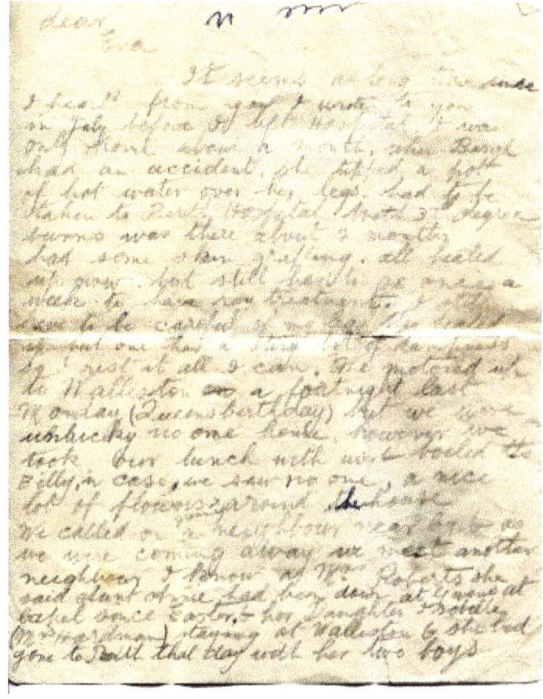

Dear Eva

It seems a long time since I heard from you, I wrote to you in July before I left Hospital. I was only home about a month when Beryl had an accident, she tipped a pot of hot water over her legs, had to be taken to Perth Hospital with 3rd degree burns was there about 2 months had some skin grafting all healed up now but still has to go once a week to have ray treatment. I still have to be careful of my legs they healed up but one has a tiny bit of dampness so I rest it all I can.

We motored up to Walliston a fortnight last Monday (Queens birthday) but we were unlucky no one home however we took our lunch with us & boiled the billy, in case we saw no one a nice lot of flowers growing around the house. We called on a neighbour nearby and as we were coming away we meet another neighbour I know a Mrs Roberts she said Aunt Annie had been down at Gwens at Capel since Easter & her daughter Isobella (Mrs Hardman) staying at Walliston & she had gone to Perth that day with her two boys

….that's was how we saw no one and Uncle Alf come down last Xmas but was most of his time down at Capel. When I was in Hospital this time last year Aunt came to see me, she looked real well. she had been shopping & bought toys for some of her grandchildren but said she did not feel well, she has suffered for years, always had one once a week at Doc at (Kalamunda) now Gwen does it having learnt nursing & Aunt told me her memory is getting bad. I am writing to Gwen to ask about how aunt is. Well I hope this finds you all well as it leaves us now, work is getting very busy at the GPO Mavis is still at Goldsborough Morts & Gordon at state works, will now say goodbye.

Wishing you all a Merry Xmas & Happy new year from us all

From your loving sister Hilda

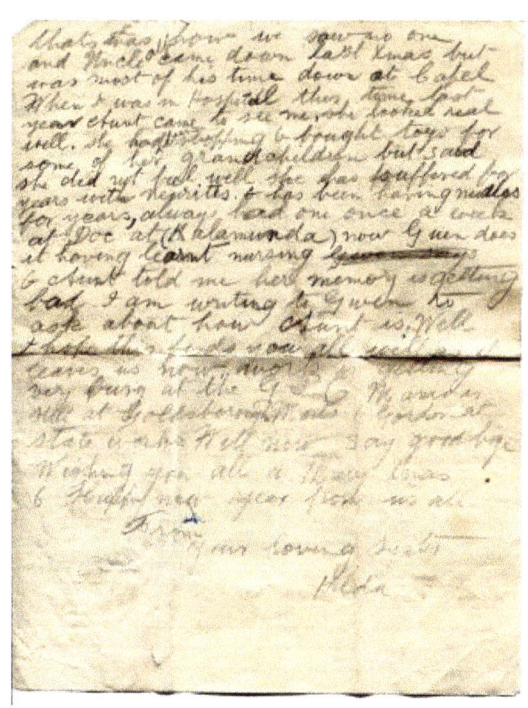

Mavis' Story

(In her own words)

Born in Newcastle Street, Perth in 1929, Mavis was the eldest of three children born to Charles and Hilda Vernon. She lived most of her life in the family home, which was on a one-acre block in Joondanna.

Mavis attended Mount Hawthorn Primary school, walking through the bush with her cousins who lived across the road from her. She and her cousin Marj were in the same class as Hazel Masterson. Hazel later became Hazel Hawke, wife of Australia's Prime Minister Bob Hawke. Marj and Mavis both subsequently went to Girdleston High School in James Street, Perth. Mavis had ambitions to study and become a teacher but was discouraged by her parents.

In her teenage years, many summer days were spent at Scarborough Beach with her cousins. They would ride their bikes to and from the beach, some nine kilometres each way and mostly uphill on the way home!

Mavis' working life was, firstly, at Goldsbrough Mort where she was Private Secretary to the State Manager, and following their merger with Elders, as Private Secretary to the General Manager of Elder Smith Goldsbrough Mort.

A keen sportswoman, on 13 May 1948, Mavis was the "poster girl" on the front page of Perth's Western Mail, representing Goldsbrough Mort's basketball team.

She was also Ladies Tennis Champion at Leederville Tennis Club in 1955.

Although there was no shortage of suitors, Mavis never married.

Mavis' involvement with care has been lifelong. Her younger sister, Beryl, became intellectually disabled because of constant attacks of epilepsy. Mavis supported Beryl at school where she was not understood, and when their parents died she was with her on her journey at home, in hostel care, and later a nursing home until her death in late 1998.

In 1968, Mavis was nominated by Elders for the position of Secretary to the "HRH The Duke of Edinburgh Commonwealth Study Conference" which had a marked effect on her life.

Forty-eight Commonwealth countries were represented, and for three weeks, Mavis became secretary to the representatives of eight of those countries.

Prince Philip, as President, played a very active role throughout the entire conference.

Mavis also had the privilege of again meeting His Royal Highness at Government House during a later Royal visit to Perth.

As a result of her work at the Conference, Mavis became involved directly or indirectly in a number of organisations, mostly involved with care. Firstly, she became Hon Secretary of Sister Kate's Children's

Home, and subsequently, Associate of the Community of the Sisters of the Church, the Order that brought Sister Kate to Perth at the beginning of the Century.

While still at Elders, she became involved in the St George's Cathedral Restoration Appeal, Meath Care (frail aged hostel), WA Arthritis & Rheumatism Foundation, WA Post Secondary Education Commission and the WA Opera Company.

Mavis had found her calling.

She became a council member at Meath Care, joined the WA Advanced Education Executive Committee (WAPSEC) as a Commission Member and the Council of Care (WAACON) as Hon Secretary.

While with the Council of Care, she was involved in the production of a video for the Celebration of Care held at St George's Cathedral. This video led to an invitation to become Honorary Secretary of St Bartholomew's House.

Mavis' capacity as Honorary Secretary led to an eight-month tenure as Honorary Director, acting in the role until the appointment of a new Director. Consequently, Mavis received the Medal of the Order of Australia, becoming Mavis Vernon OAM in 1996.

Mavis also became Honorary Secretary of the Friends of St George's Cathedral and President of the Cathedral Women's Fellowship.

Her major involvement there was responsibility for the Floral Carpet, which stretched along the entire length of the cathedral to the Altar – this Flower Festival was aptly named Journey of the Spirit.

Later, Mavis took on the role of Honorary Secretary of the Government House Foundation of Western Australia, of which the Friends of Government House are members.

Here, for twelve years, her work with His Excellency the Governor Major General Jeffery and Mrs Jeffery led to the establishment of Guides in Government House, Devonshire Teas at Open Days, and the oganisation of their Farewell Ball in a marquee on the Great Lawn in the Gardens.

In addition to the OAM, in 2001, Mavis was awarded the WA Centenary Medal for Service to the Community.

Mavis devoted her life to the care of others.

MAVIS VERNON'S PROFILE :

To write about oneself is not easy.

My involvement with care has been life-long. My sister, 18 months younger than I, became intellectually disabled because of constant attacks of epilepsy (initially, convulsions when a child). I "walked" with her at school where she was not understood, and when my parents died I "walked" with her at home, and then along the road of hostel care, and later at a nursing home until her death in late 1998.

My entire working life was as a Secretary, firstly, at Goldsbrough Mort where I was Private Secretary to the State Manager, and following the merger with Elders (the first major merger in Australia), as Private Secretary to the General Manager of Elder Smith Goldsbrough Mort. It later merged with IXL which had a profound effect on the organisation, sadly later leading to its loss of position in the community.

While at Elders, I was "donated" as a Secretary to HRH The Duke of Edinburgh Commonwealth Study Conference which had a marked effect on my life as it did to most other conferees. 24 Commonwealth countries were represented, there were 8 different countries in my group with whom I lived and worked for 3 weeks, and Prince Philip, as President, played a very active role during the whole time. Members of the Study Conference Group in WA recently had the privilege of meeting His Royal Highness at Government House during his visit to Perth.

As a result of the Conference, I became involved directly or indirectly in a number of organisations, mostly involved with care. Firstly, I became Hon Secretary of Sister Kate's Children's Home, and flowing from this I am now an Associate of the Community of the Sisters of the Church, which was the Order that brought Sister Kate to Perth at the beginning of the Century.

Brigadier Alf Buttrose with whom I worked at Elders took up the post of Chairman of Trustees of the Anglican Church which led to his and then my involvement in the Cathedral Restoration Appeal (as a result of the earthquake damage), Meath Care (frail aged hostel), WA Arthritis & Rheumatism Foundation, WA Post Secondary Education Commission, the WA Opera Co., etc. This grew into my joining Meath Care as a Council Member, WAPSEC as a Commission Member and the Council of Care (later to be entitled WAACON) as Hon Secretary. With the Council of Care, I was involved in the production of a video for the Celebration of Care held at St George's Cathedral. And as a result of this video, I was asked to become Hon Secretary of St Bartholomew's House.

My involvement with St Bartholomew's, apart from being Hon Secretary, developed into my being Hon Director for a period of eight months until the appointment of a new Director. This experience was a high learning curve for me, and I can honestly now say, *But For the Grace of God Go I*. As a result of this work, I was awarded the OAM (Medal of the Order of Australia).

Each time I visit St Bartholomew's there is a spiritual awakening and joy in me.

I was baptised as a baby in St George's Cathedral by Dean Robert Moore and was later confirmed by Dean John Hazelwood. I was Hon Secretary of the Friends of St George's Cathedral, President of the Cathedral Women's Fellowship, and am now on the roster of Flower Ladies. My major involvement here was being responsible for the Floral Carpet which stretched along the entire length of the aisle to the Altar - a wonderful sight and the Flower Festival was aptly named *Journey of the Spirit*.

During the past 12 years I have been Hon Secretary of the Government House Foundation of Western Australia of which the Friends of Government House are the members. This has involved the establishment of Guides in Government House, Devonshire Teas at Open Days, and most recently a wonderful Farewell Ball for His Excellency the Governor and Mrs Jeffery in a marquee on the Great Lawn in the Gardens.

People I love, the needs of others are always before me, and by being a Secretary over the years this has enabled me to meet many wonderful people and to keep abreast with the ever-changing world.

Mavis Vernon, OAM
17 April 2000

Family History notes found amongst Mavis' belongings

RECOLLECTIONS OF THE "VERNON TREE":

1. For some reason, the history of the family was not discussed or recorded during the time of Grandma Vernon's life. However, the following are recollections of things heard but which would need to be researched in some cases to authenticate them.

2. GRANDMA VERNON:
Laura VERNON, married Charles Molesworth VERNON in England, she being around 18 years of age. They came to Australia, Midland, when my father, Charles Molesworth VERNON, was approx. 1 year old. He was born on 1 February, 1893. Other children in the family, in order of age were - William, Bob (died single when around 24 yrs), Florence, Charles, Hickman, Dorothy. Grandfather Vernon died when Charles was 13 years old, i.e. 1906/7 when he was 42 years old. He worked on the railways, dived into the river and was staked in the neck which became poisoned and he died of blood-poisoning in the Northam Hospital. Grandmother Vernon was left to bring up the family. I understand Bob, in order to support his mother, worked day and night - he was studying accountancy as well - but died of consumption. Worked up until the day he died. Grandmother Vernon took in washing and worked at Woodbridge in West Midland as a means of support. Charles commenced work at the age of 13, and his small income went to support the family, which he did until the death of both Grandma Vernon and sister Dorothy.

Laura VERNON'S MOTHER AND FATHER:
She was nee Laura AZZONI, her father being Francis AZZONI - a merchant who spent part of his time in Florence and part in London. This was the life-style of Grandma Vernon while a child. Her father was fluent in several languages, a handsome person, tall, fair-haired, northern Italian in appearance. However, at about the time Grandma Vernon became a teenager, he lost his worldly wealth - apparently, a ship on which imports were being carried went down at sea - there was no insurance, etc. So from apparent wealth, it turned to apparent poverty. Grandma VERNON had a brother, Francis AZZONI (he may have come to Australia and lived in Sydney), and a couple of sisters, both of whom were teachers and did not marry. (I have a feeling that one was named Nina).
Grandma VERNON'S MOTHER was Eliza JORDAN before she married Francis AZZONI. I think Grandma Vernon's Grandmother's name was Laura JORDAN.

Page 2.
2. GRANDMA VERNON: (Cont'd)
There was a Marie HANCOCK who I think was a cousin of Grandma Vernon's. She and her sister retired to the Isle of Wight where they lived in a stone cottage until their death.
Dad used to refer to COUSIN JESSIE of BUNGAY, TUNBRIDGE WELLS, with whom he stayed when on leave in World War I.

3. GRANDFATHER VERNON:
He was Charles Molesworth VERNON, son of Henrietta (nee) ENGLAND-JOHNSTON (born in Dublin, Ireland, the daughter of a Church of England Minister). I do not know anything about her husband who would have been GREAT GRANDFATHER VERNON. Grandfather Vernon was born in England (it may have been Richmond), he was an only son. He at one time had a small tobacconiste shop but was not good at business, giving away his earnings, etc. He then went to sea (or it may have been the other way round) in the merchant navy, signing on as crew for various sailings. He would have visited Australia at this time.
I understand Grandfather Vernon was a handsome man and Grandma Vernon was devastated when he died at such a young age. I also understand in the hospital the comment was made of what a loss.

GREAT GRANDMOTHER VERNON (nee ENGLAND-JOHNSTON) had been married before her marriage to Great Grandfather Vernon. She married Robert MOLESWORTH while in Dublin, she was about 18 and he was about 32. He was trained in law and they came to Australia, firstly, Adelaide and then Melbourne. She had children, two or three sons and a daughter. One of the sons was named Hickman who also went into law. Apparently, the divorce tore the family apart, and she finally went to England where she would have met her husband. I think she was about 60 when she died.

4. AUTHENTICATION:
Marriage Certificates, Birth Certificates, Death Certificates would be of great assistance in authenticating dates and names. The above, however, could be a useful start.

(Mavis Vernon)
(Mavis Vernon)
(Daughter of Charles Molesworth Vernon)
10th July, 1993

58 Baden Street
JOONDANNA WA 6060

"Covergirl" 1948

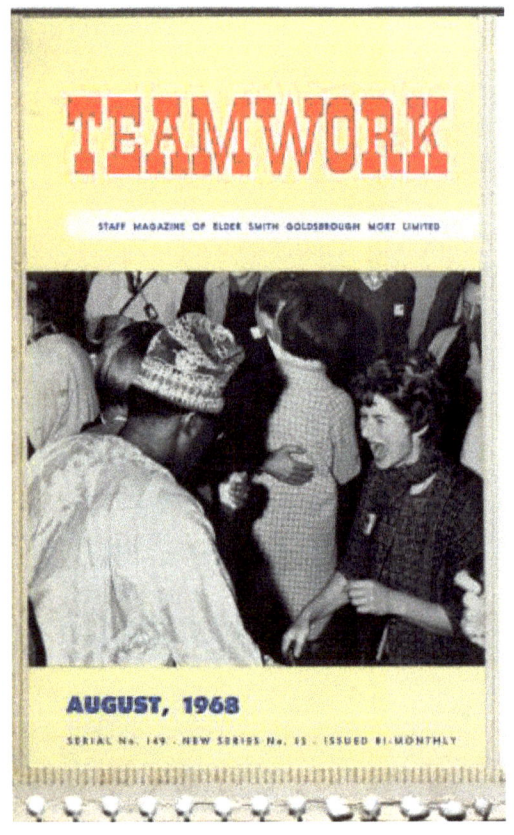

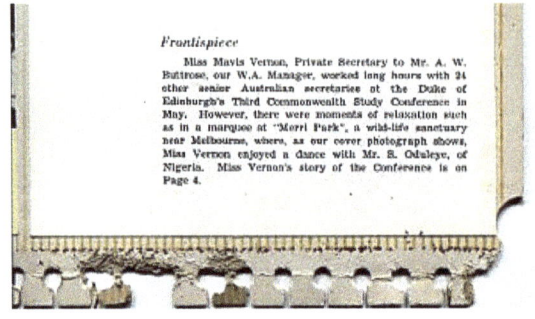

SECRETARY WORKED 16-HOUR DAYS AT DUKE'S CONFERENCE

by Miss Mavis Vernon

When asked to put down my impressions of H.R.H. the Duke of Edinburgh's third Commonwealth Study Conference, I found it so difficult to decide just where to start.

The tempo was aptly described by Mr. James Brady, of our group, in a speech he delivered at the Closing Dinner, when he said: "We were forewarned to some extent that this Conference would be no picnic. But I am sure that we were not even remotely aware that we would be called upon to display in a mere three weeks every Spartan quality we had acquired in a lifetime of no less than 25 years or more than 45 years."

If this tempo is multiplied by 23 days of an average of 16 hours each, it will be realised that our programme was a very full one—predominantly work, but interspersed with receptions, luncheons, dinners and highlighted by an outdoor day and barbecue at "Merri Park", near Melbourne, the property of Mr. C. T. Looker, Chairman of the Conference Executive Committee.

Often I have been asked, what did our Group do? What did they achieve? Perhaps the easiest way to answer this is, following briefings in Sydney and Canberra, on Australian conditions and the theme—"The Human Problems of Industrial Development and Redevelopment in Commonwealth Countries," the Group went on tour to Dandenong and Shepparton, in Victoria, to observe industrial development in practice.

Constantly they asked searching questions, wherever they went—whether interviewing employers or employees; visiting charitable institutions, hospitals, schools, families, etc.—and at the end of each day, when talking over their activities and findings, the discussions were stimulated and well-balanced by members' diverse backgrounds. These represented various occupations and eight Commonwealth countries at different stages of industrial development.

On our return to Melbourne, the results were summarised in a report which was delivered at a closed session. Members then divided into their respective commissions—education and training, application of science and technology, management of economic development, government, industrial relations and living environment—and reported on their findings throughout Australia, which were also delivered at closed sessions.

Miss Vernon and Mr. K. Iyer, a member of Study Group K, try to make friends with a wombat at "Merri Park" when members of the Duke of Edinburgh's Conference were given a day off, but still had to report back for work that night.

And the other question asked is, what did I do? Certainly, I did not have much time for myself, and it took me all my time to keep up with the group. Following the day's discussions, this had to be recorded, resulting in approximately 50 foolscap pages of reporting while on tour. This, on our return to Melbourne, had to be reduced to a 2,000-word report.

Other jobs included: acting as a commission secretary in Melbourne; duplicating—400 copies each run, and then stapling; liaising between staff and members; ushering and hostessing at functions; looking after sore throats, lost property, lost keys—doors with snap locks which meant locking oneself out with the key inside; placating members when mail from home did not arrive on time; ensuring togetherness within the group; assisting members with their returning-home arrangements, etc.

This photograph was taken during Study Group K's first working session on Monday, May 13. Seated (from left) are Mr. James Brady (Trinidad and Tobago), the Duke of Edinburgh, Mr. Ken Stone (Australia — Chairman of Group K), Mr. Byron Stevens (Australia), Mr. K. Iyer (India). Standing (from left) are Mr. John Green (British Solomon Islands), Mr. Len Fortune (New Zealand), Miss Mavis Vernon (Group Secretary), Mr. Harvey Wessner (Canada), Mr. Bruce Hiskens (Australia), Mr. Mike Gorrie (Singapore), Mr. Peter Jeffreys (Australia), Mr. Peter Cottrell (Australia), Mr. Albert Bache (Britain).

"Science, technology and modern industrial methods have brought about a greater revolution in the daily life of mankind than any other happening in history.

"Today there is a growing realisation that communities can thrive under some circumstances, but they can also become unsatisfactory and almost inhuman if set in the wrong environment.

"There are many experts in this field, but unless the future managers and administrators, unless the people who will ultimately wield authority have an active appreciation of the problems, there can be no worthwhile progress."

Glamour Job for W.A. Secretary

This photograph of Miss Mavis Vernon, Private Secretary to Mr. A. W. Buttrose, our W.A. Manager, was taken before she went Absent With Leave from May 12 to June 3 to tackle another secretarial job.

She was one of 25 senior Australian secretaries chosen to assist the organisation of the Duke of Edinburgh's Third Commonwealth Study Conference which was attended by 300 members from 26 overseas countries.

Study groups visited every State to analyse and report on the way human problems are encountered and dealt with in different communities throughout Australia.

Secretaries accompanied the groups to assist members, to compile and maintain day-to-day records of discussions and activities, and to liaise between Conference Staff and group members.

Miss Vernon's group had the task of studying and reporting on the human problems of industrial development and re-development in the Victorian communities of Dandenong and Shepparton.

"Teamwork" has asked Miss Vernon to tell us about the Conference which the Duke of Edinburgh officially opened in Sydney and closed in Melbourne. We hope to publish her story in our next issue.

Beryl & Mavis around 1932

Hickey & Jean's daughter Laura, Mavis & Beryl centre, Gordon front, around 1937

1969

Date unknown

Letter from Mavis to Gordon. 1990

58 Baden Street
JOONDANNA 6060
11th May, 1990.

Dear Gordon,

No doubt, it is God's will that I was at home this afternoon at 1.45 p.m. when I received your faxed letter. (It was not in the box this morning when I went down to collect yesterday's mail).

I understand your predicament, as I, too, find the cost of living difficult at times.

The only way I can help you at the present is to pray for you, and this I will do daily. May God show you the way to assist you.

What little money I have is invested, and at the end of each month I take out the minimum for the month ahead, leaving the other in to receive some interest, but, of course, the rates have gone down. The next due date is not until the end of May.

At the same time as I received your letter, there was one there for Land Tax for $354 which should be paid by 25th May. So that is the situation.

I saw Beryl yesterday and had lunch with her and Betty Smith who is at Graceville. She is good, but getting very much older which is showing.

I didn't tell you - there was no point in writing, but on Ash Wednesday when walking on the overway over Wellington Street to the Bus Station I was "mugged" and am indeed lucky to be alive. Nothing was taken - it is thought to be a pure act of violence - but the man tried to strangle me, and when I called out three times (no-one came to my assistance as there seemed to be no-one around) he threw me heavily onto my head, resulting in my being stunned briefly. I ended up in Royal Perth Hospital, but rather than stay there for the six hours waiting to see a doctor, I rang Dot and Len Fletcher who came in and I stayed the night with them. The next day I saw a local Doctor, who said I should be OK. So I continued on for the next few weeks with a very busy programme, but with a very sore head, shoulders and neck muscles, etc.

- 2 -

Gordon, as a result of this "accident" as I call it (but the Police agree I could have lost my life), I am not as confident catching buses, etc. at night.

Someone offered to try and restore the Mini which has been standing for two years since I was hit in Green Street, but said the cost to do so would be too much, and there would still be a doubt that the car would be completely safe.

As a result of this, only this morning, I contacted Dot Fletcher to see if she would drive me around car yards, etc. To purchase a car would mean I would reduce my savings considerably.

Gordon, there is no doubt at all that God was with me the night I was "mugged". Dot Fletcher said she had a sharp pain at almost the time the situation occurred. She immediately prayed to God and my name came before her.

May God be with you, and with me as we move forward in the coming weeks.

Until the end of May I have no money at all, except for simple house-keeping, and this is very basic.

At the end of May I will have taken a decision about whether or not to obtain a car, and here I will be asking for God's direction.

In the meantime, I will be praying for you constantly.

All my love.

Mavis

P.S. Have you been in touch with the people to whom you loaned money? Could anyone in the Church to which you have given so much time and energy help? Have you thought of going to a country town where there could be more work of a seasonal nature and the cost of living may not be as high?
In your prayers to God, please ask Him to show you the way to new directions.

Mavis 2008

2011 Cousins Laura Williams and Mavis

The rights of man

● PETER SWEENEY continues the series on ordinary people who do extraordinary things.

Sunday Times 1999 / my first cousin - daughter of uncle Charlie + aunty Hilda, sister of Beryl + Gordon

HEROES

BISHOP Michael Challen got no takers to his invitation the first time he went round the table.

He started again — but this time his plea was a lot more serious.

St Bartholomew's, an inner city house for homeless men run by the Anglican Church, needed to find a voluntary director in 1988 — or close its doors.

The previous director had to be replaced but St Bartholomew's was light on in the bank.

Mavis Vernon originally said nothing because she believed the East Perth house should have a man as the boss. But when nobody answered Bishop Challen's second call, she pondered the dark future of the men who called the house their home.

"I'll do it — but only for a month," Miss Vernon said to the Bishop.

Nearly a year later, she stepped aside as director. Today, Miss Vernon remains as the honorary secretary for St Bartholomew's House, which offers support and accommodation to homeless, frail, aged and disadvantaged men.

Miss Vernon has campaigned strongly for the rights of the men.

That's even more remarkable considering she has always been a single woman.

"I never had the time to get married," said Miss Vernon, who cares for a younger sister who is intellectually disabled and totally immobile.

☐ Alvin Cole and Albert Kerkstra with Mavis Vernon in the grounds of St Bartholomew's Home for Men in East Perth.
Picture: GARY MERRIN

"St Bart's used to be home to mostly older men who were alcoholics. Now there are younger men affected by drugs and psychiatric disabilities."

Miss Vernon, who this year was awarded an Order of Australia medal for services to the community, began her long-time involvement with the Anglican Church with the now 105-year-old Meath Care organisation.

She still goes to the Trigg-based Meath Homes every week to help look after and entertain residents as the piano player in the sing-song session.

Her organisational talents and capacity for hard work prompted the late Archbishop Geoffrey Sambell to ask her to join the Anglican Church council of care.

The church was doing a promotion on its six caring agencies and needed direction and drive.

"I'll think about it," Miss Vernon replied. But an affirmative answer was not far away and many services have since benefited from her commitment.

When not working for the Anglican Church, Miss Vernon can be found at Government House, where she's a volunteer guide and the honorary secretary of the Government House Foundation.

Mavis's OAM Medals

Tireless worker receives Honours' award

A JOONDANNA woman has earned a place in the 1996 Queen's Birthday Honours List.

Mavis Vernon has been awarded the Medal of the Order of Australia for her services to the community.

For the past decade, she has been honorary secretary for the council of St Bartholomew's House, an inner-city residence which offers support and hostel accommodation to homeless, frail aged and disadvantaged men.

During that time Mavis has been a tireless campaigner for their rights and in 1988-89 acted as voluntary director of the house.

Her concern for older people comes to the fore at Meath Anglican Retirement Home where she helps look after and entertain residents. She is a long-term member of the organisation's executive council.

Her community spirit also extends to young people.

Adding to her hectic schedule is Mavis' role as honorary secretary of the Government House Foundation.

She took up the position in 1988 and often can be found giving guided tours of the historic building.

The Duke of Edinburgh's Conference Organisation of WA and the WA Post Secondary Education Commission have also benefited from her involvement.

Mavis Vernon, of Joondanna, was awarded the Medal of the Order of Australia in the 1996 Queen's Birthday Honours List.

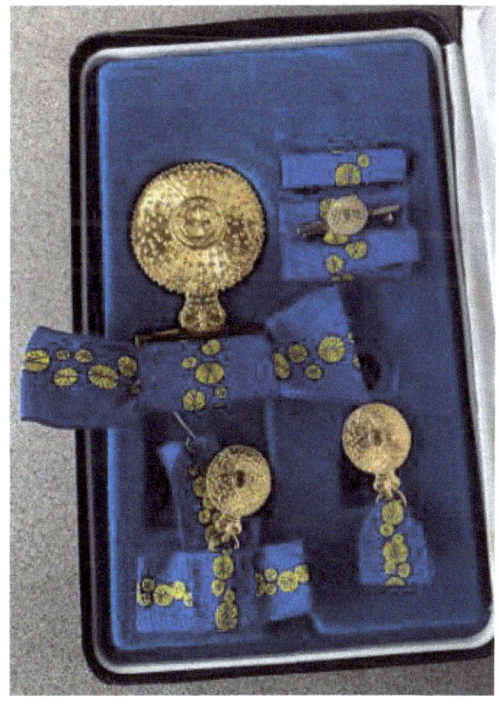

Beryl's Story

Beryl was her father's 'mate' and went everywhere with him. The following eulogy, written by Mavis, tells her story.

EULOGY FOR BERYL ISOBEL VERNON
THURSDAY, 1st OCTOBER 1998

Beryl Isobel Vernon was born on 30th June 1931 and died on 24th September 1998.

She was the second child and second daughter of Hilda and Charles Vernon who lived in 49 Baden Street - then Osborne Park, now Joondanna.

My mother's family lived in New South Wales on a farm on the South Coast. There was no telephone, no car - the only transport - a ship or a train which took a week to get to the other side.

Mum's father became ill - she travelled to his bedside, leaving a one and two year old in the care of Dad, his mother and sister. Not long after her return, Beryl had a convulsion which became the pattern of her life. Princess Margaret Hospital was the only area of care - very difficult to access without a car, telephone or taxi often late at night.

It was thought the convulsions could have been brought on by Meningitis - the only care or cure for the turns was a hot bath. This pattern continued until she became a teenager and the turns then became known as Epilepsy. At that time there was no Dilantin to lessen the spasms, but as a later teenager this became available.

Beryl attended Mount Hawthorn School until she was 14 - there were no aids to assist her for her loss of schooling through blinding headaches which often took her sight away for a time. There was no real understanding among the educationists (this was not their fault). Actually, until twenty years ago I didn't realise Beryl could read.

When I was 9, my father said I would always need to help her. I moved away but always tried to be around when needed.

Over the years as I walked with Beryl as a disabled person, I learned to feel as she did. There was a division between the able-bodied and the disabled - whether waiting in a hospital area or wherever - but this was human nature. (What you don't understand - doubt).

But with my walk there have been some wonderful people who showed love, care and compassion to Beryl as Jesus would show it -
- Professor Eric Saint
- Revd Doug Davies
- Revd Les Goode
- Dr Thomas Early
- Dr Anthony Brisbout
- Dr Michael Benness
- Graceville - particularly Major David and Eva Wilson
- Over recent times the Staff at Chrystal Halliday
- Mrs Dorothy Fletcher
- and very much so - Mrs Betty Smith.

Beryl always wanted to make a statement and be her own person; she loved flowers, animals and birds and little children; when she was younger she loved to do embroidery (most relatives and neighbours have one of her pieces); she did not communicate well; she became frustrated as her life became more limited.

Had she been born today her life would have been different.

I have always said - "But for the Grace of God go I". Beryl was one of God's Chosen Children.

I think Beryl would have loved the words Dad wrote in Mum's Autograph Album in 1957 (2 years before she died) -
> "Birds love sunshine
> Flowers love dew
> Stars love Heaven
> and I love you."

Beryl is now in Heaven with Dad, Mum and Jesus.

Mavis Vernon
1st October 1998

Beryl & Charlie, Forrest Place 1959

Gordon's Story

As a young boy, Gordon's doctor diagnosed him with schizophrenia as he was reportedly "speaking to God, hearing voices in his head", following which he received electric shock treatment. As we grew older, we understood that Gordon was 'different' and that he was a vulnerable person.

Gordon left WA in 1963, and returned in 2013/14, 50 years later. He was 28 when he left. He was already involved with the church in WA and we were told he went to Sydney to work at the Wayside Chapel.

Gordon lived an almost itinerant life in NSW for 50 years and had many different addresses. Wherever he went he became involved with the Church, working periodically, living on the dole/pension or his share in the sale of land or properties that the three siblings had inherited from their father.

He returned to the family home around 2013/14. He did not contact any of his Vernon cousins so no one knew he was there. He was feeble-minded and unable to look after himself and was cared for by a kindly neighbour.

Gordon 2016

The following is part of a letter written by Gordon's neighbour:

"Gordon told me when age 12 (at home) one day he felt someone put their hand on his shoulder and that he also audibly heard a voice say "Gordon don't be scared, Pray out loud I am with you".

Gordon felt it was Jesus/Lord talking to him directly. As a young man Gordon was admitted to Graylands Psychiatric Hospital and given Shock Treatment.

He left for Sydney 1960 living there for 50 years from age 25 to 75. Gordon came back permanently to Perth approx age 75 because Centrelink cut him off Age pension due to substantial asset of family home.

Prior to this he would occasionally come back to Perth to do firebreak on 17 Joondanna prior to 2010.

Whilst in Perth Gordon would rent at YMCA Accommodation Jewell House 180 Goderich St Perth, which was used predominantly by homeless people.

Gordon could not live at family home, was uninhabitable: full of belongings; only a sheep's trail from back door to front door; all other rooms where crammed full of belongings; brick walls collapsed (which -name deleted- repaired at no cost to Gordon for his time and I paid for the window); rat droppings everywhere; no hot water or working fridge/cooker.

Whilst living at Jewell house Gordon would come to 17 Joondanna to potter around doing gardening during the day and just hanging out with me.

I'd feed him & started to take care of him on a daily basis since he was clearly a vulnerable & at risk person with his "simple minded" mental capacity & noticeable memory issues.

He was admitted into Aged care June 23rd 2021"

On Gordon's passing, 2 September 2021, the Joondanna house and land (a full acre) became the property of a member of Victory Life Church, who had made it his business to befriend Gordon.

Gordon had signed a will giving the property to this man.

We can possibly assume that Gordon thought he was giving it to the church, which was not the case.

Hickman & Jean Vernon
Edward Donald (Don), Laura Jean (Laura), Alma Marjorie (Marj), Roberta Jessie (Bobbie), Winifred Gladys (Winnie), Dorothy Isobel (Dolly), Thelma Constance (Connie) and Eric John (Ric)

After the war, Hickey joined the WA Government Railways, where he stayed all his working life, cycling from Midland and later Joondanna to work every day.

On 16 May 1925 Hickey married Jeannie McDonald Banks from West Midland, perhaps they met at the local dances or church Sunday schools, where Jeannie played the organ. They had eight children:

- Donald,
- Laura,
- Marjory (Marj),
- Roberta (Bobbie),
- Winifred (Winnie),
- Dorothy (Dolly),
- Constance (Connie), and
- Eric.

Hickey and Jean purchased an acre of land in Joondanna next door to Hickey's mother. Charlie and Hickey made a path from Charlie's house, through his block coming out at Baden Street opposite Hickey's house.

All Hickey's and Charlie's children grew up together and attended Mt Hawthorn Primary school. They would walk together through Charlie's block and through the bush to the school.

Years later in the early 1950s, Hickey's daughter Marjory and her husband Frank Gardiner built their house on Joondanna Drive immediately next door to Charlie's. The footpath was then extended to reach the back north west corner of the Gardiners' home so the family had access to and from Hickey's in Baden Street. Most Sundays were spent at Nan's with various cousins (there are twenty-six of us!) aunts and uncles traversing through Charlie's to our house and vice versa. There was a lot of interaction with Uncle Charlie, Mavis and Gordon. We all have wonderful memories of those times.

At the time of writing, there are twenty-six grandchildren, sixty great-grandchildren and forty-six great-great-grandchildren descendant from Hickey and Jean, most of whom live in Western Australia, and one family in Canada.

A family picnic is held every year on a Sunday closest to Jeannie Vernon's birthday, 31 October.

Send Off To Examiner H. M. VERNON

PERTH EXAMINERS had known Hickman Molesworth Vernon around the Perth Depot for nearly twenty years. It was fitting therefore that they should gather together on the 9th February to bid him farewell on the eve of his retirement at 65 years of age.

Mr. Vernon is shown in the foreground of above photo receiving from Foreman L. Roberts, as chairman of the Examiners' Social Club, a token of their esteem and good wishes. Various speakers supported Mr. Roberts in recognition of the sterling qualities they had grown to appreciate in their long association with the departing guest.

Hickey expressed himself as gratified at the sentiments expressed by the speakers. He had conditioned himself to accept retirement as a means of catching up with some of his private projects. He proposed taking a good holiday in Sydney before settling down.

In his young days, Hickey Vernon was a noted swimmer, and was a State champion at Guildford. He intends to return home in time for the Empire Games to take a keen interest in the swimming events.

He served three years with the First A.I.F. in the 6th Brigade Ammunition Column.

BUILDING SCIENCE
(Continued from Page 37)

Both publications may be obtained from the Building Research Liaison Service, P.O. Box 2807AA, Melbourne.

NSB No. 43 may only be obtained from the Commonwealth Experimental Building Station, P.O. Box 30, Chatswood, N.S.W.

Hickey's Retirement

Recollections from Family Members

Marj Gardiner

First Memories	Kindergarten, Miss Margaret Graham, Miss Priest, Activities - Baden St home - piano (lessons)
Beginning School	Miss Heney, Miss Halbert, Miss Barry, Miss Manod, Mr Sawyer, Mr Warner, Mr Doug Marshall
Children at Primary school Subjects taught 3 R's	Hazel Masterson (later to be Hawke, wife of Prime Minister), Edith Casley, Una Drinkwater, Angela Dermanich, Florrie Harrison, Joy Smith, Enid Gunston, Vi Travis, Faith Clayton, Gwen Forsyth, Audrey Crews, Lois Moyle, cousin Mavis Vernon, Joan Garner, Joan Chapman, Lila House, Shirley Sissons, Gwen Taylor, Joy Woods, Gloria Pash, Iris Ashwater, June Richards, Rosa Daniele, Lorna Bruce, Molly Paterson Alan Thomas, Bill Smith (x2), Don Caporn, Harold Caporn, Doug ?, Brian Pilgrim, Peter Jowett, Peter Tidy, Lionel Smith, Cliff Hooker
Dad Railway Examiner	Annual Free pass - Busselton, Dunsborough days
Neighbours	Mrs Brown - Husband Tom; Percys; McLains(?); Grandma, Dorrie, Wilf; Mrs Shotton & Eli; Mrs Ericson - suicide
Babies coming home	
High School - Girdleston - James Street War	Tramways - no 15 from Perth City to Mt Hawthorn then change No. 16 to Osborne Park
Hartills Business College	Shorthand, typing, bookkeeping to trial Balance, Comptometer Friend Freda Oldfield
First Job	Hemingway Robertson Institute - correspondents & coaches for accountancy
Extra Job	Cafe - Break-o-Day.Hay Street nr King Street
Arthur Pidgeon	"Bird for Wireless"
War Years	My teens - Dances City Ballroom, Anzac House, Wrightsons
Scarborough Beach Days	Bill (Nobby) Miller, Alan & Ken Sawyer, Ken (Goog) Udell, Ron Coulson, Cliff Hooker, Jim Deegan American, Poms, Dutch sailors - R&R
Wars End, Onslow, Carnarvon	Falling in love, 18 years
Marriage	Scarborough - Shroeders, Laura & Len, McLennons, Don & Shirl "Little 5's" Friday nights - the house - 2 babies, 2 rooms. Sewing dresses 17 Years then work - nerves, Learning to drive. Holden EH

I really got to know my brother Don (Edward Donald Vernon) at about age 17-19 years. He is the eldest of our family. There was Don, Laura, myself, Bobbie, Win, Dolly, Connie and Ric – boy first, six girls and boy last. Don was a sailor during the war period.

I adored him and when he came home we had lots of laughs together about funny things which happened within and without our family. It never worried Don and I that sometimes dad (wonderful man) got drunk every so often after two beers. I think we understood why he did.

This is my 65th year and my first recollections of my life are from about age five years – I can remember my year in kindergarten at Mount Hawthorn with Miss Margaret Graham and a Miss Priest –lovely ladies and the first other than Mum to place regimentation on my life – which for societies' sake, we all need – what a shambles it would be if we were not.

I can remember the pasting, the drawing, the blocks, the sand pit, the singing activities of kindergarten. Pre-Christmas, there was great excitement for me making some wonderful things for Dad & Mum. Always, I think for Dad it was a Matchbox Holder, ie a piece of hessian fabric stitched down with wool with compartments for the match box. For Mum, always a needle case made up of similar material. Wow, such sexism then, ie male – matches – females – needles!!

School was next – 1st 'Bubs' aged 6yrs, 1st Std (standard) 7yrs, through to 6th Std age 12 when I finished at Mount Hawthorn. First year towards Junior Certificate – War intervened. We started in "Girdlestone" in James Street, Perth, catching a tram each morning and afternoon. It was an all girls school and slap bang next door was the all boys school, named "Perth Boys".

Girdlestone was for the Commercial field in that time, Modern School was for those following the professions and East Perth Girls School was for the domestic, seamstresses etc.

I was to turn fourteen years in April of my 2nd year of State school and Mum (bless her heart) in her wisdom decided between her and Dad to send me to Hartill's Business College (located in Hay street, just a few doors west of His Majesty's Theatre). I spent twelve months at Hartill's. Mr Hartill Snr was then the Principal. I learned my shorthand (Pitmans), typing, bookkeeping to trial balance and a very complex machine called a comptometer – a forerunner of computers

I'd say. In later office work I touched on ledger machines – another complication which is now so easily computerised. From college I gained my Certificates in Shorthand, Bookkeeping, Typing and Comptometer, then after gaining a position at age fifteen and a half with the H.R. Institute (now H&R Block). This company was previously known as Hemingway Robertson Institute – correspondents and coaches for accounting and ran a mail order system – it was the way then for people to become certified accountants and the opportunity was there for me but no-one in the establishment or anywhere else ever mentioned that to me. At that age, 15-17, I too, like today's children, didn't force the opportunities for the future.

Growing Up At 53 Baden Street – firstly known as Osborne Park then, when boundaries changed, Joondanna. (Incidentally, Connie and Ric only knew it as Joondanna). When I grew up (1929 – 1936 don't know exactly), Tyler Street was then called Trafalgar Road.

Must remember to speak of my mother – STOIC – YES. The dictionary defines this as 'a person of great self control', that was my mother. She may have had sad secrets that she didn't want to share (ie. pass on to her daughters) – let them experience life as it is. (6 of us) – I know for sure now at sixty-five years that one as an individual in 'a time of life' must not place the burdens of a previous era on the young. Sometimes all we have to say is that "I hope you'll get to see the world".

In my life (after marriage) the quiet times with my Mum were when I played Scrabble with her. I wish now she was still here to play with me. Life goes on.

Dad

I think I am a replica of my Dad. Stoic to a degree but we are romantics and cannot NOT let our heart sometimes flow from us

In my very young days all was wonderful. I cannot recall when it really set in that our family may have been a little different from others because in Baden Street we had another family – I won't name them – over the road, whose situation was far far worse than ours.

Dad was a 1st World War veteran. The VETS from that war were promised everything upon their return (if they returned). The Government, for sure, allocated Defence Service Homes but in those days there was no counselling for the terrible trauma boys of 21 years experienced, which my father was, in the fields of (foreign) France. In my growing up years, Dad was always in constant work with the WA Government Railways where a whiff on one's breath meant instant dismissal – remember these were the 'Depression Years" from 1929-33. Dad was a shift worker and his job was that of "Examiner" with WAGR. Being a shift worker, every 3rd weekend he was able to let his hair down and he did get drunk with the alcohol, which made him so frustrated and sometimes so verbally aggressive with my mother and the whole system that promised him the world before he went away to that awful war, but gave him 'nought' in return for putting his young life on the line.

Childhood – on reflection, WONDERFUL!!

The world as we new it was just that – FREE to roam without fear of molestation etc. We – 1, 2 & 3 and then 4, 5, 6, 7, 8 of us – lived at 53 Baden Street Osborne Park (now Joondanna). Our grandmother Laura (nee AZZONI) Vernon lived next door with her daughter Dorothy (my father's sister) on a property which belonged to Dad's brother Charlie Vernon and next door (west).

A LETTER FROM MARJ TO DON.

52 Kenny Drive, Duncraig.   Tues. 28th December, 1976.

My Dear family,

Today I took Mum and Win (Gaynor was with us) to visit our Dad. I cried. Tonight about 10.15 pm I heard on the radio his favourite song "Twelfth of never." I cried again. I picture him as of a few years ago when he played it on his gramaphone or heard it on radio and affiliated it with "his Bride" our Mum.

Today he looked very wan and could barely speak to us, his eyes closing all the while. The Sister in charge, who is very nice, told us that he has quite a bit of congestion on him.

When I held his hand he gave me a good squeeze and said "keep smiling." I thought about those hands which were giving me the squeeze as I looked at him with eyes almost closed..

His hands, which held the bars of his cycle which bore him to his job and back home thru' all weathers and also which kept it in good repair always so that he wouldn't miss his work or be late. The toys he made in his off time, carts, fish tins on strings, gym bars, see saw, building blocks, etc. The mending and oiling of our bikes over the years. ---- We all had a bike.

In earlier years his hands, together with "Uncle Charlies, cut down enormous trees. Today there's not a "man" who would attempt the task without the aid of a professional with expensive machinery and the only tools Dad and Charlie had were axes, wedges and crosscut saw, which tools I might add, together with tough healthy bodies and commonsense with regard to safety always, did the trick. What fun we used to have after abig old Tuart was felled.

His hands turned to when the house became too small to accommodate us all and sectioned areas off for those who he knew needed privacy at their age.

Hands which belong to his being, which in the main is Sentimental Gentleness but also a streak of great strength when it came to an issue --- in my own case, remember my "trip" to Darwin!! Perhaps there were not any other "cases" but I know (in my case) there was no way after Dad's decision, ie packed bags over the balcony at the back of the house and "You're not going and that's that, now get to bed." That I would have defied him.

His beautiful toil worn hands hardly ever laid one heavily on any one of us eight children and my goodness there were those times I'm sure when he could have flayed us, particularly when he was having his sleep afternoons in order to go on night shift. --- I can see him now storming from the main bedroom and hassling Mum with "Can't you keep those kids quiet Jean" but that was quite a long time ago.

He has said to me over the years, as possibly you've all heard also, that he was glad that our choice of partners for life were all good types. He is so proud of us but cannot show too much.

Our Dad and Mum are fighting the good fight. The world changes but in the long run nothing changes, we're born this time and pass on when our life's work is done. Love to all,
                                                                                    Marj.

Winnie Sinagra

I think Dad bought his one-acre block from Uncle Charlie and had the War Service home built on it. He had to build three bedrooms as he already had a boy and a girl. They moved in when Marj was about eighteen months I think. Before that they lived in Broome Street, East Perth. The photo of Mum and Dad on the veranda would have been taken there, possibly their wedding day as we think that was Mum's wedding dress, which we still have.

Uncle Charlie owned quite a bit of land. I think he once owned all the land between our place and Tyler Street, through to Short Street and possibly a couple of blocks on the other side towards Joondanna Drive. Not sure if Grandma's little house (next door to us) was already there when the land was bought. They were always there when I grew up and it was a pretty 'daggy' place but I guess they appreciated having a roof over their heads as life was pretty tough in those days. Grandma Laura and Dorrie (Dorothy) also lived in Prowse Street, West Perth (a house Uncle Charlie owned) before coming to Baden Street. Probably moved to Baden Street when Uncle Charlie built in Joondanna but I really don't know for sure, just assuming. Not sure if Charlie was already on his block across the road when Mum and Dad moved to 53 Baden street. I don't think Marj and Frank bought their land from Uncle Charlie but not 100% sure.

There was a dairy between Scarborough Beach Road and the bottom side of Baden Street, over Main Street. I think it was owned by Flynn's. I can't remember getting milk from them but their cows were often herded up Baden Street towards Dog Swamp for grazing. We often had to get a bucket and spade after they passed, to collect their poo for the garden and to burn on a hot summer night out on the front lawn to keep the mozzies away!

There was a market garden on the bottom side of Main Street and we often went there for veggies. Our milk was delivered by horse & cart and Mum would leave a billy can out on the front verandah with the money. The baker also delivered our bread by horse and cart.

Things did improve and update as time went by.

Dad always said they spent a lot of time swimming in Guildford and we understood his winning swim was through there. I didn't know about the engraved Fob which is now in his great grandson Elliott Jackson's care.

Charlie also had houses in Greenmount but never lived in them that I know of as they were a later addition (probably after he sold the land in Tyler Street to State Housing). I believe there was some sort of building on one of the two blocks he owned.

Dad always rode his bike to work at Perth Railway Station. I don't think he worked at Midland after he was married. He always said he worked down south digging potatoes during the depression but that may have only been a fill in till he started at Perth Railway Station. That's the only place I know of that he worked, although I think he worked with Midland Railway on a line between Midland and Walkaway as a youngster before the war.

Dad was a lovely, kind and caring man who loved his family and did he's best, for all his faults. We are none of us perfect!

Dolly Beros

I was born on 3rd October 1935 to Jeannie and Hickey Vernon. and am the sixth child of eight. Five sisters and two brothers.

Life in Baden Street was happy and free as we had lots of bush all around us, so there was plenty to do and as I had plenty of siblings, there was always someone to play with.

My father's brother Charlie Vernon and his family lived opposite, so there was also our cousins to play with. Dad's mother and sister lived next door to us.

There was plenty of bush to play, with large tuart trees, and every now and then Dad and Uncle Charlie would chop one down for firewood. Us kids loved to play in the dropped tree and look for birdie grubs behind the bark. We also played ball games on the road such as Donkey, Hoppy and Brandie. Our road was very narrow and back then we hardly saw a car go up Baden Street.

At night after tea, we had to play games or draw before bedtime. Sometimes Mum & Dad joined in; Dad loved to draw ladies with the big bustle at the back.

As Dad did shift work, I feel it must have been hard on Mum, but she never complained. On the Sundays that Dad was home, during the Autumn, we would walk to Menora (Walcott Street) along Wanneroo Road (Dog Swamp) to Roberts street, then turn up to the Reservoir and then home. It was quite a hike. During the summer on a Sunday, we would pack up and head to the Swan River at Peppermint Grove. Quite a hike, catching the No 16 tram from Osborne Park to Mt Hawthorn, change to the No 15 tram for Perth, alight at the top of the Horseshoe Bridge, head down the steps to Perth railway station, catch a train to Cottesloe, alight and walk down Leake Street to the river. It was quite a distance!

By 1940, Connie was born. I had started kindergarten and WWII had begun. I can remember Dad painting the windows black so no light could be seen during the night, also the ration books for tea, sugar, butter and, I think, clothing. It was tough times.

At night during the summer, we would lie on a rug on the grass and watch the search lights criss-crossing in the sky. My brother Don had gone off to war. I remember more of him as the letters came home to Mum & Dad and Mum making fruit cake and wrapping them up in calico and posting them off to Don.

By that time, my older sisters Laura and Marj were teenagers and would often bring home American and English sailors, or soldiers, to have dinner with us. After dinner Mum would often play the piano and everyone would sing. They were always happy to come back again when in Port.

In 1942, I started school at Mount Hawthorn Primary. My brothers and sisters also attended the same school. In 1944, the last of the eight children was born, a boy called Eric John. By now the war was nearly finished and life was getting back to normality again.

Not long after the war, my eldest sisters got married and started having babies. I was twelve when I first became an Aunty.

I attended Girdlestone High School in Perth for two years, left and started work at *Foy and Gibson* department store for six months. I then left and started work as a dental nurse in Leederville for seven years.

I got married in 1957 to Clive Beros and we had four sons. When I was thirty-two, we went farming in Eneabba and I worked at the local mine for the next twenty-seven years. We sold the farm and came back to Perth to live, where we are still today, 2023.

Connie Booth

I was born on 3 October 1940, seventh child of Hickman Molesworth Vernon and Jeannie McDonald Vernon (nee Banks).

My earliest memories are of the family home and yard and bushland surrounding, of Dad chopping wood on a chopping block set near his shed, which was a felled tree with two big branches covered with sheets of tin, and grown over with morning glory creeper.

Behind this shed was a huge almond tree and a fig tree which was a great play area for us. Two more fig trees at the front of the yard and an apricot tree kept us in jam all year round. Dad picked figs and delivered them to Raynors' Factory in West Perth on his bike on his way to work at the Perth Railway Station.

I remember my mother cooking at one end of the large kitchen table, the huge wood stove constantly burning at the other end of the large kitchen; family meals taken at the table with probably never less than seven people; Dad at the head of the table with Mum, Bobbie, Win, Doll, myself and Eric. I can't remember much of Don (who was in the Navy), Laura and Marj (who went North working when I was small).

Dad would be first up in the morning, lighting the fire – making tea and cooking toast on the fire. Milk was delivered by horse and cart and poured into a billy can and jug left out by Mum. We used to fight over the cream which settled on the top. There was no refrigerator or ice chest. A Coolgardie Safe (a metal and hessian cage kept wet to keep things cool) was on the back verandah. Mum used to set jellies in the passage way. Hot water from kettles was used for a bath. Dad had made a frame in which to set a dish of hot water over the bath. We would wash then tip the water over ourselves.

Washday was Monday – all day!. The copper was lit on the back verandah and Mum would still be washing late into the afternoon.

In my early years, our backyard was surrounded by bush for miles and miles. We would go for long walks and gather wildflowers – myrtle, hove and orchids – spider orchids, cowslips.

Dad had some chooks in the backyard when I was very small, but I don't remember them as I got older.

I can remember going on the train to be immunised (maybe somewhere in North Perth) The smell of methylated spirits still brings back the memory.

Being born in 1940, our country was at war. Our windows had to be totally blacked out at night. There were also underground air raid shelters at various places. I vaguely remember some big gas masks, but of course we never had to use them.

Groceries were delivered to the house once a fortnight from Matheson's Grocery Store in Mount Hawthorn. The Watkins man would bring his case with such things as Vaseline, Flavine, Ointments and Eucalyptus oil. Then there was the Jewish Haberdasher, Mr Berliner, who brought dress fabrics and clothing to the house. Mum paid him in time payment or with ration tickets. Food and clothing was rationed till the end of the war in 1945.

In June of 1944, our youngest family member, Eric John, was born, bringing the family total to eight children, the first and last being boys with six girls in between. Edward Donald was the first born, and by the time I came along, he was a grown lad and had joined the Navy. He served in the Second World War as a stoker on a ship called the Shropshire. He became ill and ended up in hospital in England. However he survived but never really lived in the family home again.

We all went to the Mount Hawthorn Primary School and then various secondary schools. I went to Girdlestone in the city and learnt office skills, typing etc. and worked in several different offices over the years.

With the influx of migrants to Perth in the 1950s, the city began to grow and suburbs spread further north, south and east. We lost our lovely bushland to housing, roads and freeways. We were now living in a world of automation and our lives would change forever.

The money was always short, however we were all given a chance to learn the piano. Our mother was musical – she played piano and a neighbour, Mrs Shotton, played a violin. We had many an evening singing along to their lovely music. No TV in those days! I had piano lessons for eight years and to this day still maintain my interest.

Our father served in the First World War and witnessed much horror and sadness. He (like most men who served) never spoke about it until he'd had a few drinks on a Saturday. He was a good, hard working, clean living man and he did his best raising eight children in tough times. He made us a swing and a see-saw and hill trolleys which we rode down our street – no cars in those days.

All in all, we had a pretty good life.

Ric Vernon (Eric John Vernon)

I was born on June 4, 1944, at King Edward Hospital, Subiaco. In reflection, I realise my position as eight of the eight children spread over 19½ years was quite unique. I'm not too sure why the "E" was dropped off my name, Eric, however, it just seemed to grow with me.

I always lived at 53 Baden Street, Joondanna. I think it was a war-service home and they were very proud of having it. I can recall my first bed was in Mum and Dad's room. The rest of the house was crammed with all the other siblings. Mum told me that she and her family once lived on Rockeby Road, Subiaco and I can remember her showing me the house. (I wouldn't have a clue now though). Mum and Dad also mentioned that they had lived elsewhere before the Baden Street house was built.

When I look at the 'luxurious' lives we lead today, I am amazed that Mum, Dad and we eight kids happily lived and shared the house at 53 Baden Street. Only one bathroom with no running hot water! We managed with 'birdie-baths'. You stood in the bath. Dad had built a platform which reached from one side of the tub to the other. It contained a circular cut-out which held the metal basin. You brought a kettle of hot water from the stove and filled the basin for your bath. It was excellent and certainly did the job. In later years, things were modernised and a hot water tank, shower, etc were installed.

Brother Don was eldest. I think my first memory of his being in the house was that he slept in the sleep-out Dad had built onto the back of the house. I think he had lived back east before that. He was born in 1925 and I was born in 1944, so there was a big age difference. In later years, we joked about him being the 'little big' brother because I towered over him – I was the 'big little' brother! We often joked that he was old enough to be my father! I can remember when he began courting Shirley and later, their wedding.

My six sisters, Laura, Marj, Bobbie, Win, Doll and Con were spread by age over a number of years and it was a bit of a blur for me to keep up with what was going on. Saturday afternoon bath and beauty readiness was noisy as they prepared for their Saturday night social events. Dad had the copper boiling with plenty of water. With only one bathroom and no hot running water, it was birdie-baths for all. Hair washing must have been an interesting event I think. However, I remember them all parading through the house dressed in their finery as they departed for their various dates.

A typical woman/wife of the time, Mum 'slaved' away with constant meals, clothes washing etc. Clothes washing day was generally Monday. Dad would light the fire under the copper and Mum would work tirelessly washing for hours. I can still see her wringing monstrous sheets out by hand. When I was a teenager, somehow she got a hand-wringer and she thought she'd gone to heaven.

Dad was the provider – working at Perth Railway Station as a wheelwright. They were very pleased and happy with the fact that he was employed during the Depression. He kept the woodbox topped up all the time so Mum could cook on the Ironstone Stove in the kitchen. I can only imagine nowadays what a feat that was, especially during a Perth summer. That stove was the hub of family life. It hardly ever seemed to be unlit. It was a magnet for us in cold weather. We huddled around it with our feet on newspaper warming them in the open oven doors. Dad would serve us fried bread or toast and drippings. (The thought of that now almost makes my tummy turn, but we thought it was yummy).

We'd listen to the radio serials: *Biggles, Night Beat, Bob Dyer's Pick-a-box, Jack Davie, the Goon Show* etc. One mustn't forget the noon-hour soap, *Blue Hills* by Gwen Meredith. Connie and I used to 'announce' it all the time with greatly exaggerated numbers for its episodes.

Mt Hawthorn School was my 'K-7' school. Being the last of the eight Vernons to attend, some of my siblings' former teachers were still there. I have a vivid memory of my first day in Grade 7 with the 'scary' Doug Marshall calling the roll. Vernon being almost last alphabetically, when he called my name, he lowered his head and peered over the top of his glasses and boomed, "Not another Vernon!". My brilliant red face sank below the desk top. I believe he had taught Don and a few of the other siblings. From Mt Hawthorn, I attended the brand new Tuart Hill High School and then on to Mt Lawley Senior High for grades 11 - 12.

There was a weekly chore roster. Dad always washed the dishes but we took turns drying dishes, ironing, sweeping, food preparation, wood-getting etc. Often as we all did these chores we sang along together. We loved singing "rounds" such as *Ah poor bird, Early one Morning* etc. Singing together was something we all enjoyed. In the winter months we gathered around the lounge room fire and took turns choosing songs from the famous 'Red Book'.

I was four years old when I became an Uncle! Laura and Len's first child Rod was the first grandchild for Mum and Dad and I can recall him learning to talk. I'd ask him his name and he'd say "Voddy Villiams"!

Being four years younger than sister Con, it was a bit like being an only child at times as she soon went to school and had her own group of friends. I chummed around with Barry Page who lived up on Joondanna Drive – almost the only house there. (I am still in touch with him and always visit whenever we are back in Perth). Graeme Blackman lived on the corner of Baden and Tyler Street. Barry, Graeme and I were quite 'thick friends' and rode our bikes everywhere, joined cubs, church gymnastics on Wednesday evenings etc. Other neighbourhood friends were Phil Skinner, Ken Johnson, Ray Hughes, John Hulme and Barry Arnold.

I remember sleeping out on the front lawn during the hot weather until the mozzies got us then we moved into the cool lino floor of the hallway. I will never forget our Sunday family picnics to Peppermint Grove. I really enjoyed those times. Everybody had a chore: carry this bag and that bag etc. The food alone must have kept Mum busy preparing. We walked from home to catch the bus or tram into Perth. Then onto the train to Karrakatta I think. It was quite a long walk from the station to the river. (it seemed even longer at the end of the day, being a bit sunburnt and tired!)

Under the back verandah of the house was the 'dust bowl'. We used to shuffle up and down making enormous clouds of dust – we didn't seem to get allergies though – amazing. There was a sand box too for playing in, next to our 'tame' 28-Parrot and a pink and grey galah.

Growing up, I loved the wide open space of the property and the bushland out the back; searching for mushrooms, picking wildflowers (not a good idea at all but we were totally oblivious to environmental things). Winter time lounge fires were a treat. As I got older Dad let me set and light it. Later, we'd all gather (huddle) around it and sing songs from the famous 'Red Book'. I think someone still has it. Nobody wanted to leave the coziness and go to bed, because in those days there was no central heating/air conditioning and the cold sheets gave us goosebumps.

Our yard had two huge fig trees. The figs were delicious and I used to help Dad pick boxes of them and we'd take them on our bikes to a jam factory, which I think was in Leederville.

All of us kids used to play games inside the 'tent-like' centre of the trees. To this day I love figs and fig jam.

The grape arbor around the back of the house was very attractive. It was a lovely cool place in the summer and Mum had all of her various potted plants growing there. Dad had a good variety of grapes. Big blackish-purple ones, delicious Ladies Fingers, currants and muscatels. Humans weren't the only ones who liked them. He had possum traps set around the base of the vines. I can recall leaning out of the bathroom window and enjoying a few grapes which grew close by.

On some Saturday mornings, Connie and a group of us kids would go to the Boans department store in Perth which had an auditorium. The radio station, 6PM I think, held a sing-a-long session called *The Willie Weeties Show*, sponsored by Weeties breakfast cereal. A screen up front had projected words to the songs on it and we'd all sing our merry hearts out – the original karaoke?

If we went up on stage and sang a solo, we'd receive a big box of Weeties. Of course we were all very keen to be chosen for a chance to win a box. It was broadcast live so Mum would listen at home.

What a safe environment we grew up in. We could step out the front door, 'disappear' for the whole day, and arrive back for evening mealtime. No means of communication, mobile phones etc. Sometimes, a few of us kids would get on our bikes and head off out along Main Street then onto Balcatta Beach Road and follow it out to North Beach Waterman's Bay, Trigg's Island (as it was called then), then back along West Coast Highway (which was a narrow barely paved 'track') and onto Scarborough Beach. Swims along the way, fish and chips at Peter's and a bottle of coke made our day before the ride back home to Joondanna. It sure was a hard bike ride up those hills along Scarborough Beach Road. That area was so quiet and peaceful back then.

Overnight deliveries of milk and bread were still common in the late 40s-early 50s and quite often a horse and cart was used. When I was still pretty young, Dad would 'double-dink' me on his bike and we'd cycle around the neighbourhood. He had a hessian bag and shovel and he'd collect all the good horse manure. Back home, he had a barrel of manure tea which he fed to the veggie garden. At pea-picking times he said he wanted to hear us all whistling! Every now and then he'd call out, "Eric. Are you whistling?" Of course I couldn't with a mouth full of peas!

There wasn't much traffic on Baden Street and the slope was perfect for trolley carts. We neighbourhood kids would spend hours perfecting our carts. They had ball-bearing wheels which made a great sound as they roared down the hill. We made sure we had a safe run-off before reaching Tyler Street crossing as our braking systems were not too smart.

Dad and Uncle Charlie worked as a team gathering firewood which was in constant demand for the cook stove. Once in a while they would work for a couple of weeks digging around the root area of a giant Tuart tree. When it was clear and some roots chopped, they let the strong wind blow the tree over. What a noise.

Then the job began of chopping, sawing and carting all the wood back to the woodshed area.

And the 'dunny'. (How many different names are there for that place, eh!). The lone-standing edifice in the backyard. The weekly pick-up from the 'honey wagon', red-back spider alerts.

Dad would roll up a piece of newspaper, light it, then hold it down the toilet seat hole to burn them out! Amazing how the ten of us used that one dunny! Toilet paper, as we know it now, was non-existent.

Dad kept a good supply of 'soft' paper there. Newspaper was pretty hard to take, but there wasn't much of that. The favourite in my day was the soft tissue paper that was wrapped around each individual apple.

As more nieces and nephews arrived, I seem to have crossed/blended with my siblings to them, making my 'family' even bigger. My youngest sister was four years older and nephew Rod was four years younger so it was easy for me to flow from one age group into the other and as more nieces and nephews arrived, they were a bit like brothers and sisters for me, especially as most of the married sisters and their families lived fairly close to us at 53 Baden Street.

I spent lots of time with my nieces and nephews. Sunday beach days were wonderful with us all piling into various vehicles and heading for the beach. Sunday nights, all back to 53 Baden Street for tea and the famous poker games. These were events that tied us all together. It was such a big, close family. All of us were very close and supported each other through thick and thin. Mum and Dad must have been 'bricks'.

Perth was really a very small, quiet city back in the 1950s and early 60s. We never had a car or a telephone and TV arrived in 1956. I bought Mum and Dad a second-hand TV in 1964 or so. Before that, to watch TV, I used to track up the path through Uncle Charlie's place to sister Marj and her family's home. Their TV was rented and we had to keep dropping two shillings ('two bob') into a box on the back if we wanted to keep watching otherwise the service petered out. It was a time of Westerns, *Bonanza*, *Gunsmoke* and my favourite *Rawhide*, which launched Clint Eastwood's career.

In 1967, aged 23, I set sail with three friends on a working holiday around the world – the 4-week cruise to all Australian ports, New Zealand, Fiji, Samoa, Vancouver, San Francisco and disembarking at Los Angeles was the beginning of the next phase of my life. In one of the last conversations I had about the trip with Mum and Dad, Dad said, "You'll probably get over to Canada and meet a nice Canadian sheila and settle down." My reply was, "That won't happen. We're going to travel across North America, then on to Europe before we get back to Perth in about three years."

The adventure continues ...

Footnote: Ric did exactly as his father predicted. He married Canadian Rosemary Sidall and has lived with his family in Vancouver, Canada ever since!

Lyn Brown (nee Gardiner)

My earliest memories are living in Uncle Charlie's shared house in Brighton Road, Scarborough. I think at first my Auntie Laura & Uncle Len and then my Uncle Don & Auntie Shirley lived in the front and we were in the back. I can remember having an imaginary friend 'Babbin' with whom I had lots of conversations! I used to ask Mum for a biscuit for me and one for Babbin … Mum usually obliged. Some years later, my little sister Denise also had an imaginary friend "Janery Ponce" who had an entire family … we loved listening to her adventures with them and kidding her along.

Where did we get those names?

One of my earliest memories of my younger sister Vicki was when she was a toddler and we were playing in the back yard of the Scarborough house. It was winter and we were splashing in the water coming from the downpipe. We got pretty wet and I don't think Mum was very happy!

I remember Dad taking me to Scarborough Beach for fish & chips, a meal that we also shared every now and then at our kitchen table with Shirley & Don; they must have been newlyweds as Auntie Shirley would put her elbows on the table and flop her hands around so that her diamonds were flashing for all to see … this is a vivid memory for me even now. I loved Auntie Shirley and wanted her to be my 'Fairy Godmother'!

Dad was building our house in Joondanna Drive, right next door to Uncle Charlie's block and I can still see him getting on the bus with his toolbox and planks of wood etc … as we didn't have a car. Denise and Gaynor were born after we moved there.

Living in Joondanna next door to Uncle Charlie's house was wonderful. Once we had moved in, Dad built a path from the north-west corner of our house to connect to the existing path from Charlie's house to our grandparent's house in Baden Street opposite. At the time of writing, that path still exits. I can't remember anyone but family ever using that path … such a safe environment back then.

Some of my earliest memories of Joondanna include the house to the west of Nan & Pop's in Baden Street where Pop's mother Laura lived along with his sister Dorothy – 'Dorrie'.

Florence's son Wilfred was pensioned off from the army and became itinerant, sometimes visiting Dorrie and grandmother Laura. As youngsters, we were quite frightened of him and as cruel as children can be, we called them 'Dirty Dorrie' and 'Filthy Wilfy'. (I'm sure they weren't!) … later, we understood that Wilfred was badly affected by the war (WWII) and was shell-shocked".

We went to Nan & Pop's every Sunday as did many of our aunties, uncles and cousins. Us kids would run amok around their block, climbing and raiding the fig trees having a wonderful time, gorging on figs and chatting. After tea, there were the card games … the older cousins were allowed to sit at the table and play for pennies and 'thruppences'. To this day, I still love a game of cards! If we weren't playing cards, we were running around together on the back verandah, drawing or writing our names on the brick wall, always excited to be together. The path between our house and Nan & Pop's was well-worn, and for us, it was extra special as we got to see them most days, and all of our cousins whenever they visited Nan & Pop.

Charlie's pine trees were huge and a challenge for us cousins to climb (my sister Vicki was better at this than me, I was a bit of a 'sissy' and she was the 'tomboy'). At Christmas time, Charlie would climb the tallest tree and hang coloured lights. You could see them for miles! In amongst the pines was a lot of salvage. Charlie collected stuff from building sites and demolitions – he was a real 'Steptoe', so this part of his one-acre block was a cornucopia for us kids! He also grew peas and I can remember Vicki & me filling our skirts with them and having a feast … his daughter Beryl used to come and chase us away.

I can remember us having to catch buses (not sure how many) to get us from Joondanna to Bicton to visit Shirley & Don … took us hours! We didn't have a car and no phones in those days. One of our trips ended badly when they weren't at home! Us girls were heartbroken as we loved visiting them and catching up with our cousins.

I went to Mount Hawthorn Kindergarten, aged five; walked there and back daily and once a week had a small calico bag pinned to my dress with the money inside to pay! Then went on to Mt Hawthorn Primary School, as did my mother, aunts and uncles before me and my sisters after me. I can't remember my Uncle Ric still being there, however he would have been in the 'Senior School' and me in the 'Bubs'. I can remember sitting cross-legged on the big verandah drinking milk in the mornings (sometimes warm in summer!), morning assemblies and delicious 'Oslo lunches', consisting of salad, brown bread, fruit and peanuts.

Ric and his friends would occasionally ride their hill trollies down Joondanna Drive hill, a bit steeper and more of a thrill than Baden Street! On one occasion, I can remember either me or my sister Vicki acting as 'lookout' at the bottom of the hill …

As a young teenager, I spent a lot of time with cousins Ken & Rod (Williams) who lived in Osborne Park.

We would cycle to each others' homes to spend the afternoons listening to records (Beatles!), telling jokes, raiding Nanna's fig tree and whatever other mischief we could get up to, all very innocent days. As well as Ric, I can also remember Dolly and Connie still living at Baden Street, Dolly in her hockey uniform with a black eye! And Connie with her boyfriends … Some of us older cousins were allowed to go to Connie's and Ric's 21st birthday parties which were held on the back verandah at Baden Street. Connie gave me strict instructions not to call her 'auntie' as she didn't want to be an old auntie at her 21st birthday party! At Ric's party, he came out dressed as a woman with big balloons under his jumper … he tried to balance a bowl of peanuts on them and failed!

I loved going to Nanna & Pops. I still picture Pop in the morning, sitting at that big table by the wonderful old kitchen fire (which was alight every day, summer and winter) in his trousers, braces and singlet, rolling his cigarettes for the day and putting them in an old tobacco tin. He would light his ciggies with a piece of tightly rolled newspaper (a taper) which he lit in the fire. Every now and then he would impress me with his French: "Voulez-vous promenade avec moi ce soir, Madame?" which he learned during the war … I thought that was very exotic.

I often asked Nan if I could have her button box to play with … can remember sitting for hours sorting them into colours or just running my hands through the buttons, loving the feeling. Nan taught me to sew on her old Singer treadle sewing machine, I am lucky enough to be the proud owner of that machine which is still in working order.

As I got older I occasionally went down to visit Nan for a game of Scrabble … I don't think I ever won a game against her!

Ken Williams

Sunday night was card night where all uncles, aunties and kids headed for 53 Baden Street.

Poker with matchsticks was the main game and while all the kids were playing outside the uncles and aunties would all sit around smoking and drinking and playing poker.

Hickey, my grandfather, always sat at the head of the table and Jean, my grandmother, sat at the other end and the cards went on while us kids went outside to play 'hidey' and 'chasey' and generally had good fun. We climbed the grapevines to hide; we ventured under the house amongst all the building materials Pop had stored, and came out covered in dust and black dirt.

We always wondered what was in Pop's locked room/sleep-out. We could only look over the top of the door and saw a bed where he probably had an afternoon nap.

As kids, we used to explore the fig tree, almond tree and trellised grapevines for fruit in season and scoff our findings.

Pop also had a workshop shed with the door always locked but we could see over the top. Always a mystery, and we wished we could have a look at and explore there too.

In the lounge room, we used to read and look at the pictures of Pop's World War I books, listen to the piano being played from time to time by Ric or one of the aunties and watch TV, black-and-white when they finally got one.

Nanna and Pop's main bedroom was a place where all the young children slept while they played cards. I remember going in there on the way home while Mum and the other aunties were getting the sleeping children ready to take home. The bedroom had nice wood furniture in it that I really admired.

The back veranda was also a place we played. It had a dartboard, wash trough at one end with a copper boiler, and down the other end a bathroom with a step in shower above it. On the wall behind the dartboard and written on the bricks was all the names of visitors that had been to 53 Baden Street and we all wanted to put our names up there ... which we did. The names I think were started when Ric was at teachers college and I remember putting my name on the highest brick we could reach at the time.

Another area out the back I liked was the platform lookout over the backyard that was snug and enclosed with a bench seat we could stand on to look out. A ramp made of timber went down to the brick toilet and those grape vines!

Pop Vernon like his flagon vino and would drink it out of a Vegemite glass. He would be quite tipsy by the end of a card night and many other times, probably due to post traumatic stress through his experiences during WWI. At other times, we would hear the record player that used to belong to Ric blaring out *Wolverton Mountain*, Pop's favourite record. They also had a radio and Nanna used to listen to all the popular AM stations and enter many competitions and was often successful in winning prizes.

Our playground also was to venture over the road into Uncle Charlie's open space in front of his house. There we would continue all our childhood games till it was time to go home and we were called by our parents.

Uncle Charlie, Pop's brother , used to come down and I remember he would call out the front to Nanna , "Are you there Jean?" This was usually to have a vino with his brother or to deliver a glass flagon or two of cheap wine purchased on his way home from Greenmount where he had a block of land.

As time progressed, our method of getting to Baden Street for cards changed. At first we walked, then we rode our bikes, and then we went in our station wagon. This would've been the early 60s. I remember walking home and my brother Rodney and I having a competition to see who could pee the furthest across McDonald Street where we lived at number 20, and going back the next day to check and debate who had won.

Later on, we used to ride our bikes at breakneck speed, racing to get home first. We also used the road like a blackboard and wrote and drew pictures all over the road and would come and look at it the next day.

Many of Ric's friends called in on Baden Street and I befriended a fair few of them over those years, if we were there at the same time. This would've been in the early 60s when Ric was at teacher's college and we were visiting Nanna and Pop on our way to visiting Auntie Marj and Uncle Frank and their family.

We had many a good time playing with Lyn and Vicki. Auntie Marj was always good to us, often feeding us our favourite toasted cheese sandwiches. We also, from time to time, had a feast of watermelon that Uncle Frank bought home from the markets where he worked. My love of guitars came from Auntie Marg as she allowed me to explore and marvel at her Spanish guitar that was kept in their lounge room. Also my love for music has its roots in the old radiogram that Auntie Marj allowed me to play. I think I wore out poor Lyn's first Beatle's record on that valve radiogram with its deep, clear and smooth bass sound.

Fond Memories that shape our lives.

"Kenny" Williams

Barbara Home (nee Vernon)

A visit to Baden Street to see Nanna and Pop was special. It seemed a long way from where we lived but the drive was always worth it.

I remember:

The black oiled boards of the front verandah.

Sitting on the bench under the kitchen window eating Nanna's rice pudding – the best – cooked in the oven of the large black iron wood stove.

The sideboard in the kitchen covered in ornaments and notes.

The piano in the lounge. Sometimes played by aunties and uncle when we visited.

Pop telling me that when blackberries were red, they were green. I liked that. I thought it was very funny.

Card games – poker – on Sunday nights. The adults playing for matches, pennies and small silver coins.

Writing my name on the back verandah brick wall with chalk, along with the names of my many cousins

Walking down the long ramp from the back verandah to the back yard.

The grape vines on the trellis at the bottom of the ramp, covered with sweet grapes. The currant grapes were my favourite. I also remember Lady Finger and Sultana grapes.

And of course the fabulous fig tree. To climb and play in and to sit among the branches and leaves, eating the figs, always pulling the figs apart and checking that the little "white worms" were not moving!

Running across the road and through Uncle Charlie's bush block – filled with Geraldton Wax – to play with my cousins.

And, of course, Nanna and Pop who gave me and my brothers our kind and gentle father and many wonderful aunties, uncles and cousins.

Allan Murphy

Mum and Dad would visit 53 Baden Street at least once a month but sometimes twice. Once we had said our hellos to Nan and Pop, it would be off to visit the Gardiners on Joondanna Drive, walking through Uncle Charlie's block and entering through the back gate. After spending some time with them, we would return to 53 B.

Often by this time, other families had arrived, bringing with them more cousins to play with around the old house; climbing the old almond tree on the next block; running around the lawn, playing 'hidey' and getting dirty in the black sand under the house where there were lots of hiding places.

Evening meal was taken by the adults and older cousins around the big oak table. I can only recall the tasty meat and salad dishes Nan V. would put together, followed by rice pudding for desserts.

After the meal, the adults would play penny poker with lots of chatter and laughter while us kids would read quietly or draw with coloured pencils on white butcher's paper on the floor.

On a very few occasions, there would be singing around the old piano in the lounge room. Then it would be time for us to depart for home.

Being a part of this amazing family meant there were lots of cousins to get to know and play with, and lots of uncles and aunts.

In 1963, Mum, Dad and his parents flew to Tasmania to spend some time with my Dad's sister. We were billeted out among the family – Phillip (and I think Brian) stayed with Nan and Pop Vernon; I was with Uncle Len and Aunty Laura but I cannot remember where Leanne was placed. I also spent some time on another occasion with Uncle Ross and Aunty Win and their family. (Cannot remember the year or the reason)

It was a truly great family to grow up with and I have lots of happy memories. A couple come readily to mind: spending a weekend at the Beros' beach shack on Whitfords Beach and a family picnic at Trigg Beach (?) one afternoon/evening. After deciding the wind was too strong for a meal to be enjoyed, a decision was made to move inland a bit. Upon arriving at the spot and doing a head count, it was realised Geoff Beros was missing. He was found on the beach a short time later (thankfully)!!

As we grew up, there were the family weddings, the gatherings to celebrate Ric and Rose's visits from Canada, and, in later years, the annual gatherings in Kings Park and then Belmont alongside the river.

I feel very privileged to have been a part of this family.

Laurie Sinagra

The world is bigger than you can imagine. I'm not sure exactly why I've been brought to stay at this house and I'm not too sure who these people are.

It turns out that it is my grandparents' house, and it is they who are living in it. Not too many surprises there … unless you are about three or four.

The house is dark and old. There isn't much inside that a young boy is too excited about. With the exception of a piano and a lamp that changes colours, there is nothing "modern" about this house.

There is a wood stove upon which there is always a kettle, or so it seems. The sink seems more like cupboards than a "wet" area. I don't think that hot water ever found its way through a tap to that area. You'd have to boil that in the copper on the back verandah and lug it into the kitchen sink … something we also had to do in our house that was situated around the corner.

The bedrooms are dark and dusty, like the rest of the house seems to me. It is not a place to be for a very 'scared of the dark' little boy. So I avoid them as much as I can.

There is a massive back verandah that has years worth of sump oil poured on the wooden boards to protect them. It served as a bedroom as well. There was a laundry at one end with the copper and the "wringer" along with the amazing concrete sinks. Man, that texture and smell is still with me like nothing else. The bathroom was at the other end and I hated it. Its plug hole was rusting and there was this wooden 'bench' that straddled the bath and contained things like soap and a face cloth from memory. It always looked like it was mouldy to me also. I guess I'm particular about that stuff.

Underneath the house was the playground of champions as far as I was concerned. Pop used to keep his timber underneath there and there was enough room for an adult to stand up due to the nature of the block of land falling away down a slope. Pop had extended the back verandah to create a bedroom for the eldest child as they grew. I'm suspecting that some of them never had a tenure in that room but instead married and moved straight out.

Underneath that house we would kick the black sand until you could hardly see one another. It was the best thing ever … and possibly the worst. Who knows?

Out the back of the house was the 'Rainbow Room'. It definitely was from another era as far as I was concerned. But hey, when you gotta go, you gotta go.

It was interesting to me at the time, but not as interesting as it is to me now, that the wall separating the back verandah from the internal house was a large red brick wall that had been inscribed on by all manner of family members and guests over many years. I am fairly certain that most of it was done using chalk.

There are some 'Perth-a-nalities' up there to this day although the bulk of it has faded or been graffitied on by subsequent tenants.

Directly across the road is the jewel in the crown. My pop's brother, Charlie, owned a massive block of land that stretches through from Baden Street to Joondanna Drive in Joondanna. I'm not sure if he was okay with us playing there but we did anyway. It was magnificent and scary all at the same time.

My family eventually moved back to Perth from Esperance when I was about four or five and it was at this time that really got to know my grandparents and my multiple cousins. We lived just around the corner from my Nan and Pop and we went there a lot. Sometimes I'd just walk up the street to see them or do a little odd job, probably at my Mum's request. Invariably, there was likely to be some of my cousins there too … which I'm sure was my prime motivator for going there.

Christmas Day was always a great day at my grandparents. All of the aunts and uncles would be there with all of my cousins. We'd talk about the things that we had received for Christmas, eat treats and run around like nutcases. Heaven.

Barry Sinagra

My memories probably started from about four or five years old. As we only lived down the road in 49 Tyler Street, some of my first memories are of going to visit Nan and Pop and we always had a lot of fun at their house. My sister Lesley and I used to play in the fig tree. I remember Ric's 21st birthday party a bit and I still remember him wearing the wig. I also remember going to one or two football games to watch him play.

As we got older and started exploring around Nan and Pops' place, we found some interesting things, like his old postcards from WWI and his old gas mask as well. The postcards had pictures of topless women as I expect a lot of soldiers had those in the day. I still remember the Sunday afternoon drinks that Pop and Uncle Charlie had under the back veranda. We often went from Nan and Pops' house to the Gardiners' house through Uncle Charlie's block, very often stopping and nicking stuff from Uncle Charlie's veggie garden, like fresh peas when they were in season.

We had a lot to do with the Beros family and often met them at Nan and Pops' place. We did lots of things with them, such as swimming in the river at Peppermint Grove and going to their farm in Eneabba and to their beach houses at Whitfords and Greenhead.

I stayed at the Beros house when my brother Andrew was born as we were living in Esperance at the time. It was funny watching Mum when she was driving the car; as her pregnancy advanced, her belly kept rubbing on the steering wheel of the car and I always had a little bit of a giggle at the time; it also sometimes left black marks on her clothes. When Andrew was born he was not given a name for a few days and so the nurses named him Charlie Brown so that is where he got his nickname of Chuck from.

The times we spent with the Beros' at the Whitfords shack were magical. Good times down the beach and playing in the sand. I remember going out in Clive's boat around Whitfords Island and falling into a hole around the Island – yes I was dragged out of it.

Also one time we were waiting for Dad to come home from work and he was late. We walked with our mums from the shack to Mullaloo Road at the time and did not see Dad at all. As we were walking back, there was a snake across the track; we were told to jump over it and keep walking so we did and thought nothing of it.

We often visited family during our time growing up; we often had card nights at home with the Williams's, Beros and some of Mum and Dad's friends. These were always fun and as we got older we were able to play in the earlier games as we still had to go to bed at some time. We always had a party on Guy Fawkes Night as it was also one of Mums friends' birthday so we always managed to get crackers to let off and things such as Catherine Wheels and other fireworks were always let of.

Growing up as a member of the Vernon family was amazing and always really fun except when your pants were pulled down by our fun-loving uncles at parties – that was not fun! But we always enjoyed catching up with our cousins – it was a great time – and we always had time to make sure we caught up with everyone who was there. I am sure that everyone still has a lot of time for each other as I don't remember any arguments between any of us, not saying there wasn't, but very few at least.

One of my funniest memories from home was we had the Booths around one night and the girls were playing in the lounge room with us and Dad received a phone call from one of his Italian friends. Dad spoke Italian and English in the same sentences. Nothing new to us but the Booth girls were both rolling on the floor with laughter at the way Dad spoke on the phone.

Phil Murphy

On most Sunday afternoons Mum and Dad took us to see Nanna and Pop Vernon. The Gardiner girls would join us and we would go under the house and eat grapes and play hide and seek in the grapevines and around the dunny. It was great fun. Sometimes the Williams family would turn up. We all had a great time. We also had a great time at Charlie Vernon's in the pine trees. We got told off for climbing the trees.

Cassie Mudge (nee Booth)

Growing up Vernon meant having many cousins to play with during the school holidays. Happy memories of Gaynor staying with us in York when Aunty Marj had to work, and glorious watermelon as well as other fruit and veggies from Uncle Frank when he came to collect her. It was a special treat, not something Mum would buy from the shops normally. We also had the added enjoyment of spitting the pips at each other afterwards.

Aunty Doll and the Beros boys also coming to stay with us, getting up early and watching Sesame Street on TV before the adults woke up. Riding bikes around the countryside, fighting over bikes and toys, swimming at the pool, usual mischief, fish and chips on the weekend.

Happy times interspersed with tragedy when the phone call came from Uncle Don late at night to break the devastating news that we'd lost Denise. It was a point in my life where our innocence was lost and I came to realise that the world was not a safe place to be in. I was eleven and it was the first loss of someone very dear to me. We were close; she was a special person in my life who was openly kind, loving and nurturing. She would plait my hair and teach me songs *Que Sera Sera* and *Edelweiss*. She stood up for me when others didn't. She was so patient and a special loving soul. I don't think I realised how much this loss impacted me until much later years. Aunty Marj's grief was palpable, and many nights were spent at our house with her and Mum talking and crying late into the evening.

There were lots of happy memories of visits to Perth staying at Nanna's. It was a fascinating, if not a little bit spooky, house with lots of places to play and explore. Uncle Charlie's beautiful bush block opposite with visits to sweet Mavis, sitting and chatting with her on her bed on the veranda and being frightened of Beryl.

Being allowed to stay up late at night to sit on the bench on the hill out the front of Uncle Charlie's looking at the street lights over Osborne Park, listening to him telling stories.

Visiting Aunty Win's and playing table tennis with Laurie for hours on end. Aunty Win's delicious spaghetti. Trips on the bus into the city to see a movie, then playing hide and seek with all the kids when we got home, with board games later in the night.

Funny memory, during a holiday visit from the Sinagra's to York, my friend Karen and I were giving Lesley cheek and she threw a dart down the veranda, lodging it into her forehead. Luckily, it was only a flesh wound and all fixed with a kiss and a bandaid.

Special trip to Garden Island on Uncle Theo's boat with the whole family. Such an adventure, swimming in the ocean and in a big water tank on the Island when it was open to the public. So much fun being all together over there.

A rare visit to Uncle Don and Aunty Shirl's. Uncle Don had a film of Mum and Dad's wedding day in Melbourne. I don't know where that would be now or how he ever came into possession of it. They had a pool in the backyard which was unbelievably exciting. I remember thinking they must have been really rich. Clay had a TV in his bedroom which was unheard of. It was black and white but I still thought he was the coolest cousin ever.

Visits to Aunty Doll and Uncle Clive's in Wembley, all of us kids bathing together in the same bath water. Sticking chewing gum in David's hair and getting in big trouble as he had to have a crew cut to cut it out. Dobbing each other in for peeing in the bath water. Feeding the swans down at Lake Monger and squealing when they pecked our fingers.

Holidays in Eneabba, swimming in Dynamite Bay, clambering over the rocks to find crabs, and screaming when we did.

Our families have had many tragedies over the years since, sadly, a large part of life includes loss, yet I feel very blessed to have been born into such a large diverse family, who were always happy to see us and always so warm and welcoming. No matter how much or how little any of us had there was always plenty to go around and everyone was always welcome to stay in each others' homes. Having such a large extended family gave me a comfortable sense of belonging.

Leanne Cantrell (nee Murphy)

My memories of Baden Street visits when a young child.

We arrived at Nan and Pop Vernons (usually on a Sunday afternoon) for a quick visit and a cuppa for Mum and Dad. Us kids had to play 'outside'. The huge tree in the backyard was of great interest to the older cousins and also, the grapevine was always a thing of interest if the grapes were ready but I could never reach them – the boys could though!

After a quick check around Nan's house, we headed across the road and meandered through the trees and bush and arrived at the Gardiners' place. Always great to catch up with them all if they were home.

After that visit, we piled into our car and popped around the corner into Tyler Street to see if the Sinagras were home and then on to the Williams family and had afternoon tea then headed home.

Always had a great time catching up with a few of the cousins if they were home.

Gaynor Gardiner-Sherwood

Being number twenty-two in the tribe of twenty-seven cousins meant you always had a play mate or someone to look out for you.

My mum and dad worked full-time, so during school holidays, I was 'farmed out' to wonderful aunties who weren't working, many times to Auntie Win's down in Tyler Street, Joondanna.

Laurie was only a few months older than me, and we played HOURS of ping pong and totem tennis, climbing through a gap in the back fence for the balls and getting scratched by the massive lantana.

There was a paddle pool or a run under the sprinkler to cool off on the hot days

Uncle Ross brought back baby chicks once, all different colours, all adorably fluffy. He used to call me 'little chick'.

Once Barry stirred me up, and I swore at him. Auntie Win heard me and dragged me into the bathroom to wash my mouth out with soap. Barry 1, Gaynor ZERO.

Andrew played constantly with his Meccano set on the lounge floor. I was envious of his ability to make really good car noises. I could only manage 'broom broom' and thought I should be better, because I was older, then I figured it must be a 'boy' thing.

Laurie and I used to see who could make the most bubbles in the toilet water bowl when we peed. Laurie always won! I remember,at least once, David Beros in the competition too. The Sinagra's loo always had loads of *MAD* comics it. And a sticker 'anyhow, 'ave a good wee', cut off from the *Winfields* cigarette advert "anyhow, 'ave a good weekend". I thought that was really funny.

Uncle Ross was Italian so the Sinagras had Italian bread and 'real' spaghetti. I thought spaghetti only came out of a tin with red sauce and at that young age, I preferred it that way. They also had Parmesan cheese that you had to grate and put on your spaghetti, I didn't like it and thought it smelt like spew. I loved the

Italian loaf though. Once I watched Auntie Win and her friends make real spaghetti, putting dough through a machine. I was fascinated …

I also spent many school holidays in York, then later in 'Dally' (Dalwallinu) with Auntie Connie, Uncle Gary and cousins Cassie and Alison who were about three years and six months older than me consecutively.

Mum and Dad would drive me up to York at the beginning of the holidays. We'd go via Sawyers Valley. Dad would always stop at the same green grocers and get an enormous watermelon. I guess the grocer was a client of Lanzke's Market where Dad was an auctioneer. We'd have watermelon juice dripping down our arms and watermelon 'smiles' on our faces, not forgetting the pip spitting competitions.

I remember eating lemons too, piled high with sugar to make them palatable.

I was pretty small and slept in an old cot. One time I got locked in by accident (well that's what the bigger girls told me). It was one of those cots with a fly-wire frame around it. Anyway, I screamed pretty good until I was let out.

We kids played hide and seek in that enormous house. We ran all over the neighbourhood without a care in the world ... except for the 'wicked witch' next door. We were scared of her, made sure we didn't hit the ball over the fence or do anything to stir her up.

In summer, we spent most days down at the local pool just mucking about.

There was a piano in the lounge, I think Ali and Cass would play. I'd sit at it and bang on the keys pretending I was Elton John with *Crocodile Rock* playing on the turntable.

As a little kid, I used to sing to myself all through the day. Mum thought it was great, I guess a happy kid sings, hey? Cass and Al both have lovely singing voices. Hanging out with them I realised this and stopped singing out loud, which is kinda sad for me, but better for everybody else's ears.

Some holidays some of our other cousins would join us. Darts on the porch with the older crew. Lesley Sinagra either got a dart in her foot or threw one at someone else's foot. I kept my distance from the 'big kids' when the darts were out!

In 'Dally', we played HOURS and HOURS of *Monopoly*. *Eight Days a Week* and *Please Mr Postman* were always on the radio.

At least once we made up a 'widgy board' to call in the spirits. I'm not sure if it was Cass or Al who actually pushed the glass around the board, but I thought it was for real. We were in the room where I slept, and each time a breeze came through the window and lifted the sheer curtains, we were convinced it was a spirit entering the room. I don't think I slept too well that night, keeping my eye on that curtain!

That same night, there was a wailing/howling sound from the lock up. Uncle Gary was a copper, so the Booth family lived next to the police station. Anyway, we three girls thought it was Uncle Gary making "spooky" noises to scare us. Turned out to be a drunk in the clink singing and moaning.

Ah the imagination of kids, hey?

I also had plenty of stints at Aunty Doll's and Uncle Clive's in Nanson Street, Wembley.

I remember bath time with Dave and Nigel when we were little. Aunty Doll always used to remind the boys to 'wash behind their ears' which I thought was strange. Why did the back of their ears get so dirty, I wondered?

Another memory is of David trying to convince me to let him tie my loose tooth to a door so he could slam it and pull my tooth out. I declined the offer. And later in life, Dave studies to be a Health and Safety Officer!

On the lounge floor was a cowhide. I loved sitting on it and tracing the patterns of the hairs. We played on that floor all the time. I still love cow hides today and put it down to that fond memory.

We used to walk to Lake Monger to feed old bread to the swans. Mostly it was wonderful, but once a flock of swans surrounded me and pecked at me as I couldn't tear off the bread fast enough to feed them all. I threw the whole loaf down and skedaddled back to Aunty Doll.

In later years, the Beros had moved up to their family farm near Eneabba. What a great place that was.

Mum took me and a girlfriend up there once. We were about ten or twelve. My friend and I wandered about the farm and discovered a sheep lying on its side, unable to get up. We saw its big belly and thought it was a lady sheep about to have a baby. We ran back to get Uncle Clive's assistance and he laughed and laughed as he told us it was just a fat old ram that had eaten too much.

That night we tucked into our beds in the little shed next to the house. We could hardly sleep because we thought there were aliens coming. There were strange noises and a strange light – turned out to be long distant traffic on the highway and dawn! Ah, city kids don't know much, do they? We both slept well the following nights.

I remember playing under the sprinkler on a hot day. A bee stung me through my floral bather top!

At meal times when all four Beros boys were at home, Aunty Doll put at least two loaves of frozen bread (Mother's Pride if I remember correctly, in a waxy paper wrap) into the oven to freshen them up (boy, they smelt GOOD) … … and they were always all eaten. At that stage, I think I was the only one at home with my mum and dad. It took us several days to finish just one loaf of bread, so I was amazed at how much food had to be prepared to feed us all.

Again, when the 'big' boys, Geoff and Muzz and Dave, were at home on the farm, we'd play a card game called 'Cheat'. We spent the whole night around the big table having a blast. My hands were never big enough to hold all those cards.

Oh, and the outside long drop dunny. 'Pooh Whee' that stunk!

The Sinagra and the Beros families had a holiday house in Greenhead. I spent many a school holiday up there with them. We kids spent HOURS at the beach in front of the house, mucking about on foam boards until the rash on our bellies got too sore.

Climbing through the mounds of seaweed on the beach.

Going for long walks around the bay to the sand dunes and skidding down them on bits of cardboard. Gee, it was hard work climbing back up for another slide down.

Riding or walking around to Dynamite Bay, playing in the waves, checking out the rock pools, trying to find a beach out of the wind.

Walking out on the exposed reef, one time yelling at Mum to NOT touch the pretty blue thing. I thought it was a blue ringed octopus, which it could have been, or maybe just a blue bottle stinger. Anyway, I thought I was clever 'saving' her from sure death.

And HOURS of card and board games with Laurie and David sitting cross-legged on our beds.

More watermelon dripping down our arms, watermelon smiles and pip spitting competitions in the backyard.

In the evenings after dinner, the adults playing Bridge, I think. And my mum never really getting it and being reminded how to play each time.

And a kero fridge. What a concept!

There was the occasional day or week at Uncle Don's and Aunty Shirl's too.

Barb and Paul had either left home by then or were away at work. Clay was around and introduced me to ACDC, *Highway to Hell*.

I'd hang out by the pool in the warmer weather.

I used to delight in watching Uncle Don fall asleep watching telly, leaning his chin on his hand. His elbow would always slip off the arm rest and he'd pop it back without waking.

Mum, Dad and I would go to theirs for New Year's Eve Celebrations … most years I think. It was always a hoot.

I also remember our visits with Aunty Laura and Uncle Len who used to pick me up, hold me upside down and tickle me until I squealed for mercy.

A chat with Jan's hubby Warwick later in life helped guide me away from becoming a massage therapist and instead a physiotherapist … handy that!

Visits to Aunty Bob's and Uncle Ron's as well, but no stay overs, as no kids around my age.

Then there were plenty of hours spent just down the garden path at Nana and Pop's in Baden Street.

Us Gardiner's were able to simply go from our backyard, through a gate in our fence to Uncle Charlie's, down the path to Nana's. Memories from there:

Having to go all the way down to the bottom of the ramp at Nana and Pop's place to go to the 'dunny'. I thought that ramp was so long.

David Beros teaching me to make whistles with the shaft of a wild oat weed. There was plenty of material to work with in the enormous backyard at Nana's.

Feeding the neighbour's pet kangaroo through the low wire fence.

Eating those yummy figs, and the pretty Ladies' Fingers grapes on the pergola near the outhouse. And the weird and waxy Hovea in flower.

I think we used to go there on Boxing Day. All the aunties, uncles, and cousins would be there. We'd sit around that (we thought big) oak table, us 'littlies' on the bench seat along the window, all squeezed in.

Nana still used a manual wringer to get the water out of clothes. Nan only ever had that brownish, transparent oval-shaped soap in the bathroom; I can still recall its smell, if not its name, maybe it was Pear's.

Uncle Charlie, 'Mrs Mavis' and Beryl next door: Many afternoon hours spent standing on the bench behind a seated Uncle Charlie, chatting away and me gently filling his big hat with gum nuts and seeds etc, thinking he'd never notice. We sat facing Joondanna Drive, watched the comings and goings of neighbours and traffic, listened to the birds and enjoyed sunsets, before it was time for me to go back home, just next door.

And morning teas with 'Mrs Mavis'. She always let me have a chocolate finger biscuit. Very special.

'Mrs Mavis' slept on their front porch, with a big mosquito net over her bed. I thought that was very exotic.

I spent many mornings or afternoons and even whole days playing 'cubbies' that I'd build on Uncle Charlie's bush land. My favourite ones were under Geraldton Wax trees, because they smelt so wonderful. And there was a 'small lake', or so I thought, with very exotic arum lilies in winter. It was actually a seep or drain from the house, so luckily I never dived in!

Like many of my cousins around my age I was scared of Beryl because she looked strange; she talked slowly and had such a deep voice. We didn't understand why she was different, we were just scared of that difference.

As a 'grown up' Vernon, I was able to visit the Canadian contingent of the family. Fortunately, Uncle Ric, Auntie Rose and I easily recognised each other as I stepped off the plane in Courtenay, BC. Baby Callie had just arrived to proud parents Alissa and Paul. Hayley and Aniel, just wed and Roger all grown up and handsome.

When my husband Rod and I were living in London and later Switzerland, on visits home Mum would organise an afternoon tea with all the aunties and uncles so I could catch up with them all in one go. And now we still have an "aunties lunch" a few times each year. It was also lovely to have Aunty Con visit us in Neuchâtel on Mum's first visit. Lyn and Dave were living in the UK at that time and joined us for a week together.

Aunty Win and Aunty Laura also came for a visit and, on another occasion, Rod and I went to Paris to catch up with Aunty Doll and Aunty Win. Such lovely memories and connections.

How fortunate I am, we all are, to be a part of such a large and loving and wonderful family. I love that we all keep in contact, and at least once a year meet at the family picnic.

Hayley Datoo (nee Vernon)

When I think of my childhood and what it meant to 'grow up Vernon', the first thing that comes to mind is how special it felt to be part of such a 'big club'. Even though we were far away, all the visits from various family members over the years, our own couple of visits to Perth, and all the communication in between helped us to feel connected to all our cousins, aunties and uncles.

Our Australian connections made us just a little bit 'exotic' in our small Canadian town, and Dad's Aussie musical repertoire ensured we were exposed to important favourites like *The Redback on the Toilet Seat* and *Six White Boomers. Snaggers on the Barbie* feature prominently in our summer barbecue season, and breakfast isn't 'breakkie' without Vegemite.

I have a few disjointed memories as a four-year-old from my first trip to Perth. They are all mixed together, but I remember playing with snails under the porch at the Baden Street house, and being fascinated by lemon and cumquat trees. I remember how hospitable everyone was to us and what seemed like an endless party to a four-year-old. It has been wonderful over the years to see so many members of the family in Canada – those visits instilled a sense of the importance of family ties that seems to me all these miles away to be a strong trait of the Vernon clan.

I will always be indebted to cousins, aunties and uncles who helped to make my visit to Australia as an eighteen-year-old comfortable and special. We don't tend to realise the magnitude of what people are doing for us when we are teenagers, but those months were incredibly important in my transition to adulthood, and I'm ever grateful to those Vernon clan members who went above and beyond.

Reflecting on my upbringing, I suspect several of my values are very much rooted in my Vernon heritage. The importance of family, appreciation for the simple pleasures in life, thriftiness and the healing properties of a strong cup of tea in the afternoon.

Vicki Jackson (nee Gardiner)

Growing up Vernon: how do say how I feel without being cheesy?

Before I was born: Mum sometimes talked about her childhood and youth. Those stories, snippets of Mum's journey with her family, became the beginnings of my sense of 'being Vernon'. She talked of fetching pails of warm milk from a dairy at the bottom of Baden Street, of which I can find no history. Possibly, a nearby neighbour had 'house cows' in a paddock that produced enough milk to sell to the locals.

When trying to get us ready for an outing, in frustration, Mum used to say 'it's like trying to herd Brown's cows'. I always thought that Mr Brown must have been the nearby neighbour who had the cows, but perhaps that was a reference to Browne's Dairy, in Shenton Park. It was the first commercial dairy in the

Swan River Colony, established by Edward Browne in 1886.

She talked of family bike rides to the beach (or just with Pop?), which created vivid images in my mind of girls on bikes in shorts, hair flowing behind them, lazy days at the beach and a long hot ride home.

She talked of birds in the bush, and I remember one time she took us next door to Charlie's with a torch at night to see an owl in a large gum close to our back gate. My memory is that it looked like a Barn Owl, but I can't be certain. These were a species local to Perth. I do remember it's big white face and Mum telling us to be careful and keep our distance as they could be dangerous. Stories of how she and some of the Vernon sisters went to meet WWII sailors that came to Perth on R&R and taking them back to Nanna and Pop's for a family meal and a singalong around the piano. Stories of her lying on the floor with Pop and commiserating with or comforting him as he dealt with residual horrors of WWII ... I still have some small Belgian wooden clogs, fashioned as mementos that soldiers sent home. Uncle Charlie had these inscribed.

Speaking of Pop, he was a good swimmer as a young man and, on 21 February 1914, he won the Swim Through Guildford. In the West Australian on 13 February 1914, an article about the upcoming swim through cites H. Vernon as a 'leading swimmer'. He went on to win the 2-mile event the next Friday, with a time of 59 minutes on a handicap of 5 seconds. In my 60s, I could still swim a kilometre in half an hour in a pool, so a mile would be an hour. Pop swam 2 miles in the same time! Even though he was a young man, the river is not as kind as a pool and he may not have had the same access to professional training as I did as young woman. The article also mentions a C. Vernon, presumably Uncle Charlie. This was just six months before the beginning of WWI.

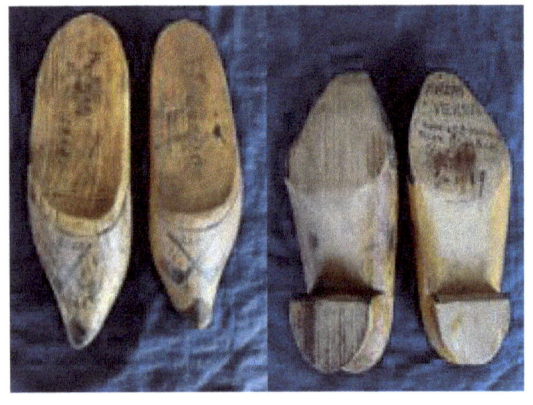

FROM C. VERNON Bousse-Lez-Walcourt near Charleroi, Belgium 6-1-19

G.A.S.C. Swim Thru Guildford 1914
2 MILES
FASTEST TIME
59 MINUTES 5 SEC
H VERNON

Growing up in the Vernon Family as a "Gardiner Girl"

After I was born, Mum and Dad moved in with Don and Shirl, who had rented a house from Uncle Charlie in Brighton Road. Barb and I were babies, and Lyn was two-plus years old. We were there until we moved into Joondanna, at which time I think I was about three years old. I have had dreams/memories about a three-sided shed on the west of the property where a beer keg was the go on a sunny Sunday afternoon. I don't recall who else was there apart from our two families, and Lyn doesn't share those memories.

Growing up with Mum, Dad and sisters in Joondanna on a quarter-acre block, next door to Uncle Charlie's bush acre, we spent endless hours building cubbies and playing at cowboys with some of the neighbourhood kids. We built metre-high forts out of the pine needles that fell from the avenue of massive Norfolk Pines, planted years before by Uncle Charlie.

We used the pines' lower (flexible) branches as bucking horses, shouting out ride 'em, cowboy', holding one arm high in the air as we bounced up and down on them. They gave us quite a wild ride! We mucked around, fossicking for treasures in Charlie's impressive 'junk piles' lined up against the western fence of his house enclosure. They furnished the 'rooms' in our fort.

At Christmas, Uncle Charlie put coloured lights in several of the trees, the tops of which could be seen as far away as the corner of Scarborough Beach Road and Main Street, perhaps even further. During these post-war years in Western Australia, these lights were quite spectacular as the practice of lighting up gardens and houses with cheap, imported Chinese lights had not yet arrived.

We rarely went into Uncle Charlie's house, but occasionally we would go into the front living room and sit with Aunty Mavis (second cousin) while she played the piano.

Aunty Mavis was always gentle and kind to us when we were young. She even came to our home in Marmion for Mum's 60th birthday, albeit she arrived at 4:30 pm when the invitation was for lunch!

Not so her brother and sister, though. I can't remember what I did to upset her, but I was once chased up Joondanna Drive and caught by Beryl. She had me by the hair and was pushing me to the ground when I managed to wriggle out of her control. I reckon I was about eight years old, and she scared the life out of me! I kept my distance after that.

Her brother Gordon was a bit of a mystery, and I was always wary of him. I remember him hanging over our back fence one day, berating my beautiful Mum, telling her she would go to hell because she smoked cigarettes and drank beer! Thankfully, he disappeared for years, so we didn't have to worry about him (we later found out he had moved to Sydney).

We had easy (and approved) access to Uncle Charlie's brown sugar figs just outside our gate, and with hearts pumping at the thought of being caught, we stole peas from his vegetable patch as soon as they showed signs of maturing (I sometimes wonder if he didn't plant them expecting us to do just that!).

Our family could pop down to Nanna and Pop's place in the next street in a jiffy. Uncle Charlie laid a brick pathway from our back gate to Baden Street, which he or one of his family then flanked with sweet-smelling daffodils and jonquils. On a warm spring day, coupled with the Geraldton Wax blossoms, flowering eucalypts and pine trees, it was like a stroll through a perfumed garden, replete with a variety of chirping birds.

Nana and Pop's was a place of intrigue. I was infatuated by the two large cane chairs on their front verandah, although I rarely saw anyone sitting there. I thought they were very exotic, like something from a Somerset Maugham book about the tropics. I also thought the same about the stand of sugar canes that grew at the back of the house.

I always received a warm welcome from Nanna and Pop, no matter when I showed up. When I was little, I loved chatting with Pop while he repaired a bike or cobbled my school shoes. I adored listening to Nanna recite *The Man from Snowy River* while she created magic, cooking with ease, knowing how to manage the flames and flues of her wood stove to get just the right temperature to gently bake a custard or to amp it up to cook a pastry dish. I was mesmerised as she ground mince and sliced her green beans with a mechanical slicing machine. I remember telling her that I loved toffee and that we sometimes had a penny to buy one in a cupcake paper from a little shop near the school. So, she promptly got out the sugar, some water, food colouring and 'hundreds and thousands' and taught me how to make it … easy!

Nanna used to save her vegetable scraps for us to feed to our chooks. She always wrapped them in newspaper for ease of transport up the path to home. One day, I went and picked them up and got distracted, mucking around in the bush. I'd left the wrapped scraps on the letter box at the foot of the brick path, and when I was ready to go home, I put them under my arm. I got about four steps up the path and started to feel multiple bites. The scraps were riddled with ants, and within a few seconds, I was running up the path screaming blue murder. Mum met me at the bottom of the stairs to our verandah, and as soon as she realised what had happened, she stripped me naked and gave me a good hosing down!

We often played in Nanna and Pop's yard. I was enchanted by Nanna's little bower with its Lady Finger and currant grape canopy that shaded her lovely array of pot plants (or were they Pop's?).

Snooping around beneath the house, I came across a beautifully carved, wooden-framed photo of Pop in his army uniform and asked Nanna why it wasn't on display in the house. She said Pop didn't like that photo much, so there it stayed under the house. At the time, I was too young to understand the cruel nature of war and the sacrifices Pop and others made. I am now the photo's privileged curator. It is proudly displayed in my home, and I can see a remarkable resemblance to Pop in my son Daniel.

Lyn and I used to climb the big fig tree in their backyard. It had limbs close to the ground, so climbing it was easy for little girls. On this day, we were still dressed in beautiful crepe paper dresses that Mum had painstakingly sewn for us to wear at a parade during a Mt Hawthorn Primary School fete. Lyn's, of course, was blue; mine was pink. Needless to say, the lovely dresses ended up in tatters, but I don't remember being chastised by anyone for ruining them, only appreciating years later the amount of effort Mum put in for us.

Nanna and Pop also had a TV well before we did, so after school, we would go and watch *Countdown*, *Johnny Young's Young Talent Time* and other shows of interest to pre-teen and teenage girls. I was also Uncle Ric's' music student for a few months. I was not disciplined enough to make the grade, but listening to Uncle Ric playing honkey tonk music kick-started my love of that music genre and which took me down the path of discovering the Blues and old school R&B music.

We loved it when Uncle Ric was our babysitter; it was so cool having him around. It didn't happen that often, but it was as we were getting a bit older and probably didn't want to be dragged around to places with Mum and Dad (and they were happy to leave us behind) but were still too young to be left alone. We were all proud of him when he graduated from high school and went to Teacher's Training College on a bursary. He was the only sibling to have a tertiary education. He then left us all behind to do his compulsory two years as a country teacher and later left for Canada as an Exchange Teacher and there made a wonderful life for himself and his family.

As we grew, Nanna's became a magnet for the family events that I'm sure we all remember. Ric's 21st, Sunday family penny poker card games and others. We loved it when these events were on as we got to see our cousins. What a mob we were. That's when we would all go to Charlie's (if daylight) and make cubbies, run amok and do skits, pantomimes on a jarrah deck in the northwest corner of the property near the Baden Street letter box.

At other times, our aunties and uncles would visit Nanna and Pop, and the cousins would come up to our place. We'd mess around there until it was time for them to go back to Nanna's and go home. We always loved it when our cousins came to visit. At time, we must have been a bit too much for Mum to handle, as I can recall her getting quite angry with Lyn and me at times, though that didn't stop us.

As kids, we also loved our visits to other aunties, uncles and cousins. It wasn't unusual for me to visit with aunties and/or cousins after school or at weekends.

We loved it when Uncle Don and Aunty Shirl visited us at home. It was a long trek then, and it didn't happen often enough. When all our families had cars, it became much easier. Mum and Auntie Shirl were great buddies and us kids loved to get up to mischief. We also loved to visit them in Bicton when we had a car.

I recall going to Aunty Laura and Uncle Len's for a party, and several of us were playing 'hidey in the dark' in the living room. Uncle Len got pretty heated up about that. It wasn't until later, as a young adult, did I get to know Uncle Len a bit more and realised that he had a wicked sense of humour.

I loved Uncle Len's garage/shed – it was so neat and clean! He even had a pegboard on a wall with painted outlines of each tool. The lawns and surrounding garden beds were always well-tended.

A few times when I was about eleven or twelve, I cycled over to catch up with Ken. I enjoyed poking around in their garden and found it unusual for them to have a pomegranate bush. Their house in McDonald Street had a large expanse of swampy land behind it, so they had a large area to explore and muck around in, too. It is now a light industrial area.

There were also a couple of events at Aunty Bob and Uncle Ron's. Again, I remember the well-tended gardens and lawns and warm nights with party lights at their Cannington home. Aunty Bob was a quiet, gentle person, while Uncle Ron's personality was larger than life. He was never without a joke or two.

I remember going to an event at Aunty Dolly and Uncle Clive's in Sasse Avenue, Mount Hawthorn, where the music was blaring 50's jive and early rock 'n roll. I thought they were pretty cool for an aunty and uncle! Also popping in after school to visit Aunty Connie in Egina Street, probably when Cassie was a baby.

There were afternoons at Aunty Winnie's in Tyler Street to catch up with Lesley. They had a big block and Uncle Ross had a big shed down the back of the block, and sometimes a very big truck snaking down the driveway. Aunty Winnie could be found making pasta and using garlic! These foods were unheard of in Mum's kitchen at the time. As you can imagine, the aunties were always welcoming and, as they are great bakers, there was plenty of lovely cakes, slices and other goodies on offer for a snack or afternoon tea.

Now I am a grown-up. We all continue to gather with cousins and visit with aunties and uncles. For me, that included visiting Aunty Con and Uncle Gary in York when Cassie was still a small, shy girl and Alison still a baby. Later, I spent time with them in Coolgardie. That was in the early 80s, which was a traumatic time for me. I travelled up on the Prospector with Aunty Dolly, who was a great comfort on the journey. The week spent with Gary and Connie was also very restorative (except for the damn town rooster that insisted on crowing at regular intervals from 4:40 am and started of the cacophony of the rest of them!).

There was also a trip to visit Esperance and staying with Aunty Winnie over an Easter I recall, in her 'transportable' home, and catching squid off the jetty in the freezing weather.

There were trips to Dolly and Clive's farm, firstly, staying overnight with them in their 'tin shed' home, the simplicity of which I loved – it felt like being on holiday. We went roo-shooting with Clive on one occasion. Over time, Clive showed us the progression of turning the land from native bush into a productive farm while protecting areas of environmental importance. Hearing stories about how the emu mobs mowed down his crops. Also, ditching the tin shed in favour of a brick and tiled family home, the construction of which was not without the usual delay problems. While there, we usually headed over to Greenhead for some fishing and snorkelling before travelling back to Perth.

And now.

We Vernons are a fine bunch. We are good communicators, keep in touch, are non-judgmental, and have respect and love for each other. I am grateful for the understanding, love and help I've had over the years from sisters, aunties, uncles and cousins. Collectively, we have a rich and diverse history that has eclipsed the new vernacular of 'diversity and inclusion'. We've been living it since birth.

I am extremely grateful for being born into the Vernon family and place a high value on 'being Vernon' as my experiences with being part of other families tells me we are very special indeed.

With Love, Vicki

In Memorium

Denise Kaye Gardiner

31-1-1958 - 17-9-1973

Our beautiful daughter, sister, granddaughter, niece and cousin

We all felt the pain

For 2 families, life must go on

By Alan McIntosh

What is it like to live in a suburban street where the teenage son of one family murders the pretty teenage daughter of the family opposite?

"Life goes on; we just have to keep going," said Mrs Alma Gardiner, mother of 15-year-old Denise Gardiner who was murdered by a teenage neighbour in September this year.

"I don't bear any malice towards the boy's parents, but I can't find it in my heart to disagree with the verdict.

"He had a fair trial."

Yesterday Philip Emil Fruet (16) was sentenced to death for the murder of Denise Gardiner.

His mother, Mrs Dorothy Fruet, said today: "We used to be neighbours sharing a cup of tea and that and doing favours.

"I feel so sorry for Mrs Gardiner but I don't know if I should go and see her."

The houses of the two families are almost directly opposite in Joondanna Drive, Joondanna. The two teenagers knew each other, though they had never gone out together.

Mrs Gardiner said today Denise was a gentle young girl who was not as forwardly confident as her two married sisters.

Family pictures show her as a pretty, smiling girl.

Mrs Gardiner said Denise had been extremely fastidious about her appearance.

"She pressed her uniform every day," Mrs Gardiner said.

Denise loved horse-riding and swimming, had learnt to water ski, was a member of the West Perth Football Club cheer squad and was a

◆ Denise Gardiner.

"normal average student," according to her mother.

"She played records—they were always blaring," Mrs Gardiner said.

To get over their tragedy the Gardiners have adopted the philosophy that life must go on.

On the wall in their kitchen hangs a little scroll that somebody put there after the tragedy.

It says: "Today is the first day of the rest of your life."

Mrs Gardiner said: "Life has to go on.

"At first you could talk about screaming or doing something, but the law had to take its course.

"My husband is terrific. We are a very close family.

"We didn't know if we'd move from here or stay. At first we were going to move and now I don't know what we will do, but we have been here 19 years.

"You go on living but memories keep coming back..."

Mrs Gardiner said she and her husband went to the trial to make certain there was no defamation of Denise's character or suggestion of a liaison between the boy and her daughter.

There had been no evidence of this in court.

Mrs Gardiner said that Denise's little sister Gaynor (8) knew that Denise was dead, but did not know the details.

Photo Album

*Believed to be taken on
Jean & Hickey's Wedding Day*

The Early Days

Wedding Day Sept 1900 Jeannie McDonald Thomson (age 36) & John Robert Banks (age 29)

Circa 1910 Grandfather Robert Banks

Isabella McCartney O'Brien, nee Thomson (Tibby). Jeannie's cousin

Jeannie McDonald Banks Snr

Jeannie McDonald Banks (Snr) around 1900 baby could be either Roberta or Jeannie (Jnr)

Jeannie McDonald Banks (L) & Roberta Banks (R) 1906

1910 The Banks Family Home - 223 Hamersley Road Subiaco

Grandmother Jeannie MacDonald Banks

Grandfather Robert Banks

Roberta (L) and Jeannie Banks Circa 1916

Jeannie Banks Circa 1916

Jeannie Banks Circa 1920

Charles Molesworth Vernon
1862 – 1907

Laura Vernon (nee Ellen Laura Amelia Amy Azzoni)
1866 - 1960

1915 Hickey. Notice license plate MJ1 ... Midland Junction 1

A young Dorothy (Dorrie) Vernon Circa 1910

Circa 1924 Dorothy (Dorrie) Vernon with her mother Laura Vernon

Sister and Mother of Charlie & Hickey

Jeannie & Hickey Vernon with baby Don Circa 1926

Circa 1929
Rear: brothers Bill (L) and Hickey Vernon.
Centre: Ettie Vernon and children, Jeannie with Laura holding a doll and Don.
Roberta Gleed (nee Banks) with maybe Noel and Phyllis.
Other children unknown.

Circa 1936 Grandfather Robert Banks

Circa 1941 Grandfather Robert Banks

Grandfather Robert Banks

1948 Grandfather Robert Banks, with Robert Gleed (nephew of Jeannie Vernon)

Don Vernon aged 1, 1926   Marjory Vernon aged 1, 1931   Circa 1933 Laura, Don & Marj

Circa 1933 Charlie with bike, Hickey with kids at 51 Baden St. Joondanna
L-R Beryl, Mavis, Charlie, Jeannie (rear, leaning on picket fence) Laura, Marj & Hickey

1931 Jeannie

Circa 1933 - Jeannie and sister Roberta (Bobbie) Gleed. Taken in front of Commonwealth Bank, Murray Street, Perth

*Circa 1933
Florence Vernon's son, Wilfred*

Bobbie (rear), Marj & Winnie
Circa 1938

Marj, 1938

Circa 1937? Charlie, Hilda, Jeannie and Hickey (obscured)

Family Group at Baden Street circa 1937?
Rear: Hickey, Jean;
Middle: Beryl, Mavis, Laura, Marj, Winnie;
Front: Dolly, Connie, Gordon

Circa 1950? Sisters Roberta (Bobbie) Gleed and Jeannie Vernon

Circa 1950? Jeannie Vernon

1940 Grandmother and Grandfather Banks (perhaps in Singapore?)

1944 Don on HMS Shropshire

Circa 1942 Don

Circa 1942? Don & Hickey

1941 L-R Laura holding Connie, Bobbie, Winnie, Dolly sitting on fence, and Marj.
Front gate at Baden Street

1943 L-R Dolly, Marj holding Connie, Bobbie, Laura, Winnie
Front gate at Baden Street

Vernon Family
Rear, Bobbie, Hickey, Laura, Don, Marj;
Centre Winnie, Jeannie holding Ric, Connie and Dolly standing in front.
Taken at the rear of Baden Street, Circa 1946

1944 Marj, aged 15, photo taken outside 53 Baden St, Charlie's block in background

1946 Marj, aged 16

Circa 1946 Connie, Winnie and Dolly

Circa 1946 Connie, Winnie and Dolly

1948 Jeannie & Hickey

1948 Marj Vernon & Frank Gardiner, sweethearts, under the bridge at Carnarvon

Frank Gardiner

1947 Jeannie & Ric, front yard, Baden Street

Circa 1950s Beachgirl Jeannie

Circa 1950 - Dolly & Winnie

Circa 1952 - Eric & Connie

Circa 1950

Vernon Siblings and their Mother

Rear - Dorothy, Hickey, Bill and Charlie Vernon Front Laura Vernon (nee Azzoni)

Hickey, Marj, Eric, Jean, Connie

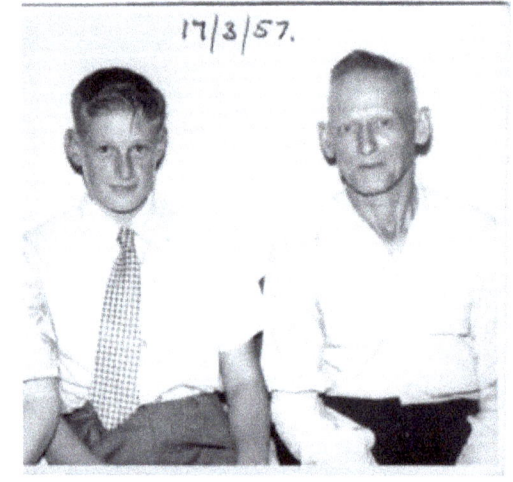

1957 Eric & Hickey

Weddings

&

The Next Generation

Laura Jean Vernon married Albert Leonard Williams
2 August 1947

Alma Marjory Vernon married Frank Leonard Gardiner
22 April 1950

Roberta Jessie Vernon married Ronald Douglas Murphy
2 September 1950

Edward Donald Vernon married Shirley Constance Calley
17 May 1952

Winifred Gladys Vernon married Ross Charles Sinagra
9 June 1956

Dorothy Isobel Vernon married
Clive Anthony Beros
13 July 1957

Thelma Constance Vernon married Gary
George Booth
17 March June 1962

Eric John Vernon married Rosemary Frederica Siddall
4 July 1970

The Next Generation

1951 - Frank & Marj with baby Lynette

1952 Laura with Ken & Marj with Lynette

Frank Gardiner & Don Vernon,
Circa 1951
Forrest Place Perth

Hickey & Laura Williams with Rodney Williams 1951

1952 L-R Hickey, Laura, Marj holding Lynette, Shirley, Don, Jeannie, Noel Gleed, Roberta Gleed (Jeannie's sister) Ernie Gleed, Len Williams holding Ken.

Front Rodney Williams, Ric Vernon

Don & Shirley's Wedding

17-May-1952.

L-R Dolly, Marj, Laura, Bobbie, Winnie, Connie in front

Circa 1955 Sisters-in-law Shirley and Marj

*Hickey & Jean Vernon,
Circa 1950
Forrest Place Perth*

*Lyn Gardiner, Vicki Gardiner in pram,
Barbara Vernon 1954/55*

Circa 1955/6 Lyn Gardiner, Barbara Vernon, Vicki Gardiner

Circa 1956 Vicki and Lyn Gardiner

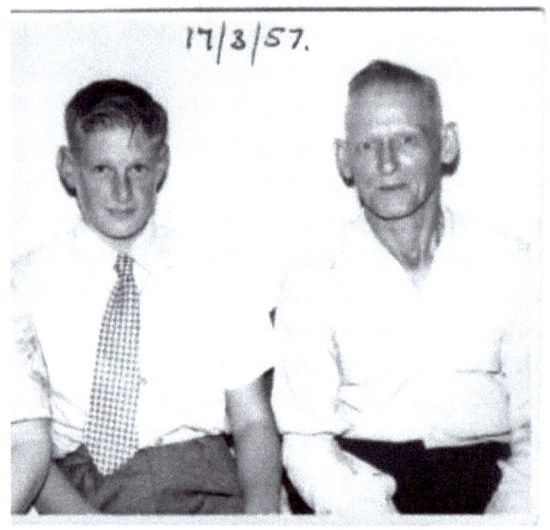

Circa 1957 Ric & Hickey

Jean & Hickey Circa 1960

1961 Connie's 21st
Rear: Ross Sinagra, Marj Gardiner, Clive Beros holding Murray, Don Vernon, Ric Vernon,
Len Williams, Ron Murphy
Centre: Winnie Sinagra, Frank Gardiner, Dolly Beros, Bobbie Murphy, Jeannie Vernon
Front: Shirley Vernon, Connie Vernon, Laura Williams with Jan and Hickey Vernon with Denise

Connie's 21st.

In-Laws Clive Beros, Ron Murphy, Shirley Vernon, Len Williams, Ross Sinagra, Frank Gardiner

1961 Connie's 21st

"Bookend" Brothers Eric & Don Vernon

Ric Vernon with nephew Geoff Beros
circa 1960

Circa 1961
Denise Gardiner, Geoff Beros and Lesley Sinagra - all born in January 1958 - Lesley and Denise a few hours apart!

Circa 1964 Rear: Cousins Denise Gardiner, Geoff Beros, Barry Sinagra. Murray Beros on bike.

Circa 1970
Jean & Hickey
Front garden Baden Street

L-R Hickey, Charlie, with brother-in-law Ernie Gleed (Jean's sister Roberta's husband) and their neighbour Mr Shotton at a wedding?

Jean & Hickey 1970

Jeannie's 80th Birthday

Cousins: Circa 1971

Rear - Barry Sinagra, Lesley Sinagra, Denise Gardiner,

Front - Laurie Sinagra and Andrew Sinagra

Cousins. Circa 1970

From Rear top - Denise Gardiner with Marj, Geoffrey Beros, Barry Sinagra, Vicki Gardiner, Lyn Gardiner, Gaynor Gardiner (obscured), Murray Beros, Lesley Sinagra, Jan Williams, Laurie Sinagra, Connie Booth holding Alison

Front - Ken Williams, David Beros & Unknown

Various Family Gatherings

1971 - professional family photoshoots!
Commemorating Ric & Rosemary Vernon's first Wedding Anniversary
Held at Don and Shirley Vernon's home in Bicton, WA

Rear: Barbara, Paul and Clayton Vernon
Front: Shirley and Don Vernon

Rear: Jan, Ken and Rodney Williams
Front: Len and Laura Williams

Rear: Denise, Lyn and Vicki Gardiner Front: Marj, Gaynor & Frank Gardiner

Rear: Murray, Geoff and David Beros
Front: Dolly and baby Nigel Beros

Rear: Allan and Brian Murphy Front:
Bobbie and Leanne Murphy

Rear: Barry and Lesley Sinagra
Front: Laurie, Winnie and Ross and baby Andrew Sinagra

"All the Vernon Girls" - (well not quite!)

Taken at Rodney & Dot Williams' Wedding 20 May 1972.

Rear: Marj Gardiner, Dolly Beros, Jeannie Vernon, Bobbie Murphy, Laura Williams, Shirley Vernon, Barbara Vernon, Lyn Gardiner

Front: Leanne Murphy, Gaynor Gardiner, THE BRIDE Dot (Harris) Williams, Connie Booth, Denise Gardiner, Winnie Sinagra

Missing for one reason or another:
Vicki Gardiner, Jan Williams, Alison Booth, Cassie Booth and Lesley Sinagra

Missing because of distance: Rosemary Vernon (Canada)

Two more Vernon girls were born after this photo was taken: Alissa and Hayley, daughters of Ric and Rosemary Vernon

And the Beautiful Bride wore Hotpants!

1980 - Bobbie & Ron's 30th Wedding Anniversary, Connie, Bobbie, Ron, Don, Marj and Jeannie in front

1988 Six Sisters: Laura, Connie, Dolly, Marj, Winnie and Bobbie

1992 Family Picnic

Party Girls Marj & Connie 1993

1980 something? Ric & Rosemary's visit

1995
Ric & Rosemary's visit, the 8 siblings in the order they were born
Don, Laura, Marj, Bobbie, Winnie, Dolly, Connie, Eric

L-R Winnie, Marj, Bobbie, Don, Dolly, Connie and Laura

1999

L-R rear Laura, Winnie, Bobbie, Don, Connie and Marj
Front Ron Murphy, Shirley Vernon and Clive Beros

2002

L-R rear Ron Murphy, Bobbie, Marj, Laura, Don, Winnie, Dolly and Clive Beros
Front Shirley Vernon and Connie

2004

*2005 Ric & Rosemary visit - Family picnic at Matilda Bay...
all the boys above and all the girls below*

2005 Ric & Rosemary Visit

"Bookends" Ric and Don

8 siblings Winnie, Dolly, Connie, Ric, Don, Laura, Marj and Bobbie

2010
Dolly, Rosemary Vernon, Ric, Winnie
Don and Laura

2010 Ric & Rosemary visit

2018 Six sisters - Marj, Connie and Winnie, Front Dolly Bobbie and Laura

2019 Ric & Rosemary visit

Rosemary & Winnie

Ric, Gaynor & Rosemary

Ric & Dolly

2019 - A Visit to 53 Baden Street
Home of the Vernon family for many years

(with thanks to Laurie & Lisa Sinagra for organising and to

the current owner Nadia for the privilege)

Above - The front door and verandah

L-R Rosemary Vernon,
Lyn Brown,
Nadia (current owner)
Gaynor Gardiner-Sherwood,
Winnie Sinagra and
Ric Vernon behind

The beautiful old double wood stove still there

Jeannie's old kitchen, not much has changed
L-R Rosemary Vernon, Nadia (current owner) and her brother, Ric Vernon and Winnie Sinagra

The famous "Wall" on the back verandah, untouched all these years ... many visitors and cousins added their name to the wall

The "Rainbow Room"

Vernon Family Tree

Descendants of Jeannie MacDonald Vernon & Hickman Molesworth Vernon

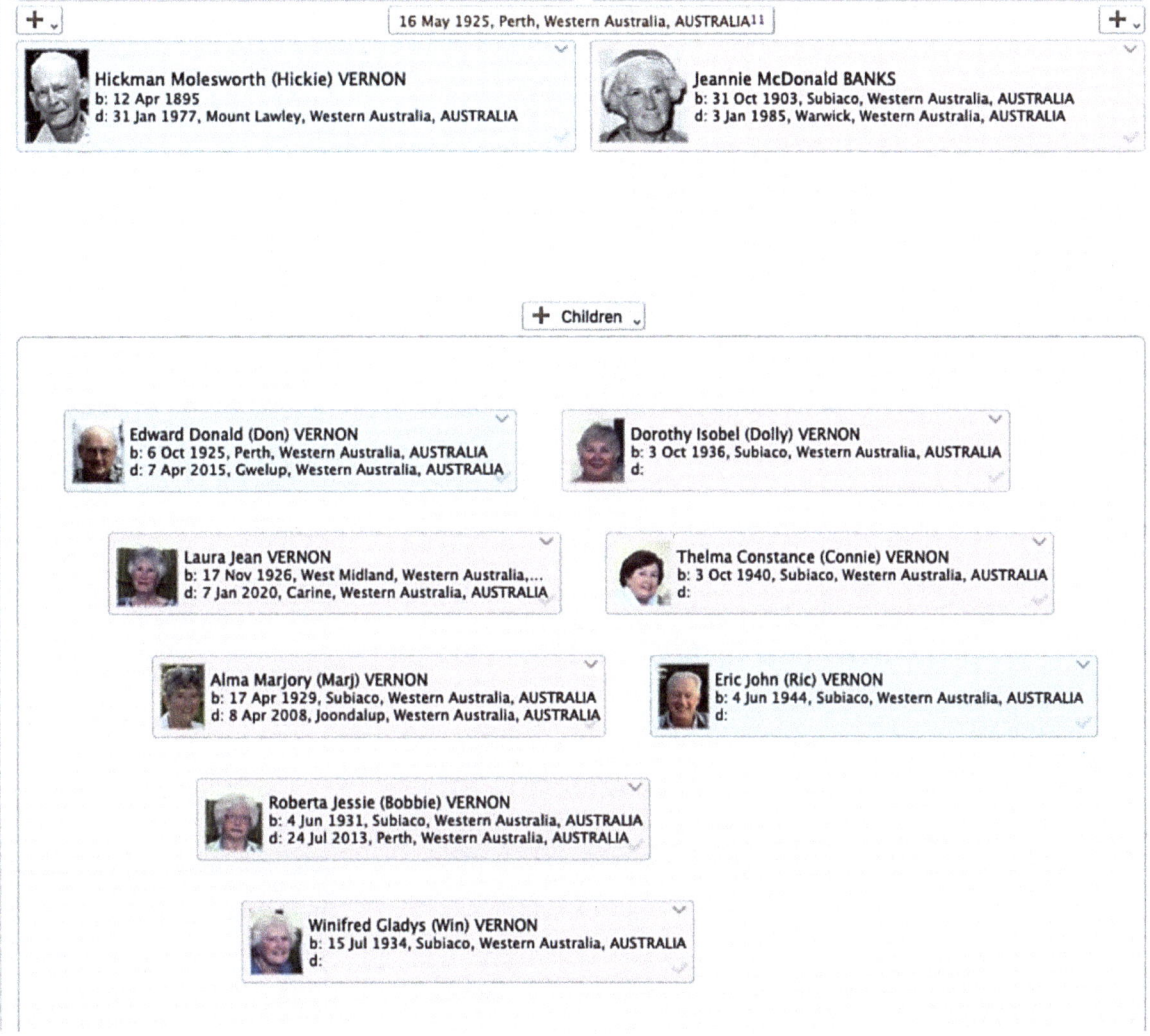

Edward Donald (Don) Vernon

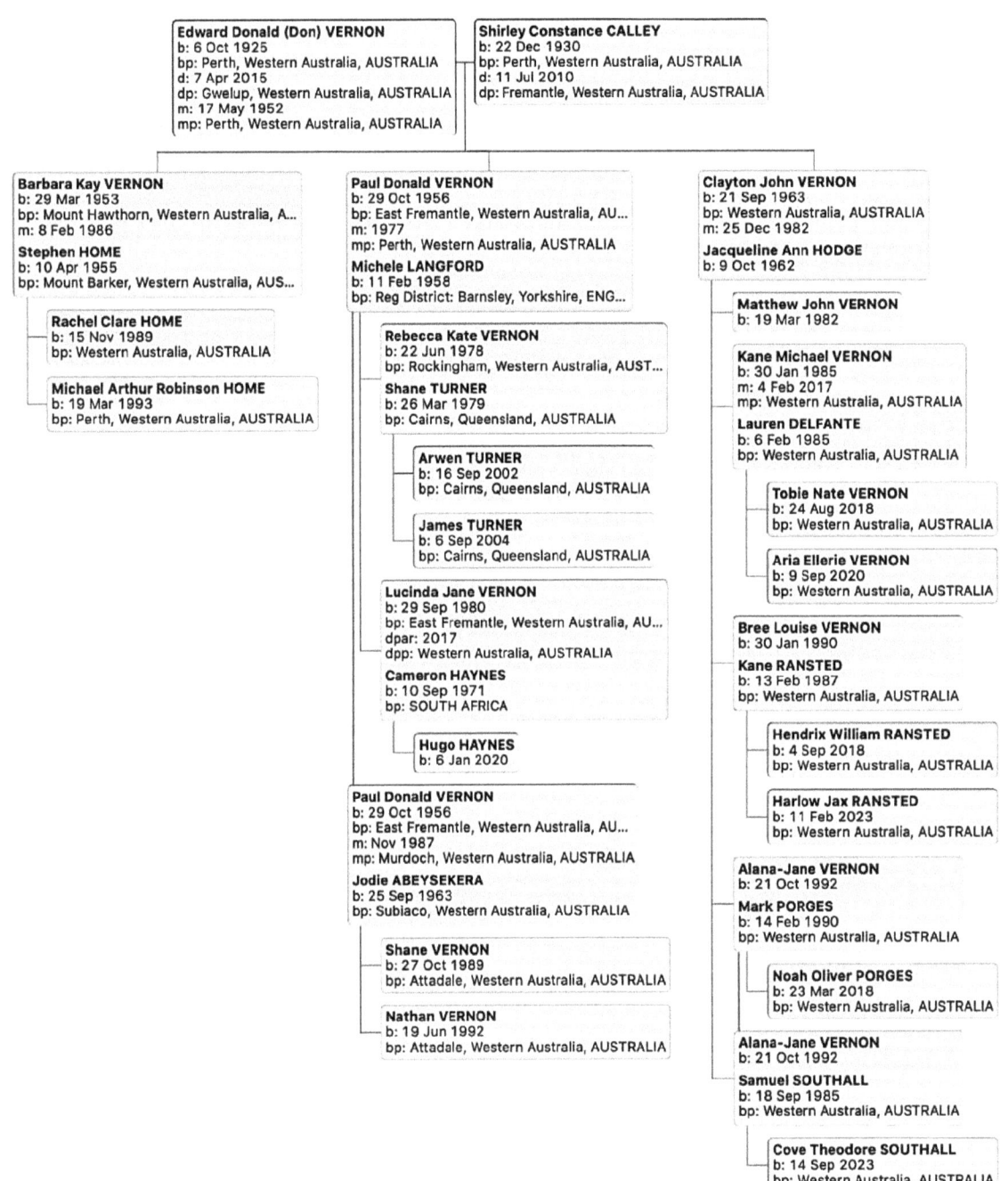

Laura Jean Vernon

Albert Leonard WILLIAMS
b: 6 May 1924
bp: Spalding, Lincolnshire, ENGLAND
d: 18 Feb 1996
dp: Perth, Western Australia, AUSTRALIA
m: 2 Aug 1947
mp: Perth, Western Australia, AUSTRALIA

Laura Jean VERNON
b: 17 Nov 1926
bp: West Midland, Western Australia, AUS...
d: 7 Jan 2020
dp: Carine, Western Australia, AUSTRALIA

- **Rodney Norman WILLIAMS**
  b: 12 Nov 1948
  bp: Subiaco, Western Australia, AUSTRALIA
  m: 20 May 1972
  mp: Bunbury, Western Australia, AUSTRALIA
  Dorothy Joan (Dot) HARRIS
  b: 21 May 1952
  bp: Bunbury, Western Australia, AUSTRALIA

  - **Mathew Bradley WILLIAMS**
    b: 16 May 1973
    bp: Subiaco, Western Australia, AUSTRALIA
    Virginia Mary RING
    b: 25 Oct 1974
    bp: Camden, New South Wales, AUSTRALIA

    - **Jessica Emily WILLIAMS-RING**
      b: 24 Aug 2000
      bp: Campbelltown, New South Wales, AUS...

  - **Mathew Bradley WILLIAMS**
    b: 16 May 1973
    bp: Subiaco, Western Australia, AUSTRALIA
    m: 8 Mar 2008
    mp: New South Wales, AUSTRALIA
    Belinda BALL
    b: 27 Jul 1981
    bp: Blacktown, New South Wales, AUSTRALIA

    - **Ava Harli WILLIAMS**
      b: 22 Jul 2010
      bp: New South Wales, AUSTRALIA

    - **Coble Rose WILLIAMS**
      b: 27 Apr 2012
      bp: Penrith, New South Wales, AUSTRALIA

  - **Amanda Jayne WILLIAMS**
    b: 24 Sep 1976
    bp: Subiaco, Western Australia, AUSTRALIA
    m: 10 May 2003
    mp: Brunswick Junction, Western Australi...
    Steven Amando CARBONE
    b: 17 Apr 1977
    bp: Bunbury, Western Australia, AUSTRALIA

    - **Connor Steven CARBONE**
      b: 29 Apr 2004
      bp: Bunbury, Western Australia, AUSTRALIA

    - **Erin Marisa CARBONE**
      b: 30 May 2006
      bp: Bunbury, Western Australia, AUSTRALIA

    - **Lucas Amando CARBONE**
      b: 11 Sep 2009
      bp: Bunbury, Western Australia, AUSTRALIA

  - **Kim Michael WILLIAMS**
    b: 12 Jan 1980
    bp: Bunbury, Western Australia, AUSTRALIA
    m: 1 Mar 2003
    mp: Australind, Western Australia, AUSTRALIA
    Kelly Janelle MEACHAM
    b: 5 Mar 1980

    - **Mikayla Darcy WILLIAMS**
      b: 8 Sep 2004
      bp: Bunbury, Western Australia, AUSTRALIA

    - **Ruby Joy WILLIAMS**
      b: 12 Feb 2007

- **Kenneth James WILLIAMS**
  b: 7 Jun 1951
  bp: Subiaco, Western Australia, AUSTRALIA
  m: 20 Dec 1977
  mp: Greenwood, Western Australia, AUST...
  Charmaine Rosalie BROWN
  b: 4 Aug 1953
  bp: Subiaco, Western Australia, AUSTRALIA
  d: 20 Oct 2003
  dp: Perth, Western Australia, AUSTRALIA

  - **Owen Mark WILLIAMS**
    b: 3 Jul 1981
    bp: Osborne Park, Western Australia, AUS...
    Jeannine SHELLEY
    b: 9 Jan 1981
    bp: Brisbane, Queensland, AUSTRALIA

    - **Joshua Heath WILLIAMS**
      b: 14 Jun 2006
      bp: Wagga Wagga, New South Wales, AUS...

    - **Isabelle Rosalie WILLIAMS**
      b: 21 Feb 2008
      bp: Townsville, Queensland, AUSTRALIA

  - **Rachael Joanne WILLIAMS**
    b: 26 Aug 1984
    bp: Subiaco, Western Australia, AUSTRALIA
    m: 24 Jul 2010
    mp: Adelaide, South Australia, AUSTRALIA
    Lachlan HAZELDINE
    b: 16 May 1982
    bp: Lilydale, Victoria, AUSTRALIA

    - **Chloe Ann HAZELDINE**
      b: 24 Jul 2012
      bp: Subiaco, Western Australia, AUSTRALIA

    - **Thomas James HAZELDINE**
      b: 14 Dec 2014
      bp: Bairnsdale, Victoria, AUSTRALIA

  - **Kyle James WILLIAMS**
    b: 30 Apr 1986
    bp: Subiaco, Western Australia, AUSTRALIA

  - **Ryan Nathaniel WILLIAMS**
    b: 11 Sep 1988
    bp: Subiaco, Western Australia, AUSTRALIA
    d: 23 Jun 2015
    dp: Rockingham, Western Australia, AUST...

  Kenneth James WILLIAMS
  b: 7 Jun 1951
  bp: Subiaco, Western Australia, AUSTRALIA
  m: 24 Sep 2005
  mp: Perth, Western Australia, AUSTRALIA
  Rosemary Jean CARR
  b: 21 Jul 1953
  bp: Geraldton, Western Australia, AUSTRALIA

- **Patricia Jan (Jan) WILLIAMS**
  b: 26 Aug 1957
  bp: Mount Hawthorn, Western Australia, A...
  m: 2 Dec 1979
  mp: Scarborough, Western Australia, AUS...
  Warrick Anthony WELSH
  b: 21 Dec 1955
  bp: Nedlands, Western Australia, AUSTRALIA

  - **Bianca Jan WELSH**
    b: 23 Apr 1985
    bp: Subiaco, Western Australia, AUSTRALIA
    m: 12 Nov 2011
    mp: Yanchep, Western Australia, AUSTRALIA
    Gary CONNOLLY
    b: 21 Jun 1982
    bp: Durban, Natal, SOUTH AFRICA

    - **Cooper Gary CONNOLLY**
      b: 27 Oct 2015
      bp: Glengarry, Western Australia, AUSTRALIA

    - **Brodie Marc CONNOLLY**
      b: 8 Mar 2019
      bp: Glengarry, Western Australia, AUSTRALIA

  - **Marc Anthony WELSH**
    b: 30 Aug 1988
    bp: Glengarry, Western Australia, AUSTRALIA

  Patricia Jan (Jan) WILLIAMS
  b: 26 Aug 1957
  bp: Mount Hawthorn, Western Australia, A...
  Glynn CARTLEDGE
  b: 5 Dec 1953
  bp: West Midland, Western Australia, AUS...

Alma Marjory (Marj) Vernon

Frank Leonard GARDINER
b: 10 Jan 1925
bp: Perth, Western Australia, AUSTRALIA
d: 7 Jan 2005
dp: Perth, Western Australia, AUSTRALIA
m: 22 Apr 1950
mp: Perth, Western Australia, AUSTRALIA

Alma Marjory (Marj) VERNON
b: 17 Apr 1929
bp: Subiaco, Western Australia, AUSTRALIA
d: 8 Apr 2008
dp: Joondalup, Western Australia, AUSTRALIA

- **Lynette Joyce GARDINER**
  b: 21 Apr 1951
  bp: Subiaco, Western Australia, AUSTRALIA
  m: 29 Jan 1972
  mp: Mount Hawthorn, Western Australia, A...
  Terry Raymond GOOCH
  b: 31 Aug 1949
  bp: Mount Lawley, Western Australia, AUS...
  - **Vernon Terry GOOCH**
    b: 23 Nov 1975
    bp: Perth, Western Australia, AUSTRALIA
    d: 11 Jul 1978
    dp: Perth, Western Australia, AUSTRALIA
  - **Laurie James GOOCH**
    b: 18 Jan 1978
    bp: Perth, Western Australia, AUSTRALIA
    Susan Pojen (Suzi) BOONE
    b: 20 Sep 1987
    bp: PHILLIPINES
  - **Brett David GOOCH**
    b: 23 Dec 1979
    bp: Perth, Western Australia, AUSTRALIA
    m: 5 Jan 2018
    mp: Perth, Western Australia, AUSTRALIA
    Carolina DA SILVA RODRIGUES
    b: 8 Jul 1986
    bp: BRAZIL
    - **Oliver Jacob GOOCH**
      b: 25 May 2015
      bp: Joondalup, Western Australia, AUSTRALIA

  Lynette Joyce GARDINER
  b: 21 Apr 1951
  bp: Subiaco, Western Australia, AUSTRALIA
  m: 20 Jan 1991
  mp: Scarborough, Western Australia, AUS...
  David Michael BROWN
  b: 28 Jun 1948
  bp: Newcastle under Lyme, Staffordshire,...

- **Vicki Lorraine GARDINER**
  b: 19 Nov 1953
  bp: Subiaco, Western Australia, AUSTRALIA
  m: 21 Apr 1973
  mp: Perth, Western Australia, AUSTRALIA
  Leo Glen ROSS
  b: 10 Dec 1950
  bp: Perth, Western Australia, AUSTRALIA
  d: 3 Apr 1983
  dp: Perth, Western Australia, AUSTRALIA
  - **Daniel Shane ROSS**
    b: 8 Oct 1978
    bp: Perth, Western Australia, AUSTRALIA
    m: 19 Sep 2009
    mp: Broome, Western Australia, AUSTRALIA
    Rachel Victoria PEARSON
    b: 16 Oct 1978
    bp: Newman, Western Australia, AUSTRALIA
    - **Eli Thomas ROSS**
      b: 23 Nov 2010
      bp: Broome, Western Australia, AUSTRALIA
    - **Abbie Lee ROSS**
      b: 8 Jan 2013
      bp: Broome, Western Australia, AUSTRALIA
    - **Otis Frankland ROSS**
      b: 13 Nov 2015
      bp: Perth, Western Australia, AUSTRALIA

  Vicki Lorraine GARDINER
  b: 19 Nov 1953
  bp: Subiaco, Western Australia, AUSTRALIA
  m: 9 Feb 1985
  mp: Perth, Western Australia, AUSTRALIA
  Ian Stanley JACKSON
  b: 17 Nov 1945
  bp: Riverton, South Australia, AUSTRALIA
  - **Elliott Frankland JACKSON**
    b: 1 Mar 1985
    bp: Perth, Western Australia, AUSTRALIA
    Chloe AMANDINE
    b: 3 Jan 1990
    bp: BELGIUM

- **Denise Kaye GARDINER**
  b: 31 Jan 1958
  bp: Perth, Western Australia, AUSTRALIA
  d: 17 Sep 1973
  dp: Perth, Western Australia, AUSTRALIA

- **Gaynor Louise GARDINER**
  b: 21 Jun 1965
  bp: Osborne Park, Western Australia, AUS...
  m: 7 Jan 1989
  mp: Perth, Western Australia, AUSTRALIA
  Rodney Cameron SHERWOOD
  b: 4 Jul 1964
  bp: Denmark, Western Australia, AUSTRALIA

Roberta Jean (Bobbie) Vernon

- **Ronald Douglas MURPHY**
  b: 10 May 1928
  bp: Port Pirie, South Australia, AUSTRALIA
  d: 11 Jan 2019
  dp: Armadale, Western Australia, AUSTRALIA
  m: 2 Sep 1950
  mp: Perth, Western Australia, AUSTRALIA
- **Roberta Jessie (Bobbie) VERNON**
  b: 4 Jun 1931
  bp: Subiaco, Western Australia, AUSTRALIA
  d: 24 Jul 2013
  dp: Perth, Western Australia, AUSTRALIA

Children

Allan Roy MURPHY
b: 12 Feb 1953
bp: Victoria Park, Western Australia, AUST...
m: 23 Jan 1981
mp: Forrestfield, Western Australia, AUST...

Jennifer Lee FENWICK
b: 17 Apr 1959
bp: Subiaco, Western Australia, AUSTRALIA

- **Felicity Jane MURPHY**
  b: 23 May 1982
  bp: Bentley, Western Australia, AUSTRALIA
  m: 6 Mar 2010
  mp: Bunbury, Western Australia, AUSTRALIA

  Damian Andrew FARNELL
  b: 4 Jun 1977
  bp: Bunbury, Western Australia, AUSTRALIA

  - **Anneliese Christine FARNELL**
    b: 23 Jul 2018
    bp: Subiaco, Western Australia, AUSTRALIA

- **Caleb John MURPHY**
  b: 23 Jul 1985
  bp: Bentley, Western Australia, AUSTRALIA
  m: 8 Jan 2011
  mp: Bunbury, Western Australia, AUSTRALIA

  Stephanie Angela FURCHOW
  b: 9 Jun 1986
  bp: Kalgoorlie, Western Australia, AUSTRALIA

Frank Phillip (Phil) MURPHY
b: 26 May 1954
bp: East Victoria Park, Western Australia,...
m: 11 Feb 1978
mp: Cannington, Western Australia, AUST...

Kerry Anne NEWING
b: 19 Oct 1957
bp: Burwood, Victoria, AUSTRALIA

- **Melissa Narelle MURPHY**
  b: 17 Aug 1979
  bp: Bentley, Western Australia, AUSTRALIA
  m: 21 Mar 2015
  mp: Western Australia, AUSTRALIA

  Stephen Mark SMEDLEY
  b: 11 Jan 1965
  bp: Seven Hills, New South Wales, AUSTR...

- **Justin Michael MURPHY**
  b: 14 Jul 1981
  bp: Subiaco, Western Australia, AUSTRALIA
  m: 4 Aug 2018
  mp: Western Australia, AUSTRALIA

  Penelope Ann PIERCE
  b: 10 Dec 1986
  bp: Subiaco, Western Australia, AUSTRALIA

  - **Lachlan Phillip MURPHY**
    b: 14 Jan 2016
    bp: Rockingham, Western Australia, AUST...

- **Justin Michael MURPHY**
  b: 14 Jul 1981
  bp: Subiaco, Western Australia, AUSTRALIA

  Christine Ann BENNETT
  b: 17 Apr 1985
  bp: Bentley, Western Australia, AUSTRALIA

  - **Ella Jane MURPHY**
    b: 3 Sep 2008
    bp: Armadale, Western Australia, AUSTRALIA

- **Glen Robert MURPHY**
  b: 22 Apr 1983
  bp: Subiaco, Western Australia, AUSTRALIA
  m: 11 Oct 2008
  mp: Western Australia, AUSTRALIA

  Rachael Eve CARBONE
  b: 23 May 1986
  bp: Subiaco, Western Australia, AUSTRALIA

  - **Asher Declan MURPHY**
    b: 11 Nov 2023
    bp: Western Australia, AUSTRALIA

- **Nicole Maree MURPHY**
  b: 23 Aug 1986
  bp: Subiaco, Western Australia, AUSTRALIA
  m: 16 Nov 2019
  mp: Western Australia, AUSTRALIA

  James Peter CHRISTENSEN
  b: 12 Jan 1984
  bp: Armadale, Western Australia, AUSTRALIA

  - **Jesse Robin CHRISTENSEN**
    b: 26 Sep 2024
    bp: Western Australia, AUSTRALIA

- **Brett Anthony MURPHY**
  b: 13 Jul 1990
  bp: Subiaco, Western Australia, AUSTRALIA

  Lauren TALBOT
  b: 1 Dec 1985
  bp: Attadale, Western Australia, AUSTRALIA

  - **Eshne Victoria MURPHY**
    b: 31 Oct 2018
    bp: Armadale, Western Australia, AUSTRALIA
  - **Bridie Elizabeth MURPHY**
    b: 16 Feb 2022
    bp: Western Australia, AUSTRALIA
  - **Cora Lyla MURPHY**
    b: 9 May 2023
    bp: Western Australia, AUSTRALIA

Brian William MURPHY
b: 15 May 1956
bp: Western Australia, AUSTRALIA

Julie CARTWRIGHT
b: 22 Oct 1956
bp: Subiaco, Western Australia, AUSTRALIA

Leanne Gail MURPHY
b: 10 Oct 1959
bp: Western Australia, AUSTRALIA
m: 27 Feb 1988
mp: Morley, Western Australia, AUSTRALIA

Robert James CANTRELL
b: 21 May 1953

- **Blake Robert CANTRELL**
  b: 23 Dec 1993
  bp: Subiaco, Western Australia, AUSTRALIA
- **Sophie Louise CANTRELL**
  b: 24 Aug 1997
  bp: Subiaco, Western Australia, AUSTRALIA

Winifred Gladys (Winnie) Vernon

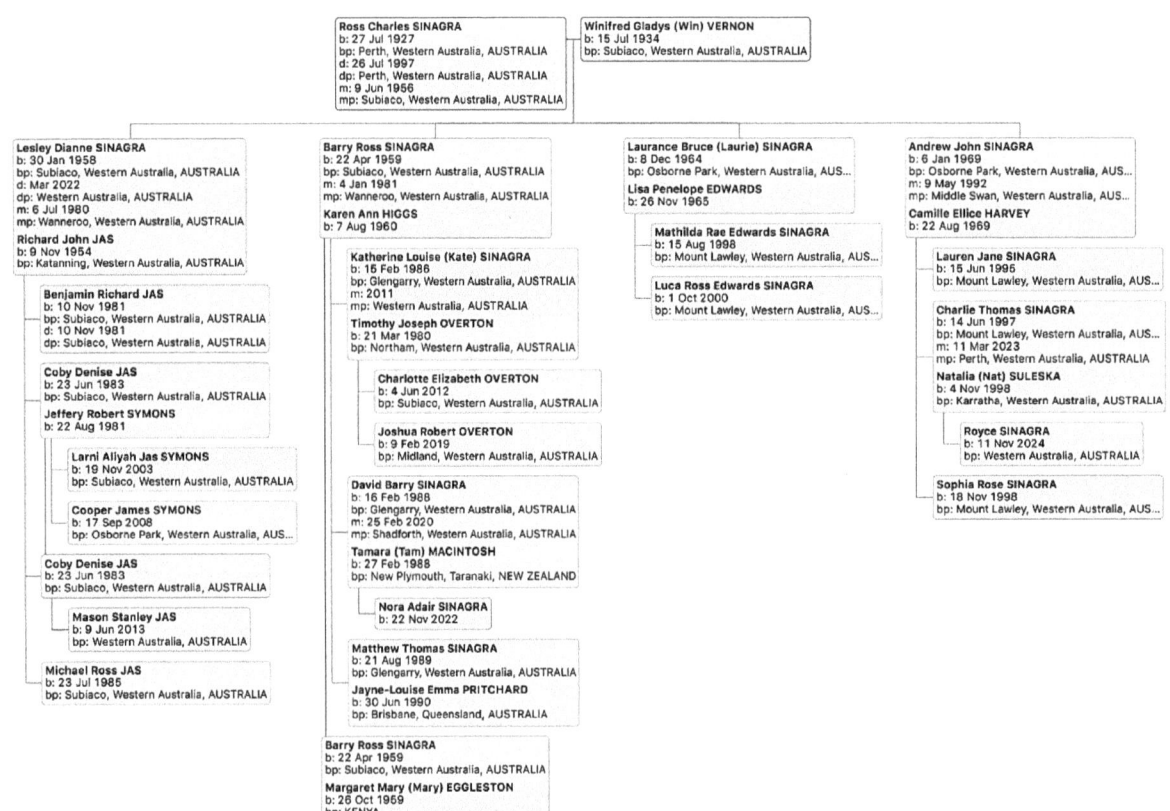

Dorothy Isobel (Dolly) Vernon

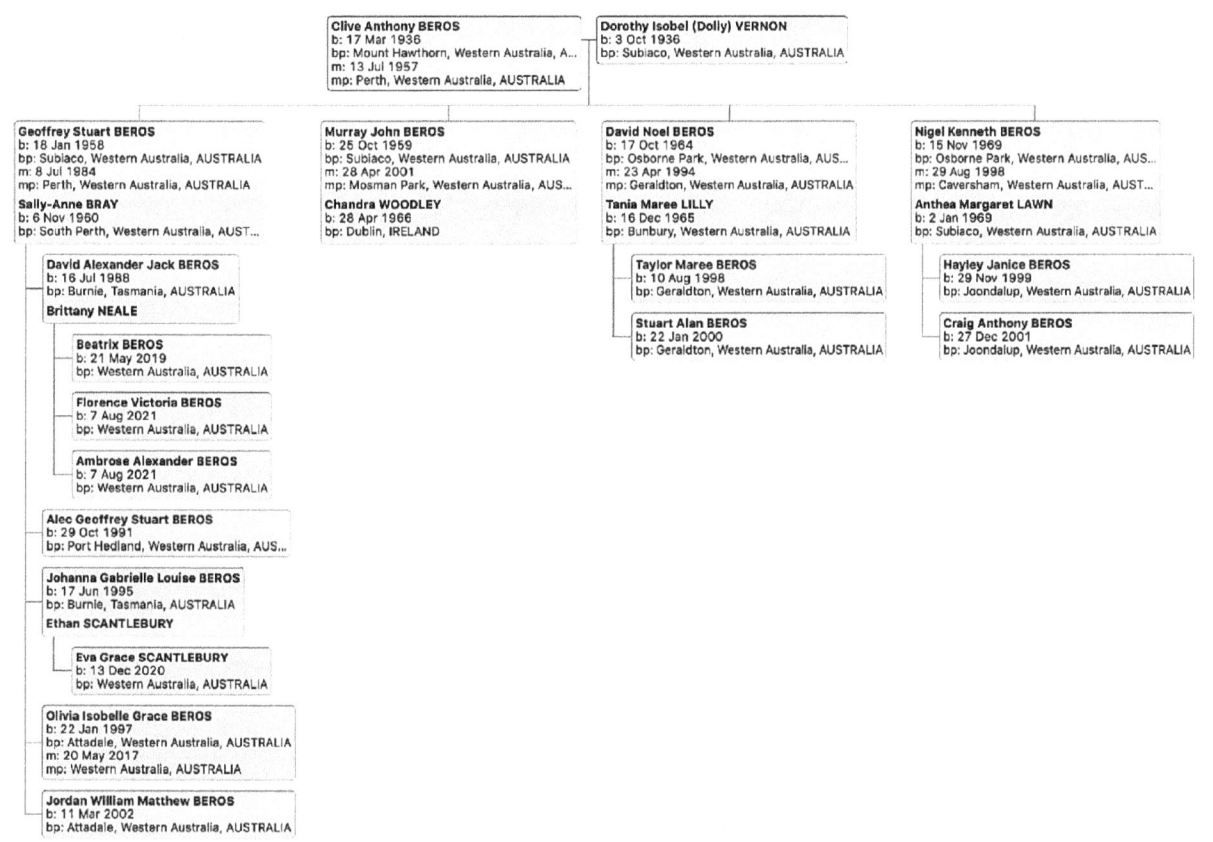

Constance Thelma (Connie) Vernon

Gary George BOOTH
b: 22 Aug 1940
bp: Northam, Western Australia, AUSTRALIA
m: 17 Mar 1962
mp: Hawthorn, Victoria, AUSTRALIA

Thelma Constance (Connie) VERNON
b: 3 Oct 1940
bp: Subiaco, Western Australia, AUSTRALIA

Cassandra Jane BOOTH
b: 30 Sep 1962
bp: Melbourne, Victoria, AUSTRALIA
Stephen Grahame HOOTON
b: 25 Sep 1957
bp: Auckland, NEW ZEALAND
d: 26 Jul 2016
dp: Stirling, Western Australia, AUSTRALIA

Alison Jean BOOTH
b: 1 Dec 1964
bp: Osborne Park, Western Australia, AUS...
m: 23 Nov 1991
mp: Perth, Western Australia, AUSTRALIA
Bruce Graeme GOULD
b: 23 Nov 1959
bp: Geraldton, Western Australia, AUSTRALIA

Chelsea-Jade HOOTON
b: 9 Mar 1987
bp: Auckland, NEW ZEALAND
d: 27 Jul 2012
dp: Fremantle, Western Australia, AUSTRALIA

Jack Aiden GOULD
b: 9 Dec 1996
bp: Subiaco, Western Australia, AUSTRALIA

Emily Kate GOULD
b: 20 Mar 1998
bp: Subiaco, Western Australia, AUSTRALIA

Cassandra Jane BOOTH
b: 30 Sep 1962
bp: Melbourne, Victoria, AUSTRALIA
m: 12 Nov 2004
mp: Perth, Western Australia, AUSTRALIA
Nigel David MUDGE
b: 15 Jan 1974
bp: SCOTLAND

Eric John (Ric) Vernon

Eric John (Ric) VERNON
b: 4 Jun 1944
bp: Subiaco, Western Australia, AUSTRALIA
m: 4 Jul 1970
mp: Courtenay, Vancouver Island, British...

Rosemary Frederica SIDDALL
b: 6 Jun 1946
bp: Sheffield, Yorkshire, ENGLAND
d: 7 Oct 2022
dp: Courtenay, Vancouver Island, British C...

Alissa Judean VERNON
b: 30 Nov 1973
bp: San Juan de Marcona, PERU
m: 8 Aug 1998
mp: Gabriola Island, British Columbia, CA...

Paul Joseph Mundell PRATT
b: 10 Jul 1970
bp: Ontario, CANADA

- **Callie Lauren PRATT**
  b: 14 Jan 2007
  bp: Comox, Vancouver Island, British Colu...

Hayley Claire VERNON
b: 8 Jun 1977
bp: Comox, Vancouver Island, British Colu...
m: 18 Aug 2006
mp: Courtenay, Vancouver Island, British...

Aniel Kenneth DATOO
b: 11 Nov 1977
bp: Vancouver, British Columbia, CANADA

- **Eamonn Alexander (Kyra) DATOO**
  b: 18 Jan 2009
  bp: Nanaimo, Vancouver Island, British Col...
- **Malaika Rose DATOO**
  b: 2 Aug 2011
  bp: Comox, Vancouver Island, British Colu...

Roger John VERNON
b: 25 Aug 1980
bp: Comox, Vancouver Island, British Colu...
m: 7 Sep 2015
mp: Courtenay, Vancouver Island, British...

Caroline BERNARD
b: 6 Mar 1980
bp: Fort McMurray, Alberta, CANADA
d: 31 Aug 2021
dp: Bowser, British Columbia, CANADA

- **Alice Joelle VERNON**
  b: 15 Nov 2016
  bp: Comox, Vancouver Island, British Colu...

Molesworth (wife) v. Molesworth

The Molesworth Connection

Henrietta Johnson was married in 1840 in Dublin, Ireland to Robert Molesworth, who later became Sir Robert Molesworth, a judge of the Supreme Court in Melbourne, Australia. They divorced in November 1864 on grounds of adultery.

They had 8 children:

*Hickman	1842 - 1907
Robert Arthur	1843 - 1920
Wilhemina Jane	1844 - 1844
Elizabeth Josephine	1846 - 1900
George Gerald	1851 - 1853
MaryJane Sophia	1854 - 1855
Richard Johnson	1848 - 1848
Henry	1848 - 1848

Charles Molesworth Vernon 1st was born out of wedlock in England in 1862 and was originally named Charles Vernon Smythe.

BIRTH 21 October 1862

Birth Certificate - Charles Vernon Smyth

Baptised - George Charles Vernon Smyth

Born at 1 The Green, Richmond, Surrey, UK

Father: Charles Smythe

Mother: Henrietta Smythe formerly Johnson, Residence: 1 The Green, Richmond

Note: Johnson (or England-Johnson) is Henrietta Molesworth's maiden name.

BAPTISED 22 Feb 1863, Twickenham Middlesex, UK

Child: George Charles Vernon

Parents Christian Names: Charles Vernon and Jane Smythe Abode: Queenstown, Ireland

Trade: Merchant Captain

Note: Birth Certificate states Father as Charles Smyth and also Smythe, also mother's name changes from Henrietta to Jane Smythe on baptism certificate.

Our family is not directly related to Sir Robert Molesworth. However Henrietta's illegitimate son George Charles Vernon, (recorded on his marriage certificate as Charles Molesworth Vernon), is a half sibling of her children with Sir Robert Molesworth. Henrietta is the grandmother of William, Robert, Florence, Charles, Hickman, and Dorothy Vernon.

The following pages are transcripts from the divorce case Molesworth vs Molesworth which was taken from daily reports in the *Melbourne Age* in 1864. You might assume from these pages that Henrietta was quite a character!

> **HICKMAN MOLESWORTH:*
>
> *Hickman Molesworth was the preferred defence Attorney for Ned Kelly and much effort was made to gain his services by the Kelly family. While at the same time the police and Government went to great lengths to prevent Hickman from defending.*

Molesworth (wife) v. Molesworth

DIVORCE COURT

Thursday, 17th November.
(Before the Chief Justice, and a Special Jury of Twelve)

MOLESWORTH (WIFE) v. MOLESWORTH

Extract from *The Age* Melbourne, Friday, 18th November, 1864

> A petition by Henrietta Molesworth for a judicial separation from her husband, Robert Molesworth, one of the judges of the Supreme Court.

Mr Dawson and Mr Wood instructed by Messrs Klingender, Charsley and Liddle, appeared for the petitioner; and Mr Billing and Mr Michie, Q.C., instructed by Mr McKean, for the respondent.

Mr Wood explained that the jury were called upon merely to decide certain issues of fact. The substance of the respondent's allegations, as stated by the learned counsel, was that the conduct of the petitioner with Richard Davies Ireland, in the middle of April, 1855, was unduly familiar for a married woman; that, on or about the 6th July, 1855, she committed adultery with R. D. Ireland; that, between March and May, 1861, she committed adultery with a person named Hawker in England; that, when living at or near Melbourne, before the month of June, 1862, she committed adultery; and that, at the latter part of the year 1862, at or near Richmond, in England, she was delivered of a male bastard child. The petitioner denied all these allegations, and affirmed that, for a period of nine months prior to September, 1855, by a course of unkind conduct, the respondent rendered her life miserable; that they cohabited together until the 29th September, 1855, and that on that date he promised to provide suitably for her maintenance during her absence from the colony; that he had subsequently promised to forward £300 a year to England, but had neglected to do so; and that on one occasion he had violently assaulted her.

Mr Dawson, in stating the case to the jury, said he was quite sure they would all participate in the feeling of regret which pervaded the whole profession, that a case like this should have been brought before the court. It was a matter of regret, not only to those entrusted with the due administration of justice, but it was a matter of regret, he might say, to the whole colony that its honour should be impaired in such a manner.

He thought he was right in making this observation, because he believed it would transpire in the course of this most melancholy inquiry that the simple reason why the case was brought before the court, and through the court before the colony and the whole world, was that the respondent had declined to furnish his wife with something like £300 or £400 per year, and that the only obstacle to the adjustment of the difficulty was a question about an amount of some £100 per annum. Mrs Molesworth had been challenged and provoked to take this step, having no other alternative; and it would be his painful duty to lay before the court a course of conduct on the part of the respondent, which it would be impossible for him to justify, and which had compelled Mrs Molesworth to adopt this course, and appeal to the court for a judicial separation.

He went on to explain that Mrs Molesworth had been married at an early age, when she was between seventeen and eighteen years of age, and that soon after their union the frightful passion of jealousy, which had hitherto dictated Mr Molesworth's conduct, which he had characterised as cruel and barbarous, had broken out.

He then related several acts of this nature, which were afterwards deposed to by the respondent, and remarked that, in 1855, he was jealous because of some alleged familiarities between Mrs Molesworth and Mr Ireland, but he should be able to prove that this accusation was, like the rest, an unfounded one. He believed that Mrs Molesworth, on one occasion, tortured by the indignities he had heaped upon her and exasperated by his cruel conduct, snapped her fingers at him; and, in order to revenge herself, told him that she had committed adultery with Mr Ireland. She said it, however, simply out of bravado, and merely as a retaliation for the long course of annoyance to which she had been subjected.

He had deposed her from her proper position in the family, treated her in the most cruel manner, and, indeed, played with her in quite a feline spirit, being sometimes kind to her and at others behaving to her in the most outrageous manner. Irritated by this injustice, she had made a statement that she had committed adultery; but she afterwards denied the charge, and it would be proved that her husband believed her denial. In 1855 she went to England for his personal convenience, and was promised an allowance of £300 per annum, but, after she had been in England a short time, she was actually divested of that pittance by him.

The learned counsel next explained the circumstances under which she had taken a second voyage to England, and the manner in which she had been received on coming back the first time, all of which were afterwards fully given in the evidence.

After referring to several occasions on which it was said the respondent had treated his wife with the greatest cruelty, and, in one case, subjected her to the grossest indignity, he concluded by remarking that the petitioner, driven from her home, abjured by her children, and denied a suitable allowance by her husband, had no resource but to appeal to the court as her sanctuary and to the jury as her deliverers.

The first witness called was Dr. Howitt, who proved that he attended Mrs Molesworth at Bignell's Hotel, on the 29th June, 1858. She was suffering from a black eye and a cut on the lip. These arose, most probably, from a blow; if they had arisen from a fall, the parts would have shown more signs of abrasion. Prescribed the usual remedies, and all the indications passed off in a few days.

Henrietta Molesworth, the petitioner, was examined by Mr Dawson. She stated: I am the petitioner in this suit, and the wife of Mr Robert Molesworth. I was married to him in January, 1840, when I was between seventeen and eighteen years of age. Mr Molesworth is about seven years my senior. Some years after our marriage, there was a difference between us about a ball which took place at Mr Longford's, in Ireland. I got two tickets, which were given me by a gentleman when I was out walking one day. The second ticket bore no name, and I asked my husband to take it and accompany me. After a good deal of persuasion, he declined, but promised to take me to the party and bring me back. He, however, did not do so; and, when I got home, I asked why he had not come to take me, as he had promised. He made some reply, and we had one or two words.

He then locked the door of the bedroom, and pulling me down by the hair of the head, beat me on the head and leg with a hearth-brush, which he broke several times. I said nothing at all, and did nothing, as I was quite powerless. He then took a knife off the table, and held it in front of my throat. I said: "For God's sake, Robert, spare my life; I am not fit to die."

He then in a passion threw the knife to the other end of the room, and made me go to bed, locking the door. He afterwards brought me some dinner and a glass of wine to drink. After he went away, I made up my mind that I could not live with him any longer, and as soon as I could get away I went to a friend's house at Dublin. He followed me and apologised for his conduct, and I went back to him. I had to send for Dr. Beattie, for I was beaten very severely.

In 1852, we came to South Australia, and lived there a year or two. We brought out a servant with us named Mary Hickey, now Mrs Dollard. In 1854 we came to settle in Melbourne. Our family made the acquaintance of the Irelands. Mr Molesworth introduced me to Mr Ireland, and the families became very familiar, as all Irish people do. (Laughter) I remember having a little girl, either in 1854 or 1855. Mr Molesworth on that occasion behaved in a very singular way. He was very kind to me up to this time, but the morning the child was born, he went out of the house, and never came back until the evening. He never took any notice of the child, and behaved in such an extraordinary manner that we were on very cool terms afterwards. Everyone noticed his neglect of the child, and Dr. Patterson commented on it.

I was not aware at that time that he was jealous, but it appeared he was. I remember a conversation about Captain Clarke, the Surveyor General. It took place at a dinner party which we gave at our house, at St. Kilda, during our intimacy with the Irelands. It is what is called in this country a "state dinner," so we had all the "nobs" there. (Laughter.) Captain Clarke spoke to me a good deal, and when we went into the drawing room we sat together in a corner, there being at the time a great many persons in the room.

Afterwards Mr Molesworth came to me and said I talked too much with Captain Clarke; but, as I had a manner of making myself agreeable, he would excuse it. I laughed at him and asked what he meant, and he had nothing to say. There was also an unpleasantness about Mr Cruikshank, who came out in the early part of 1855, and had some station up at the diggings. We had known him at home, and Mr Molesworth gave him a general invitation to the house. I asked him to come and dine on Christmas Day, and when I told my husband, he said that he did not want him, and that if he did come he would go and dine at an hotel.

He went out in the morning with the children, and I excused him to Mr Cruikshank, by saying that he had business to attend to. We sat down to dinner at about four o'clock, and presently there was a ring at the bell. Mr Cruikshank told me afterwards that I got as white as a sheet, for I did not know what Mr Molesworth might do. He, however, said he was very glad to see Mr Cruikshank, and ordered some champagne to be brought, which we all drank together.

When Mr Penfold, my brother-in-law's brother, came out, Mr Molesworth invited him to the house, and told me to make myself agreeable. He gave Mr Penfold a horse to ride, and told him to take me out with him. One night Mr Molesworth broke open my bedroom door – we occupied separate rooms at this time – and rushed in with nothing but his nightdress on. I said, "What brings you here?" He sat down on a chair and became as white as a sheet, and said, "What keeps Penfold here?" I said, "That is a pretty to do, seeing that you invited him."

I looked at him, and he said, after a little conversation, "I see by your face that you are innocent, but you have such a manner, that he (Penfold) has taken advantage of it to be kind to you." He insisted on his leaving the house, and he accordingly left.

He was going to Sydney, but the machinery of the vessel broke down, and he had to come back, when Mr Molesworth again invited him, and insisted on his receiving some money.

About 1855 he repeatedly invited Mr Dunne to come to his house, and it was arranged that he should come out one Sunday. I told him that Mr Dunne was coming, when he said, "That is the way you have of asking every sort of fellow to my house. "Well, Robert," I said, "Mr Dunne said you asked him to come." He said, "Well, I don't want him, and I won't be at home." When Mr Dunne came, Mr Molesworth said he was delighted to see him, and had some wine brought out.

Presently, out of a brown study, he said, "Dunne, it is rather an awkward thing for me to say, but my wife is in the habit of asking people to the house without my wish, and I certainly shall not be at home to you today." Mr Dunne got up and went away without saying anything, but I was so vexed that I threw myself upon the bed and cried. I remember going to Castlemaine on circuit with my husband. Judge Williams had said it was a strange thing that Mr Molesworth should leave me behind always, and on this occasion I went with him.

We went all together in Cobb's coach. I had a nurse, and took the baby with me. Mr Ireland was going too, so my husband asked him to join us at breakfast and dinner every day. He said he should be very happy to do so, and we all went up together. At the hotel I occupied one bedroom, and Mr Ireland and my husband occupied the other. We all dined and breakfasted together every day; and at breakfast Mr Molesworth would say, "Well, Ireland, you have not got much to do on circuit, take Mrs Molesworth out and show her the place." He went out with me frequently, and we walked in the streets together. There was a ball at the hotel, to which I went. Mr Molesworth did not want me to go at first, but after a good deal of pressing, from Mrs Bull and other ladies who were going, he allowed me to go. Mr Ireland did not go but took me in the afternoon to a shop, at my husband's request, for me to get a ball dress. Several months afterwards, Mr Molesworth told me that he followed us to the shop and looked through the window to see if we were really there.

I sat up one night when Catherine, the servant, went out. When we were at dinner, Mr Molesworth said to Mr Ireland, "Will you sit up with Mrs Molesworth tonight; I feel rather tired and will go to bed." Mr Ireland said he would have no objection, and he did sit up with me. He was drinking whisky punch and smoking a pipe during the evening. We were sitting on chairs at opposite sides of the fireplace, and sometimes Mr Ireland would get up and lean against the chimney place. I heard a noise several times, and called twice to my husband to know if he had called; but he mumbled something, and said he did not. The third time after

I heard the noise, Mr Molesworth rushed out of the room in his night dress, and crossing over to where Mr Ireland was sitting, grasped him either by his collar or by his hair. Mr Ireland was perfectly collected, but Mr Molesworth attacked him in the most awful manner, calling him all the names he could possibly think of. Mr Ireland asked what was the matter, and Mr Molesworth told him he suspected him of making love to his wife. He flew about the room, asked for a knife, and there was an awful scene. I never stirred; I was so astonished, and Mr Ireland either went downstairs or was kicked down. Mr Ireland's hat was left in the room, and I went and threw it to him in the street.

Mr Molesworth came up to me and said, "Go into your room at once; you are not to blame, but go into your room." I went there and stayed until Catherine came home.

The next morning we had to start early for Melbourne, and we all went again in the same conveyance. Mr Molesworth asked me what conversation had passed between Mr Ireland and myself. I told him it was about some family matter, and he appeared perfectly satisfied. He said he had listened through the keyhole, and had heard a word or two which had caused him to misunderstand the conversation. He then went and apologised to Mr Ireland, and they became fast friends.

He gave me another state dinner, at which Mr Ireland, his wife and sister were present. In fact, there were as many Irelands as would have filled table. (Laughter.)

One morning, after I had been out riding on an untrained horse, lent me by Mr Goslett, I returned very tired, and went to sleep. Presently, I felt all the clothes pulled off me, which woke me up; and I said, "Robert what's the matter?" He said, "I have found out that you are a -----;" and called me most opprobrious names. I said: "What do you mean?" He said: "I have been examining your clothes, and I find that you have been improper with somebody."

I did not know what he meant; and he sat upon the edge of the bed and explained it to me. I said, "Oh, Robert, how can you say so? I have ridden a horse that has hurt me very much." With that he examined my person. (Sensation.) He afterwards apologised, and said he was sure that what he had accused me of did not occur.

Two or three months after the affair at Castlemaine, another disturbance took place with Mr Ireland. One evening Mr Molesworth gave me some money to pay a bill, and just as I was going out Mr Ireland came in. Mr Molesworth said to him, "Will you walk down with Mrs Molesworth to pay the bill?" Mr Ireland did not seem very willing to go and I suggested that we should all go down together. Mr Molesworth went to get his hat, and was away about a quarter of an hour. Suddenly he burst open the door in great haste. I thought he looked rather queer, but he did not say anything and we went out together. When we got outside the gate he suddenly took hold of Mr Ireland and hit him. Mr Ireland said "I shan't let it pass this time as I did at Castlemaine," and they commenced beating each other awfully on the side of the road. They afterwards both went home, and Mr Ireland, after this, never again came to the house.

I led a miserable life afterwards, but nothing would persuade Mr Molesworth but that Mr Ireland and I were intimate, although he took no pains to discover if it was the truth or not. He always went out at different times and places to what I did, and on one occasion went in the carriage to a dinner at Government House, leaving me at home, but giving no reason for not taking me. I had a conversation with him about Mr Ireland some six weeks after this. I said, "Robert what would you give to know whether Mr Ireland and I are intimate?" He said he would give anything to know. I then told him a story about meeting Mr Ireland under a tree, and his trying to be intimate with me. He asked me to write a note to Mr Ireland, and I did so. I began the note – "Dear Mr Ireland, - Come down and meet me under the tree tonight." He said the note would not do, and I must write a second one, commencing – "Dear Richard," and stating that my husband would be away that night. I began a fresh note, and he took possession of the first. As soon as I had written the second one something struck me, and I asked him what he was going to do with the one he had got. He said, "Now I have got Ireland in my power, and can show that you and he are guilty."

I solemnly declare this was not so, and told him I had merely made the statement I did to annoy him. He, however, kept the note, and I afterwards wrote one to Mr Ireland to explain the circumstances of the first being sent.

I at first determined to deliver it myself, but Hickey promised faithfully to take it, and I gave it to her.

Instead of delivering it she gave it to Mr Molesworth, and Mr Ireland is not aware of the whole circumstances from that day to this. [The letter, which the petitioner said was directed by the respondent, was produced and read. It was as follows: - "My dear Mr Ireland, - Robert is to be out tomorrow evening. Will you meet me under the tree? Send me a line to fix the hour."]

I never met Mr Ireland under the tree. Sometimes I used to speak to him at the gate, and there is a tree near. He used to come there to ask how I was getting on with Mr Molesworth, and if we were better friends. He never gave me any reason for suspecting my being intimate with Mr Ireland, but, as I was not then living with him as his wife, he said he suspected I was living with some other man. He first accused Mr Penfold, and then Mr Ireland. Soon after the last affair with Mr Ireland, I went to live at Mrs Poole's, at Prahran, and was occasionally visited by Mr Molesworth.

I used sometimes to dine at his house, by his express invitation. He would sometimes treat me very kindly, and at other times very unkindly.

One evening I went with him into the sitting room, and after locking the door, he made me sign a paper promising to go to England, and on the 29th September, 1855, I sailed in the "Donald Mackay". For a month before this time, and after writing the letter I was intimate with Mr Molesworth. He made one remark at this time, which I remember, that he hoped I should not be in the family way. He said if I pleased him in going away he would give me lots of money. He and his two sons accompanied me to the "Donald Mackay". We had luncheon together, and he fell on his knees in the drawing room and said:- "Henrietta, I am very sorry it has come to this, but as I have paid your passage, I think it is better for you to go. I never believed there was anything in that about Ireland." He came to the ship with me, and, taking me in his arms, cried and sobbed as if his heart were breaking. (After a pause, in which the petitioner appeared to be overcome by her feelings, she continued) - He said distinctly that when I returned I was to live with him as his wife. I arrived in England sometime in December, and had no money except £10 10s, which he gave me on the ship.

I stopped at the Adelphi Hotel, at Liverpool, and after about three days I got a letter from Mr Kent, enclosing £20, which he stated was the first instalment of an allowance of £80 per annum, which Mr Molesworth was going to give me. I then went to my relative at Woolwich, Mr Penfold, the Accountant-General. I next went to Sir Richard Bethell (Lord Westbury), and, in consequence of the advice he gave me, I returned to the colony.

I came back in the "James Baines", and arrived in March, 1856. All the money I got in England besides the £20, was an additional sum of £25 which I obtained in advance. I went to Mr Molesworth's house the day I arrived, and told him I had come out by the advice of Lord Westbury, to get maintenance from him. He called me a ---- ---- and a ---- ----, and, before Mr Rose, insisted on my leaving the house. I said I would not leave, unless he got a carriage and pair of horses. He got the carriage, and I went with Mr Rose to town. On starting, Mr Rose gave me £5; but I have a temper sometimes, and I threw it away amongst the flowers.

We went to Bignell's Hotel and dined, drinking a bottle of champagne between us. Mr Rose shortly afterwards left, and I soon after ordered the carriage and followed him to Mr Molesworth's house.

I knocked at the drawing-room door, which he had locked, and said, "It's me, Robert, won't you let me in?" He opened the door, and called me again most barbarous names, Mr Rose standing by without saying a word.

I said, "What am I to do, am I to starve in the streets of Melbourne?" After a little time, he said if I did not go he would kick me out. He then caught me by the shoulder, and putting his knee in my back, kicked me from the fire place to the door, and from the dining room down the passage, before all the servants. We had no words, as I never opened my mouth. He kicked me to the gate, and said he would make me get into the carriage. When I got into the carriage, he turned round and gave me a dreadful hit in the eye and another in the mouth.

I said, "For God's sake don't knock my teeth down my throat," and threw myself under the carriage, hoping the horses would go over me. I was severely bruised by the blows, and it was for these injuries that I was attended by Dr Howitt.

Next morning I got a letter from Mr Molesworth, in which he said I was to get £300 a year and to have one of the servants, on condition that I did not live at St Kilda; but my children were to be allowed to see me as often as I liked.

I afterwards thought it would be best to go back to my friends, and on condition of receiving £300 a year, I sailed back in the "James Baines". Mr Rose saw me off, and gave me twenty guineas when I started. I only got £200 a year in England, but received two presents of £100 each, from Mr Molesworth, on writing to say that I was heavily in debt and hard up.

I remained in England five years, and during that period, my daughter Josephine arrived, Mr Molesworth having asked me to take care of her, as she wished to go to England. I got a writing master, drawing master and French master for her, and she remained with me altogether for nearly twelve months. I came back to Victoria in 1861, in consequence of not getting my remittance.

This closed the examination of the petitioner, and the court was adjourned for half an hour.

On resuming, the petitioner was cross-examined by Mr Billing. The following are the most material points:-

Mr Billing: Did you not say to Mr Molesworth at Castlemaine that you had no regard for him, that you had no religious feelings, and little regard for public opinion, and that you were only kept by a feeling of delicacy from being bad?

Witness: No; I never discussed the question of religion at all.

Mr Billing repeated the question.

Witness: That is all moonshine.

Mr Billing: Was nothing said about public opinion?

Witness: I never had much regard for public opinion. (Laughter.) I had no conversation to that effect.

Mr Billing: Now, what were the relative positions of Mr Ireland and yourself when you sat up together at Castlemaine, and he was drinking and smoking?

Witness: He was sitting opposite to me. He was not the worse for drink. I never saw him drunk. He can take a good drop, you know. (Great laughter.) I was sitting conversing with him for an hour or so. I remember the topics of conversation.

Mr Billing: Do you remember talking about any celebrated crim. con. case?

Witness: Yes, that was the principal subject of his conversation with me. We were not talking about this long, for it was just about this time that Mr Molesworth came out of his room. I don't remember the other topics of conversation.

Mr Billing: Did anything like this take place. Did he say, "What if you have a boy by me?"

Witness: I swear that nothing like this was said. He was talking about his own family affairs, about his mother-in-law having eloped with another man.

Mr Billing: So that was the conversation. Mr Ireland drinking and smoking, and amusing you with a story about this?

Witness: Yes, that was the subject of the conversation.

Mr Billing: Nor was nothing said about provision for this child?

Witness: There was not (excitedly). You appear to be like the wolf in Little Red Riding Hood, Mr Billing, ready to swallow me up at one mouthful. (Laughter.) No judge can make me swear what did not take place.

Mr Billing: Did not Mr Ireland say something about being able to bear being away from you for a month?

Witness: No; he never said anything of the kind, and I am so much in the habit of receiving compliments from men, that, if he had, it would have gone for nothing. It would have gone up the chimney like the smoke of his pipe.

The witness was cross-examined with reference to the treatment by her husband, when he had suspected her of improper conduct, but she adhered to her statement.

Mr Billing: When you were in company with Mr Ireland, on the 4th of July, 1855, did you not say to him, "You have ruined me, and you know. I should be ready to beg through the world with you?"

Witness: I did not make use of such words. I might have said something like it in reference to my name being ruined by what had appeared in the papers. Something had appeared about two leading barristers, and about a lady being in the case. He said he was sorry that my name had been brought in, and I might have said, in the course of conversation, that he had ruined me in public opinion. I never made use of the expression that I should be ready to beg through the world with him. I would not like to beg with any man, even if he was the handsomest young fellow in the world. (Laughter.)

Mr Billing: Do you remember Mr Ireland sending you a letter the day after the second scuffle?

Witness: I don't remember his doing so. I never saw any of his handwriting. I remember the evening of the children's party in our house on the 6th July, 1855. Mr Ireland and I went out a short way together on that evening.

Mr Billing: Notwithstanding previous transactions?

Witness: Mr Ireland was in the habit of coming to the house often. He walked to the gate, but did not pass it. We were there only a few minutes. He was very anxious to know whether Mr Molesworth and I had made terms.

Mr Billing: I am obliged to put the question Mrs Molesworth; but did you on that occasion commit adultery with Mr Ireland

Witness: I am astonished at you Mr Billing. I did not. He never took the slightest liberty with me.

Mr Billing: Never on the 6th of July?

Witness: Never on the 6th of July. I never said he had so directly. I said to Mr Molesworth, "What would you give to know that I am intimate with Mr Ireland?"

Mr Billing: Did not you say to your husband that you had been guilty of adultery with Mr Ireland once only – on the night of the children' party, on the 6th July?

Witness: I deny it. I said, "What would you give to know that Mr Ireland and I are intimate?"

Mr Billing: Did you say that Mr Ireland was a wonderfully cunning man; that he had got you completely under his management, and that he had commenced to make love to you in the previous October, when walking home from his house?

Witness: No.

Mr Billing: Did you tell your husband that your going to Castlemaine was concocted between you?

Witness: Oh, no. It was Mr Molesworth that asked me to go.

Mr Billing: Did you not tell him that, when going to buy the dress, Mr Ireland had kissed you?

Witness: He never did kiss me.

Mr Billing: Did you tell your husband that you had intercepted a letter from Mr Ireland to him on the 5th July?

Witness: If I intercepted the letter it is very likely I told him so.

Mr Billing: Did you say that Mr Ireland had succeeded once with you when you were intoxicated?

Witness: No; I swear we never had any intimacy.

Mr Billing: Did you not say you wanted to punish Mr Ireland, and suggested writing the note in order to do it?

Witness: No; Mr Molesworth suggested the note. My only object was to play a hoax upon Mr Ireland and having done so I repented and wrote the note of explanation, which you have got. It is a most material note to me, and would explain all this business. (Letter handed in.)

This is the answer. It is, "I will meet you under the tree, at half-past six o'clock." I don"t know that this is his handwriting. I never had the letter in my possession before. Mr Molesworth said he kept it for the purpose of commencing an action against Mr Ireland. He kept it in his desk and I tried to get it one night but could not. My husband did not require me to leave the house on account of my committing adultery with Mr Ireland. On the contrary it was on account of his conduct that I left. I left the house when he was out of town; and he was surprised to find that I had done so.

Mr Billing: Did you not meet Mr Ireland at Prahran?

Witness: I never saw him at Poole's but I met him once in Prahran, and spoke to him. I wish it to be distinctly understood that I cut the intimacy with the Irelands. They bothered me out of my life, these Irelands did. (Laughter.) I was never so sick of a family before. I was as sick of them as of a pair of old shoes. (Renewed laughter.)

Mr Billing: Did you throw a half-eaten apple at Mr Molesworth in his house?

Witness: I swear I did not. I threw it into the hall, but not at him.

Mr Billing: When he struck you, did you not call him an old cuckold, and say that you might have cuckolded him twenty times if you had liked?

Witness: I said nothing like it. I remember smashing the lamp of the carriage, but I did not break the windows of the house as was stated.

Mr Billing: When did you go to Plymouth?

Witness: I went to Plymouth in 1858. I knew a gentleman of the name of Hawker. He was a surgeon and a married man. His wife's name was Margaret Hawker. I was living with them at one time. The letter produced is my handwriting. Mrs Hawker found it in her husband's pocket-book, I believe.

The letter was put in and read as follows:-

"My Darling, - it was not the present trouble of my purse I meant when I wrote you my last letter; it was as to what a wretched position I would be in if I were in the family way, and you know there is a chance of that. Oh, Tom, it is when I am here alone I am almost mad to think if it should be so; for then what would become of me? You would not come and live with me, and I would be ruined. Now, darling, though I love you, what am I to do? Had I not better not be to you more than a fond friend? I believe you love me a little. Now, don't be angry I said speak – but look at our passions, madly in love – and how it is to end?

You will come here this evening, and all will be forgotten, and I will be to thee a miserable undone woman again; I can't resist you, for you get pale with passion and love, and I am ruined by you then. Oh! if I had been your wife; but no, like Hinda, in the Fire Worshippers, my love is shame.

Oh God! what is my future? – a dark blank – a wretched woman. This is the stake I played for and lost. If we talk this over, will you see this as I do; and oh! think of my future fate – Yours ever, LOVE." [Envelope addressed, "For you, My Darling."]

Mr Billing: Well, what do you think of that?

Witness: It is quite a love letter. Mrs Hawker said she found it in her husband's pocket book, but she did not tell him directly. I wrote this letter to Mrs Hawker:-

"Saturday morn. – Dear Mrs Hawker, – I am sorry to hear you are poorly – so am I too. As my unfortunate letter was never dictated to be seen by you or yours, I think you told me yesterday you would feel satisfied if I would prove to you the party that letter was intended for. It is a hard trial to my feelings to show up an admirer, but, if you solemnly swear that you won't divulge his name to mortal, and, further, place in my hands my letter, I will.

It is a passed circumstance now between us, and as he is a single man, and one I liked I will name him to you, but on no other terms. My letter in your possession was written to him two months ago. Yours very sincerely, MOLESWORTH." [Envelope ad-dressed, "Mrs Hawker."]

Mr Billing: Now tell me why you sent that letter.

Witness: I sent it under peculiar circumstances. Mrs Hawker found the letter in her husband's pocket-book, and annoyed me in every way. She sent for me at about two o'clock in the day, when Mrs Wills and Mr Hawker were there. She read the letter, and I said Mr Hawker must have taken it from my portfolio. He looked up and said, "The very thing I told my wife two hours ago."

Mr Billing: That is your explanation of the two letters.

Witness: The letter is in my handwriting, but I never wrote it. It is a copy of a letter found in my apartments, and if a man puts it in his pocket-book for several months, how am I to know anything about it? I found it on the floor of the drawing room after a party.

Mr Billing: What did you take a copy of it for?

Witness: Because I could hardly read the original, it was so crumpled up.

Mr Billing: But you kept the words on the envelope, "For you, my darling?"

Witness: Yes.

Mr Billing: What did you do with the original?

Witness: It was a very crumpled piece of paper, and I threw it into the fire after I had read it.

Mr Billing: But what was your object in preferring a copy of this letter to the original?

Witness: Because I could hardly read the original, and I thought the letter was a very unique one. I wanted occasionally to read it over when looking through my portfolio.

Mrs Wills was not examined before the commission.

At this stage, the cross-examination of the petitioner was adjourned until the following morning, at ten o'clock.

Molesworth (wife) v. Molesworth

DIVORCE COURT

Friday 18 November, 1864
(Before the Chief Justice, and a Special Jury of Twelve)

MOLESWORTH (WIFE) v. MOLESWORTH

Extract from *The Age*, Saturday, 19th November, 1864

> Petition for judicial separation. This case, partly heard yesterday, was resumed this morning, the cross-examination of the petitioner, Mrs Molesworth, being proceeded with. Mr Dawson and Mr Wood for the petitioner; Mr Billing and Mr Michie for the respondent.

Mr Billing read the following letter:-

"Tuesday morning, the 18th (?June 1861). - Dear Mrs Hawker, - I did not answer your last letter, as it was an uncalled for one. My object in now writing to you is this – to ask you to return my letters. They can be of no use to you, and under these circumstances, I don't see what good you can derive from holding them in your keeping. On the first day I visited you on your return home, I told you that letter was mine. We used to be friends. I don't now dwell on this. I merely ask, have I deserved all the unkindness I have met at your hands in consequence of writing a letter to a young man?"

Witness: The letter is in my handwriting. I gave an explanation of it yesterday. I reminded you yesterday that the letter, without date or signature, was made use of by Mrs Hawker as a cause of jealousy between me and my husband. Under these circumstances I sent an evasive letter about a young man, in order to get possession of the letter, and it shows what a base woman Mrs Hawker was to associate her husband's name, who is now dead, with mine. There are many Toms in the world. There are tom tits -

The Chief Justice (interposing): Attend to me, Mrs Molesworth. You are a witness, and, if you were not a party to this cause as well as a witness, I should adopt a different course with you, but I do beg of you not to use such expressions as "tom tits."

Witness: But Mr Billing deserved it.

The Chief Justice: It does not matter whether he deserves it or not. You are not to make use of such expressions here.

Witness: I am to sit down and say nothing?

The Chief Justice: No; but you are to answer the questions.

Mr Dawson remarked that the witness had been provoked by the interruptions which Mr Billing had made.

\Mr Billing appealed to the court if he had not conducted the examination in a fair spirit.

The cross-examination proceeded.

Mr Billing: You said yesterday that the intimacy between your husband and you took place between the 28th and 29th of September.

Witness: I did not say any particular day. It was some time in 1855, during the time I was stopping at Mrs Poole's, at Prahran. There has been no intimacy between us since.

Mr Billing: Do you remember, in the year 1861, having a photograph taken?

Witness: I cannot say whether I did in 1861 or not, I had so many likenesses taken. I daresay I have had them taken in various years. (Several photographs of the witness were put in and recognised by her.

Several letters were also handed to her, some of which she denied having written. None of them were read in court.)

Mr Billing: You saw Mrs Penfold in the autumn of 1862.

Witness: Yes; in England.

Mr Billing: Did you give her any address to write to you?

Witness: Yes; Mrs Tolley, at Twickenham, Holly House. I told her to write to me, under cover, to Mrs Smyth, an acquaintance of mine staying at Tolley's.

Mr Billing: Who was Mrs Smyth?

Witness: She was the wife of a captain in the merchant service?

Mr Billing: Had the captain any residence in England?

Witness: No; no regular residence. Mrs Smyth had no settled residence. She generally lived in Liverpool, but not constantly; sometimes she resided in Cork. I know she resided there, because I have visited her there. Her address was on the parade. She had lodgings there.

Mr Billing: Did you give Mrs Penfold any other address? Did you ever tell her to write to you at Miss Hutt's?

Witness: Yes; her residence was on the green at Richmond; No. 1, I think. I once resided at No. 1 Alva Cottages, Twickenham. Mrs Pitman resided there. I never remember mentioning to Mrs Penfold the name of Mrs Evans. I never heard her name. I swear most solemnly I never knew a person of that name. I never met Mrs Haling. I never resided at Mrs Tolley's. I intended to, but never did. I never said I resided there, but I said I intended to do so.

Mr Billing: Did you tell Mrs Penfold that you had been residing at Richmond and Twickenham?

Witness: I told Mrs Penfold that I was living at Mrs Tolley's, because I thought she would consider it very queer if I lived at any other place. I did not tell Mrs Penfold that I was living at Miss Hutt's. I told her to direct her letters to Miss Hutt's under cover to Mrs Smyth.

Mr Billing: Do you say you did not know a person of the name of Sophia Evans?

Witness: How could I when I never saw her? I never heard her name except from you.

Mr Billing: In the month of November, 1862, were you confined of a child?

Witness: I distinctly deny it.

Mr Billing: Or October?

Witness: Or October.

Mr Billing: Or at any time in the latter end of 1862 - in October or November?

Witness: What! two children in two months! (Laughter.) No, I did not. (The question was repeated several times, and on each occasion replied to in the negative).

Mr Billing: In company with Mrs Tolley, did you ever pass under the name of Mrs Smyth, of Twickenham or Richmond?

Witness: No. I never gave the name of Mrs Smyth to any person.

Mr Billing: Did you ever apply to anyone to suckle a child for you?

Witness: How could I when I never had one.

Mr Billing: But I ask the question, did you?

Witness: No.

Mr Billing: Did you not apply to some one to suckle a child in the month of September, 1862?

Witness: No.

Mr Billing: What time was it that you went to Mrs Tolley's house?

Witness: I never went at all. I never visited there.

Mr Billing: Did you ever say to Mrs Tolley that your name was Smyth, and that you were a cousin of Mrs Molesworth's?

Witness: How could I say that when I am here as Mrs Molesworth.

Mr Billing: Or that you were the wife of Capt. Smyth of the merchant service - did you say that?

Witness: No; I swear it. I never said anything to Mr or Mrs Tolley. I did not know them. I never left any jewellery, or sent it to Tolley's house.

Mr Billing: Did you ever send or leave any jewellery for Mrs Haling?

Witness: I don't know Mrs Haling, so I could not. I never slept at Miss Hutt's; but I have been in the house. I visited Mrs Smyth there, either in October, November or December, and one day I sent there to get some letters of mine. I never saw a person of the name of Rosina Ann Haling. I never knew a medical man named Hassell at Richmond. You see that if I have had no other blessings, I have had good health. It has not cost me five pounds for medicine during the last six years. No medical man attended me, because I was not sick, and did not require one. I had not enough money to pay for one, and I don't think any medical man would have attended me unless I paid him, except Dr. Patterson, who has been very kind to me, and goes upon tick. (Laughter.) I have been a tenant of Tolley's. I rented a house from him on the Yarra. I know the name of it. It was Elmsbank cottage, Nelson street.

Mr Billing: Where were you in the latter end of 1862?

Witness: I was in the body, I suppose.

Mr Billing: Where did you reside?

Witness: Let me see? I went to Liverpool first, and then I went to Dublin. Then I went to Cork, where I was for a few days; and then I went to Queenstown. I think I was in Queenstown at the time you speak of.

I lived there a very short time - a fortnight or three weeks. I was there in the month of September. I went afterwards to Plymouth. I was not there long, because I did not know many persons there. I went also to Teignmouth, and was there a month or five weeks; and on leaving there, I went to London, through Bristol, by the train. I remained in London until, I think, February. I resided on the Strand, but not all the time. I resided in different parts - once in Norfolk street, Strand, No. 9, living with a Mrs Pearce, whom I had known some years before. I was there a couple of months. I was there in October and November, and a part of December, because it was a cheap sort of place and I had no money to spare. When I left there I went to live near the Victoria Railway Station - just for the change. Anything for a change, you know, Mr Billing. Only remained there a short time, because they were more expensive lodgings than the others.

After that I went very suddenly to Queenstown. I think it was in February, 1863. I went back again to Cork for a few days, and from Cork I went again to Queenstown and down to Liverpool from Plymouth, and by train to London. I embarked from Liverpool. I have been once at Kinsale, but not latterly. My sister, Mrs Penfold, did not live there, but she used to visit the place. I met Mrs Smyth five years ago. I have told you I met her during the year 1862. I never met her out here.

I did not meet her on shipboard on my way to England. She was not a fellow passenger of mine.

Mr Billing: Is this letter in your handwriting?

Witness: Yes; it is my handwriting.

The letter was as follows:-

"14th May, 1864. - Robert, - It has come to my knowledge you suspect me of being the mother of a child during my last visit to England. It is not so. On leaving here, Mr Tolley, foreman of Mrs Finlay's, gave me his father's card, and asked me to see his friends, as I then rented a house from him in South Yarra. I had intended doing so, but a friend of mine, a shipmate, going to London, I forwarded Mr Tolley's card to her; and, on hearing from her that the place would not suit me, I did not go. She went; and, as I lent her several of my clothes, hence the misapprehension. Her husband is a sea captain, now in China. You can act as you please as to the mistaken identity. I simply tell you the facts. I never visited these people, as I heard their habits would not suit me.

I am extremely sorry you have lost such a sum of money in the last action. We have been a truly unfortunate couple. Rest assured it is not my wish to injure you. My letters, both from Ireland and London, if you refer to them, will show you this. I don't point out to you what you are to do, I simply give an explanation; act for yourself. If I have been, through fate, the unwilling tool of others, I shall right it through life. My present existence is a miserable one. I hope all alimony will be handed to myself. I often want a shilling. This is not your fault, as I might live on the income settled. -Your unfortunate wife, H.M."

Mr Billing: Who did you allude to in that letter?

Witness: I alluded to Mrs Smyth.

Mr Billing: Then how do you explain your former statement that Mrs Smyth had not been a shipmate?

Witness: I distinctly told you that I did not know Mrs Smyth had been a shipmate, but she told me she had made a voyage with me; and I have made voyages with so many people that I did not recollect. I wish you had been a shipmate with me - we could have had something more than cold water together. (Laughter.)

The following letter was then handed to the witness, who admitted having written it:-"3 Wilmot terrace, Queenstown, Ireland. My dear sir, - I have just received your letter, and am obliged for yours and Mrs Tolley's kindness. A cousin of mine, Mrs Smyth, will be with you tomorrow, being Wednesday, the 17th.

You will kindly show her some lodgings that will suit us, and I will join her in a fortnight, as business detains me here for that time. Will you also take her in for a night, in compliment to me? She also knew your family in Melbourne, and will tell you all about them, as she was a fellow voyager with myself. Yours, most obliged, HENRIETTA MOLESWORTH.

I cannot fix the hour for her arrival, but think it will be about seven o'clock. G. Tolley, Esq., Little Holly House, Twickenham, near London."

Numerous other letters were handed in, but were not read.

Witness: When I wrote my letters I generally wished Mrs Penfold to look over them. Mr Molesworth wrote to me and told me that every letter I wrote he put on a file, and my answer was that every letter of his to me I read at arm's length with the tongs, and as soon as I had read them threw them into the fire.

It then occurred to me that I should keep his letters, and I afterwards kept them all, and put them at the bottom of a drawer. I sent all my letters to Mrs Penfold and my mother to see that I did not commit myself, for I very often write letters without ever reading them over.

The cross-examination of the petitioner then closed.

Mr Dawson, in re-examination, asked the witness if she was travelling with Mrs Smyth about autumn, 1862.

Witness: I don't remember.

Mr Dawson: Were you intimate with her?

Witness: I was very intimate. If we had not been intimate we should never have settled to go into lodgings together.

Mr Dawson: What kind of a person was she?

Witness: A very large and stout woman; fat, and with fair hair and brownish eyes.

Mr Dawson: Did she ever get anything from you?

Witness: I made her a present of two articles of dress - a bonnet and a black dress, for I was never stingy. She had a box of mine, and sometimes she took some of my clothes to wear, but not very often.

This closed the examination of the petitioner.

Richard Davies Ireland, examined by Mr Wood, said: I am a member of the Irish bar and of the bar of this colony.

I arrived in this colony in January, 1853, with my family. Mr Molesworth and his family did not arrive at that time, but shortly afterwards. I was not acquainted with them in Ireland, but made their acquaintance immediately after their arrival. I met Mr Molesworth as a brother barrister. They came to live at St. Kilda, and, from their proximity, and from belonging to the same profession, we became intimate.

We frequently visited each other, as did the ladies of the two families. I dined frequently with Mr Molesworth, and he was often at my house. I remember going on circuit to Castlemaine. I was in the dressing room of the bar. Mr Molesworth, who was then Solicitor-General, came there and asked me if I was going to Castlemaine. I said, "Yes; I have got briefs there." He asked me if I would join him in taking a carriage, as he intended to take his wife, nurse and child to Castlemaine with him. There was a coolness between my wife and Mrs Molesworth at this time, and I did not at once accept the offer. We found that it would cost some extraordinary price, something like ȷ30 or ȷ40, to get a private conveyance, and next morning I said I would prefer going in Cobb's coach. We all went in the coach the next morning.

I went in a separate coach as far as Taradale, when some passengers got out of the coach, and I joined the rest of the party. We proceeded on to Castlemaine, and stopped at the hotel where the coach pulled up. I got out, and was about to proceed to the Castlemaine Hotel, where I was in the habit of staying. In fact, I had ordered rooms some time previously; but Mr Molesworth insisted upon my going to the same hotel, which I reluctantly did, as I was cautioned before leaving town, not to go with them, and was aware of his peculiar temper. I did not want to go, but, being two barristers on circuit, I did not like to refuse. (The witness described the position of the rooms occupied by the party, as stated by the petitioner the previous day, and remarked that at the time he thought it a rather peculiar arrangement.) We had meals together, and frequently walked out together. The circuit lasted, I fancy, some days.

Mr Molesworth, as Solicitor-General, was prosecuting, and there were several civil actions, and I was in them all. He and Mrs Molesworth and I sometimes walked out together in the bush, where the Mechanics' Institute now stands. I remember there was a ball to take place, and the night before we were all sitting together.

Mrs Molesworth had spoken about it several times, and said she did not wish to go, but about twenty minutes to eleven, when I was about to go to bed, she suddenly said, "I will go to the ball." Mr Molesworth seemed to be very dissatisfied with this proposal, and it was a rainy kind of night. She said, "I am determined to go tonight." She meant to get a dress for the ball.

She said, "I must get a skirt; the brother of my dressmaker in Melbourne is living here, and I will go." I said the place would be closed at that time of night. When she turned round to me and said, "what is that to you?" Mr Molesworth said, "let Ireland take you." I said, "come along with your wife;" but he said he would not take her. She put on her bonnet and shawl, and said to me, "will you refuse me?" I did not like to refuse her, and went. We travelled all over the place, and I knocked up the man by throwing a stone at the door, and we went in to get the dress. She and I came back about eleven o'clock, and found Mr Molesworth sitting there. I went to bed immediately. The next night Mrs Molesworth asked me to go to the ball, but I declined to go, and her husband went with her. The next day we all walked about together, and, as we were going away in the morning, she wanted to ask a gentleman, a friend of hers, to dinner, but Mr Molesworth would not agree to it. When we were going to dinner, at about a quarter to six o'clock, we resolved to invite him, and a letter was written to ask him. The dinner was put back, and we waited until a late hour - between seven and eight o'clock - but the gentleman did not make his appearance. There was a jug of beer on the table, and Mrs Molesworth took some. I was going to take some, when Mr Molesworth said, "This is the last day we are going to be here; let us have some champagne." I said, "With all my heart;" and champagne was brought up. We then had dinner, and after dinner we had some port wine. I took very little of it - it was very bad. (Laughter.) I said, "I will have a glass of punch;" and he said, "So, will I." We had a couple of glasses of punch together. There was some champagne in a bottle on the table, and he took a pull at it - on the top of the punch. (Laughter.) About nine o'clock in walked the gentleman who had been invited. He apologised for being late, and Mr Molesworth asked him to sit down, and there was another supply of punch, but Mr Molesworth drank wine then. We sat down quietly for some time, when all at once he said to the gentleman, "You are a most unreasonable person to stay here to this time of night."

Mrs Molesworth rose and got into a towering passion, and said, "you are very wrong to be rude to my friend." The gentleman then bowed himself out, and Mr Molesworth proceeded to bed, she scolding him. I was going too, when she said, "Don't go; the nurse has gone to the circus, and she will be in about ten minutes. Wait till then."

I said, "I was going down stairs to smoke, and I don't like to smoke in the room where you are."

She said she liked it, and I then said if I smoked at all I would smoke up the chimney.

I smoked in this way, sending the smoke up the chimney. Suddenly I heard some rubbing on the wall. I said, "What's that?" and she said, "I am afraid Robert has fallen out of bed." (Laughter.) I said, "You had better go and see." She accordingly went, and said he was just jumping into bed when she went in. We thought this strange, but we soon changed the subject, and talked about my brother-in-law, Dr. Carr, and what he had said to Dr. O'Sullivan about her. As I was sitting in this position Mr Molesworth opened his door and rushed in in a long night dress, crying out, "My wife, my wife, you have seduced my wife;" and running to the side board said, "Can I get a knife?" I thought he was mad, his conduct and manner was so extraordinary.

He tried to spit in my face, but was so feeble and in such a state that he could not.

I pushed him down on to the sofa, and said, "For God's sake, Molesworth, be quiet; the house is full of people." He, however, called out louder "Murder," and, as I heard the doors of the rooms opening in all directions I slipped down stairs. I called from the street to Mrs Molesworth for my hat, and she gave it to me, and I then walked away to put an end to the affair.

Mr Wood: You had been drinking something that night?

Witness: Certainly; I had been drinking to some extent.

Mr Wood: You were smoking too; taking a puff, and drinking at intervals?

Witness: That's it. I was as cool as I am now. I saw no more of them that night. We had no conversation about crim. con. at all. The next morning I was in the verandah, and saw Mr Molesworth. I said, "You behaved, sir, in a manner to me that I shall not allow to pass; and don't leave your house tomorrow till nine o'clock, as it is my intention to send a friend to your house." We went down in the same coach, but not together. I think I rode outside and the others inside. I came home, and next morning there was a paragraph in one of the papers about a squabble between two eminent barristers about a lady at Castlemaine. I went to look for my friend, and desired him to go to Mr Molesworth, and get him to name one.

My friend went - I saw him go between seven and eight o'clock in the morning, but Mr Molesworth had left his home. I came into Melbourne, and; as soon as I got to my chambers, I found that Mr Molesworth had been there shortly before ten o'clock, and had left his card, with a message that he would call again at about one o'clock. I went out and returned shortly, and he came in while I was there. He said, "Ireland, I have come to say how I regret what occurred at Castlemaine. I was the worse of drink, I hope you will think nothing more of it. I thought I heard a conversation, but I have spoken to Mrs Molesworth about the affair, and I am in error." I said, "I am sorry for her," or something of that sort. We shook hands and he went away.

Mr Wood: Did you, in the interval, send to Mrs Molesworth?

Witness: No; I think she sent for me, but I would not see her. On Sunday, Mrs Ireland and my sister-in-law avoided Mrs Molesworth - did not walk with her as usual; but immediately after church, Mr Molesworth followed me to my house and came in and sat in the parlour, in the presence of my wife, and said, "Ireland, I want you to come and dine with me." I looked at my wife and she did not seem to like the idea, nor I either, so I said, "When?" He named a day, and I made an excuse, and he named another. I went then and met a large party, and talked with Mrs Molesworth as usual, and as if nothing had appeared in the paper at all.

Mr Wood: Were your families on the same terms as before?

Witness: No; my wife was not asked. The ladies of the family were not on the same terms as before, but Mrs Molesworth came to the house and I tried to make it up as well as possible. The next feature in the case was this: I was going one evening to take my sister-in-law home, and, seeing a light in Mr Molesworth's window, I thought it a convenient time to go and see him. Mr Molesworth said, "Come in Ireland, come in." There was a bottle of claret on the table, but I said I was in a hurry. He said, "You must take a glass of wine." I did take a glass. It was then getting on for ten o'clock, and I said, "I must be off." Mrs Molesworth said, "Robert, where is the cheque you gave me this morning, for the child's schooling?" He said, "I don't know where it is." She said, I would accompany her to take it. He seemed annoyed at this, and I said, "Mrs Molesworth, do you know that it is after ten o'clock? She said, "I have got a clock and a watch in the house too." I said, "Molesworth, come down," but he would not.

I said to Mrs Molesworth, "You are not on terms with my sister-in-law, and how can I take home two ladies who will not speak to each other?"

I then said to Mr Molesworth, "Come on," and he went out to get his hat, dashing out of the door. As soon as he had gone Mrs Molesworth came across to me, and, after my experience at Castlemaine, I told her to stop where she was. She said, "How dare you join with him against me. I won't be tyrannised over by any man, and would rather beg my bread than submit to it. You are the last man that should assist him, for you ruined me at Castlemaine when you got my name in the papers."

I begged her to sit down, and just as she was doing so, he came in at the door, with his hat and gloves on. I said, "I am glad you are going," and we then walked out. I took care to put him in the middle, and I walked outside. When I got a few yards from the gate I said, "I will be off now. They will think me a very queer man if I knock them up at this hour of the night." "So you are," he said, and suddenly I found his hand on my throat. I pushed him from me, and said, "Don't attempt to repeat the Castlemaine business with me." He made a kick at me, and then struck at me. I was so exasperated that, as a precaution, I threw away a loaded whip which I had in my hand, and I pummelled his head for ten minutes, and kicked his shoes off and rolled him in the mud.

Thinking I saw a policeman coming up I went away. Next morning, I was standing at the bar moving a motion, when Mr Molesworth came in with a handkerchief tied round his face, which was in a perfect jelly.

He went into the room behind, and the bar went into see him. I went on with my business. I had not met with a scratch or a hurt of any description.

Next morning Mrs Molesworth was at my house crying, and in an awful state of excitement, saying her husband wanted me to go there.

I refused to go there, and said I would have nothing more to do with them, as I was sick of it. However, she came one night, and was in a state of intense excitement, and called for wine, which I would not allow to be brought in, as I could see she had taken some already. I had never observed her in a similar condition before. She implored me to go down to the house, but I said I would have nothing more to do with him. She pressed me very much, and I said if he wanted me he must come up to me. She went away and he came in about fifteen minutes. I said, "Well, what in God's name do you want?"

"Well," he said, "you know the time I went out for my hat I knelt at the keyhole and listened, and heard the expression, "You ruined me."

"Well," I said, "It is not very easy to remember a conversation of the kind, but, as far as I can remember, all she said was, that I had ruined her name about the Castlemaine affair." I said I would do anything he liked to satisfy him, and submit to any inquiry.

He said, "I must go home first". I said something sharp, and he went away. That was the last time I met him. After this occurrence Mrs Molesworth was constantly coming to my house, but Mrs Ireland would not allow her to come inside. She used to send her servants with messages and letters, and I have frequently walked with her to my gate, and to her house, Mr Molesworth being there all the time.

On one occasion she told me she was going down to Johnson's to get some poison to put an end to herself, which terrified me out of my wits. She said, "I have been blasted in the public papers, and you are the only person that knows I am innocent." She was a very peculiar, hasty, and good-natured woman, and she was always coming to tell me what she said, and what her husband said to her. Messages and letters were frequently brought to me and all the members of my family knew it.

I went down there repeatedly, and she came to our house as often; and, rather than turn a lady away from the doors, I went down to speak to her.

On one of these occasions, she said, "Well, do you know, I think I will give Robert something to think of. He has driven me to madness, and I will make up a tale."

Mr Michie here interrupted the witness, and suggested that the statement he was making could not be considered evidence.

Mr Dawson submitted that Mr Ireland was entitled to explain any of his interviews with the petitioner.

Ultimately Mr Michie waived the objection.

Re-examination continued:

One evening when I was at dinner, Mrs Molesworth came, and I went to see her at the gate. I said, "I hope Mr Molesworth and you have made all matters right between you." She said "I have given him something to think about. I told him I committed adultery." I said, "With whom?" She said, "With you."

I said, "Thank you, you have given me a nice return for all I have passed through," and I walked away.

When I had gone a few steps, she called out, "But I told him immediately afterwards that it was all a lie, and he did not believe a word of it." I told my family about it immediately afterwards. I never heard until yesterday what it was that I was accused of, and I could never, during the last nine years, ascertain anything about it.

Mr Wood: Do you remember getting a letter from Mrs Molesworth after this, and sending a reply.

Witness: One night the woman who was in the habit of bringing messages came up with a note, and I remarked something strange in her manner. The letter was from Mrs Molesworth, but I instantly knew, from its style, that she had never written it wittingly. When I looked at the window she turned away and behaved very suspiciously. I went away but immediately afterwards she turned round and said Mrs Molesworth wanted an answer in writing. I then either wrote or told her that I would meet Mrs Molesworth in the evening at half past six. When I went out I took a whip, thinking that I would find Mr Molesworth watching for me.

If I had I would have made him go home very quickly. I was sure the letter was not written by Mrs Molesworth voluntarily, and I was perfectly well aware that a trap had been laid for me.

Mr Wood: I have one other question. I won't ask you if you ever committed adultery with Mrs Molesworth, but have you ever been guilty of any impropriety with her?

Witness: Never in my life of any character or description whatever. I swear it, and defy any man to come up and prove it.

Cross-examined by Mr Michie: I went out to keep the appointment the same evening I received the note.

Mr Michie: I think if you read over the note you will see that the proposed assignation is for "tomorrow".

Witness: (after reading the note) : Yes: I must have been in error about that.

Mr Michie: Then you might have other errors in the course of your evidence?

Witness: I might.

Mr Michie: It was after careful reflection and deliberation that you went out to keep this appointment under the trees?

Witness: Well, I suppose so. I cannot remember. I did go out.

There was a big tree before his (the respondent's) house, and I expected to find him there watching for me. I went out to see if I was right in my conclusion that he was watching for me. I did not see Mrs

Molesworth, and I felt satisfied she was under his influence, and had been made use of to trap me.

Mr Michie: How long were you out altogether?

Witness: A very short time. The time I took to go and return and a few minutes beside. It was more than ten minutes. I don't know if it was more than half an hour.

Mr Michie: Did Mrs Molesworth give you any explanation of the matter the next morning?

Witness: I don't think I saw her the next morning.

Mr Michie: Why did you not treat all the notes you received from Mrs Molesworth as coming from an idle woman?

Witness: Because this related to a quarrel between her husband and me.

Mr Michie: What do you call the quarrel?

Witness: The Castlemaine transaction.

Mr Michie: The notes did not all refer to this quarrel at Castlemaine?

Witness: They had to do with subsequent quarrels.

Mr Michie: It was then a sort of chronic quarrel?

Witness: You have just described it. They led a cat and dog life all the time I knew them.

Mr Michie: You were like the chorus in the Greek tragedy, always coming in at the wrong time? (Laughter.)

Mr Ireland: Not exactly that.

Mr Michie: Over what period did the correspondence extend?

Witness: I cannot tell.

Mr Michie: Months or years?

Witness: Months, I believe. I cannot tell the exact time.

Mr Michie: Did you ever inquire if the message, taken by Mr Gardner, had been delivered or not?

Witness: He never told me that he had delivered it. The letter produced is in my handwriting.

Mr Michie: And you say that you did not impute anything to Mr Molesworth, for not calling upon you till one o'clock, in consequence of the message he had received from you?

Witness: No; because I knew he did not get it.

Mr Michie: And yet you send the following letter:-

"Sir, - Nothing can be further from my mind than the idea of treating your dastardly, unprovoked inhospitable assault upon me last night otherwise than I should deal with the act of an assassin. I, upon one occasion, recognised your position as that of a gentleman, by sending you a message.

The result in that case was, as I have no doubt it would be in this, were I to adopt a similar course, an apology.

You must distinctly know that I am about to proceed to Melbourne, for the purpose of consulting as to what legal or other steps I ought to take, and should not feel it necessary to consider my course for a moment were it not for the respect and sympathy which I entertain towards your unfortunate wife.

You have acted like a ruffian, and I shall deal with you, and have dealt with you, as such. - Your obedient servant, R.D.I."

Witness: I knew he did not get the message, because he left the house two hours before it was delivered. I referred to the result of my sending the message.

Mr Michie: Is this note in your handwriting (handing up a letter)?

Witness: It is.

The letter was as follows:-

"13th August, 1855. - Sir, - My last letter was written to you under an impression that you had received a message from me, through Lieut. Gardner, which message I felt justified in sending owing to your unaccountable conduct at Castlemaine. Since then I have learned that the message did not reach you, and I therefore have to withdraw the expressions contained in it in reference thereto, which I can easily conceive, were most offensive.

I take this opportunity to withdraw anything offensive in my note, although I most emphatically say that nothing can justify your former conduct."

Witness: When I found he had not got the message I, of course, at once wrote an apology. I cannot say how long Mrs Molesworth and I were in conversation on the occasion at Castlemaine. There was no long discussion about a crim. con. case. Nothing about it was mentioned.

Mr Michie: If Mrs Molesworth has said that such a conversation did occur, she must be in error?

Witness: Yes.

Mr Michie: Was nothing said about a lady going away from her husband?

Witness: That might have occurred.

Mr Michie: Does not that savor of crim. con.?

Witness: We certainly talked about that, but not about any crim. con. case.

Mr Michie: Do you remember a letter from Mr Molesworth, specifying a charge of improper intimacy and daring you to bring an action?

Witness: He wanted me to bring an action against him for libel, in order to vindicate his wife. Mr O'Farrell, his solicitor, called at my chambers and brought me a letter, but I declined to receive it, as I did not want to have his abuse.

Mr O'Farrell stated the purport of the proposal contained in the letter, which was that Mr Molesworth should go round and circulate amongst a number of mutual friends certain statements relative to my conduct, and I was to bring an action for slander and thus enable him to vindicate himself. I said, "What an ass he must be. He is a confounded fool." I did not want to be blackguarded by him, and then to get no redress myself. I think I wrote him a letter, but I did not read any portion of his to me. I tore it up.

The following was the letter referred to, which the witness persisted in stating had been written in consequence of Mr O'Farrell's statements, and not in reply to any letter:-

"34 Temple Court. - Sir, - I am in receipt of your letter of the 31st ult., in reply to which I have only to reassert my denial of the charges contained in it, and to decline the proposal made by you. - I am, &c, R.D.I. - 3rd September, 1855."

The court here adjourned for half an hour. On resuming -

Mr Dawson stated that he was prepared to make an offer of compromise, rather than let the case go further.

Mr Michie said he must decline to entertain a proposal made at such an extraordinary time.

The case for the petitioner closed with the evidence of the following witness:-

James Ennis, a coachman formerly in the service of the respondent, examined by Mr Wood, deposed: I have seen Mr Ireland frequently at Mr Molesworth's house. He frequently walked with Mrs Molesworth. I never observed any misconduct between them. I remember when Mrs Molesworth returned the second time from England, the respondent told me to lock the gates, as Mrs Molesworth had returned, and I was to take any message that might come over the gates.

The respondent told me to go for a constable to take Mrs Molesworth in charge.

Mr Michie then addressed the jury on behalf of the respondent, remarking that it would have given him great satisfaction to have been able with propriety to accept the suggestion which had been made by his learned friend, but he confessed it seemed such an extraordinary one, coming as it did after his client had been assailed for two days in such terms, that it could not possibly be entertained.

He made every allowance for the natural ardour of learned gentlemen for their clients, but he thought his learned friend would excuse him for saying that he had been scarcely justified, upon the authority of mere statements, in making use of the terms he had thought proper to use. He was not going to retort. He should rely upon the facts, and he thought, they would find, before the case was concluded, that these facts spoke more strongly than any counsel.

After remarking upon the demeanour of the petitioner in the witness-box, which he considered, to say the least of it, hardly becoming for any one in her position, he explained the various issues to the jury, and remarked that they would have to find upon each of them in accordance with the evidence.

Excepting little differences of temper, and occasional violence, he could not see that there had been any cruelty on the part of the respondent.

The petitioner and Mr Ireland had both given their version of the intimacy which was alleged to have subsisted between them, and it would now be for the other side of the question to be heard, and Mrs Molesworth would be distinctly contradicted by her husband as to the statement she made with reference to a guilty connection with Mr Ireland. If there was any doubt, he asked them to give her the benefit of it; but, if they had no doubt, then their duty would be to pronounce their verdict upon the issue before them.

Mr Molesworth did not deny having committed an assault upon his wife, but the affair had been greatly exaggerated, and, if the act could not be excused, there were many circumstances which would palliate it. He next referred to the contradictory statements which had been made by the petitioner, with reference to the letter commencing "My darling," and remarked that he failed to see how she could reconcile the two explanations with reference to it.

The evidence he was prepared to submit would prove that Mrs Molesworth had resided in England for some time under the name of Mrs Smyth, and that, while sheltered by this concealment, she had given birth to a child. He would not dwell any longer upon the case, but would at once call his evidence.

The evidence taken before the commission which sat in England was put in; but a portion only, and that not material, had been read, when the court rose.

Molesworth (wife) v. Molesworth

DIVORCE COURT

(Before the Chief Justice, and a Special Jury of Twelve)

MOLESWORTH (WIFE) v. MOLESWORTH
Saturday 19 November, 1864
Extract from *The Age*, Monday, 21st November, 1864

Mr Dawson and Mr Wood for the plaintiff; and Mr Billing and Mr Michie, Q.C., for the respondent.

This suit, a petition for judicial separation, was proceeded with.

The reading of the evidence taken before the commission in England, which had been commenced the previous day, was now concluded. The following is the substance of the testimony:-

John Gaisford, a photographer, of 82 George street, Plymouth, said that he carried on business at that place in 1861. Mrs Molesworth several times came to his establishment in June, July or August to be photographed. (Three photographs were returned in the commission which Mrs Molesworth, on Friday, admitted were likenesses of her. Some objection was made to their being taken as evidence, but His Honour decided to admit them; taking a note of the objection. The photographs were marked P1, P2 and P3.)

The witness went on to say that Mrs Molesworth told him that she was living at 3 Wyndham place, Plymouth. He called upon her and saw her there, when he delivered the portraits. She came to his studio once with a lady aged about sixteen or seventeen, who, she said, was Miss Georgina or Josephine Molesworth. She said the lady was the daughter of Judge Molesworth, of Melbourne. He saw Miss Molesworth at Wyndham place. He knew a Mrs Penfold, wife of Mr George Penfold, a paymaster in the Royal Navy.

Cross examined; he could give no date when he took photograph P3. He only took one copy. He made no entry of the party's name. The copy he produced was a duplicate taken on the preceding week. He had not endorsed the name of the party on the plate, but he entered her name in a book, "Mrs Molesworth, 6th August, 1861, £2 15s 6d."

Jane Penfold of No. 3 Chelsea road, Southsea, Hants, deposed that she was the widow of the late George Penfold, a paymaster in the Royal Navy. Her father was the Rev. Joseph Johnson of Glin, in the county of Limerick. One of her sisters died about ten years ago; the other, Henrietta, was the wife of Robert

Molesworth. Her mother married one Samuel Harding after her father's death. Her sister in 1860 lived at Plymouth, at No. 8 Wyndham place, with her daughter Elizabeth Josephine. Portrait No. 1 was the likeness of her sister, and also No. 2 and No. 3, though the latter was not so like as the others. In August, 1862, witness was residing at Vilmount Terrace, Queenstown.

Her sister visited her there, and when she departed in the autumn, her address was Mrs Smyth, Mr Tolley's, Little Holly House, Twickenham, Middlesex. Used to write to her sister under that cover, and subsequently used to write to her under the cover of Miss Hutts, The Green, Richmond. By writing "under cover" meant that she put an envelope inside an envelope; but she did not always do this. The replies she received were sometimes dated London, and sometimes not dated at all. She afterwards addressed her at Mrs Pittman's, No. 1 Alver Cottages, Twickenham Common.

Did not think her sister was in the family way when she went to England, and never heard of her being ill at Richmond.

Remembered Mrs Molesworth telling her about a Mrs Evans in 1863, but could not swear that the conversation had reference to a child. Did not remember having written to Mrs Evans about Mrs Smyth's child, but did write to a Mrs Hailing about Mrs Smyth. Would not swear that letter No. 7 was not in her writing; it certainly was a very good imitation. Mrs Molesworth came to see her again in March, 1863, witness having been very ill just before. She came unexpectedly in consequence of witness being ill.

Mrs Penfold's examination proceeded:-

Q. Have you any cousin of the name of Smyth? .

A. Not that I remember

Q. Who is the Mrs Smyth to whom you refer?

A. Pray spare me.

Q. Before your sister left England did you see a child?

A. No

Q. Did she speak to you of a child?

A. You must spare me. You must excuse my answering that question.

Q. Did she speak to you of one?

A. I would rather not answer that question.

Q. Did not your sister tell you that she had been living at Richmond and Twickenham?

A. No; not directly.

Q. What do you mean by not directly?

A. She did not tell me.

Q. Did you know that she had been living there?

A. Yes; she told me so.

Q. Did she mention the names of the persons she had been living with?

A. Yes.

Q. Who were the persons she mentioned?

A. Mrs Tolley and Miss Hutt.

Q. Did your sister mention to you a child of the name of George Charles Vernon Smyth?

A. You must excuse my answering the question.

Cross-examined: she could not remember if when she wrote to her sister in the name of Mrs Smyth, she directed the inner envelope.

Sophia Evans, the wife of Joseph Evans, a labourer, residing at 2 Delhi Cottages, Twickenham, deposed that she was confined of a child in November, 1862. A lady who gave her name as Smyth, came to her cottage in December, 1862, accompanied by Mrs Tolley, and asked her if she would suckle a child, about six weeks old. She said the baby was her own, and that she had been living at Miss Hutts, Richmond Green.

She went there, and saw Mrs Smyth with the baby, which she was suckling. Mrs Smyth gave her a reference, "Mrs Penfold, Vilmount Terrace, Queenstown, Ireland." She sent a letter to Mrs Penfold, and received an answer. Nursed the child for a week, when Mrs Smyth took it away, but engaged her daughter about a fortnight after to nurse it in the daytime.

Mrs Smyth was then living at Mrs Pittman's, Alver Cottages, Twickenham. Portraits No. 1 and No. 2 are likenesses of Mrs Smyth, the mother of the child. Her daughter remained in Mrs Smyth's service until March, 1863, when the lady left Twickenham.

Re-examined: Would swear she saw Mrs Smyth suckle the baby. Never saw Mrs Smyth in the dress of portrait No. 1. She generally wore a black silk dress. Her hair was not dressed like it was in the portrait, but was worn in a net. She was certain the portrait was that of Mrs Smyth directly she saw it. No. 3 was not so like as the other portraits were. Would not swear that it was intended for her. Mrs Smyth told her that she was going to Mrs Penfold's in Ireland.

Cross examined: The child was a boy.

Margaret Hawker, of 16 Kildare terrace, Westbourne Park, Middlesex, said she was the widow of Thomas Hawker, late of the Royal Naval Hospital, Plymouth. Her husband died in March, 1862. In 1860 she was living at Plymouth, and became acquainted with a lady calling herself Mrs Henrietta Molesworth. She said her husband was Mr Justice Molesworth, of Melbourne. Portraits P1 and P2 resembled her. She was living at 8 Wyndham place, Plymouth, with her mother, Mrs Harding. Mrs Harding left for Queenstown in December, 1860. Her daughter Josephine and a governess resided with her part of the time. The landlady of the house in which Mrs Molesworth lived was Mrs Johns. Persons could go to Mrs Molesworth's apartments without being seen by other inmates of the house.

People could turn the handle of the door and walk in without ringing. In the beginning of May, 1861, witness went on a visit to her father and mother at Guernsey.

Her husband remained at Plymouth. Returned in about a month, and the day after she found a letter in the pocket-book of her husband, which was lying in a cupboard where he usually kept his papers. Recognised it at once as being in Mrs Molesworth's handwriting. It was enclosed in an envelope which had been wafered, but which was open when found.

Witness sent for Mrs Molesworth, who came, and admitted the letter, stating that she knew every word that was in it; that it was for an unmarried man who was her acquaintance, and was not intended for witness nor anyone belonging to her. Mr Hawker was in the room at the time, but he said nothing, and shortly afterwards left.

Mrs Molesworth asked for the letter, but witness declined to give it to her. Mrs Molesworth never said that it was copied from a letter she had found. Witness received a letter from her next day, 20th May, which, with the others, she handed over to Mr Powys (Mr Molesworth's solicitor). A few days after the receipt of this last letter saw Mrs Molesworth at Teignmouth, and asked her to give the gentleman's address to whom she had written the letter found in Mr Hawkers pocket-book. First of all she said she would give the address in writing, and witness replied that if she would, and would bring up a candle, the letter would be burned before her eyes.

Mrs Molesworth then wanted the letter placed in the hands of a friend of hers, but witness objected, and wanted it to be given to her father or brother, who would give it up when the address was made known.

Mrs Molesworth repeated that it was for a young unmarried man of her acquaintance but did not state that she had copied it from another. The result was that she did not give any address, nor mention any name. Witness afterwards wrote several letters, and received replies, some of which she gave to Mr Powys.

She subsequently communicated with Mr Justice Molesworth. Portrait No. 3 was that of Mrs Molesworth.

Had seen her in a dress similar to that in which she was represented. Was positive of this.

Cross examined:

Never noticed any impropriety between her husband and Mrs Molesworth. Had made no memorandum of the date of the finding of the letter, but believed it was 29th May. Spoke to her husband before sending for Mrs Molesworth. He denied that the letter was addressed to him. Mrs Molesworth did not hesitate for a moment to admit that it was in her handwriting, even though she was not told where it was found. Witness's husband always denied that any improper intimacy took place between him and Mrs

Molesworth. Would not undertake to swear that Mrs Molesworth never said that she copied the note from another.

She did embrace the offer to have the letter burned if the address of the person for whom it was intended was given up; on the other hand, she wished it to be placed in the hands of a friend. There might have been a word or two corrected in that letter.

Mr Hawker explained that he had become possessed of the letter in this way - he said he had been visiting at Mrs Molesworth's and whilst she was out of the room he lifted a portfolio from the table and under it was a letter with the peculiar address, "For you, my darling." His curiosity being aroused he took it up, intending to replace it, but Mrs Molesworth came into the room and he then put it in his pocket.

Re-examined:

Saw a small photograph of Mrs Molesworth, in a brooch, at her lodgings. She said she had had her photographs taken at Gaisford's.

William Todderich Kent, of 51 Rutland square west, Dublin, solicitor, said that the portraits P1 and P2 were taken from Mrs Molesworth or some negative or picture resembling her. Witness was the agent of Mr Molesworth, and as such had paid moneys to the petitioner. He produced a letter from her, dated 8th February, 1856, acknowledging receipt of £25; and one dated 31st March, 1856 for a similar sum. Witness also remitted her £25 in June, 1856. He also sent her £50 in November, for which she thanked him by letter.

Mrs Molesworth was paid at the rate of £200 per annum whilst she was in England, from 1857 till 1861. (The witness was examined at some length as to the handwriting of a letter marked No. 8, dated from 3 Vilmount terrace, Queenstown, Ireland, 2nd March, addressed to Mrs Tolley, and signed "J Smyth." He thought portions of it were in Mrs Molesworth's writing, both from his knowledge of her and from comparison with letters he had received from her. This letter was not read in court.) The witness added that Mr Molesworth had paid to Mrs Harding, petitioner's mother, £52 per annum for the last eight or nine years.

Mr Dawson objected to the statement as irrelevant.

The next witness on the commission was George Tolley, of Albion House, Twickenham, secretary to the Richmond Conveyance Company.

He said that his house was formerly called Little Holley House. He had a son named George Tolley residing in Melbourne, Victoria. Witness received a letter, marked No. 5, signed Henrietta Molesworth. (This document Mrs Molesworth, on Thursday, acknowledged to be her writing). It is as follows:-

"10th September, 1862. 3 Wilmot terrace, Queenstown, Ireland. My dear sir, - When I left Australia, three months since, I got a card of introduction to you from your son, whom I knew for the last seven years. He begged of me to go and see you and his mother, and he said for his sake you would be friendly disposed to me.

Could you manage to take two rooms for me in your neighbourhood? I would require a sitting room and bedroom, with attendance. I would rather they were reasonable lodgings in a quiet way, and would not wish the people of the house at present to know my name, wherefore you are taking the lodgings weekly for a lady. If you would allow me to stop with you one night, on my arrival in London, it would be a great accommodation, and we might then settle permanently of this matter.

I send you a card, in his (your son's) handwriting, he gave me. You will, no doubt, recognise his writing. He also promised to write of me to you as an introduction. An answer will much oblige me, addressed to the above address. I would go up about the 16th or 18th of this month. - Yours most truly, Henrietta Molesworth (Mrs Molesworth)." [The envelope was addressed to "Mr George Tolley, Little Holly House, Twickenham, near London, Middlesex." Witness answered that letter and received another on the 17th of September, 1862, dated as on the previous day. (This letter appeared in our issue of Saturday.) A lady came to the house on the evening of the day he got that letter.

Portraits P1 and P2 were very correct resemblances of that lady, and he had no doubt were taken from her. She said her name was Smyth, and she had come at the recommendation of Mrs Molesworth, who had written to witness. She added that she was a cousin to Mrs Molesworth and Mrs Penfold, and was wife of Captain Smyth, of the merchant or naval service, and her son was on a voyage to India with her husband. She said Mrs Penfold lived at Queenstown.

She mentioned George Tolley, of Melbourne, and said she had spent many pleasant evenings with him. She lodged with witness for about six weeks. He saw the name of Molesworth gummed on one of her boxes. When she left she said she was going to her cousin's in Ireland. One Sunday evening, about a month subsequently, witness had been out with his wife. When he returned home his daughter gave him a paper containing jewellery, and said Mrs Smyth had been there, and wanted an advance of a little money on it. It was wrapped up in an old envelope. In consequence of seeing an address on the envelope, he went to Miss Hutt's, No. 1 Richmond Green. Saw Mrs Smyth. She appeared surprised to see him, and asked how he knew her address. He said by the envelope containing the jewellery. He told her it was no use trying to deceive him, for he thought she was really Mrs Molesworth, and not Mrs Smyth. She replied, "For God's sake don't name Mrs Molesworth."

A child was brought in, but it was not said whose he was. Witness said it was a very fine child and like her. She did not express any surprise. A few days afterwards, Mrs Smyth came to ask Mrs Tolley to recommend a wet nurse for the child. Witness went with her to Mrs Evans on Twickenham Common. Shortly before Christmas she came to Holly House with the nurse, the child and the cradle. Witness saw her suckle the child several times. Mrs Smyth afterwards went to lodge with Mrs Pittman, at Alver cottages, and on one occasion she told witness that she was going to India, and intended to place the child at Plymouth or Queenstown.

No person answering the name of Molesworth stopped at his house in 1862 or 1863, nor was any one stopping with him except Mrs Smyth.

The child was christened George Charles Vernon Smyth.

Witness, his wife and his son stood sponsors, and he gave a dinner on the occasion. The Rev. Mr Master, the vicar of Old Church, Twickenham, performed the baptismal ceremony. Mrs Smyth gave the particulars for registration. She left Twickenham a short time afterwards.

Cross-examined: His age was 73. Did not notice the address on any of the trunks but the one. Did not know or suspect that the lady was in the family way when she first went to his house. She had not the appearance of being so.

Never saw Mrs Smyth write.

First saw the photographs P1, P2, and P3 about three weeks previous to giving his evidence; but he had seen a small portrait sent him by his son from Melbourne twelve months before. It was returned to his son. Had seen Mrs Smyth in a dress similar to the one in P2. She also wore her hair in the same way as was represented in the likeness. She always gave the same account of herself as being Mrs Smyth.

Re-examined: She principally wore a red coloured loose dress called a Garibaldi, loose round the body, and appeared to wear a large crinoline. Could not swear if she asked for a wet nurse for "the child" or "my child".

Rosina Ann Hailing, wife of Henry Hailing, residing with her father, Mr George Tolley, of Albion House, formerly Little Holly House, Twickenham, deposed that she was living with her parents at the same residence, in the year 1862. On Wednesday, the 17th September, a person calling herself Mrs Smyth came to the house.

She afterwards said her christian name was Jane. She said she came from Queenstown, and that her husband was an officer at sea. She spoke of Mrs Molesworth and Mrs Penfold as her relations. The portraits produced are the portraits of the person calling herself Mrs Smyth. She stayed with us about four weeks. I saw the name of Molesworth on one of her boxes, and when I asked her about it, she said Mrs Molesworth had lent it to her. She said Mrs Molesworth and Mrs Penfold were her cousins, and that the latter stayed at Vilmount Terrace. Mrs Smyth wore a black silk dress and Garibaldian jacket, white chip bonnet, with scarlet velvet and white roses and a scarlet cloak, trimmed with black velvet rosettes.

Q. Do you recollect when the person calling herself Mrs Smyth resided at your house received a letter from your brother, from Australia?

A. Yes; I do.

Q. Did that contain a letter addressed to Mrs Molesworth?

A. It did.

Q. What became of the letter from your brother?

A. My mother was reading the address, and said, "Here's a letter for Mrs Molesworth," and Mrs Smyth jumped up, and said, "My dear Mrs Tolley, I will forward it to her." When she left she said she was going to a Captain and Mrs Carey at Brixton.

One Sunday in November she came back to our house and said she had come from London and must go back there again. She said she was in a great deal of trouble, as the mail had not arrived and she was without means.

She left some jewellery with me to give to my father to get money upon. The paper containing it had the address:- "Mrs Smyth, Miss Hutt's, No. 1 The Green, near London." In the course of the week she came to our house again and said she had had a baby. She said she had been confined after leaving our house. I saw her afterwards at Miss Hutt's, nursing and suckling a baby. She called on my mother after that and asked her to engage a wet nurse for the baby. After leaving Miss Hutt's Mrs Smyth was living at Mrs Pittman's, No. 1 Alver Cottages, Twickenham. She spent the afternoon at our house on Christmas day, and Eleanor Evans nursed her baby. Mrs Smyth left about March, 1863, and said she was going to Queenstown to remain there for a time, and then going to India to meet her husband. I wrote afterwards to Mrs Penfold and got in reply the letter marked No. 9. The child's name was "George Charles Vernon Smyth." Mrs Smyth said she had come from Australia and that she had rented my brother's house, Thames Bank Cottage, there.

Sarah Anne Hutt, of No. 1 The Green, Richmond, deposed:

In the month of October, 1862, a lady, giving the name of Mrs Smyth, called upon me, for the purpose of taking the rooms. She occupied a bedroom on the first floor, and occasionally the dining room underneath. Soon after she arrived she was confined, but I was not present. I did not see Dr. Hassall call, but occasionally I saw the child in the hall, or in the room which Mrs Smyth occupied. I cannot say whether Mrs Smyth was ill while at my house, but a woman named Ann Hedges came to attend her.

I believe she is a nurse, but I can't say what sort. She attends patients. I could not say how long this lady remained in my house, nor where she went afterwards. I saw her very seldom, as she kept herself to her rooms, and I had another house. I never saw her suckle her child.

Cross-examined: I will undertake to swear I saw Mrs Smyth with a child. I saw it in her arms. She always represented herself as Mrs Smyth, and I never knew her under another name.

John Drew Dudmesh, a clerk in the copyhold commissioner's office, proved that, while clerk to Mr B. W. Powys, he posted a certain letter to Mr P. A. C. O'Farrell, then the respondent's proctor.

Bransby William Powys, solicitor for the respondent in England, produced a certified copy of a register of baptism, purporting to be the register of baptism of George Charles Vernon Smyth, son of Charles Vernon and Jane Smyth. He also proved receiving several letters from Mrs Hawker, which he forwarded to Mr O'Farrell, copies of which he produced.

Richard Hassall, a doctor of medicine at Richmond, Surrey, deposed: In the autumn of 1862, in the month of October, a lady named Mrs Smyth called upon me to engage me to attend her in her accouchement. I attended her about the 20th or 21st October, at Miss Hutt's, Richmond. I recommended a woman named Hedge, as a nurse, and she attended her. The confinement took place in the upper room, on the first floor. The child was a boy.

Q. Do you think you could recognise the portrait of the lady you attended? (Portraits handed to witness.)

A. I should say she is this style of woman. This gives me an impression of the lady whom I did attend.

Q. How often did you see the lady?

A. Not many times, because, having attended her, my assistant saw her in my place.

Q. When you saw her she was in bed?

A. I think when I went into the room on the first occasion, she was sitting on the bed side, and afterwards in bed, with the blinds pulled down.

She was about forty years of age. I attended no other person in her confinement at that house about that time. I attended no other person of name of Smyth at any other place about that time. I do not know any other person of the name of Hutt, or similar name, living on Richmond Green, who lets lodgings.

Cross-examined: What was the length of the interviews with Mrs Smyth when she called about her accouchement?

Witness: I suppose a very few minutes. I don't remember.

Q. Was Mrs Smyth in a ball dress, or morning dress, similar to that in the first two portraits, when she called upon you?

A. No; I don't remember how she was dressed.

Dr. Hassall was called as a witness for the petitioner, and gave similar evidence with reference to portrait No. 3, as he had done regarding the two others.

This closed the commission.

The first witness called by Mr Michie was, Mary Dollard, who deposed: My name was formerly Mary Hickey. In the year 1855 I was in the service of Mr Molesworth, at St. Kilda. I remember seeing Mr Ireland there frequently. He was there mornings and evenings. Sometimes by the time the courts were over (at five or six o'clock), and sometimes later. I have known him to be there as late as ten o'clock. I have known him to be there when Mr Molesworth was absent. Sometimes his visits on these occasions were short and sometimes he stayed for perhaps an hour. I remember hearing about an affair between Mrs Molesworth and Mr Ireland at Castlemaine. Mr Ireland came frequently after that affair. He came more than once a week.

I remember a fracas taking place between Mr Molesworth and Mr Ireland. A few days afterwards there was a children's party at the house. Mr Molesworth was keeping his room at that time. Mrs Molesworth gave me a note the same evening to carry to Mr Ireland. I cannot tell the exact time. It was after nightfall, as the lights were burning. It might be about nine o'clock.

I delivered the note personally to Mr Ireland in the hall. After that I got another note from Mrs Molesworth. Mr Dopping brought a note to Mr Molesworth's house, and I was then sent with the second note to Mr Ireland. I delivered the second note into his hands and he came down with me to the gate. I cannot recollect whether Mrs Molesworth was standing at the gate, or whether I told her he was there, but when I went in I left them both standing at the gate. I told some brother-in-law of hers that Mr Ireland was standing at the gate, and he went out, but when he came back he told me he could not see them. I afterwards went back to look for Mrs Molesworth, but could not find her. The omnibuses used to pass the place. I went about a dozen yards from the gate, but could not see her, and went again with the same result.

The second time, I went about a dozen yards further in the same direction, and I saw Mr Ireland coming from under the fence. I said, "Where is Mrs Molesworth?" He said, "I think she is gone in." I went back and she was in before me. She was out about an hour, more or less. There was a sort of park or field the other side of the fence. Mr Ireland was coming out of the field.

I had not been out on the second occasion more than five minutes. I am sure Mrs Molesworth was not in when I went out. I don't recollect if there were many houses near, or if there were any trees.

Some weeks after this I was called into a room; Mr and Mrs Molesworth were there. When I went in Mr Molesworth asked if I was aware that Mrs Molesworth had been seduced by Mr Ireland. I said I was not, and he asked Mrs Molesworth if she had told me. She said she had not. Mrs Molesworth was writing, and she gave me the letter to take up to Mr Ireland. I took it and delivered it to Mr Ireland. I have stated that all that passed in the room before I took the note. He told her to tell me what she had told him, and she then said that Mr Ireland had seduced her on the night of the children's party, that he caught hold of her and threw her down under the tree. I delivered the note to Mr Ireland in the hall. He gave me an answer to the note, which I brought back. I gave it to either Mr or Mrs Molesworth, who were both together in the room.

The next day Mrs Molesworth gave me a note to take to Mr Ireland. I did not take it to Mr Ireland, but gave it to Mr Molesworth. She went away, either the next day or the day after, to Mrs Poole's, at Prahran.

She came back the same evening, when Mr Molesworth was away.

I remember Mrs Molesworth going to England. In June, 1856, I saw her again at the house, at about six o'clock. Mr Molesworth had given orders that she was not to be admitted. I saw her coming in through the fence. She came in through the back yard, through the kitchen, straight into the dining room. She asked for a glass of wine, and had some; and, in a short time, Mr Molesworth came in - in about half an hour she remaining in the dining room. There were some loud words, and something was said about a carriage. A man went into Melbourne to get a carriage, and Mr Rose accompanied her into Melbourne. Mr Rose came back and went to dinner, and, in about an hour after, Mrs Molesworth came back. She again went into the parlor, but I don't know what occurred there. I heard a noise like breaking of glasses, and I went to the gate and saw her sitting down there. Mr Molesworth, Mr Rose, the governess and some of the servants were there. The carriage lamp was broken, but I cannot say who broke it. She walked down as far as the other gate, and then threw herself into the street, bringing a great crowd of people about her. I then persuaded her to get up, and accompanied her to town, and stopped at Bignell's Hotel all night with her.

Cross-examined by Mr Dawson:

The fence was a common open post and rail fence. The road was a frequented one, traversed by the omnibuses in the day time. Mr Molesworth was very much excited the afternoon Mrs Molesworth returned, but he did not call her a ----, I never said so to Mr Liddle, or that Mr Molesworth had kicked her out of the gate.

To the Jury: I don't remember if the night of the children's party was dark or light. It was not moonlight. I could see across the road, but I don't know whether I could see further.

I was in the middle of the road when I saw Mr Ireland come from the fence. I was close to the fence. I cannot say exactly my reason for going out to look for Mrs Molesworth. I don't know it is usual for servants to look after their mistresses, but I was anxious about her, as there was a great deal of unhappiness in the family at the time, and I did not want her to be out. I never saw any undue familiarity between Mrs Molesworth and Mr Ireland. I went with Mrs Molesworth in the carriage, of my own accord. After the row with Mr Molesworth I did not see any signs of a scuffle about her clothes, but there was dust on her mantle.

When Mrs Molesworth went out on the night of the party, she had on my cloak and bonnet, which she took from me at the gate. I did not see any evidence that Mrs Molesworth had been drinking when she made the admission of being seduced by Mr Ireland. The same evening, when we were sitting in the room, she told me that Mr Ireland was always saying something to her about one thing or another, and that from the first time he saw her, he had fastened his eye upon her, and would go to any part of the world with her. I was never aware of any cruel conduct on the part of Mr Molesworth. They always appeared to be happy until this time.

A Juror: Did Mrs Molesworth ever give you any reason for making the confession?

Witness: She said it was because Mr Ireland had refused to take her to a party at Mr Fellows's.

A Juryman: You mean that this was in a spirit of revenge?

Witness: Yes; she told me the same night.

To Mr Dawson: I applied to Mr Ireland, when he was Attorney-General, for a place for a relation. It was not at the suggestion of Mr Molesworth.

Alexander O'Grady Rose, examined by Mr Billing:

I am associate to the respondent, and a relative of his. I first met Mr and Mrs Molesworth in the colony in 1854 or 1855. I came down from the diggings, and spent a day or night with them. They were living on the beach road. They appeared then on good, and even affectionate, terms. I then left Melbourne, and did not come down for a year; and I was quite astonished to hear that Mrs Molesworth had gone away. This was in October, 1855, and in 1856, I became Mr Molesworth's associate. At this time he was living in a larger house, in a street the name of which I forget. About half past three or four o'clock, one afternoon in June, I saw Mrs Molesworth come through the fence and enter the house. We shook hands, for we had been very old friends. She said it was an inhospitable reception, and called for some wine, which was brought her, and she had some glasses. She called the servants, and questioned them about the children in a very imperious way. She told me she had taken Sir Richard Bethell's advice, and had come out to take her place as Mr Molesworth's wife, and that she was determined not to move unless she was put out. I told her, He will be back about six o'clock, and you will be put out, and there will be a row."

She said all she wanted was to be put out, and she would go out quietly and make no row. In about an hour Mr Molesworth returned, and she told him what she had told me, and that she would assert her rights. He said he would put her out. She said she must have a carriage. I sent for one, and took her to Bignell's Hotel, in Melbourne, where we had a bottle of champagne.

The wine was opened, and I just put it to my lips. She wanted me to stay and dine with her, but I would not, and I went back to town. Before Mr Molesworth arrived I had offered her £5, and told her Mr Molesworth would make proper provision for her. She refused the money; but when I again offered it to her, at Bignell's Hotel, she took it.

I went back immediately, and arrived rather more than an hour after starting. When I got back they were done dinner, and some was brought to me on a plate. I had scarcely finished when she burst into the room a second time. She was in a very excited state and spoke very loud. She had an apple in her hand which she threw, but I did not see that it hit any body. She was very abusive, and spoke in a very irritating way to Mr Molesworth. I think the first words he said were "Out of the house, harlot."

She continued to abuse him, and after the scene had lasted some minutes he seemed to lose all control of himself, and taking hold of her by the shoulder he rushed her to the gate.

She said she would be his ruin, and would run him into debt every where. She then took one of the lamps out of the carriage and broke it against the wheel, saying "You will have to pay for that." The carriage was not the one we went into town with. She was going to take the second lamp out, when the coachman took it from her, saying "Oh, no, Missus, that is my property."

She then threw stones at the window and called Mr Molesworth names, saying what a pretty judge he was. She also called him an old cuckold, and he then struck her. I only saw one blow given. When she was struck she threw herself down near the gate, and, after crying for some time, she went further off and threw herself down again, screaming louder than before. Some one said she was in a fit and slapped her hands. She got up and asserted her dignity, saying she was a judge's wife, and the man who assisted her was only a hatter.

I saw her the next morning and she had a black eye. She said she was afraid she had ruined herself in the estimation of the people of Melbourne, and I said, I was sure she had.

She said it was all my fault, for if I had remained with her the previous night it would have been all right, but that immediately I had left she finished the whole bottle of champagne. She was not kept in bed long, but her eye was very bad. She talked about going to law, and I told her there was no law in the colony that would give her so much alimony as Mr Molesworth was voluntarily paying her. It was arranged that she was to have lodgings, and £6 per week was to be paid to her upon a particular day.

She objected to all the lodgings I selected, except those that were very expensive, and after a short time, she said she was so miserable, no one coming to see her, that she thought she would rather go home. Mr Molesworth said he would not give her more than £200 per year, as £200 in England was equal to £300 here, and, at last, she agreed to go home, on the condition of getting £300 per year. When it was arranged that she should go, she went down to Brighton and stayed there for some time, and insisted that on the voyage home she should have a cabin to herself. This was done, and she went home in the "James Baines." I went to wish her good bye. The next time I saw her was on board the "Eliza Ann Bright", in November 1861. I accompanied her to Bignell's Hotel, and she told me she had found it impossible to live on £200 a year, and she had come out to get alimony.

Cross-examined by Mr Dawson:

I tried to stop Mr Molesworth from rushing his wife out of the house. I said "don't" several times, but I could not have prevented what occurred. I afterwards persuaded him to go in. I did not consider at this time that Mrs Molesworth was entitled to her rights as a wife. I did not see Mr Molesworth drinking that day, and he did not look as if he had been drinking. He was sober as to wine, but he was in an outrageous passion. I picked Mrs Molesworth up several times, and so did the servants, but she threw herself down again.

I told her she was disgracing herself and the family. I did not tell the respondent he was disgracing his family. He had been appointed as a judge about eight months.

Mr Dawson: You did not consider him to be disgracing himself by making this disturbance in the street?

Witness: I considered her (the petitioner) to be the cause of the row.

Mr Dawson: Now, Mr Rose, was Mrs Molesworth the worse for drink on that occasion?

Witness: She was drunk, if you want to know. She came back drunk, violent, and excited.

Mr Dawson: You gave her some money?

Witness: Yes; I gave her a £5 note.

Mr Dawson: Did you say that was all she was to get?

Witness: No; I told her provision would be made for her every week. Mr Molesworth had told me so before.

To the Jury: Mr Molesworth told me, before Mrs Molesworth came, that he expected her arrival and would turn her out.

A Juror: Do you consider any amount of provocation would justify a man in striking a woman?

Witness: It is hard to say.

A Juror: Would you have struck her yourself?

Witness: I would not.

William Dopping, examined by Mr Billing: I know the families of Mr Ireland and Mr Molesworth. I remember on the 6th July, 1856, bringing a note from Mr Ireland's house to Mr Molesworth's. I am not sure of the date, nor whether it was a note or a message. I was to give it to the woman Mary Hickey. I delivered the note to her.

At this stage the examination was adjourned until Monday morning at ten o'clock.

Molesworth (wife) v. Molesworth

DIVORCE COURT

Monday, 21st November
Extract from *The Age*, Tuesday, 22nd November, 1864
(Before the Chief Justice, and a Special Jury of Twelve)

MOLESWORTH (WIFE) v. MOLESWORTH

> Petition for judicial separation. Mr Dawson and Mr Wood for the petitioner; Mr Billing and Mr Michie, Q.C., for the respondent.

This case, which had been partly heard on Thursday, Friday, and Saturday last, was resumed. The first witness called for the respondent was George Tolley, who deposed:

Mrs Molesworth rented a house from me in March, April, and part of May, 1862. It was in Millsden street. No person of the name of Smyth rented a house from me. I don't know such a person.

Robert Molesworth, the respondent, was then examined by Mr Billing. He said: I am the respondent in this suit, and a judge of the Supreme Court.

Mr Billing: Mrs Molesworth has spoken about some conduct with regard to a child in the early part of your union. Do you remember any of the facts?

Respondent: It is the first time I ever heard anything on the subject. I never heard her make any observation as to my treatment of the child.

Mr Billing: And such a thing did not take place?

Respondent: I, perhaps, was not a particularly affectionate father. I was never in the habit of taking much notice of infants, but there was nothing between us on the occasion to attract my notice.

Mr Billing: Do you remember any communication that took place between you in the month of November, 1854?

Respondent: I recollect one night in November, 1854, she told me that she was afraid she would become bad; that she had very little affection for me; that she was not much under religious influence, and had very little regard for public opinion. I afterwards endeavoured to resume the subject of the conversation, but she seemed disinclined. I never before expressed jealousy; and I never did until we were separated, except as to a belief in the criminality of Mr Ireland and Mr Penfold.

Mr Billing: What was the origin of your acquaintance with Mr Penfold?

Respondent: He was a brother of my brother-in-law. He came out here with no previous acquaintance. His name was Henry Penfold. He came here in January, 1855. He stated he was passing through Melbourne, going to Sydney, and would remain only a few days. I invited him to my house. Mrs Molesworth and he got into quick intimacy, calling each other by their Christian names. He stayed ultimately about six weeks in the house. Mrs Molesworth and I were going on a visit to an acquaintance, and she arranged that he should be included in the invitation.

She asked her friend to ask him, so that he went with them, and there was more familiarity between them than I liked.

I had to go on circuit, and he had an order to get money from me if he wanted it.

I gave him 10 pounds in such a way that he might understand I would not expect to find him on my return, in fact that he would want the £10 before I returned to take him to Sydney.

On returning, I found him at my house, still living in the same way. After some time I had to go on another circuit – to Castlemaine; and the morning before I went I told Mrs Molesworth that I thought this man was staying unaccountably long and I did not like his motives for staying.

She said he had wanted to go, but she pressed him to stay. She first asked, "Are you jealous of him," and laughed at the notion of jealousy. I said I did not believe there was anything criminal between them, but I thought his stay was from wrong motives. She promised that she would no longer press him to stay, but she took some pains to disabuse me on the subject. I returned in about a week, and learned that he had that day started for Sydney. He, however, returned in the evening, stating that there was something wrong with the ship, and that he could not sail for one or two days.

When the ship did start, he was with me on the verandah as the hour approached. He was waiting for an omnibus. I told him, "You are apt to lose your passage; this is not the highway; go down to the corner where the omnibuses are in the habit of passing, and you will get one quickly." He still loitered for a quarter of an hour and then started.

He returned that evening, having been too late for the ship, and there was no other opportunity of going to Sydney for a week or some time after. On his return I received him very coldly. His deportment to Mrs Molesworth continued the same. A couple of days after this, there was a conversation between Mrs Molesworth and me about a young lady, a distant relation of hers, with whom we had been intimate in Ireland, and whom she wanted invited to my house. Mrs Molesworth refused to invite her, and said, "Why don't you invite her yourself?" I said, with a look at Penfold, "It is the business of the lady of the house to invite female visitors, and of the man to invite male visitors." We had some further altercation on the subject, and a couple of evenings after she proposed to Mr Penfold to take an evening walk, which they did. The next morning I told Mr Penfold that his visit had lasted longer than I expected, and he left the house.

Mr Billing: Mrs Molesworth has alluded to some circumstances in connection with the name of Mr Dunne. Do you remember what they were?

Respondent: Well, Mr Dunne is a gentleman, whose presence in the house I never had the slightest objection to; but I wished my servants to have the opportunity of amusing themselves on Sunday, and frequently expressed my disinclination to have company on Sunday. On Saturday, Mrs Molesworth told me Mr Dunne had invited himself to dinner next day, and she could not well help it. I expressed some annoyance at this. My servants were kept at home in consequence, and Mr Dunne did not come after all, at which I expressed increased annoyance.

The ensuing Saturday she told me she had been in town, and asked Mr Dunne to dine next day. When Mr Dunne came I told him the facts, and said that at any other time I should like to have the pleasure of his company, but that I should not sit with him that day.

That was the systematic kind of annoyance to which I was subjected. If it had not been so I should not have taken such a strong course with regard to it. Mr Dunne and I have always been good friends since. I told him at the time that he had been invited in spite of me.

Mr Billing: Some allusion has been made to a difference between Mrs Molesworth and Mrs Ireland.

Respondent: The cause of the quarrel was a cart belonging to Mr Ireland coming into the yard and injuring my pump. It was simply a ladies' quarrel, but, however, it led to a total estrangement. Mr Ireland has talked about some scratched plates or dishes, for which he paid £14, but I never heard anything about it.

Mr Billing: Mrs Molesworth has alluded to the circumstance of her riding on a horse borrowed from Mr Goslett. On what day was it?

Respondent: Well, in April 1855 – on Good Friday. She and I rode out together, she on a horse borrowed from Mr Goslett. She was unused to riding, and complained afterwards of being galled. The next day went to Castlemaine, and I don't think it necessary to add anything to her evidence about it. We went to Castlemaine on Saturday. There was to be a ball on Tuesday, and on Monday evening Mrs Molesworth took it into her head to go to this ball, and to get a make-shift dress. I gave her £5 for the purpose, but I would not go out with her. Mr Ireland did. I had then no suspicion of him.

Mr Billing: Is it the fact that you followed them out?

Witness: No; I never followed them, or thought of following them.

Mr Billing: Or in fact had any suspicion?

Respondent: Well, trifling. Of course if I had had any serious suspicion I should not have allowed them to go out in that manner. On Tuesday Mr Ireland, by my request, did go out with her, and show her the gold-washing, and so forth. On Tuesday, we were at the ball, and were kept awake all night by it. On Wednesday, Mr Ireland, Mrs Molesworth and I walked out together, and their deportment made me very jealous – that is, her separating from me and leaning on him, and so forth.

Well, when we returned, there was a gentleman named Chapman, who was her acquaintance and who had a situation at Castlemaine, and she urged me to invite him to dine. I was quite opposed to it, but agreed at last. I wanted her to accompany me to Mr Chapman's to invite him, but she refused, saying she was tired, or something of that kind. I went to Mr Chapman's and left an invitation for him to dine. I returned, and found that Mr Ireland and Mrs Molesworth had gone out together in the dark. I had then become intensely jealous.

As to our drinking at dinner, I don't think it was I who proposed champagne. As to punch, I think I took one tumbler only, and that was hollands. I rather think Mr Ireland was drinking hollands, and not whiskey.

Mr Chapman came, not to dinner, but about half past nine in the evening. He was remaining very long, until, I think, about half past ten o'clock. We were to start for Melbourne next morning at, I think, about five o'clock. It was drawing very late, and I told Mr Chapman that we had been up all last night, and were going away early next morning, and we wanted to go to bed; so he went away.

Mrs Molesworth had given permission to our servant to go to some theatre or circus there, of which I was not at all aware. I was not aware of it until after my fracas with Mr Ireland. I was anxious then to get to bed, and equally anxious for Mrs Molesworth to get to bed. I never requested Mr Ireland to sit up with her. They were, however, remaining together. I did not close the door of my bedroom.

Their conversation was faint, and I got to the door to listen to it. I heard, as I thought, Mr Ireland say, "If you have a boy by me," with some expression about a "wealthy provision." I also, as I thought, heard him say, "I will bear to be a month together without seeing you."

I made some slight noise, and Mrs Molesworth came to the door. I returned to my room, and was getting into bed. She returned, and closed the door.

Sometime after this, I rushed out, much as has been described, and charged Mr Ireland with attempting to seduce her. I don't wish to say anything contrary to the testimony already given relative to subsequent matters. The next morning we started in the same carriage – I and Mrs Molesworth, the servant and child being in front; and Mr Ireland at the back. Mr Ireland used the expression to me, "You shall answer for this."

He used no expression whatsoever about my staying at home, in order to receive a message from him. Nothing of the kind. That day, Thursday, we came to Melbourne. On Friday night I went to the carpet bag where Mrs Molesworth's linen was kept, and I saw one garment of hers which I thought was evidence of criminality. I went into her bedroom and woke her, and she started up. I called upon her then to explain what her conversation had been with Mr Ireland the day before. She said they had been talking about a great many things and principally, she said, about a specific case of adultery.

Mr Billing: A case of crim. con. that occurred some years ago?

Respondent: Yes. I asked her particularly as to the overheard words, and she totally denied them.

I then went into the next room and brought out the article of dress, of which I have spoken, and asked her what she could say to that. She at once said it proceeded from her having been galled, and said "You may examine my person if you think fit, and see if it is the fact." I never attempted to examine her person. I felt so completely answered, in the latter point, at all events, that I apologised for having said anything about it. I left home for Melbourne at the usual hour, about eight o'clock, and called on Ireland. I found him not at home, and left word that I would call again in the afternoon. I did meet him, at about one o'clock in the afternoon, and did apologise to him, saying I had offered him a very gross insult; that I had some reason, at all events, to doubt my suspicion, and that I felt a most ample apology was due. He then stated the subject of their conversation in the same way as Mrs Molesworth had done. I never said anything to Mr Ireland about my having been drunk. I never said so.

About a week after I went on circuit to Portland, and during that interval I never entered Mr Ireland's house, nor asked him to enter mine. When I returned, Mrs Molesworth told me Mr Ireland had twice been there, the first time leaving a newspaper, which referred to our fracas, and the second time telling that the reason which he had given of our fracas was, that we were all drunk, and had a quarrel about a broken pump. About a month after that Mr Ireland was invited to a large party at my house.

Subsequent to that I, one evening, had a communication with him on a professional business, upon which we were both engaged, and, subsequent to that, at Mrs Molesworth's instance, I invited him to dine at my house. I was not aware that he visited my house otherwise.

Mr Billing: Well, we come now to the 4th July.

Respondent: The evening of the 4th July Mr Ireland came in and we had a glass of wine together. After some time, Mrs Molesworth proposed that she and Mr Ireland should go out together about some bill that she wanted to pay. Mr Ireland gave her no encouragement, and, after some time, she proposed that we should all three go, and it was so arranged.

There was a large cracked pane in the window where he and she were, with the blind drawn over it. I heard her say twice, very loud, "You have ruined me," and after that, as I thought, "I will beg through the world with you." We then went out, and a struggle took place between us about which I don't want to contradict his evidence.

That evening I sent him a written message, and the next morning I got a letter, which has been produced, from him – the letter containing the expression about ruffianism.

It came with nothing but a wet wafer on it. At a subsequent period, Mrs Molesworth told me that she had intercepted the letter and read it before I got it. On 6th July, two days after this fracas, we had a children's party in my house. I had a black eye, and did not appear. I had many conversations with Mrs Molesworth as to the overheard conversation. I had also communications with Mr Carr, Mr Ireland's brother-in-law, who came on behalf of his sister.

Mrs Molesworth after that requested that I would see Mr Ireland, and hear his account of the evening's conversation. I communicated with Mr Carr, and it was arranged that we should hear his (Mr Ireland's) account of it. I met him, and he made his explanation. He said the expression, "You ruined me" had reference to the injury to her character which had resulted from the previous fracas. He admitted the words "Begging through the world." The result of the interview was to make me say to Mrs Molesworth that I did not believe her to be guilty. Further consideration made me dissatisfied, and I expressed myself so to her. I told her I thought she had better go to England.

She consented to go, and I took a passage for her in the "Marco Polo", for which I had to pay one hundred guineas. After the passage was engaged, she changed her mind upon the subject, and ultimately refused to go. The passage money, of course, was forfeited. We continued after this in the same state of suspicion.

She often urged me to administer an oath; but, in answer to her, I stated I would not rely upon her for it. I ultimately said to her I would administer an oath, but it should be a very solemn oath, in the form of an invocation, and that if she took it I would act upon it. Well, she said she thought it a sin to take any oath of that kind; that she was quite ready to kiss the Bible or go before a clergyman or magistrate, but would not take such an oath as I proposed. I told her that I must consider her refusal as clear evidence of guilt. After that I told her that, if she insisted upon staying in the house, I would not again go into company with her; that she might go to any company that would receive her, but that I would not go along with her.

Mr Billing: We come to the 24th August. Do you remember what occurred on that date?

Respondent: On the 24th August, immediately after dinner, she desired the children to leave the room, and we were left alone; and she then stated that she had been guilty of adultery with Mr Ireland. I asked her when it was, and whether it was at Castlemaine. She said, "No, not at all. It was on the night of the children's party."

She stated to me that Mr Ireland's first love-making to her was in the preceding October, and that, when bringing her home from his house in the evening, he had talked love to her. She said he had told her that from the first time he had laid eyes upon her, in 1853, he was determined she should not escape him. She stated that our going to Castlemaine together was a matter pre-arranged between them. She stated that, as to the conversation which I thought I overheard, I was generally right about it. She stated that as to the expression "I could be a month without seeing you," that she had said she could not live with two men at the same time, and that his answer was, "I would be content to live a month together without seeing you."

She stated that the morning she came up she sent a note by one of the children to tell him what account to give of the overheard conversation.

She stated she had sent a great many notes to him, by his directions, to his chambers instead of to the house, and that she then arranged with him the account to be given of the conversation I had overheard, and had also got him to make an apology to me; that she sent a note to him by Mary Hickey, and that Mr Dopping brought an answer to it.

She stated that he and she went out a considerable way from my house, and she attempted to describe the place they went to, but could not make me understand it. We did not then speak about places in St. Kilda by streets. We spoke about such and such a person's house, and, as soon as we got a distance beyond the houses, we knew it was difficult to describe any place; but she made me suppose it was some half mile or so away from our house. She said they had had intercourse. I asked her if it was rape, and she said no. She stated that he had solicited renewals of the intercourse, but that she had refused, and that was the only occasion on which she had been guilty. She stated she was intoxicated at the time; and that she had afterwards told Mr Ireland that, only that she was tipsy, he would not have succeeded with her, and that he laughed at that.

She stated also that she had told Mr Ireland that she had refused to take the oath, and that Mr Ireland said she was a great fool not to swear anything. She said she had intended to confess the entire matter to me if she had sailed by the "Marco Polo". She said that she and Mr Ireland had been in concert before the meeting, which Mr Carr arranged, as to what he (Mr Ireland) was to tell me. She stated, as to Henry Penfold, that there was not the slightest ground of suspicion. She expressed a great desire to have Mr Ireland punished, saying he richly deserved it, and she asked if she would be permitted to give evidence against him, if I took proceedings against him. I told her that she could not.

Mr Billing: Do you remember anything about the word "cunning"?

Respondent: Oh, yes. She said he (Mr Ireland) was an excessively cunning man, and that he had got her completely under his management, and could wind her round his finger, or something of that sort.

Mr Billing: Anything about his being afraid of being found out?

Respondent: She said she had threatened him with disclosing the affair, and that he was very much afraid of her.

Mr Billing: Was there anything about a motive for meeting that night?

Respondent: Oh, yes. She wanted him to apologise. She stated that the letter which came to me next morning she had intercepted. At last I said, if she wanted to punish him, the best way to do it, would be to write him an assignation, and get an answer to it that might commit him. She readily consented to that, and I dictated to her that document which has been given in evidence, asking him to meet her under the tree.

I was going to make a copy of it, but she herself made a copy, so that both parts were in her handwriting. Mary Hickey was called into the room, and I told her that Mrs Molesworth had confessed her criminality with Mr Ireland. She said it was what might have been expected, for he never out of the house. I then told Mary Hickey that we both wished her to convey that letter to Mr Ireland and bring back a written answer.

During her absence Mrs Molesworth caught me by the hand, and said she had always respected me, but had never loved me. Mary Hickey returned with the scrap of paper appointing the time of half past six. It is in Mr Ireland's handwriting.

She stated that Mr Ireland had given her a very kind reception, had given her a glass of wine, seemed very glad to see her, and wrote that scrap of paper.

Mr Billing: Do you remember if there was any particular conversation the next morning?

Respondent: Well, the next morning Mrs Molesworth had changed her views. She did not deny the confession, but said she was very wrong in making such a statement.

She said that no woman who had had to do with a man ought to have betrayed him in the way she had betrayed Mr Ireland; but said nothing whatever intimating that her former statement was untrue. The day after that, on Sunday morning, she said, "What is to become of me?" and, "Let me fly from this country."

On Sunday afternoon, for the first time, she retracted the confession. It was on Saturday that Mrs Molesworth wrote the letter to Mr Ireland, which was afterwards handed to me, stating, "Let nothing prevent you coming to me." Mary Hickey, instead of carrying it to Mr Ireland, brought it to me; and, on the Saturday, Mr Ireland and I came out in the same omnibus accidentally, so that I was not absent from home. Mrs Ireland had got hold of his part of the assignation, and she wrote a letter to Mrs Molesworth, as angry as might be supposed, enclosing a copy of the assignation, and threatening to give me the original.

Those three letters were in one place in my desk – Mrs Ireland's letter, the copy of the assignation, and the letter which Mary Hickey handed to me. On the Sunday night Mrs Molesworth got my keys from the dressing room, and went to my desk for the three letters. She told me so the next day. However, she did not find the two documents that are now produced, as they were in a different place.

On the Monday, I told her she must leave my house, and she agreed to do so. On the Tuesday, I went to look for lodgings for her about St. Kilda; but, in the meantime, she had arranged to go and stay with a person named Poole, with whom we were acquainted; and I found that she had gone to the Pooles' when I came home. On Wednesday, she came to my house accompanied by Poole. I then ordered her to get out, and she refused. I then took her, and forcibly and publicly put her out, in Poole's presence. Poole is since dead. Shortly after that, she consented to go to England.

Till she consented to go, she was partly excluded from my house; but she came to the house stealthily. She did not come in my presence. She afterwards wrote a note, stating that she would go to England.

I got that note, because it in some degree diminished the danger of my being treated as in the case of her promise to go by the "Marco Polo". About that time I wrote the letter which is referred to as having been delivered by Mr O'Farrell. I exhibited that letter to a great many of my common acquaintances, Mr Mitchie, Mr Higginbotham, Mr Gurner and others. With reference to Chapman, I went into the bar dressing-room adjoining the court, Mr Ireland and Mr Chapman being together in the room. I handed a copy of the letter to Mr Chapman and requested him to read it.

Mr Ireland got very pale and did not attempt to assault me. I then got what purports to be an answer to that letter. That answer, which was in Mr Ireland's handwriting, has been read. At the time Mrs Molesworth consented to go to Europe, she came more to my house, and latterly I asked her to stay to dinner.

She, however, ceased to be altogether mistress of the house. She came to the house, and was at first tolerated, and, as the period of her departure arrived, she was better received. So far as I know, she never slept in the house; but I think that, on the last night of her stay in Melbourne, she did sleep in the house. She was to sail on the 29th of the month. She slept in the house.

Those were the only two occasions of intercourse between us – on the evening of the 28th and the morning of the 29th – on the evening of her departure and on the morning of her departure. After the first she asked to be allowed to sleep with me and I distinctly refused. She said something about me ordering a nice luncheon on the 29th, but that is all nonsense. Of course she had luncheon.

She also describes me as falling on my knees and apologising to her, and expressing myself favorable to her. here is not a particle of truth in her statement in that particular. On the 29th I walked with her from

St. Kilda to Sandridge to go on board the vessel. During our walk, I stated to her that, from what had occurred, my feelings were so far changed towards her, that I thought it not improbable I might bring her back to reside in Melbourne, but I did not say anything to her about coming to live with me as my wife. She then asked if that would be from any change of my opinion as to her criminality – my being satisfied as to her innocence. I did not give her an answer to that question. Throughout the journey she repeatedly protested to me that she never met Mr Ireland from the time she left my house. She said that from that time she had never seen him.

She put this forward as an argument in favour of her innocence. An argument of this kind – could it be supposed that if she cared for him it would be so – that she would not have seen him. On board of the ship we went into her intended cabin, and she then threw herself on her knees and protested her innocence, and that in a very loud voice, calling out "I am innocent, I am innocent," – in a state of great excitement, and she would not be checked as to the loudness of her tones.

I was very unwilling that her fellow passengers should hear her so expressing herself, because of the inference they would draw from it, and so I took leave of her and withdrew. After her departure from the colony, I received several letters from her, but I did not write any letter to her which she could receive before her departure from England. This is one of the several letters I received from her:-

"Gosport, 4th March.

Dear Robert, - I wrote you a letter by the last mail, mentioning it was my intention to return to Melbourne. I have now settled to leave this the 5th April, and to go back to the place which contains my children. I hope you will receive me as your wife into your house, and that we may meet as friends. I came from Melbourne to gratify and pacify you for a time, sacrificing my feelings to your pleasure.

I have accomplished that object now, and, as no income would ever oblige me to leave my own children, I now return to where they live. You are under the impression I was a faithless wife. I am not. What I said in violent, deep, concentrated passion – the natural passion of weeks, to madden you, feeling you wronged me, and when I saw you did feel it I then told the truth, which is I am innocent of all men, and had no occasion to err – never been provoked to do so by word or act.

Now, this business can't be proved but on our own assertions, and this is the case. If you do not believe me it is useless dwelling on a subject that can never be cleared up, but as I am not ashamed to return to Australia, I am determined to go back, and, if you don't wish to receive me as the mother of my children there is but one course to be adopted, namely, we separate with this proviso that you allow me a suitable allowance, take a respectable lodging or home for me, and I have the privilege of daily seeing my children, this I wish the world to know. I pleased you by coming unprotected to England for a reasonable time but as I have my character, in every sense of the word, to maintain, I too wish the world to judge am I or not guilty; and it can soon be seen if my conduct or acts will show a desire to levity; but as this unfortunate business occurred in Melbourne it is there that I have to be righted. Now as in all this business, I have acted openly, I feel it right to acquaint you with my plans. You recollect saying you were the person to redeem me or not.

Now, if you don't so, I must only see that I be supported by you as your wife and the mother of your children.

If we separate let it be a joint consent. When I arrive in Melbourne I hope I will not be thrown on the world, and that you will have made arrangements as to my future plans. I do not want to live with you if you don't please, but I will not submit to be put on the world without a suitable maintenance out of your power altogether. You did what you could to prove me guilty. I forgive you but I won't make myself so when I feel I am not."

On going to the ship from St. Kilda I did not ask her anything as to her guilt or innocence. From the time she made the confession, I never in any way intimated to her that I had the slightest doubt of its truth. I did not on the 29th of September promise to provide suitably for her maintenance out of this colony. There was some mention of maintenance, and I said I would send her £100 a year, quarterly. She said that would not be sufficient. No arrangement, however, was made as to suitable maintenance. When she was going by the "Marco Polo" I said to her that she knew enough of me to know that we would not be likely to differ about money matters.

When she was going away by the "Donald Mackay", she said "the allowance must be so much out of your power." Those words were never forgotten, "out of your power. I refused to make any allowance out of my power. I did not say that I would send for her in twelve months to return to cohabitation with me. I said I might send for her, but I gave no promise of cohabitation, and there was no definite period fixed. She sailed on the 29th September. She was in England about four months, and, during that time, I paid her twice £25. She got another £25 by an order. She did not exactly get it, but she left her sister an order for £25, which was to be forwarded to my agent. She got two sums of £25 regularly, and one sum of £25 irregularly, making £75 altogether.

I gave orders that, on her return, the house should be shut against her. When I went home, on the day of her return, she was at the house before me, and so we met. I asked her what brought her there. I said I would not receive her, and insisted that she should leave the house. She said she would not leave but to go to an hotel; and I said she might go to an hotel.

She then said she would not leave but in the carriage, and I said the carriage would be got for her. The carriage was got for her, and she and Mr Rose went to an hotel.

In the interim I was informed of the manner in which she had conducted herself in the house – that she had assumed the tone of its mistress.

She came back to the house the same evening and insisted on seeing me. Our conversation was then of a very angry character. I think she was abusive to me; but I cannot recollect any precise expression of abuse. I know I was abusive to her. I told her, I think, I would not permit a whore of a wife in my house, any more than I would any other whore. I required her then to quit my house, and she refused. As I was in the room, and she was in the hall at the door of the room, she threw a half-eaten apple at me, which struck piano behind where I was standing.

I took her then and rushed her out of the house. I did not kick her. I used my knee to put her out of the house, but I did not kick her. I forced her out of the hall and out of the gate. At the gate I struck her a single blow in the face. The instant after I struck the blow – the instant after – she called me an old cuckold, and said she might have cuckolded me twenty times if she had liked.

She then smashed one of the lamps of the carriage by which she had come out, and I returned into the house, leaving Mr Rose with her. A servant went out to her afterwards. She was vociferating, and had attracted a great crowd. She was shouting out, "A hundred a year" was what I heard most. She attracted a great crowd, but at last she was induced to depart. She wrote me a letter next day. It begins, "I am sorry there was a fight last night between us." This is the letter:- "Dear Robert, - I am sorry there was a fight between you and me last night, but you struck me violently in the eye, and my mouth is this day quite swelled. I am very ill indeed. I hope you will be reasonable; and, as I prefer making direct communication to yourself, if you allow me 300 pounds a year I will accept the offer. Of course this sum will only permit me to hire one servant and lodgings; but, having no wish to have my children's good favor before the public damaged, I prefer this sum rather than going to law with you, it must only reflect on your wife if she has not the common necessaries of life. You need have been under no apprehension as to my taking possession of your house, as that was not my design. I merely went to speak to you, but really I think you get so excited by seeing me, it is better not.

I was six months out of nine at sea, this must prove to the world my affection for any particular individual was not of a strong quality. But you are aware I took this voyage with the strict commands of you, and of you only. Now, no one can blame a mother to see her children, and with this object I have come out. Perhaps that is enough now to say. Had you taken a lodging for me, all this would have been spared, but you would not; and if you don't do so, who am I to ask now?

Again, saying I was in a passion, and of course not accountable for what I said, I did not mean to run you in debt, or to be unreasonable; I merely wish the children to be near me. I assure you I am perfectly indifferent to other acquaintances. I have shown this, and to prove it I would not mind returning home again if it pleased you."

I answered that letter by a draft. That is the only letter I ever wrote to her about money allowance. She was examined about this letter. I employed Mr Rose to carry the letter to her. I furnished Mr Rose with money to give her on her arrival - £5 or £6, I think, and for some time I think I gave him £5 or £6 a week for her, but that ceased very soon. It is not a fact that, in 1856, I wrote her a letter offering her £300 a year. The letter I wrote to her about money referred to her having arrived in an expensive place, but I did not state what my intentions were with respect to any allowance.

Mr Rose informed me that she was not disposed to remain here, but would go to England, if she got £300 a year. I told Mr Rose, if she would go to England, it should be £200 a year, and that this should be a permanent arrangement. I authorised Mr Rose to make this offer.

The whole subsequent arrangements were between her and Mr Rose, and he informed me that those terms were accepted.' Mrs Molesworth is in error as to many of the facts of the ball at Mr Putland's. It was not a ball of Putland's, but was an archery ball. She there abused me for about half an hour, without any answer on my part, and she flung a cup of coffee in my face. I did beat her then; but it was with the handle of a fire screen, one of those small fire screens that ladies hold in their hands. As to using a knife, I did nothing of the kind. This transaction occurred in 1847, at Dalkey, near Dublin. She afterwards, in her indignation, smashed a lamp that was in the hall.

My daughter several times expressed a wish to go to England, but I refused to let her go. She, however, fell into ill health, and the doctor recommended a long sea voyage and change of climate. I then consented to her going to England, and engaged the lady who had been with her as governess to accompany her, and to bring her back again. The arrangement was that my daughter was to have medical attendance in London. She did not go for the purposes of education.

On the contrary, I ordered that her education should be suspended during her illness. I said she was not to stay in England for a longer period than six months, and that the lady who accompanied her to England should return with her. I said that for all or part of the six months, if it was consistent with medical arrangements, she might remain with her mother, as I had no reason to believe there was any other criminality but the one instance, and as she was living with respectable people.

Accordingly, I did permit my daughter to join her mother in England. I may mention, though perhaps I do not exactly know it, that, after my daughter remaining with her mother till about March, she was sent to school. When I heard of this, I sent peremptory orders for her to come back, and stated that all money orders should be stopped till the lady who accompanied her home returned with her. At last she did come out, and at the last moment, my wife got into the same ship and came out with her. Precisely at the same time there came a communication from Mrs Hawker. This was the letter No. 8, attached to the communication and what is now produced.

I am sure this letter was written by Mrs Molesworth, though it is not in her natural or usual handwriting. [The witness here mentioned the several pieces of resemblances in the letter to the handwriting of Mrs Molesworth, as the t's, q', n's, w's, etc]. On the whole, I have no hesitation in saying that the letter was written by Mrs Molesworth, though to a certain extent, it is not in her ordinary handwriting. The letter was produced and handed in, but not read.

Cross-examined by Mr Dawson: Mrs Molesworth is a woman of a very excitable temper. Not eccentric, but very wayward. It is on the back that I struck her the blow at Putland's. I cannot say that I did not strike her anywhere else, as I am only certain of that. She did not sleep in the house that night after the beating, but went to a poor woman's house opposite. None of the servants came into the room during the beating. Not until after.

I do not remember either locking or unlocking the door. However, the servants did not come in, and she did not sleep in the house that night.

I remember a female child being born in 1854. It died afterwards.

That child was alive at the time of the fracas between me and Mr Ireland at Castlemaine. I had two medical advisers to attend the child. Dr. Patterson first, and also Dr. Motherwell afterwards. I never was reproached by Mrs John Thomas Smith about having caused the death of the child. I never had a word with her. She never was with Mrs Molesworth during her confinement with that child. Mrs Smith never had the most remote conversation with me at all on the subject; in fact, I never had any conversation with Mrs Smith on any domestic topics.

The letters produced are mine. Mrs Molesworth was not in a state of great excitement when she made the confession to me – not at all. I put a number of questions to her, several of which were leading questions. She commenced the conversation herself, entirely unsought for by me, and then the conversation went on with a number of questions and answers. She did not exactly convey to me the distance she went out on the night of the children's party, but I inferred from the whole of the conversation that she had gone altogether about half a mile with Mr Ireland.

She said, "He took me by degrees a long way from the house." I wanted her to describe the place and she failed to let me know the particular locality. She said it was near a house, but I did not know in what direction, though I was led to infer that it was in the direction of the Brighton Road. I could not distinctly understand the direction or the locality from her description. We were not living on good terms at the time, but most unhappily.

I went into the house after striking her on the road to St Kilda, and left her on the road with the servants, and a crowd about her. My income in 1855 and 1856 from all sources, was more than £2,500, it was near £3,000.

Mr Dawson: You admit that before your wife sailed for England you had intercourse with her. Now, do you not know, as a judge, that that restored her to her position – unequivocally to her position and rights as a wife?

Mr Molesworth: In point of law, I am not able to give you an answer.

Mr Dawson: If you were on the bench, and the question were put to you, would you say you did not know if that restored a wife to her conjugal rights?

Mr Molesworth: The point is a doubtful one.

Mr Dawson: And you give yourself the benefit of the doubt. Do you not know that one of the things that makes adultery so heinous is that it bastardises the issue?

Mr Molesworth: Yes.

Mr Dawson: And yet you acted with the deliberate knowledge that the child might not be your own, if a child were born within the proper time? This took place you know before she went to England?

Mr Molesworth: Yes; I am much better informed on the law of the subject now than I was then. In fact, I did not think of the law of the subject at the time at all.

Mr Dawson: Nor of your wife's feelings?

Mr Molesworth: Oh, I did.

Mr Dawson: Now, is it not all for a matter of maintenance that this case has been allowed to come into court?

Mr Molesworth: No; it is because the topics of your speech have been sedulously circulated throughout the country, and because your client was induced to file an affidavit on the records of the court, to the effect that I dared not bring the case into court.

Mr Dawson: But before my speech was made at all?

Mr Molesworth: Because she would not come to terms satisfactory to me. I allowed the case to come into court because she would not accept what I considered her character and conduct only entitled her to.

Mr Dawson: Now it comes to a difference of £100?

Mr Molesworth: No; a difference much more than that. The case at different times assumed different aspects.

Mr Dawson: If you had allowed her £300 a year in England would this painful case ever have been brought here?

Mr Molesworth: I do not know. I believe that whatever I might have submitted to I would have been dragged here, unless I had consented to her demands from time to time. I offered her £200 a year, and she accepted of it, and then broke through the arrangement. We were not on good terms when I gave her the £200. We were at arm's length then. When she made the claim I gave her £200 a year, and she accepted it. Considering her position at home, £200 a year was equal to what she had as my wife till we came here.

I had £500 or £600 a year at home during her well-conducted life. I thought that when she was ill-conducted I did enough for her in leaving her in the same position as when she was a well-conducted wife.

I did not consider that she should share in any augmentation of my income that occurred after she became an ill-conducted wife. Our scale of living was not much better here at first than at home, owing to high prices. What I gave her was inadequate for a well-conducted wife, and it was less than I might have given her if she had been civil. If she had been civil and well-conducted afterwards, I should have raised her income to considerably more than that.

Mr Dawson: Then you persevered in this because she would not be civil?

Mr Molesworth: And because I could not succeed in making an arrangement with her by any offer. When she came out from England, with the imputation of additional adultery, I said I would continue the same income if she would remain away. The largest amount I ever offered to allow her was £200 a year. When she came out the last time I offered her £200 a year. My daughter, when I sent her to England, was about fourteen or fifteen years of age. My sons are grown up.

Mr Michie: After you offered the £200 – that was after you received the information as to what took place with Hawker – you were about to answer, when you were stopped, much more as to the cause of the matter not being settled.

Mr Molesworth: That she had made an affidavit that I dare not bring the case before the court, and because the points in Mr Dawson's speech had been circulated throughout the country. I believe she was attended by Mr Howitt, not so much on account of any injury she had sustained, as that she might secure him to give evidence.

By the Jury: I did not see Mrs Molesworth on the night of the children's party, after her return from seeing Mr Ireland. I am not sure, for I had a black eye, and probably did not come downstairs. I am not distinct about it. I think I did not see her at all after. I did not know she was out. I had no idea that she and Ireland had met till she made her confession. She appeared a little intoxicated before she went out.

Upon her return from England she did not seem intoxicated. On her second visit not very intoxicated. I did not particularise the style of oath I should require her to take, but I said that it should be one of a very solemn nature. I think I used the word imprecation. That in the oath I should require her to take she would call down injuries on herself. She said she would not take such a form of oath as I proposed, but that she would kiss the book or go before a clergyman or arbitrator. I reminded her that a few days before she had wished all manner of curses on her head if she did not go by the "Marco Polo". I reminded her of that.

Mr Dawson: And you knew you would have rendered yourself liable to punishment if you had administered an oath not as a judge?

By the Jury: The cause of our not living as man and wife prior to our going to Castlemaine arose from a whole lot of petty squabbles such as Dunnes affair.

My motive for declaring to Mary Hickey what took place between my wife and Mr Ireland was that I wished her to go with a note to Mr Ireland, and because I wanted her as a witness.

By Mr Michie: Mary Hickey had been in our service for many years, and had lived with us in Ireland and in South Australia, and was almost as one of the family.

This concluded the case.

Mr Dawson then remarked that a number of letters had been put in and not read, because they only referred to domestic matters, and merely went to show the pleasant terms in which Mr and Mrs Molesworth corresponded with each other.

Mr Michie tendered as evidence the various letters and documents which had been read. Those which had been objected to were rejected; but after some argument, the court decided to receive the photographs as evidence.

Mr Michie then rose to address the Jury on behalf of the respondent. He said he might not unreasonably have asked the indulgence of being permitted to address them on the second occasion on the following morning, having to reply upon, or rather to sum up, such a vast body of evidence elicited from a considerable number of individuals during several days.

He confessed it would have been a satisfaction to his own mind had he been able to have a few hours to judge carefully the whole of the evidence before making his final observations upon it. That disadvantage under which he labored he had no doubt they would do their best to correct, by the careful attention they would bring to the weighing of that evidence when they retired to their room. They had now heard the whole of the evidence on both sides, and if his learned friend, in opening his case, had been justified in appealing to their sympathies on behalf of his client, he thought he had equal grounds for making the same request on behalf of the respondent, for, from the statement of his learned friend, or at any rate from the manner in which the petitioner had attempted to prove her case, he, the respondent, had been put upon his trial for the career of his life.

He asked them at the outset how far they thought, from their experience and observation of life, any individual could be more successful, or as successful, in going through that ordeal. They would bear in mind that, before Mrs Molesworth was put in the box, there must have been some interviews between her and her professional advisers, as to how she was to prove her case, and that after that consideration, she had begun at the beginning of her married life, and, as far as he had learned from her manner and demeanor in the box, had disparaged and demeaned her husband to the utmost. Whatever she might have said, she had accepted him as her husband.

She had full opportunity to ascertain whether there was any disparity of tastes between them, and might have rejected the man she accepted; and he called upon them, in considering the case, to dismiss from their minds any preconceived prejudice or passion they might have entertained. He thought they would not hesitate to recognise the true and golden principle that when a woman did accept a man she should honestly endeavor to fulfil the obligations of married life. This was not the only case in which disparity of temper and difference of tastes had occurred, but he had yet to learn that it was to be an excuse for misconduct.

The petitioner, to speak in the most moderate manner, was a woman distinguished by a peculiar levity. Her husband was a man of grave and studious habits, and possibly did not enjoy the same kind of amusements that were acceptable to her.

She had full opportunities of judging of these things, the same as other women, and it was her bounden duty, in that relationship so contracted between them, honestly and scripturally to observe those relations, and not unreasonably to rebel against the authority her husband chose to bring to bear upon them. He referred to the exaggerated account that she had given of the assault in Ireland, and remarked that, whatever its character might have been, it had been condoned by her, and they had afterwards lived amicably and happily together.

If the graveness of his pursuits prevented him from participating in the amusements she liked, she ought to have known that men of his profession, whose duties engrossed them for many hours in the day, and whose minds were exhausted by the toll of their profession, were not likely to enter into such pursuits. In fact, he might say, that men of that profession could not, if they wished faithfully to perform their duty to the public, indulge in such amusements, and all that could be required from a man in that position was that he should not cruelly prevent his wife from indulging in reasonable enjoyments.

The whole of the evidence, however, proved that he was neither a cruel nor an unkind husband. On the contrary, he was satisfied that he was a kind and indulgent husband, and, if he had once or twice been guilty of harsh conduct, it was only when his suspicions had so tortured him as to dethrone his reason. He could not say that he lives in bliss, who is certain of his fate and loves not his wronger, but how miserable he must be.

Who dotes, yet doubts; suspects, yet fondly loves. They came out here, and were happy; and would possibly have been happy yet, but for the unfortunate acquaintances made by them. They had heard from the witnesses called on the part of the petitioner, the origin and history of that unhappy intimacy. It was possible that one informant might have prepossessed them to a certain extent in favor of the account he had given of that intimacy.

They had heard, subsequent to that, the accounts other witnesses had given of that intimacy; and, now that they had the whole facts before them, he asked if it was a reasonable, or even a decent thing, for that witness to state in the box that he was pursuing a reasonable and merciful course of conduct to the woman he had injured in that long course of correspondence between them.

He confessed that, whatever opinions they had contracted or adopted with respect to other parts of the case, he was utterly unable to understand the operations of that witness's mind, when he said in answer to a question put by Mr Wood, that he had not recollected having done anything that could savor of what could be denominated an impropriety with Mrs Molesworth. That, nevertheless, was his evidence.

It might not have appeared an impropriety to him, but he (Mr Michie) believed he was addressing husbands, and he appealed from that witness's evidence to their judgement and consciences, and he would ask them, one and all, what would they say to a man who went backwards and forwards behind their backs, carrying letters, receiving them, answering letters – this self-constituted medium – this self-constituted sort of father-confessor, who seemed to think he had some sort of special commission for the purpose of reconciling matrimonial disputes?

What would they say if they were woke up, after a considerable number of months, to the discovery that there was this sort of thing going on; and that, with the view of reconciling them to their wife, there was this constant passing backwards and forwards and forwards and backwards? What would they think of it themselves? He put it thus to them, for that was the way in which the witness had put it, and yet still said it was reasonable to take the course he did.

If he had, in the course of his correspondence with Mr and Mrs Molesworth, suddenly lighted upon the discovery that she had conceived even the slightest preference, either for his person or his company, and had lighted then, or soon after, upon the further discovery that something like jealousy appeared in the mind of her husband, he asked them, as rational men, whether they did not think the conduct of that witness should have been peculiarly prudent, peculiarly abstinent of any exhibition of even apparent intimacy, and a careful and constant abstinence of being seen alone in her company.

Was not that, he asked, the right, the safe, the only prudent course? But he (the witness in question) had given them an account of the course he thought proper to adopt, and he had also given them a description of the scene at Castlemaine. They had heard Mrs Molesworth's version, Mr Ireland's version, and Mr Molesworth's version of that interview, and they were now able to arrive at a tolerably correct estimate of the result of that interview. They had heard Mr Ireland's version of it, and he had asked them was it reasonable that Mr Molesworth should ask him to sit up with her (Mrs Molesworth)? He gave his other evidence also in the same manner, and told, flippantly, decisively, and unhesitatingly, how he took up his whip and hat and went out to meet Mr Molesworth.

From the confident manner in which he gave this evidence, they would have believed him, had they not seen how he broke down under the cross-examination. They must have observed how he broke down under it, when he (Mr Michie) placed the note of assignation in his hand; and, from the way in which he broke down, he asked them to reject his evidence when he told them that Mr Molesworth asked him to stop up with Mrs Molesworth, after her husband had retired to bed. He asked them to reject it, because he set his client, and his demeanor in the box against Mr Ireland's testimony; and, as he found a direct conflict of testimony on that point, he asked them to believe Mr Molesworth and disbelieve Mr Ireland.

When Mr Molesworth had honestly admitted assaulting his wife, and had passed through that ordeal, painful as it was, truthfully, he would ask them to give his evidence every consideration, and accept his denial of Mr Ireland's statement that he was drunk.

The learned counsel next noticed the discrepancy between Mrs Molesworth's and Mr Ireland's account of the interview at Castlemaine, observing that the former, not-withstanding the latter's denial of the fact, had admitted that a crim. con. case was one of the subjects of conversation, and remarking that, even if Mrs Molesworth had introduced the subject, he should have endeavoured to divert the conversation to other topics. After characterising the evidence of Mary Hickey as one of the most trustworthy description, he again appealed to the jury as to whether Mr Ireland's conduct had been marked by any degree of propriety. If they had observed persons walking together in a secluded situation for an hour, would they not have thought it a monstrous thing for a man, when he knew the husband was confined to his house in consequence of the violence he had himself inflicted, to act in this manner?

The learned counsel directed the attention of the jury to the admission of guilt made by Mrs Molesworth to her husband, and asked them to accept it as true, unless they were prepared to accept another and still more dreadful alternative.

Could they suppose that she, with the knowledge and conviction that she and Mr Ireland were innocent, circumstantially informed her husband that she had been guilty of the act of incontinence once – once only she said – upon the night of the children's party? They must accept the statement of her guilt, unless they were prepared to believe in an amount of heartlessness and depravity which he, for one, would not believe in, unless it was carried to absolute demonstration. No; they must necessarily believe that she thus told her husband was grievously true, and that she did not invent this narrative as to the circumstances under which the interview took place.

She had left upon her husband's mind the conviction which had never been purged from his mind, and which probably never would be until his dying day – that she had on that occasion committed adultery with Mr Ireland. She had transformed him from the moderate man, in all his intellectual operations, into something that he himself feared to think of, and it was not to be considered at that when in that state of mind he had committed acts which in another frame of mind he would not have been guilty of.

After referring to the difference in the statements made by Mr Rose and the petitioner as regarded the dinner at Bignell's Hotel, the learned counsel referred to the petitioner's career in England, and asked if any credit would be given to her account of her residence there. He again referred to the letter found by Mrs Hawker, remarking upon the improbability of the petitioner's story upon this point, and contending that the evidence adduced before the commission, supported as it was by the unmistakeable testimony of the photographer, was satisfactory proof that the petitioner and Mrs Smyth were the same person, and that, in England, at the time mentioned, she had given birth to a child. The learned counsel concluded a powerful appeal to the jury by asking them to give a verdict in accordance with the evidence adduced on behalf of the respondent.

Mr Dawson then proceeded to address the jury in reply. He commenced by stating that the respondent was to be congratulated on this ground, if on no other, that he had secured an able palliator of his conduct. His learned friend, however, was very unfortunate in his reference to the Moor – in his quotation from "Othello" – for in this case the respondent was the self inventor of his alleged wrongs.

There was one point in particular to which he desired the jury to attend, and that was that, after all this painful suspicion in the over wrought mind of the respondent, he could have sexual intercourse with his wife. Was this man to be compared to the Moor of Venice? A man who could send his wife back to England with the full knowledge that she must become a prostitute. And there was his own handwriting for that. What on the other hand was the conduct of the Moor? What did he say in his case - I had rather be a toad. And live upon the vapor of a dungeon, Than keep a corner in the thing I love For others' uses.

But the respondent in this case could keep a corner in the thing he loved for others' uses and his own. Let there not, then, be any quotations from Shakespeare. Let there be no pathetic allusions, but let the question be answered – was the woman to be sent adrift upon the world – and, whatever this woman may have been, was her conduct owing to the conduct of her husband towards her. Let the jury say that, throughout this trial, she would be assisted by them, and assisted and maintained by her husband.

His learned friend had glossed over the facts of the case, and he sought to seduce the attention of the jury from its main features.

She complained that she had been treated cruelly, and she had proved it, and the way the respondent defended his conduct was by reviving a trumped up story nine years old. He said she had fallen, and he would drive her on the world – drive her into the jaws of that fate he anticipated for her, and therefore he would not give her a single sixpence. His learned friend said that they must not be too hard upon human nature because sometimes a man might be transformed beyond his nature in moments of passion. So he might.

But if he committed acts of cruelty to his wife in such moments, was his wife to have no right to complain? Had she no right to complain of the treatment she received because she wanted to go to an archery ball? It was not denied that on that occasion he took her into a room and beat her with a stick – it was no matter whether it was with a broom handle or not. It was said she should have known what her husband's temper was before she married him. But was it not also his duty – he was some fifteen years her senior – to have known her temper before he married her? Was he to have all the consideration and she to have none?

Was he, her senior, and a wiser man than she was a woman, not to see to her character? Did he take her for his wife without knowing all her eccentricities of character? She being so much younger than he, and he so much her senior, and so much wiser than she could be expected to be, he had the moulding of her character. It was said that he, being a man of a studious character, should not have been induced to go into company. Well, if so, there was surely some other way of treating his wife than by beating her with a stick. She was a young girl at the time, and for a man to take her into a room, and beat her with a stick, was an outrage that no man, who did not forget his manhood would be guilty of. She flung a cup of coffee at him, forsooth. Well, even so. He supposed that that was not done without some cause. What was the nature of the beating was easily seen, from the fact that she did not sleep at home that night, but was glad to get shelter in a neighbor's house. Yet, this conduct was sought to be palliated as a mere ebullition of temper – a mere escapement of human infirmity. She had to flee from her home, and no man would attempt to palliate or justify such conduct.

There were no motives for it except that there was some disagreement as to whether she should go to a ball or not. Then it was said that they lived happily for years after this, and, that all her conduct was condoned. This was the meanest defence that could be set up, for a wife was entirely in the power of her husband.

A certain intercourse with a wife was even a condonation of adultery on the part of the husband.

He supposed the petitioner had done what many other wives had done. She had, rather than expose her husband, submitted to the treatment she experienced at his hands. So much for the first part of the case, and, with respect to it, the respondent stood convicted on his own confession of having, at the commencement of his married life, committed a brutal outrage.

Here there was no provocation whatever. In her own house, she was treated to outrages of a most brutal character. For instance, there was the case of her relative Penfold, who was sent away from the house in an ignominious manner, and yet the respondent had admitted that there was no other ground for jealousy than that they called each other by their christian names. Then there was the case of Mr Dunne, the barrister. Why were they to have names dragged before the public in that way? It was the respondent's fault. The petitioner was bound to drag those names forward. Driven to assert her rights, she was bound to drag those names forward. In one of his letters the respondent complained of occasional tipsiness; and yet they found him complaining of her not having wine on the table.

Those, they might believe, were only samples of his conduct, and that the whole atmosphere of her life, as a wife, was destroyed by his conduct. She felt herself unworthy to sit at his table; and blushed to look at her children when she found the position in which she was placed; and yet, when this culmination of temper got up and he struck her a blow, he was to be let off because it was an escapement of temper. All that took place before the affair with Mr Ireland. As her letters stated, she lived a most unhappy life; so much so that she and her husband occupied different beds. And for what reason? It might have resulted in a most condemnatory answer; but it did not, for it was only because of some petty squabbles.

Mr O'Grady Rose said they lived very happily. That was his opinion of happiness, and it seemed to be much the same as his opinion of cruelty to women, for he did not think the treatment she received could be very bad, seeing she did not take to her bed.

As to Mr Ireland, the respondent could not himself make up his mind, and yet he asked the jury, after so long a period, to make up theirs upon it. As to the frequency of Mr Ireland's visits and notes, they know that nine years ago there was not so much regard paid as to the hours at which visits were made as was the case now.

People visited at all hours then; and they found that the respondent himself asked Mr Ireland into his house one night at ten o'clock.

Then they went to Castlemaine with Mr Ireland, and a change took place there, yet they afterwards found him going to Mr Ireland, and insisting on his friend Mr Ireland coming to his house and having a glass of wine. However, as to Castlemaine affair, instead of acting as he did, he might have suggested to her that it was inconvenient for her to be sitting up so late; and, indeed, there were a hundred ways of acting otherwise than he did. If he had seen her falling, or supposed she was falling, was it not his duty to have put forth a hand to help her, and prevent her falling.

Some words escaped, and he, hearing them, was jealous, and now he said there was nothing in them. She went on the previous night to Butterworth's, and he pressed Mr Ireland upon her, and he got up and followed them.

He denied that, but Mr Ireland was as much to be believed as he was. Now, all this was on the unfounded suspicion of Mr Molesworth himself, and it was put down by his learned friend as being a mere ebullition of temper - an escapement of human infirmity.

Coming to the case of confession, the learned gentleman referred to the case of Robinson v. Robinson and Lane, and quoted "Bridget's Hand Book on Divorce," where it was stated that confessions, though not inadmissible, were to be regarded with the greatest distrust, and went on to refer to the canon law, which said that faith was not to be placed in confessions. Then Lord Cockburn, in the case of Robinson v. Robinson and Lane (Swaby and Tristem, vol L, p325), made use of the following expression:- "No doubt the admission of a wife unsupported by proof should be received with the utmost caution, on account of the probable existence of sinister motives, &c." That was the principle that applied in this case. An admission was made the one day and was contradicted the next. After all his tentative examination, for that was what it was, he could not elicit the spot where the offence was committed.

The fact was, she could not tell him the place, for the offence never occurred. His taking the domestic servant into the room at once, and telling her that Mrs Molesworth had confessed, was evidently for the purpose of nailing her to her confession. Yet, after that, he made his wife a tool to entrap Mr Ireland.

Mary Hickey conveyed the note, and got the answer on the slip of paper with "half past six" upon it. Amongst those muniments of shame folded up in a judge's despatch box – out of that Pandora's box from which hope had long before escaped – was found the slip labelled No. 2, with half past six upon it.

It became all the more cruel that, after the scandal had been hanging over people's heads for nine years, it should be raked up, and when it came to the proof, there was no proof in it. Then, as to the night of the children's party, Mrs Molesworth went out in her evening dress, and, in passing Mary Hickey, borrowed her shawl and bonnet. On her return, no portion of her dress exhibited any disordered appearance. The confession, then, was merely a piece of bravado.

When she came in she went up stairs with Mary Hickey, and, in the course of their conversation, it appeared there was some pique against Mr Ireland, and so she mentioned his name to gratify her pique, and, at the same time, annoy her husband because of his jealousy. He then referred to the intimacy between the petitioner and the respondent on the night and morning before she sailed to England, and remarked that, with respect to whatever points there might be doubt as to condonation, there was no doubt as to condonation by such intimacy. He used her as a mistress, and then cast her off, sending her to England and allowing her £100 a year.

By this act she was disgraced in the eyes of her people, who would naturally ask her where was her income and where was her position. However, she found out that she had committed a mistake in going to England, and so she returned, and that on the advice of the highest legal authority. They were told that, when she went into the house, she acted in a most imperious and domineering manner, and as if she were mistress of the house. So she was. At that time, she was the mistress of the house and was Mr Molesworth's lawful wife. In the eyes both of God and man she was his lawful wife.

The exemplary coolness of Rose was all of a piece with his conduct throughout. He could not have a heart, though he might have some gristly substance that performed the functions of a heart.

Rose, when he saw her, asked her what she had come there for; and she had told him she had come to assert her rights. Poor Rose, he did not know what had taken place, and so he was to be excused; and poor Rose said, "Oh, he'll put you out; there'll be such a row." Rose seemed to be like the stormy petrel, he always felt right in the prospect of a row.

He could not understand such conduct on the part of Mr Rose; for he had always found him, in his official capacity, most courteous and obliging. Something extraordinary must have come over him. Well, the respondent came home; some words passed, and Rose got £5 to give her. Give her £5 and send her into the next street. Was that the way to treat a wife? They were told that the language used was something of this style:- "Out, harlot; out of my house, harlot. Avaunt!" And Mr Molesworth admitted that he called her a whore.

He had hoped that the blow might have been explained, but it was not. He said he did not kick her, but merely put his knee to her back – to expedite her movements, he supposed. The blow was not explained. No; he knocked his wife down in the public street, and left her there. He knocked her down, and withdrew into the house; and, as he had been told, he actually sent for a policeman to take her away. If it had been the merest drab he could not have acted worse. The respondent said it was a single blow. It might, but it was a knock down one, and he would ask them to fancy the effect of such a blow on the temper of a lady in the presence of a number of people.

She was of course transformed in temper at once, on account of that, and no doubt then used the word "cuckold" in answer to his charge that she was a whore. In the letter that she wrote next day, the spirit of the woman and of the wife spoke out, and not only that, but in the same letter she asked that Mary Hickey might be allowed to come and live with her. Was that, he asked, what a woman who was unfaithful would do? That letter, he submitted, was a most proper and womanly letter, and he also asked the jury to contrast it with the unfeeling conduct of the respondent. Though he knew she was under the necessity of having a doctor, he said that she called in Dr. Howitt that he might be a witness in the inquiry.

She went away again in 1856, and from that time to 1861, there was no imputation against her. He maintained that under all circumstances of the case she was entitled to maintenance.

During this time, between 1856 and 1861, he actually sent his daughter Josephine home to be under his wife's protection, though previous to this he had accused her of tipsiness, and suggested the probability of her becoming a prostitute to her seducers. He maintained that whatever course a woman pursued after that, the husband was himself to blame for it.

As to Mrs Hawker's letter, he held that a document of such a kind was no evidence, unless it was corroborated. The letter began, "Dear Tom," and, because of that expression, the jury was asked to believe that she had committed adultery with somebody, but his learned friend, Mr Michie, could not make out from it that there had been adultery committed with anybody – not even by the evidence of that jealous woman, Mrs Hawker, or any one else who was living in the same house with Mrs Molesworth. Mrs Hawker never suspected Mrs Molesworth until she found the letter in her husband's pocket-book. Mrs Molesworth, when questioned by Mrs Hawker about the letter, gave an answer, and Mr Hawker said it was just what he had told his wife two hours before. It was all very well to say that he seized on Mrs Molesworth's answer as being glad to get hold of anything to get off, but it must be remembered that he gave the same answer two hours before Mrs Molesworth went into the house.

The fact was that the letter was picked up in Mrs Molesworth's room, and before Hawker had time to replace it. Mrs Molesworth came down stairs, and so it was found in his pocket-book.

Every act of Mrs Molesworth was only capable of equivocal explanation because of her husband's conduct. As to the evidence obtained under commission, something more was necessary to render it sufficient and decisive as to criminality. The petitioner having lived for five or six years without any criminality, or complaint of criminality, the jury were bound to give her the benefit of her good character during that time. All the evidence before the commission, while she was at Plymouth, was that she conducted herself in a most careful manner; and was it to be supposed that a woman who had conducted herself properly during her daughter's absence, would act otherwise when her daughter was present.

As to the photographer, he asked if Mrs Molesworth was to be condemned because she was not like her own likeness, for that was what it came to, as far as the photographer was concerned. It was absurd to say that a photograph could not be mistaken for anyone but the person whom it purported to represent. They all knew in their own experience that many photographs were so unlike the original that, but for some suggestive look by the person showing it, there would be no difficulty in recognising it.

As to the evidence of the commission, it was evidence against a woman in her absence. How would it have been, he would like to know, with the witnesses if Mrs Molesworth had suddenly entered the room while the women were giving evidence in such a beautiful piece of scandal? Would they not all have been a little confused?

Now, it was not by the evidence of a photograph that a criminal was tried and condemned, but by the witness swearing to the identity of the criminal in the dock; and, if the witness said that there was only a resemblance between the prisoner and the guilty party, a jury would give the prisoner the benefit of the doubt; much more so would they do that where a photograph only was produced. He claimed, therefore, that, where the witnesses could only swear to a resemblance, the persons accused should be acquitted – and the witnesses before the commission swore only to a resemblance.

He next came to the birth of a child in October, 1862. Mrs Molesworth left Australia in June of that year. A child was born on the 21st October following. Now it might from that be suggested that she left because she was enceinte.

If so, previous to June, 1862, she must have been living in adulterous communication with some one, but where was the proof? There was not a tittle of evidence of that, and consequently they were launched on an inquiry 16,000 miles away, conducted in the absence of the accused.

He did not attempt to explain it. All he would say was, that it was not impossible, under her circumstances, that she might have become acquainted with some woman, wandering and neglected, and have lent her her clothes and her name to enable her to conceal her disgrace, for there was a sort of freemasonry amongst women so circumstanced; and if she met with a woman so situated, who was to blame but her husband – he who had disgraced her?

There was nothing impossible or improbable in that. As for the letter signed Smyth, he cared not whether it was written by Mrs Molesworth or not.

It seemed monstrous, if she were passing under an assumed name, that she should allow her boxes with the name of Mrs Molesworth upon them to go to the house; and she also had with her jewellery with her own name upon it. That, he thought, did not much look like deception.

Beyond all question, he maintained that he had a right to ask that her testimony in this matter should be accepted by the jury, for it might be true in spite of all the evidence taken before the commission. If it were so, it came to this – that she had been a party to screening some unhappy woman with whom she had met, and that was the worst that could be said. Where was the impossibility of that? Were there no women in the world in such a position who would take advantage of a woman like Mrs Molesworth in order to screen themselves?

As he had said before he said again, that general issues like this were not to be decided except on clear and decisive testimony. The jury, he felt sure, would pause long before they would say that, strange as her conduct might seem, they were not unwilling to convict her of perjury, and brand her as a harlot, and that on the ground that somebody had a portrait that was said to be hers, but which might be the portrait of somebody else.

He would now leave the case in the hands of the jury, who had to decide a most momentous issue. In coming to a decision, they would have to consider the relations of husband and wife.

They would have to trace her from the time of her leaving Australia to the time she came back, still invested with the rights and privileges of a wife. The respondent desired to cast his wife on the world, and he asked the jury to weigh in the scales of truth and honour such flimsy evidence as he had been able to bring forward. He implored the jury not to be worse, not to be more cruel, to the petitioner than her own husband had been. She had her fate before her; but she had a woman's affections. She had children, and in a distant land she had her mother and sisters. The darkness of grief overshadowed their house now, and he asked the jury not to let that shadow become darker by adding to it a lingering and lasting shame. He trusted, and not in vain, that justice would be done to his client. That the claim was made here on the holiest grounds, he was there to say. Whatever wrong she was guilty of, her husband was guilty of, and he called on the jury not to visit on an innocent woman the punishment that should be visited on the guilty. Let them not find a verdict that would drive her into misery and exile.

The Chief Justice intimated that at that late hour (half past five o'clock) he would not proceed with his charge to the jury.

The court then adjourned until the following day, at ten o'clock.

Molesworth (wife) v. Molesworth

DIVORCE COURT

Tuesday, 22nd November.
(Before the Chief Justice, and a Special Jury of Twelve)

MOLESWORTH (WIFE) v. MOLESWORTH

Extract from *The Age*, Wednesday 23rd November, 1864

> Petition for judicial separation. Mr Dawson and Mr Wood for the petitioner; Mr Billing and Mr Michie, Q.C., for the respondent.

The respondent's case had concluded the day previous, and counsel had addressed the court on both sides, but his Honour's charge to the jury had been reserved until this morning.

The Chief Justice, in making his charge, explained that the jury had to determine upon certain issues which had been sent down from the Supreme Court, in its divorce and matrimonial jurisdiction, for their decision.

They would observe that they were now discharging a purely ministerial duty; in fact, they had simply to determine upon questions of fact, upon which the court would afterwards draw their conclusions. In the course of the eloquent addresses which they had heard on both sides, and in the voluminous evidence which had been given, the whole case had been gone into, and naturally too, he thought, because they would have to consider the conduct of both petitioner and respondent throughout their married life.

Therefore, simply to have presented these issues before them in the dry and formal way he should have to put them, would not have put them in possession of the whole facts of the case; and, although the facts ranged over such a large period of time, they would have to find on the issues in the manner in which they had been presented to them, and say either aye or nay. Some would require more attention than others; some of the evidence was conflicting, and some was not; but to all of these eighteen issues he must have an answer. He thought it necessary for him to explain this point; for, generally speaking, these issues consisted of one or two questions of particular conduct, and not, as in the present instance, of transactions that had been sub-divided, he would not say complicated, into eighteen distinct questions.

Although they were numbered in the order in which they had been taken from the petition and answer, he had put them in chronological order, according to the evidence;

and he thought that would be a more convenient mode of taking them. They would see that there were charges on one part, and counter-charges on the other, and the issues showed that the petitioner charged cruelty against the respondent, and that the respondent charged adultery against the petitioner.

The learned judge then enumerated the various issues which the jury had to consider, and remarked that they simply had to answer these questions, and they must answer all of them. He could not take an answer upon one or more issues; it would be an insufficient verdict. They would, no doubt, experience some difficulty in finding upon them all, but it was their duty to answer them all, and so prevent a repetition of this evidence in a court of justice. All these questions, arising out of this particular branch of the court's jurisdiction, were peculiar in themselves.

Generally speaking, in the courts of law, it was simply a question as to whether there was a promise or not, or whether there was a particular contract or not. But here there were charges of adultery on one side and cruelty on the other.

They must remember that unkind conduct, or what the law in these cases called unkind conduct, did not consist in one act of cruelty, but in a series of small, minute, and what, under other circumstances, would be considered insignificant acts; and they would have to make their own allowance as to what importance ought to be attached to each.

It was for this reason that the court considered it advisable that these questions should be submitted to a jury consisting of a larger number than the court, and being men who were practically acquainted with life. He was aware that it was a hackneyed thing to say, and perhaps it was hardly necessary to say it, but it was his duty to tell them to disabuse their minds as much as possible from any impressions that might have been made upon them by the discussion of the question out of doors. They had, no doubt, acquired predilections of their own, and had formed their own opinion of the case, and entertained particular sentiments with regard to it. He must ask them to divest themselves of all those predilections, to annihilate them, and to crush out all their sentiments on the matter, and to consider the question fairly and justly – simply as a matter between the plaintiff and respondent. They were, in point of fact, deciding a question outside any principle as to the proper conduct of persons in married life, and had simply to decide the questions which had been submitted to them.

The first issue was, "that for the period of nine months prior to September, 1855, by a course of unkind conduct towards her, he rendered her life miserable." The time, they would see, was limited to a period of nine months anterior to September, 1855, which they would remember was the period when she first left for England, but they must nevertheless take into consideration how much his conduct during that time was likely to resemble that of previous years, for it must be remembered that the habits and tempers of people did not suddenly change.

As regarded these charges themselves, the jury would have to consider whether they were unjust or not, and whether they had been made from unfounded jealousy. They would remember, in considering this part of the case, that the plaintiff herself said that she had never wanted money until she had left the colony – that her wants were supplied by her husband, and that her bills were paid by him, and that she never wanted money until she went to England.

She also spoke of her husband being kind to her, except in reference to these charges. The evidence pointed, so far as this period was concerned, to a number of unfounded jealousies, and there was no question whatsoever that false accusations made by a husband against his wife were, perhaps, the most irritating kind of annoyance that could be imagined; for, if a wife was really devoted and attached to her husband, the least thing she would suppose was that she should not be suspected;

and, on the other hand, if her husband was a man of peculiar temperament, and became jealous of any person without cause; it was her duty to be as circumspect as possible, and if by her acts she caused him to entertain suspicions, however unjust they might be, she brought upon herself all the consequences of her conduct, and if she was afterwards treated with unkindness it was her fault.

In the very commencement of the evidence of this case, it appeared that the petitioner and respondent were married in 1840, but the jury did not know anything of their life until 1847, when the petitioner said that, in consequence of her wishing to go to a ball, a dispute arose between her and the respondent.

They did not know whether any suspicions clouded his mind at the time, but she certainly appeared to have got the tickets in a peculiar manner – without any name to them.

Whether it was that the respondent considered it unbecoming for her to go to the ball, or simply did not wish her to go, they did not know; but an angry recrimination took place, which culminated, she said, when throwing a cup of coffee at him. But no matter whether that occurred or not, something followed which he considered should not have taken place. He struck a blow, and, whether it was with the handle of the fire-screen as he said, or the brush as she stated, did not so much matter. It was the indignity of the blow that was to be considered – an indignity which was so severely felt by the petitioner that she left the house.

They must consider how far this was brought upon the petitioner by her own conduct, and not as to how far what then took place consisted in deciding what took place after, for although the evidence on the point had been listened to, it was quite outside the issue. Well, after that, she returned to their house and they lived together, and the jury must say if they did not think that, had there been any actual charges of criminality, they would not then have been brought. Then they would say if it was not so, was it not singular that charges should have been made after the wife had become the mother, and they had lived for a number of years together. After that, they heard nothing more of their new life until they came to South Australia, and until they had been in Victoria some time, they knew nothing about them. Then there were a series of charges; and, he thought, they would now see the importance of the observations he had addressed to them about the duties of husband and wife.

She gave her evidence about these charges, and, although certain names were introduced that need not have been, he did not like to stop it. But, however, gentlemen's names had been introduced – gentlemen who had nothing to do with the matter, and to whom it was very unpleasant to be mixed up with such charges, and who had not been in any way implicated. He would not mention the names again, but they would remember that she had stated that she had been insulted by a relative of hers having been turned out of the respondent's house. Well, two versions had been given of that affair, and they must say which of the two they believed, because, if the connection of hers was asked to the house, and even if they called each other by their christian names, if no undue familiarity occurred, there was no cause in the action he took.

But if the husband thought there was an improper degree of familiarity, and told his wife so, and she gave her husband cause to suspect – even if nothing serious occurred, and her conduct only arose from the love of admiration – and he took strong measures to get that person out of the house, they would say how far he was justified in the matter. He said that he had observed a dangerous familiarity between them, and warned her, and that after that she asked the person to remain in the house contrary to her husband's wishes. Whether this was the case or not, if he thought there was any danger of improper intimacy between them, he only did his duty in warning her.

There was another case in which a gentleman was intimate with the respondent, and who still entertained friendly feelings towards him. In defiance of her husband, the petitioner had invited him to dine on Sunday. This setting at naught her husband's authority was what no husband should submit to, and he took a course which he would not otherwise have done. That was the respondent's statement; and the petitioner's was, that her husband was jealous of this man, and that, because he had offended him in her presence, he had been guilty of unkind conduct towards her.

There was another person who had also been asked at Castlemaine, but the matter was of such a trivial character that he hardly considered it worthy of consideration. Then there was the conduct of the respondent towards the petitioner as regarded Mr Ireland. That involved two questions – in fact three - but they would confine themselves to two.

The petitioner alleged, as he understood, that the respondent's conduct to Mr Ireland was peculiarly unkind, as he was quarrelling with him in her presence, and, in fact, that he was jealous of this gentleman without cause. This involved, too, a distinct question, which they would afterwards have to consider, namely, whether her conduct with Mr Ireland, during the period referred to in the issue, had been unduly familiar for a married woman. There was also the specific charge of adultery which would have to be considered afterwards, but, in the present issue, they must bear in mind they were not considering him, but her and her conduct.

This charge arose, it appeared, out of the fracas at Castlemaine, and the whole course of his conduct towards her for months. The respondent said he was first jealous of him, and not then of any one else, but that he afterwards became jealous of Mr Penfold. There were several different versions given of the affair at Castlemaine. The petitioner and Mr Ireland said that the respondent invited him to go to Castlemaine; and the respondent, as he understood, said he wished his wife to go, but did not think one way or the other about Mr Ireland's going. There was no jealousy existing then, according to the respondent; but, at the outset, he must remark that it appeared a singular thing that a married man should have been asked to accompany him with his wife and child. If there had been jealousy before, and he had asked the person of whom he was jealous to accompany his wife, it would give a very grave aspect to the question.

Mr Wood: He said he had a trifling feeling of jealousy.

The Chief Justice: He advisedly said that he was not jealous at the time. However, he said that so little suspicion had he that he allowed his wife to go with Mr Ireland to buy this dress or skirt. They came back together, and he did not hesitate to say that, if he had been jealous in the ordinary acceptation of the term, the very last thing he should have done was to let them go out together in that way. If a woman was wayward, it was the husband's duty to check her; and, if he saw her going, it might be to ruin, and did not hold out a hand to her, he deserved the greatest amount of censure.

If the respondent's wife chose to go out to purchase this skirt with the person whom her husband was jealous of, he was most culpable to allow it.

There was a point of the testimony in regard to this matter on which there was a direct conflict. She (the petitioner) said he allowed them to go out, and then followed them in order to watch them. He said he did no such thing; that he was not jealous at the time; and that, either from indolence or thoughtlessness, or from not liking to go out, he let them go.

Afterwards, he said, he became jealous from his wife taking the arm of Mr Ireland. If the three were living together, and walked out together, the mere taking his arm was a matter of courtesy. It might have been done innocently, or from a love of admiration, or it might have been done in a different way. He said, afterwards, that he wanted her to go out with him to invite a person to dinner, but that she declined, on the ground of being tired, and that, when he came back, he found she had been walking out with Mr Ireland late in the evening.

That might have been perfectly innocent with regard to Mr Ireland, but, if the respondent's version was true, they must say whether or not it was right for her to walk out at that particular hour. He then became, as he stated, intensely jealous, and then followed the scene at the hotel; and here, he must remark, the conduct, both of the respondent and the petitioner, required very grave examination. It was only natural that husband, wife and every one should want to go to bed early, considering the time they had to get up the next morning.

Whether the petitioner, at this time, gave leave to the servant to go out in thoughtlessness or in simple kindness he did not know, but he could not see why she should have sat up in the sitting room; and he did not see, on the other hand, why the husband, being intensely jealous, should have allowed his wife to sit up, and not compelled her to go to bed. This conduct required particular attention; because, if the wife, from motives of vanity, wished to spend a pleasant evening in this gentleman's company, the husband, being jealous, ought at the outset to have checked all opportunities of the kind, and stopped any chance of improper conduct or any intimacy between his wife and this man. He did not know why she should sit up on the one hand, or why she should have been allowed to sit up on the other.

They must go back and examine the feelings of both, and say what were the motives throughout, and whether or not the petitioner brought this unkind treatment upon her by her own conduct. They were not considering, at this stage, the third person. He was simply the medium by which the unkind treatment was brought about.

After this there was a reconciliation, whether merely for appearance sake or not, he could not tell, but there was still a suspicious feeling, or jealousy in the mind of the respondent, which, although to a certain extent allayed, was not removed.

There was a subsequent transaction of a similar kind at St. Kilda, to which they would apply the observations he had just made. There was no doubt that the wife knew that her husband was jealous, and there was no doubt that he was really jealous, and that the jealousy continued. The jury would have to say what their respective courses ought to have been. The husband's duty was to stop the intimacy as far as possible, and the wife's duty was to conform to her husband's instructions, and cut off the intimacy as much as possible. A similar scene to that which had formerly occurred again took place, and different versions of the same event were again given by the petitioner and respondent. According to the respondent's version, his wife and Mr Ireland were left together, and the respondent, why, he (the Chief Justice) did not know, listened at the window, a pane of which was cracked. Whether he heard one word, and was then induced to stay on, he did not know, but to allow the woman and this man to remain together, in his absence, was just as inexplicable as his conduct at Castlemaine.

The opportunity should not have been allowed. Words were overheard, and it seemed that even then there were doubts in the respondent's mind, for if he had heard them unmistakably he would have rushed out at once. Subsequently to that there was a suspicion about some person, and, according to the version of the petitioner, there was a scene which it would be revolting to inquire into. According to the version of the respondent, what had been alleged by the petitioner to have taken place did not occur, and although solicited by the petitioner, he neither did it nor offered to do it. The wife, it appeared, afterwards left the house, and when she returned was sent out. If there was a reason for this course, the respondent was, no doubt, fully justified in taking it; but, if there was no reason, he was not justified.

He would come to that afterwards when considering the confession, but the culminating point of his turning her out could only have been justified by her adultery.

Until a mutual separation took place, the husband was bound to allow his wife to remain in the house whatever his suspicions might be. It might be an irksome load to bear, but such would, nevertheless, be his duty, and nothing but adultery justified the separation. He must leave them to say how the case stood between the respondent and petitioner. That there might have been conduct that must be considered unkind, there was no doubt. Did she bring it upon herself and was therefore to blame, or was he simply to blame?

Then with regard to her conduct with Mr Ireland in 1855. That referred, as far as he understood, to the case at Castlemaine. They had heard her statement that she had never been guilty of any familiarity, and his statement to the same effect. The respondent had told them what first gave rise to his jealousy at Castlemaine, and, if his version was correct, their going out together was not justifiable. In addition to this, there was also the evidence arising from the wife's confession that, when they walked out together, Mr Ireland kissed her. He would ask them to take that confession as a whole, or reject it as a whole. Although they might be inclined to accept some portions of it, and reject others, yet they must take it as a whole; and as regarded that admission and the whole of the plaintiff's confessions to her husband, he thought the observations made on behalf of the respondent, by his counsel, deserved very great consideration.

In regard to the other points, there was a direct conflict of testimony, and if they could not believe the petitioner on one point it would be hard to believe her on others, unless corroborated by other persons.

Now, with respect to the proof of adultery, with Mr Ireland, in 1855. At first they might consider the evidence in support of that charge most satisfactory, but professional men, whether wisely or not, did not look upon that kind of testimony in that light. No man or woman ever accused him or herself without a motive. There was an instinct of concealment in the human mind, and the same motive that led to sin led to its concealment.

He called it a confession, because it purported to be one, but they must say whether it was a confession or not. They had on the one side a confession made by the petitioner; that confession adhered to for one or two days, and on the third day withdrawn and denied; and the facts relating to it denied by the party implicated.

On the other, they had the confession itself, and certain circumstances which appeared suspicious, but on which, without the confession, they would not for a moment act. They would naturally ask themselves what was the object of that confession. It was attributed to the mere spirit of revenge. Did they think that likely? Did any woman bring shame upon herself merely out of pique or from petty spite? or was it not generally the case that a woman's heart was in favor of the very man who had wronged and ruined her? Was there sufficient reason, in their minds, to make them believe that this confession, deliberately and voluntarily made to the respondent, was no confession at all? According to the petitioner she never admitted her guilt – she said, "What would you give to know;" but, according to the respondent's version, which was corroborated by the servant, the confession was actually made and then withdrawn.

Could they act upon that confession? She said it was done out of mere pique; but her husband at that time would not present her as his wife, and, in a moment of remorse, she might have confessed all to her husband, in the hope of being forgiven and reinstated in her position.

Some men could forgive and forget such an injury, and some men could do neither one nor the other, and she, who knew her husband best, might have made the confession in the hope of obtaining forgiveness. They had nothing to say to the paramour, as he was not a party to the record. They had heard his statement, and would attach that weight to it which it deserved.

The next issue was as to whether the respondent had required her to leave his house as having committed adultery with Mr Ireland. He required her to leave his house, unquestionably, and for the reason assigned.

The question of his intercourse with her had next to be considered. With the effect of that they had nothing to do, but it was a strange circumstance to consider.

Did it point to a doubt in the respondent's mind as to his wife's guilt?

Did they think that, such a very short time after the manner in which she had outraged his honor, he would have taken his wife to his arms if he had believed her to be guilty? She had told him that in a moment of weakness she was taken advantage of, and had resisted all further solicitation. Did they believe that? and, if they did believe her, did they think a repetition of that to her husband was calculated to soften his feelings?

But, in deciding upon this point, they were not to consider what really did take place between the petitioner and Mr Ireland, but what the respondent believed had taken place, and upon which he acted. The respondent was not deliberately cruel. Indifference and jealousy could not co-exist; and, although jealousy might go on for a long time, it could not exist without love. They, therefore, had to consider whether this intercourse was to be attributed to affection, to a relenting on the part of the respondent, or to a doubt as to his wife's guilt.

The next issue was almost involved in that which they had just been discussing, namely, whether the respondent believed at the time that his wife had been guilty of any impropriety with Mr Ireland; and the jury would, therefore, consider them together. Then, as to his promise to provide suitably for her in her absence from the colony. He admitted that he had promised to provide her with a suitable allowance. But the question was what meaning was attached to the word suitable? He might have supposed that to be a suitable allowance. But of course that allowance was given her contingent on continued propriety of conduct.

As he understood it, the only contest about maintenance was that the one put it unconditionally and the other put it absolutely. The petitioner stated that, on the 29th September, 1855, when she was about to visit England, the respondent promised to send for her to return to cohabitation; but the respondent denied that. He said there was no such promise, though he might have used language that would lead her to believe that he might send for her to return and live in Melbourne. That was a question which might appear to the jury, in comparison with others, to be of very little importance, but it was not so. None of the questions must be disregarded. The jury must take them all into their consideration.

She said that, relying on such promise, she went to England in September, 1855. If such promise were made, it was only reasonable to suppose that her going to England was on the faith of that promise; but, if no such promise were made, she could not have gone on the faith of it; and, therefore, there must have been some other reason for her going; and it might be that she found herself miserable here by living in an isolated position, and without society, and so she might have desired to return to England to be with her friends.

Between September, 1855, and her return from England, she said she received the sum of only £20 quarterly. He said she received £25. It was not necessary to dwell much on that. She also said the respondent promised her, in writing, to remit her £300 annually, but the respondent denied that, and said that the only letter he wrote to her on the subject of money was the one of which a draft was put in, and which stated that he would give her £300 annually so long as she lived in Melbourne, but not in England, because, considering the difference between the cost of living in England and in Melbourne, £200 in England was an equivalent to £300 here; and, therefore, as he put it, he was not justified towards his children, in giving her more than £200 a year – a sum that he considered reasonable and suitable.

There were the opposite statements as to the amounts, and there were reasons given on either side for them. The jury would consider those statements and reasons, and say whether a promise of £300 in England was or was not made. At any rate, there was the fact that she returned to England at that time.

The next issue he came to was one on which they must find for the petitioner. It was the issue alleging that the respondent, in June, 1856, beat the petitioner violently and blackened her eye. But the jury would say whether under all the circumstances that took place, that was a violent beating or not. A beating was admitted by the respondent. He said it was only a single blow, and the jury would say whether that blow amounted to a violent beating or not. She said that on that occasion she gave no provocation. On her first visit, she obtained all that she required – acting on the advice of Sir Richard Bethell – she was put out, and thereby had a ground of action established. Why she went back to the house a second time after that he could not tell, but it might have been from a feeling of loneliness, being in an hotel amongst strangers. She said she did not use any abusive language on that occasion.

The respondent was not quite clear whether she did or not, but Mr Rose was very decided on the question – that she did use abusive language. No doubt she must have been excited after the blow, which was shown by her fracturing the lamp. Well, was the beating a violent beating? It was said that the blow knocked her down; but, according to her own statement, she was not knocked down by the blow. She said she was pushed out, and had her eye blackened and her lip cut by the blow; but she did not say that the blow knocked her down. She said he gave a great hit. That was her description of it, and they had heard Rose's description.

He would ask the jury to say, then, whether it was a violent blow. That she did use irritating language after the blow there could be no doubt. Whether she used irritating language before the blow was struck or not was not so distinct; but they had Rose's evidence on that. The respondent was not sure, he stated, that the apple was thrown at him, and she said she did not throw the apple at him. An answer in the affirmative as to whether irritating language was used before the blow did not amount to saying that such language justified the respondent in striking the blow. He wished the jury to bear that in mind.

What he wanted to know from the jury was this – was irritating language used or not before the blow was struck? was she beat violently? was her eye blackened and her lip cut? The use of irritating language after the blow was struck was quite another matter. They must take care and not do what was very often done – try the cause when they were trying certain issues. The court would try the cause, and it was the issues only upon which the jury had to pronounce. He could understand their feelings in dealing with a case of this kind, and that they would frequently have to go back and, as it were, check their feelings, and ask themselves again and again, if such and such a thing really occurred.

The petitioner, during her residence in England in 1861, it was alleged, had committed adultery. No person was specified, and, in his opinion, no person could be specified. The question, therefore, was simply this – was adultery committed? Was it the person referred to in the letter? If she committed adultery, it might have been with Hawker or some other person. Was the letter that was found a letter to her paramour or not? That the letter was in her handwriting there could be no doubt. She admitted it was.

But was the letter written by her with the purpose of being sent to some one else? If they believed that the letter was written by A. to B. there could be no doubt that it was written by A. to a paramour, for it referred to occasions of intercourse, and suggested even illegitimate intercourse. There were two excuses put forward for the letter being found in her possession.

The first was that it was not addressed to Hawker, but to some other person. Now that was no excuse, for it was simply a shifting of the blame from one person to another. If adultery were committed it was immaterial who was to blame.

If it were not committed then they were limited to the explanation by the petitioner in the box, which was that the letter was a mere copy of a letter she picked up, and which she wished to retain as a copy, but which was taken possession of by Hawker, and afterwards found in his pocket-book.

The jury would deal with that explanation as with the other facts of the case. There were some facts in the letter itself which it was difficult to reconcile with the statement. The copying, for instance, was not confined to the letter, but extended to the address on the envelope. Besides, the envelope had been sealed. Mrs Hawker said the envelope had the appearance of having been wafered, and of having been opened. There was also a misspelling in the letter which was referred to. It would be for the jury to take all those matters into consideration, and to try and reconcile them. If they thought it was improbable that the letter was written by her for a paramour, they would reject it; and, on the other hand, if they thought it was probable, they would say so. If the jury could not accept of the explanation, he asked them to say if they had any doubt as to the guilt of the person who wrote the letter. As to the respondent's opinion with respect to the petitioner's guilt the jury would consider the fact that he allowed his daughter to visit her mother in England.

The petitioner said that the respondent wrote to her and asked permission to send the daughter to her, that in the meantime he sent her money, and that he sent his daughter to her for education and for the benefit of her health. The respondent denied that he sent her for the purposes of education, but that, under medical advice, he sent her for the benefit of a long sea voyage. He said he made no mention of education.

He gave her permission to see her mother. Her mother sent her to be educated; and, as soon as the respondent heard of that, he ordered his daughter to return.

The jury would say whether it arose from a disbelief in the petitioner's guilt, or out of consideration for the feelings of a mother that he allowed his daughter to visit her mother. No doubt it would have appeared very hard if he had not allowed her to see her mother, but that was one of the difficulties a parent had, under certain circumstances, to contend with. There could be no doubt that it was very pardonable for a father to allow a daughter and mother to see each other, but there could be no doubt also that it was a most dangerous thing to allow a daughter growing up to visit a mother who was guilty of adultery.

The jury would say to what they attributed the permission. So far as they knew, the respondent had been an affectionate and considerate father. It was not easy to decide why the permission was granted.

Motives were attributed, and it would be for the jury to decide one way or the other. It was very easy to lay down rules as to what a father should do, but it might not be so easy, as a father, to carry them into practice. The jury, however, would say whether they believed that his conduct in this matter supported a belief in her guilt. There were certain other circumstances on which he had commented, and the jury would take them altogether into consideration, and say whether they thought the respondent doubted the guilt of the petitioner or not.

The other issue was as to adultery having been committed in June 1862, at Melbourne, where the petitioner was living; and there was another issue as to her having been delivered of a bastard child in England – the one following from the other. If there was no intercourse with the respondent, and yet she was delivered of a child, there must have been adulterous intercourse.

If the jury found that she was not delivered of a child, then, of course, they would find that there was no adulterous intercourse. Those two issues went together.

The question of the identity of the petitioner with Mrs Smyth demanded some consideration. There was no doubt that a woman calling herself Mrs Smyth was delivered of a child by Dr. Hassell, at Mrs Hutt's.

There could be no doubt that the petitioner left the colony in June, 1862, and was in Great Britain or Ireland – for she was continually moving about – at that period.

Was her identity with Mrs Smyth established or not? There was no apparent reason for her leaving Victoria at that time. It would have been well that her leaving at that time had been explained, if it could be explained. She came here from England because, as she said, the annual sum allowed her for maintenance was insufficient, and she again left for no assignable reason, so far as had been stated. There were several allegations as to the identity of the petitioner with the Mrs Smyth who was delivered of a child. With respect to the likenesses, all of which she admitted to be hers, three of the witnesses examined before the commission said that two of them were very like the Mrs Smyth who was delivered at Mrs Hutt's, and that the third was a very bad likeness.

The respondent stated herself that two of the likenesses were good and that the third was a very bad one. This was almost substantially a repetition of the words of the witnesses examined in England – two were good likenesses and one a bad likeness of the lady who went under the name of Mrs Smyth.

Well, it might be said that a sun likeness could not lie – that, in fact, a copy was as good as the original. But, he thought that, with respect to those likenesses, they could not say so, for two were better than the third. The witnesses might have been mistaken with respect to Mrs Smyth. The petitioner described her as a large, fat woman, with brown hair. Did the jury think then it would be safe to act upon those likenesses?

He did not think they could disregard them, for they were in evidence to go before them; but, acting upon them, and considering them as a portion of the whole evidence, were two different things. He made those remarks, not because there was no other evidence, but because a conclusion might be arrived at that the likenesses were proved, a conclusion that might be too hastily arrived at. Two people swore as to Mrs Smyth being confined, and that these were her likenesses.

Apart from that, there was the fact that a person was confined, and that the boxes she had with her bore the name Mrs Molesworth. Then there was the singular desire manifested not to be known as Mrs Molesworth. The moment the letter to Mrs Molesworth was produced, she said she was her cousin, though she was not described as her cousin; and again, when charged by Tolley, she said, "For God's sake, do not mention the name of Mrs Molesworth." And then there was her sister, who, when asked respecting her before the commission, said, "Oh, spare me!" She was not pressed on the point; but he thought she ought to have been pressed.

Then there was the other letter – the most difficult to get over – No. 8, which, if the jury believed to be written by the petitioner, and addressed by her to Mrs Tolley, and signed J. Smyth, in which she spoke of her son as Mrs Tolley's godson, there was certain internal evidence in the letter to go to the jury as to the identity of this person. If the photographs were struck out, there would still be evidence by that letter to go to the jury as to the identity of the petitioner with Mrs Smyth. He did not think it necessary to detain the jury longer, but would only further ask them to consider the points he had thrown out, and to return answers upon them; and an answer must be returned upon each issue, otherwise all their work would be thrown overboard.

The jury then retired at twenty minutes to twelve o'clock, and were re-admitted, at their own request, at ten minutes to four o'clock.

The Foreman then said that the jury had agreed to a verdict on all the issues save one, and on that issue they were equally divided. They wished to know if their decision so far could be taken.

The Chief Justice said he could not take it. It was not a verdict. It was not a finding. The Foreman said they were equally divided – six to six.

The Chief Justice said he should not hear that. It was one of the secrets of their position which should not be divulged.

Mr Billing suggested that his Honor should ask as to what issue the jury were disagreed.

The Chief Justice asked if the other side had any objection.

Mr Wood thought it was not desirable that the jury should state the issue upon which they disagreed.

The Chief Justice did not see what was to be gained by it.

The Foreman: The jury would rather not give the issue.

The Chief Justice then said he must ask the jury to return and deliberate again. He could not assist them in any way but by referring to questions of evidence. What they differed upon was a question of fact. There was no law in the matter.

The jury then again retired at five minutes to four o'clock.

Mr Billing then proceeded to bring under the notice of his Honor several instances in divorce causes, heard before the English courts, in which the verdict of the jury was taken on several issues only, and contended that, as the jury were agreed on all the issues except one, they must have come to a finding on the material issues of adultery. If they had agreed on one of the issues of adultery, their finding on the others were immaterial.

In support of his argument he referred to several cases, but in particular to Narricut and Narricut, 3, Swaby and Tristem, p.480, where the jury found on the issue for adultery, but not on the issue for alleged cruelty, and the finding was received. He also referred to Nicolson v. Nicolson in the last number of the Law Journal, and with respect to civil cases to that of King and Johnston, 5, Adolphus and Ellis, and a case in Bligh, 1 p.255 &c.

He remarked that in ordinary civil actions the objections to receiving a finding on a portion of the issues only, arose because of costs, but in a divorce case the question of liability as to costs did not arise, as under any circumstances the husband was the party liable for costs.

Before the learned gentleman had concluded it was intimated that the jury had agreed; and they were accordingly called in.

The Foreman then announced the finding of the jury on the issues, in the chronological order in which they were arranged by the Chief Justice, to be as follows:

1. That for a period of nine months prior to the month of September, 1855, by a course of unkind conduct to her, he (the respondent) rendered her life miserable.

Answer: No.

2. That the conduct of the petitioner with Richard Davies Ireland, in the middle of April, 1855, was unduly familiar for a married woman.

Answer: Yes.

3. That, on or about the 6th July, 1855, the petitioner committed adultery with R. D. Ireland.

Answer: No

4. That the respondent, on or about the 28th day of August, 1855, required the petitioner to leave his house as having committed adultery with R. D. Ireland.

Answer: Yes.

5. That on or about the 29th September, 1855, he stated to her that he did not believe that she had been guilty of any impropriety of conduct with one R. D. Ireland.

Answer: No.

6. That the petitioner and the respondent cohabited together until the 29th day of September, 1855, and that on two occasions, between the 28th of August and the 29th day of September, 1855, the respondent had connubial intercourse with the petitioner.

Answer: Yes.

7. That, on or about the 29th of September, 1855, he promised to provide suitably for her maintenance during her absence from the colony.

Answer: Yes.

8. That, on or about the 29th day of September, aforesaid, he promised to send for her, to return to cohabitation, at the expiration of twelve months next thereafter.

Answer: No.

9. That, relying on such promise, she did accordingly sail for England in the month of September, 1855.

Answer: No.

10. That, between December, 1855, and the petitioner's return from England to Victoria, in the year 1856, the sum of £20 quarterly only was supplied to her.

Answer: No

11. That the respondent, in the year 1856, promised the petitioner, in writing, to remit her to England £300 annually to maintain her.

Answer: No.

12. That, relying on such promise, she did accordingly sail to England in the month of November, 1856.

Answer: No.

13. That the respondent, on the 26th June, 1856, beat the petitioner violently, blackened her eyes and cut her lip.

Answer: Yes.

14. That the petitioner did not give to the respondent any provocation for the matter in the last issue, further than by going to his residence to demand that provision should be made for her, and that she did not use any irritating language to the respondent.

Answer: Yes; that she did use irritating language.

15. That, in consequence of the respondent not remitting to her such annual sum, she returned to this colony.

Answer: No; it was from other reasons.

16. That the petitioner, between March and May, 1861, committed adultery with a certain person referred to in a letter, a copy of which, commencing "My Darling," and signed "Love," is attached to the depositions.

Answer: Yes.

17. That, when living at or near Melbourne, before the month of June, in the year 1862, the petitioner committed adultery.

Answer: Yes.

18. That the petitioner, at the latter end of the year 1862, was delivered of a male bastard child.

Answer: Yes.

The jury were then discharged, and the court adjourned sine die.

***